THE BEST
GOLF
STORIES
EVER TOLD

For my parents and sister, who have instilled in me my passion
for the art of storytelling.

THE BEST
GOLF
STORIES
EVER TOLD

Edited by

Julie Ganz

Foreword by

Tripp Bowden

Skyhorse Publishing

Skyhorse Publishing books may be purchased in bulk at special discounts for sales promotion, corporate gifts, fund-raising, or educational purposes. Special editions can also be created to specifications. For details, contact the Special Sales Department, Skyhorse Publishing, 307 West 36th Street, 11th Floor, New York, NY 10018 or info@skyhorsepublishing.com.

Skyhorse® and Skyhorse Publishing® are registered trademarks of Skyhorse Publishing, Inc.®, a Delaware corporation.

Visit our website at www.skyhorsepublishing.com.

10 9 8 7 6 5

Library of Congress Cataloging-in-Publication Data is available on file.

ISBN: 978-1-62087-570-4

Printed in the United States of America

CONTENTS

FOREWORD: WHAT MAKES A GREAT STORY GREAT?

TRIPP BOWDEN

"What makes a story great?" asked my muse, champagne flute in hand, a wicked little smile on her face. Wicked, as in you're up to something and you know *exactly* what that something is.

I smiled, too. How could I not?

"You mean, what makes for a great story?"

"No," she said. "What makes a story great? Two *very* different questions."

I laughed. Surely she must be joking, to pose such a question to a former Augusta National Golf Club caddy and teller of tales taller than a loblolly pine. The answer was as obvious as the nose on my face, and my nose is big as Texas.

"Well?" she asked.

"Well, there's your answer."

"You're stalling." That wicked little smile again. "You don't know, do you?"

"Of course I know. I'm a writer, by God. I tell stories every day. Good stories. Some even great, if I do say so myself."

Silence hung in the air like bats in a cave, the sun hours from setting.

I waited for my wife to make the next move, a move that I knew, deep down, wasn't coming. My silver tongue was temporarily tarnished. I glanced around, eyes ex-con shifty, searching through my mental file cabinets, drawers, under the bed, for the elevator speech—that quick little 30-second comebacker chock-full of decorative, picture-painting words like euphoric, mesmerizing, alluring, captivating, moving, memorable, unforgettable. The elevator speech. Where the heck was it? I didn't know. In fact, I was coming to realize I didn't know much at all.

But I did, and do, know one thing.

I know a good story when I hear one.

How could I not, having grown up listening to tales at the bended knee of my Twainesque father, the good Dr. Joe, and Freddie Bennett, Augusta National's legendary Caddy Master?

Man, could those boys tell a story.

And this is how.

And this is why.

Grit makes a story great. Just like in golf, the reader expects you to grind it out, to never give up, regardless of where the story might lead. Happy place, sad place. Doesn't matter. As a writer, you are obligated to take us there. Those are the kind of stories we want to hear again and again, just like great rounds of golf, where we turn 82 into 76, because we never gave up.

Vulnerability makes a story great. Just like in golf, sometimes you gotta take one for the team, open yourself up like a lunch box and let the reader see what's inside. In no sport are you more vulnerable, more visible, more you-can-bump-and-run-but-you-can't-hide than on a golf course. Great storytelling demands transparency, the wound laid open, no secrets hidden.

Belief makes a story great. Just like in golf, you have to believe in your abilities, regardless of skill level. You have to believe in your story, have to believe your story needs to be told, needs to be shared, deserves to be shared, must be shared. With a friend, a neighbor, the world. And because *you* believe, the *reader* believes, and we want to file your story away so we can tell it again and again and again.

Great storytelling doesn't beat the dead horse. Great storytelling wakes that horse up, walks him around the farm, and promises the glue factory will never be in his future. Great stories inspire us. They make us laugh, think, ponder, wonder.

So whether it's Francis Ouimet's story behind his first big match, Gary Player's story of the 1965 British Open, or J. Douglas Edgar's story of how he found "The Secret," great stories, golf or otherwise, give us something very few things can.

Great stories give us hope.
Regardless of our handicap.

INTRODUCTION

As a tennis player growing up, I had never really considered taking up golf, a sport that tends not to be as accessible to girls in high school. Not to mention the fact that dedication to both tennis and golf requires a *lot* of time and resources, and thus the two appeared to be mutually exclusive . . . at least for a kid in this day and age, when you have a plate full of other academic, extracurricular, and social pursuits.

Yet I have always been drawn to golf and have considered the two games to be quite similar, mainly in the concentration, patience, and mental strategy required of the individuals who play them. I've also always found both golf and tennis to be "sports for the ages"—games that many pursue well past retirement. Perhaps due to these similarities, golf has always intrigued me.

When I began compiling *The Best Golf Stories Ever Told*, I initially approached the project with some trepidation. Nevertheless, it didn't take long for me to identify the cream of the crop of golf stories from throughout the game's history. As Tripp Bowden addresses in his foreword, I was challenged to answer the question, "What makes a story great?"

In the end, I thoroughly enjoyed the process of finding, reading, organizing, and learning from these stories, all of which happen to be quite different in scope from each other, but also are quite similar in their themes. Through solid storytelling and clear passion, the authors have all successfully highlighted many of the core elements of golf—the competitiveness, the frustration, and, of course, the excitement.

I hope they inspire you, as they have me, to go out and pick up a club—whether you're a seasoned pro, or as "green" as the grass that you're playing on.

—Julie Ganz
February, 2013

Editor's Note: While some of these are whole chapters from full-length books, others are short stories, and yet others are shorter than chapter-length excerpts from full-length stories or books. The Editor has aimed to capture the best parts of these longer stories, and has worked to preserve the original language.

Hemera/Thinkstock

WARMUP: THE ETHICAL AND PHYSICAL ASPECTS OF THE GAME

BY CHARLES B. MacDONALD

ONE evening some little time ago, at "The Players" in New York, several men drew around and entered into a discussion upon the merits of the game of golf. Each having had a "try" was attempting to explain the special fascination the game had for him, and each in his way happily expressed one of the many attractions of the game. The opinion was then ventured, which Rider Haggard has expressed so well, that "Golf, like Art, is a Goddess whom we woo in early youth if we would win her."

I think this is true; for one not having played the game in youth, though attracted by this or that feature to an enthusiastic degree, can not fully appreciate its many sides and rarely becomes a first-class player. Golf requires the delicacy of touch and nicety of judgment incident to billiards, and the strength necessary to make a brilliant play at baseball or cricket. There is the exercise and exhilaration of riding, the companionship of an adversary or partner, animated by the same pleasure as yourself. Wandering over the links, inhaling and enjoying the fresh air of the country, the senses are awakened, and all alert, one takes pleasure in the landscape, watching the varied shades of sunlight and shadow, which become gentle features of the game, until with sunset, happily tired, he is primed to enjoy a good dinner and a restful evening. No game gives a player's better nature a wider scope, and herein is its charm.

Today it is played in all quarters of the globe, a sure indication of its intrinsic merit. It is a self-contained game, and sufficient to satisfy physically the strongest men, as well as appeal to the most cultured minds.

Thomas Proudfoot, B. Sc., says, in one of his books: "No out-of-door game approaches within measurable distance of golf in bringing out all the best qualities, physical, intellectual and moral, of its devotees. *No really foolish or wicked or intemperate man can ever play golf or hope to do so.*"

The game of golf is a gentleman's game, though democratic in its spirit and traditions. The Duke of York, afterwards James the Second, did not hesitate to take John Patersone, a shoemaker, for his partner to sustain the honor of Scotland and the game.

Andrew Lang, in "History of St. Andrews," pays tribute to Tom Morris as "the Nestor of Golf and wale o auldman"—chronicling his merits on the same pages with those of Queen Margaret, Mary Queen of Scots, Cardinal Beaton, Robert Bruce, John Knox, Doctor Johnson, and a host of other St. Andrews celebrities. No history of St. Andrews, or article on Golf, would be perfect without mention of genial Tom Morris. *No game brings out more unerringly the true character of the man or teaches him a better lesson in self-control.*

The game appeals alike to all classes—professors, clergymen, jurists, poets, artists, the army, tradesmen, and artisans. A practical illustration of this can be seen on any golfing green on a medal day.

I can well remember my first game of golf. It was in 1872, with Charles Chambers, son of Robert Chambers, the publisher. I was being directed how to hold a club and strike a ball by two of the best known professors of St. Andrews University. Never have I known two professors to take the pains to teach me any other lesson. Apropos of this, it is told of a St. Andrews professor, who, being taught the game by his caddy, was lamenting his lack of skill and wondering at his want of success, that he turned to his caddy and asked his opinion. The reply was: "Oh, sir, ye see onybody can teach thae laddies" (meaning the students of the University), "onybody can teach thae laddies Latin and Greek; but Gowf, ye see, sir, Gowf requires a heid."

In Scotland the caddy, besides carrying the clubs, is a golfer's mentor and a most characteristic figure on all greens. With unsurpassed opportunities of studying human nature, he acquires a keen sense of the strength and weakness of his master, and is prone at all times to express himself freely. Caddies represent largely the humorous side of golf, being to it what the typical figures *Puck* and *Punch* are to their respective papers.

Familiar figures on the St. Andrew's Links in those days were Principal Tulloch, Principal Shairp, Mr. Whyte Melville and his son, George Whyte Melville, the novelist, "A. K. H. B." of "The Recreation of a Country Parson" fame, Bishop Wordsworth, brother of the poet, Doctor Baynes, editor of the Encyclopedia Britannica, the Blackwoods, and the Chambers, as well as all the professors of both colleges. So much for the game and its adherents "at home."

As for America, everyone interested in the physical beauty and intellectual vigor of our men and women must welcome with the keenest pleasure the introduction of golf into this country. It is truly an epoch. Nothing has heretofore induced men, in all kinds of weather, to steal from their offices or leave their clubs, to take hours of exercise in the open air, enlarging the muscles and broadening the sympathies. Golf certainly fills a long felt want.

In Chicago one small social club has already wound up its affairs, owing to the men deserting it for golf and the country, and the receipts of the leading clubs are materially less for the same reason.

In Greece, closely interwoven with the highest civilization the world has ever known, were the Olympian and Pythian games. There was no greater influence in moulding the natural character of the Greeks than these public contests. Games should be no less a factor in the higher civilization of mankind today than they were centuries ago. England in its way has long followed Greece in encouraging outdoor sports of all kinds, greatly to her benefit, while America has but lately awakened as to what they can do for a nation.

In the intensity of business life in America (few there are as yet who escape its thraldom), persons of strong individuality pass one another unsympathetically in the so-called social life in our great business centers, judging one another solely from an office standpoint. Let these same men spend a day golfing and they will quickly discover unsuspected qualities in one another which they will love and respect. In this sense, as Matthew Arnold expresses the advancement of the higher life, golf, it may be said, "maketh for righteousness."

As for the game, it is not violent. It can be played with more or less vigor in accordance with one's desires, and while absorbing does not engender great fatigue. Three rounds of 18 holes on the Links briskly and earnestly played will give one a good day's serious exercise. Should one feel too tired for exertion, he can putt on the ladies' green (probably with much improvement to his game), which requires little more effort than croquet. Men, women, and children can all play and be interested, expressing, maintaining, and developing their individuality. Notwithstanding the "Golf Widow" stories, it does not divorce a man from his family; it is no unusual sight abroad to see son, father, and grandfather playing in the same foursome, and in America mixed foursomes are an every day occurrence on every course. Children take as keen a delight in the game as their elders, and with them it means a splendid development of chest and figure.

In the adoption of the game in this country it was feared the tradition and spirit would be Americanized out of it; happily, innovations have been rare, and not half as much fault is found with American golf as one frequently hears the "Englished" golf.

So far in America there has appeared no disposition to modify or accentuate any of the points of the game. The game has been played in Scotland for many centuries, and, like most other things in life, in its simplicity lies its beauty.

The formation of the United States Golf Association while the game was yet in its infancy, has done much toward ensuring its healthy development. Fortunately, for golf, the Association secured an ideal president in the late Theodore A. Havemeyer, Esq. Under him the association commanded a representative authority — insured uniformity in rules and became a final court in matters of controversy. The golfing world has much to bless his memory for. Old errors are difficult to remedy, but the association was formed before errors became habits, and by enforcing rigid adherence to the rules it has preserved the game to us in all its pristine excellence.

The ideal first-class golf links has yet to be selected and the course laid out in America. No course can be called first class with less than 18 holes. A sandy soil sufficiently rich to take turf is the best. Long Island is a natural links. A first-class course can only be made in time. It must develop. The proper distance between the holes, the shrewd placing of bunkers and other hazards, the perfecting of putting greens, all must be evolved by a process of growth, and it requires study and patience.

Mr. Horace Hutchinson says: "Of all known rollers, beaters and levellers of the ground, none is so good as the human foot in sufficient frequency;" and that is true.

The Chicago Golf Club's course is a first-class inland course—probably no better inland course in existence—but the ideal course must be by the sea and on links proper.

I wonder what Eastern club will first grasp the situation!

Good golf can now be found at Meadowbrook, Newport, Shinnecock, Morristown, Knollwood, St. Andrews, etc., etc., but it is far from being ideal golf.

In concluding this article I wish to refer to three frequent errors made in speaking of the game. The implement played with is called a club and not a stick or a bat. There are 18 holes in the course on the links and not 18 links on the course. Links was originally plural, but now to golfers it signifies the ground the game is played over, and is, therefore, also used in the singular. Jamieson in his *Etymological Dictionary of the Scottish Language* gives it as a Scotch word, originally meaning the numerous windings of a river.

> "The Lairdship of the bonny Links of Forth
> Is better than an Earldom in the North."
>
> —Nimmo's Sterlingshire.

Secondly, it meant the rich ground lying among the windings of the river.

"Attune the lay that should adorn
Ilk verse descriptive o' the morn,
When round Forth's Links o' waving corn
Frae broomy know to whitening thorn,
He raptured ran."

—McNeil's Poems.

Links is also applied to the sandy, flat ground on the seashore usually covered by bent grass, furze, etc. Later the name was transferred, but improperly, to ground not contiguous to the sea, the probable reason being that it having been customary to play golf on the Links of Leith and on the Links of St. Andrews, the name came to be applied to any ground on which the game of golf is played.

I once asked an Oxford professor the pronunciation of a word about which there was much dispute, dictionaries disagreeing. Giving me the pronunciation, I asked him his authority, to which he replied: "The authority of the University of Oxford. We know no dictionary." In the old university town of St. Andrews the word golf is pronounced "Goff." In the latter part of the 16th, and in the 17th century, the word was spelled goff, gowff, gowf and gouf, but most commonly goff, and such is its pronunciation today.

—Dec. 15, 1897

PART I

GOLF HISTORY

THE STORY BEHIND THE RISE OF AMERICAN GOLF

ROGER HENRY WETHERED, JOYCE WETHERED

In these days, when sport looms large in the public eye and is even conducted upon a scale of international rivalry, golf has by no means lagged behind in popular favour. France has for many years been represented in our championships, and other countries have also played their part; but it is only recently that American golfers have sprung to such great prominence as almost to threaten our golfing supremacy. In the summer of 1920 I had the good fortune to accompany Lord Charles Hope and Mr. Cyril Tolley in a golfing expedition to the United States, and we had ample opportunities to study the American amateurs playing on their own courses and engaging in important matches among themselves. It was both interesting and illuminating. It is true that crowds of spectators watched their play on the links of Hoylake and St. Andrews last year, but not many keen followers of the game in this country have recently been privileged to see them similarly engaged under their own conditions; and it is there, I think, that they are to be seen at their fullest advantage and displaying their real genius. For this reason I have ventured to introduce a chapter on American golf, even if it only professes to be little more than a record of the impressions which I gathered there, together with occasional references to the methods of British golfers, in so far as they present a contrast to those more generally employed across the water. These comparisons, I might mention, will deal only with amateur players unless a statement is made to the contrary.

At the outset I should like to make it clear that my attitude is not that of an alarmist, but rather that of a sincere admirer of American golfers and of the grand manner in which they play this game of difficulties. We enjoyed a unique experience in seeing our friendly rivals make the game look supremely easy upon their own intricate courses. It was possible to observe their methods with some care while they were contesting their own Amateur Championship; and I am not overstating our feelings when I say that we received something of a shock on that occasion. The prospect of a successful invasion of this country no longer appeared an unlikely event. The Final was in some ways the most impressive display of golf I have witnessed; and it is no exaggeration to describe the golf of Mr. Evans and Mr. Ouimet as not only brilliant, but brilliantly consistent. Against Mr. Evans that day par golf was worse than useless; and although Mr. Ouimet stuck rigidly to the correct figures, he was beaten on the twenty-ninth green. In this way the favourable rumours of American golf were verified with a vengeance, and we Englishmen returned home in October much chastened in spirit, and convinced that we had seen amateur golf played in the manner of the best professionals.

The next year the American batteries were unmasked at Hoylake and St. Andrews; and although the result did not lead to Great Britain's complete discomfiture, it became evident enough that the United States had of recent years built up a first-class school of golf without the assistance of very old traditions or the advantages which we are supposed to enjoy in this country.

The record of the Americans' achievements last summer may be briefly reviewed. They won the Amateur International Match without the slightest difficulty. It would indeed have been a triumphal procession had it not been for Mr. Tolley's fine performance in the top match, which did much to restore our confidence in view of the Championship during the following week. America outplayed us in the foursomes. Here, at any rate, we might have been expected to hold our own; but tradition availed us nothing. As a distinguished golfer remarked with some justice after the foursomes that morning, 'Duncan and Mitchell should have played Evans and Jones.'

The Amateur Championship title was retained on these shores, and our fighting spirit worthily upheld by Mr. Tolley, Mr. Graham, Mr. Darwin, and others, who did great execution in the American ranks. But it must in all fairness be said that at no time during the week did our adversaries display anything of that form which won for them the International Match of the previous Saturday. Either they were stale, or the unfamiliar terrors of Hoylake had by then made their presence felt. At any rate, their severest critics could not maintain that they showed their true form, even in those matches which they succeeded in winning.

The Open Championship Cup has crossed the Atlantic for the first time, and the pride of British golf has been dealt a severe blow. The invaders were all there or thereabout, and they accomplished beyond the shadow of a doubt a very notable achievement.

This is how the situation in Great Britain stands in relation to American golf. For the rest, our amateur champion made a gallant effort to restore our prestige in the States, but climate and conditions were necessarily against him. Duncan and Mitchell were likewise unable to secure the highest honours in the American Open Championship. Britain had for the first time in the history of the game come off second best.

These are the bare facts of the case, and it seems probable that our golfing supremacy has been definitely threatened. In looking for the causes I can suggest that it is due probably to one of two things, or perhaps a combination of both. Either British golf has deteriorated, in that, despite a high standard of excellence, it is for the moment unable to create sufficient players of commanding genius; or the United States has actually produced, in their leading exponents of the game, players of a very exceptional merit. I do not believe that our present golfers of the front rank, professional or amateur, have maintained the standard of Vardon, Braid, or Taylor amongst the professionals; or that the level of Mr. John Ball and Mr. Hilton, when at the height of their fame, has been approached in the amateur ranks of today. Individual performances may compare in a favourable light with the exploits of the past, but that element of consistency, which is a part of real genius, is noticeably absent. One consideration, however, must be borne in mind, that owing to the far greater number of competitors engaged nowadays, golfing ability has developed into something of the nature of hit or miss. To survive these large fields demands a sustained brilliance, whereas steadiness of a high order of merit might in past years have proved sufficient for the purpose. Against this it must be admitted that

Hutchison, Barnes, and Hagen generally take it in turn to capture the various American championships in which they compete; and upon those occasions, when they have been debarred the highest honours, they have nevertheless secured places high up on the list. This fine level of consistency is also noticeable amongst the American amateurs. The title has been generally held amongst a small group, including Mr. Evans, Mr. Ouimet, Mr. Travers, and Mr. Gardiner. The victory of Mr. Guildford was not altogether a surprise, and the championship may be said to be well within the grasp of Mr. Jones, Dr. Paul Hunter, Mr. Wright, or Mr. Wood Platt, who hold distinguished positions in American golf by reason of the consistency of their performances. The same thing can scarcely be said of British amateur golf. It has been in a state of flux since the war, and the chief events have been of a very open description. There are indeed no certainties in golf; but British golf especially has recently been of a more uncertain character than usual.

It is because of this great virtue of consistency that American golfers are well worth a close study. They seem to have contributed something towards the determination of correct golfing methods. Their play has not developed on haphazard lines. With typical thoroughness they have sought to extract the essential principles of the various strokes and to establish a particular style. During the last twenty years they have learned their lesson from the practical examples of the great masters of the game in this country; and all that was known in British golf was transplanted to American soil by professionals who went to reside there or to compete in their championships. The knowledge stored up in books was available for their well-being or their undoing. They had no lack of material upon which they might build up their own school, and in the process of assimilation they seem to have exercised an admirable discretion.

In my attempts to lay stress upon the chief characteristics of American golf, it will be seen that the principles upon which they have worked are constructed upon the orthodox lines advocated in this country, but with this additional precaution, that they have endeavoured, as far as possible, to cut out the non-essentials—those golfing frills and unnecessary trick shots—which lead to the downfall of many a promising player, and to concentrate solely upon the perfecting of one special shot with each club. In this way the game is made easier, and there is no doubt that under American conditions and upon their own courses this simplification reaps its reward.

In the first place the courses conform to a type which we associate with 'inland golf.' The fairways are narrow or moderately so, and the drive in this case must always be straight. If excursions to the heavy rough flanking the fairway are indulged in, the penalty is usually the loss of a clear stroke, since the chances of a big recovery are reduced to a minimum. Owing to the calmness of the weather conditions the drive from the tee can therefore be reduced to a mechanical process, and clean, straight hitting may be employed time after time without the interference of disconcerting blasts of wind at awkward angles. Similarly, there is seldom occasion to make use of a cross wind in order to gain an extra yard or so with the wooden clubs. Straightness, therefore, is the outstanding virtue from the tee. The second shot is usually anything from a driving-iron to a mashie niblick. The green is often built up upon a plateau, and is strongly fortified with deep bunkers, usually to the side, leaving a narrow opening for a running shot if it should be attempted. The American golfer as a rule finds the all-air route the safer, provided he can impart sufficient back spin; and this is the stroke which he plays with the regularity of clock-work with all his clubs. He has developed this shot in such a manner that, provided he is a finished player, he can hit ball after ball with that gradually rising flight which denotes the application of back spin; and since each shot is played easily he becomes a fine judge of distance. Those American amateurs, whom I had the good fortune to watch in their championship matches, seemed able at their best to pitch their full iron shots in exactly the right place with the precision of a professional executing a short approach. The back spin which they imparted had no side spin, so far as it was possible to see, and the ball upon its bounce proceeded in a straight line in prolongation of the direction of the stroke. If any slight error had been committed, the tendency might be observed for the ball to pull up upon its pitch from right to left. In Great Britain this shot usually comes in from left to right; in fact, such a tendency is regarded as a hall-mark of good iron play. With a mashie niblick the amount of back spin imparted by the Americans is terrific, and I have seen Mr. Bobby Jones obtain this result without the assistance of ribs or slots cut in the face of his club. It is the practice of this one and the same shot with all iron clubs that has—up to a point—made the Americans perfect. Their attention has not been unduly attracted to those variations of stroke that delight the golfing critic here. The lack of wind in which to hold up the shot may account for a certain absence of such artistic feats abroad, and the determination of the American amateur to stick sternly to business may dissuade him from attempting them.

One or two characteristics in the American manner of playing the game may be worth noticing. They are mannerisms, but they are a means to an end—the simplification of golf. Particularly noticeable is the minuteness of the waggle. The golf books and our instructors would have us believe that a judicious freedom in our preliminary address assists in loosening the wrists, and suggests something of the rhythmic requirements of the swing. I will not maintain that this embraces all the argument in favour of the supple waggle, but I would point out that any initial stiffness of the wrists would have worked off before many holes had been played, and that if the rhythm of the swing is not already present in the mind, the fullest waggle cannot recall it. What, then, is the importance of the waggle? Surely it is only this: that by waving the club slightly over the object ball it is possible to determine whether you are standing at your customary and comfortable distance from it, and whether your stance is in accordance with your meditated stroke. If this be the whole truth, then the insignificance of the American's preparation to strike the ball is sufficient for the purpose. On the other hand, the danger of the large waggle has not been generally recognised. It tends to disturb the balance of the body, induces a slackness of the right knee, unless care is exercised, and is inclined to exaggerate the turning movement of the shoulders and upper part of the body, which should only operate late in accordance with the relentless pull of the arms during the swing. The waggle, therefore, that some of the leading American players affect only serves the useful purpose of establishing a comfortable position and no more.

Connected with the address of the ball is the facing of the club, and on this point the accuracy and thoroughness of the Americans are again shown. The method we are accustomed to adopt is roughly this: When once the stance for the shot is taken, with every regard for direction, the facing of the club correctly may be said to become almost automatic, and it only remains, in the case of irons, for the face of the club to be turned out slightly in order to counteract a presumable turn of the right wrist at the moment of impact. This turning is a dangerous practice, and one which I suspect the Americans have partly rejected. Their way of regarding the matter is that if the club is first soled behind the ball in the proper position, the feet will of necessity take up their right stance, and any indecision at the last minute with regard to them will be in this way avoided. The Americans do not, as a rule, allow for the turn of the right wrist during the swing, but trust rather to the truth of its orbit during the stroke. They therefore place the face of the club at an exact right angle to the line of the shot. Such preliminary movements as are necessary before the striking of the ball are reduced to a simple formula by Mr. Bobby Jones. First he soles his club, looks at the line, and adjusts it accordingly. His feet fall into their places naturally. He lifts the club head and moves it over the ball once or twice, soles it carefully again, glances at the line and back again, and then swings without more ado.

Having dwelt on these minor but nonetheless important details, which help to induce that frame of mind in the player necessary for the confident hitting of the ball, it will not, I think, be time wasted if we inquire into the nature of the American swing. The golf swing is always a difficult motion to analyse. Instantaneous photography has exposed, and at the same time ruthlessly exploded, maxims which were thought to be inviolate. It has also shown what has always been suspected, that there are many ways of executing an apparently perfect shot. The truth of the matter is that rhythm, and rhythm only, is the secret of correct timing. The American players appear to have approached the principles of rhythmic swinging from a sound and common-sense point of view. In order to compel the club head to a very high rate of speed at the moment of impact without sacrificing these sensations of rhythmic movement, they have allowed themselves, broadly speaking, to cultivate a large and deliberate back swing with a correspondingly long recovery in the follow through. By this method the club head is allowed in the all-important down swing ample time gradually to increase its pace until it reaches its greatest velocity at the moment when the ball is struck. There is a wide distinction between a punch and a slap, and it is in this particular that the Americans differ somewhat from us in their manner of striking the ball. In a punch the swing is necessarily a short one. The backward movement of the arm is of a secondary importance, provided that it is contained within the smallest limits. The power in a punch is developed at impact, and immediately afterwards. It is this irresistible push which contributes to the weight of the blow. The slap, on the other hand, is dependent upon correct timing for its effect, and the greater the distance from the point of its delivery to its objective the greater will be its sting at impact. For golfing purposes the longer and more rhythmic movement is particularly suitable, because in no other game does any ball respond more readily to accurate timing than the rubber-cored ball. In order to hit it great distances, the quality, that we know as sting, is of greater value than all the force of human physique applied in the form of a punch.

This, I think, is the argument in favour of the long swing. It may be criticised as tending to inaccuracy, but the difficulty of its manipulation can be overcome; and indeed has been overcome in the most convincing manner by our friends across the Atlantic, even taking into account the clemency of their weather conditions. In this country there is a tendency to discourage young players who are able, by the means of a long swing, to hit the ball sweetly with their more lofted iron clubs; and I am not sure that British golf is not being robbed of its individuality and natural grace by an insistence upon cast iron principles of rigid swinging, which only allow those in possession of abnormally strong wrists and forearms to secure the best results.

The most noteworthy points in the American swing—particularly with wooden clubs—are to be seen in the first movements of the back swing, the straightness of the arms throughout, the remarkable control of the body, and a certain litheness of the shoulders. It is at such an early stage of the swing as the very first movements of the club head that disaster may be spelt, because it is at that point that the preliminary impetus to the rhythmic motion of the swing is set in action. It is easy to see that at the commencement of a long swing the faintest suspicion of snatching may ruin the best intentions afterwards. To take the instance of Mr. Ouimet, the club is lifted back for the first foot very low to the ground, and with the utmost deliberation, while as yet the wrists have not begun to operate. His left arm is straight even in the address; and it is this arm that initiates the swing from the very beginning. This slow movement may appear a trivial point upon which to lay especial emphasis, but it is none the less worthy of observation. Just as the speed of the club head increases gradually in the downward swing, so does the same rule apply with equal force in the upward motion. For that reason it is necessary to start as quietly as possible, or otherwise the final stage of the back swing will be conducted at too great a speed for comfort or efficiency. The top of the swing is reached with a taut left arm, and it is only the bend of the left wrist, without any bend of the left elbow, which has allowed the back swing to attain its full dimension. It is important to remember that the bend of the wrist has only been brought about gradually and smoothly until the final state of tension has been obtained.

At the top of the back swing there is no pause, only what may be termed a poise, sufficient to permit of the recovery of the club head and to start it forthwith upon its downward path without checking its momentum. The maximum speed at impact is obtained by a delayed wrist action, which means that the bend in the left wrist is not straightened out by the right hand and forearm until the last moment, when the final impetus is thus added. All this while the left arm has been as straight as a ramrod. The right arm then becomes rigid in its turn, and straightens out in the follow through, until the pull on both arms becomes so strong that the necessary reaction ensues and the finish becomes absolute. The Americans make no particular attempt to retard the pace of the swing when once the ball has been struck, but allow the club to subside naturally over the left shoulder, even when the pull on the arms indicates that, for better or for worse, the shot has been played. In this way the rhythm of the swing is preserved throughout.

Body movement seems to be eliminated as far as possible. The hips are very firm, and the Americans stand well up to the ball. The chief movement seems to be left to the shoulders, which turn with exceptional freedom according to the requirements of the swing. To put it plainly, I think this may be chiefly accounted for by the fact that most of their players wear a belt and play in their shirt sleeves, which enables them to obtain their pivoting movement without unduly turning the lower portion of the body. They do not appear to move their heads in the slightest degree. It seems as if the whole mechanism works round a central column, of which the head is the only visible projection.

It is generally agreed that the most marked distinction between the play of professionals and amateurs is found in their strokes with the more powerful iron clubs. The difference is chiefly discerned in the flight of the ball. Amateurs seem unable to reproduce with any consistency the shot that starts low and gradually gathers height, until all its energy seems to be exhausted in the air, when it finally descends almost vertically upon the heart of the green, and definitely remains there. And it is this shot which the professional expert plays with unfailing regularity, and apparently without thinking. It is second nature to him, and makes the game look very easy compared with the efforts of most amateurs. We have come to believe that part of the secret of this stroke lies in the compactness of the professional's swing, and in the strength of his forearms and wrists. You may judge, then, how great a surprise it was to discover that the American amateurs, by means of a long, free swing, were securing a similar trajectory and an identical type of shot. There are indeed many ways of doing one and the same thing.

One definite principle in connection with this particular iron shot holds good—that the ball must be struck first and the turf afterwards. This method of iron play applies even more in the United States than in this country, owing to the nature of the ground; because the turf, although it exists in abundance owing to watering and other precautions, consists of a coarse mat established upon a veritable bed of concrete. If turf is taken, therefore, before the club meets the ball, it is reasonable to suppose that a slight skidding of the iron head at once takes effect with a disastrous result. What is a wise precaution even upon our own soft and springy turf becomes a golden rule in the States.

Back spin, and the soaring flight associated with it, is imparted by means of a downward blow, and partly by what is more obscure, the retention of the ball upon the face of the club for a longer period than usual. If a golf ball moves up the face of a lofted club while it is being hit, it is obvious that a backward rotary movement of the ball takes place; and it is for this reason that the club face should be moving in a downward direction. It is also clear that the longer the ball has the opportunity of remaining in contact with the face of the club, the greater will be the spin which it gathers during this process. To take the two types of shots. If the ball is hit while the club head is proceeding in an upward direction, the swing accords more with the loft of the club, and the ball is inclined to fly direct from the point of impact. But if, on the other hand, the swing is directed more abruptly downwards upon the ball, and at impact proceeds as low as possible, it must follow that the loft of the club allows the ball to remain a little longer upon its face. Taking as an analogy certain letters of the alphabet, the two most suitable examples seem to be, for the regular swing, a wide **U**; and, as representing the swing that applies the most back spin, the letter **L**, so far as it can be adapted to the purposes of a golfing stroke. It is with this last style I wish to deal. To the outward eye there is little difference in the driving swing of the American amateur from that which he employs with his irons, except that in the one case the ball is hit cleanly and in the other the turf is definitely grazed, if not actually taken. The slight waggle, the very accurate soleing of the club, and the straightness of the arms are principles which are still rigidly observed. The main differences are the transference of weight more on to the left foot, and perhaps a little more use of the right hand. In order to acquire the more direct downward action the stance is taken up with the ball rather nearer the right foot. The weight is distributed more upon the left leg at the commencement of the upward swing, in order to permit of the club being lifted up at a more acute angle from the ball, without in any way interfering with the straightness of the left arm. Furthermore, I am inclined to think that there comes a stage in the downward swing, just before the ball is struck, when the left arm as far as the wrist is practically pointing straight at the ball, and the bend in the left wrist itself has not yet been straightened. The ball is struck, and both hands follow through low in the line of flight without any deliberate straining or stiffening of the wrists. The reactionary pull of course becomes severe, but, in playing this shot, there does not seem to be the same studied effort to finish the sweep of the club head, probably because the use of the right hand has become more pronounced.

The virtue of this method of iron play seems to lie in the fact that the rhythm of the swing has been maintained in much the same manner as with wooden clubs, and that, owing to the still considerable length of the back swing, the slap has been administered rather than the more clumsy punch.

In the more delicate parts of the game upon the putting green the work of the American golfers was particularly to be admired. Their clean hitting and decisive holing-out made this alarming department of the game look comparatively easy. The firmness of their putting in this country was due in all probability to confidence gained upon the slower greens of their home links. There, the ball must be struck firmly for the back of the hole; and the danger of running out of holing distance is a contingency remote enough to be almost disregarded. In England they adopted the same method with slight modifications upon our shaven seaside greens, with the result that their holeable putts hit the back of the hole smartly in the centre and dropped into the bottom of the cup in due course without hesitation. It is quite conceivable that this quick and confident striking of the ball, with a further acquaintance of our glassy putting surfaces, might have been replaced by our more uneasy methods. However, no flaw could be detected in their manner of wielding the putter. It was characterised by all that makes for sound putting: an immovable body, stiffish arms, and free wrists. The ball was hit with the clean tap, which only the golfer who is sure of himself may administer. The whole procedure was a joy, even for jealous eyes to behold.

We are able to learn from this example little more than we knew already, unless it is to confirm the suspicion already present in our minds that the secret of putting lies in confidence; and that confidence once gained can overcome difficulties that might well appear insurmountable.

We may very well ask ourselves, how far do these principles of American golf apply to us who play the game under different weather conditions, and over differently constructed courses? The long swing in a gale of wind may be a slender reed upon which to rely; and it might reasonably be argued that we have developed our own styles of hitting the ball for the best of reasons, that no other way has been found suitable. It is a mistake, however, to be dogmatic, and in matters of golfing methods especially. In this perplexing game there are no final conclusions. The open mind is everything. I do not think we should, as a golfing community, close our eyes to the possibility that the methods of our rivals may help to develop our national style upon broader lines. There may be considerations of real interest and practical value in the American point of view.

To sum up, we have referred in particular to four details of method. The simplification of the waggle and, secondly, the accurate soleing of the club are both of first-rate importance. No conditions can detract from their possible worth. Facing the club head true to the hole has the virtue of simplicity, although there will be no advantage gained unless the swing subsequently conforms with this initial accuracy.

Then again the rhythmic motion, which is bound up with the longer swing. Whether or not it is adapted to the variable conditions of this country, where sun, rain, and wind hold sway alternately, remains to be seen, in so far as its rhythmic advantages can be attuned to our shorter back swings and less adventurous finishes.

Finally, the back-spin stroke, which may well replace the cut shot. All the advantages are in its favour. With side spin, direction is difficult to obtain by any other hand than that of a master. We are over-much inclined to play for strength rather than for direction with our approaches. We must harden our hearts, hit the ball straight at the pin, and trust to the back spin to find the strength for us.

Perhaps the most instructive comparison of all lies in the respective attitudes adopted by the rival countries towards the game. Of the two—and I am referring to amateur golf—I think the American attitude is the superior. At least it is the more likely to secure the best results. Just as the confident golfer can almost dispense with method and effect miracles when the glow of inspiration fires him, so a businesslike attitude may do much to eliminate those mischievous thoughts and rash intentions which are liable to upset the even tenor of a round. We are too prone to indulge our golfing fancy; and it even delights us to discover difficulties which sometimes do not exist. The wind plays havoc with our shots; yet in the spirit of adventure the misguided golfer seeks to chain this fickle creature of the air to his chariot wheels, and exercises his ingenuity in attempting to make it serve his purposes by needlessly elaborate devices. In most instances he finds it an unruly subject, but years of experience will as often as not fail to convince him that he is dealing with too treacherous an element in the game to warrant idle liberties.

The American example in the usual avoidance of trick shots might often be followed with advantage. I believe I am correct in saying that the principle which they for the most part adopt is one shot with each club, and each shot hit in as genuinely straightforward a manner as is possible. It is true to say that the golfer who pulls off the big things in golf is often the player who is equipped with a greater variety of strokes than his opponent; but it is equally true that had it not been for previous errors he would never have had the need to resort to their use. As a means of recovery such shots are invaluable, but it would be wise to reserve them only for the desperate occasions. Kirkwood, who is rightly supposed to have more trick shots at his command than any other living golfer, chiefly impresses the onlooker, not by the exercise of these peculiarities, but by the magnificent safety of his tactics. In this connection I remember that a keen follower of the game was discussing with a famous professional the chances of a rising young amateur, and ventured the opinion that he had not sufficient shots in his bag. The reply was, 'He is none the worse for that.' And subsequent events proved the correctness of the remark.

What is known as 'shot play' can only reduce a round to a confused jumble of individual strokes, some excessively brilliant, and the others, in racing language, 'nowhere.' A good round is one that is accomplished by a logical sequence of the easiest possible shots, each hole being linked together by the solid assurance of complete steadiness. In the same way a good score is built up hole by hole, and the homeward half must not hang disconnectedly upon the outward. Play for your fours, and the threes will take care of themselves. It is in this willingness of the professional to take what the gods offer, as opposed to the amateur's tendency to strive for brilliant results, that the wide gap dividing their prowess has come about. The American amateur is more like a professional in this respect, because he has succeeded in grasping something of the professional's frame of mind, to play golf simply for necessity's sake. For instance, he makes a habit of counting his strokes throughout the round of even a friendly game. Whatever else may be said for this custom, a vast amount of demoralising fancy play is cut out in the process. Such an attitude may indeed rob the game of many of its pleasures. The golfer who can play with his head among the stars, and attempt the game as it might be played in the Elysian fields, has his moments of sublimity. He may possibly never be efficient, but at any rate he never will be dull. Between the two alternatives there lies perchance the happy medium, and that may present at once a pleasant and a practical solution.

Brand X Pictures/Thinkstock

THE STORY OF THE FIRST TEN YEARS OF THE OPEN LADIES' CHAMPIONSHIP

MAY HEZLET

The first Open Ladies' Championship meeting was held over the links of the Lytham and St Anne's Club on Tuesday, June 13th, 1893. The weather proved favourable, and everything possible had been done by the Council for the convenience and comfort of the competitors and their friends. The greens were in excellent order, and a large crowd assembled to watch the start off. The meeting therefore commenced under most auspicious circumstances, and foreshadowed the success which has since attended all the efforts of the Union. Thirty-eight competitors had entered, the favourites being Lady Margaret Scott and Miss Issette Pearson. All through the week Lady Margaret Scott displayed decided superiority over her opponents, playing excellent golf, and winning the majority of her matches by a comfortable margin. She was never pressed in the slightest, and, in fact, had never to play the two concluding holes on the course. Miss Pearson was also in good form, and one of the best matches of the week was that in which she was opposed to Mrs. Catterall. Both played excellent golf, and the result was only decided after an exciting struggle had taken place and an extra hole had been negotiated. Miss Pearson eventually won the tie hole in five to Mrs. Catterall's six.

Miss Pearson and Lady Margaret Scott were therefore left in to fight out the final round, and so confirmed the opinions of those golfers who had ventured to predict their success before the meeting took place. Miss Pearson, however, did not do herself justice in the final heat, and Lady Margaret Scott had a somewhat easy victory. From the first the latter had been chosen as the winner, and her play fully came up to the expectations of the spectators. She has a beautifully easy swing, and her style is one of the best for beginners to imitate, as it combines grace and ease with power and skill to a wonderful extent.

The second contest for the Ladies' Championship Cup took place at Littlestone-on-Sea in 1894. By kind permission of the Council the matches were played on the men's links, the total length of the holes being 4,286 yards. The entry list numbered ten more than in the previous year, and the average standard of play had considerably improved. In the first round Mrs. H. C. Willock and Mrs. Wilson Hoare, who have both since earned many laurels, had an exceedingly close and exciting match, the latter only being successful after two extra tie holes had been played. Lady Margaret Scott, the champion, was again among the competitors ready to defend her title, and her form seemed if anything better than in the previous year. After several exciting contests those left in to the final round were Lady Margaret Scott and Miss Issette Pearson, who for the second time had thus proved superior to all their adversaries. This year, however, the final round proved much closer, and it was only on the sixteenth green that Lady Margaret Scott managed to gain the victory, and so carried off the cup for the second time in succession.

In 1895 a new era of ladies' golf commenced when the championship for the first time was held in the Emerald Isle, at the links of the Royal Portrush Golf Club. This meeting is of special interest, as it proved to be the last appearance in public of Lady Margaret Scott, and also the first appearance of Miss Sybil Whigham, the famous Scotch player. The visit of the English golfers to the Emerald Isle had a far-reaching effect. Up to that time the game had been played by ladies in Ireland, it is true, but in a very half-hearted manner. They had not realised the pleasures and possibilities contained in the sport, but had regarded it simply as a pastime to while away an idle half-hour. On seeing the skill and science of the English golfers, however, their opinion changed rapidly, and from that time they determined to devote themselves to the study of golf in earnest, and so fit themsleves to rank as formidable adversaries. The effect has been wonderful: golf has improved more rapidly in Ireland than in any other country, and the standard has been raised beyond all knowledge. Certainly the game is one worth cultivating, as many have experienced who have derived incalculable benefit from it. The Portrush links were in perfect order, and the championship week opened brilliantly. Another incident of this meeting was the presentation by Mr. T. H. Miller and Mr. Smith Turberville to the Ladies' Golf Union of the great flag, which is such a well-known landmark to all regular competitors since that time.

A preliminary medal round was held, in which the scratch prize was won by Miss S. Whigham with the fine score of eighty-nine. The chief match in the first round was between Lady Margaret Scott and Miss M. E. Phillips, and after a most exciting struggle, the former proved victorious at the last green. Miss Phillips, although defeated, played a grand game, and can always remember with triumph that she was the first lady in any championship match who forced Lady Margaret Scott to play the last two holes.

In the third round Lady Margaret Scott and Miss Pearson, not having had the luck to be in separate halves of the draw, were opposed to each other for the third time. It is unfortunate that Miss Pearson can never do herself justice in a championship match, but she has always so much trouble and worry over the arrangements that her game suffers considerably. This was the case in her match against Lady Margaret Scott, and the latter had a somewhat easy victory. Miss Whigham and Miss Dod, who have since often met as foes, were opposed in the third round, the latter proving successful by two up and one to play. Miss Dod, however, in a later round fell a victim to Lady Margaret Scott. In the semifinal round Miss Lythgoe defeated Mrs. Willock, and Lady Margaret Scott, although being four down at the turn, pulled up wonderfully, and managed to snatch the match from the grasp of her opponent, Mrs. Ryder Richardson. In the afternoon Lady Margaret Scott played perfect golf, and defeated her opponent, Miss Lythgoe, by six up and five to play. She thus for the third time in succession secured championship honours, and so created a record, which has never yet been, and is never likely to be, broken. Her style was perfect, and throughout the meeting she never showed a trace of nervousness, but played with great calmness and ease. Other players who competed in that championship and have since become famous were Miss Whigham, Miss R. Adair, Miss Dod, Miss Phillips, Mrs. Willock, Miss Pearson, and many others.

In 1896 the championship meeting took place at Hoylake over the links of the Royal Liverpool Golf Club. Most of the better players of former years were present, with the exception of Lady Margaret Scott, Miss Whigham, and Miss Dod, the absence of these fine golfers being greatly regretted. With the absence of Lady Margaret Scott it became a very open question who would prove the ultimate winner. A number of new names were on the entry list, among them being Miss Moeller of Ilkley, Miss Aitken, and Miss Kennedy. Only one of the few representatives of the Emerald Isle, namely, Mrs. Lepper, reached the third round, and one Scotch representative, Mrs. Crawford of Portobello, reached the fourth round. All the honours were carried off by the Wimbledon Ladies' Club, as three out of the four semifinalists were members of it, and its representatives had good cause to feel proud of their prowess. Large crowds of spectators watched the final and semifinal rounds. In the semifinal Miss Pascoe and Miss Moeller had an exciting match. The latter at the outset looked certain of victory, as at the seventh hole she was four up, but Miss Pascoe made a splendid recovery, and rapidly reduced her adversary's lead, eventually gaining the match by three up and two to play. In the other half of the draw Miss L. Thomson somewhat unexpectedly defeated Miss Pearson by one up. Quite three thousand spectators followed the final round between Miss Thomson and Miss Pascoe. After a very good match the latter lady proved the winner, securing the cup and gold medal with the title of Open Lady Champion for 1896. The chief feature in Miss Pascoe's game is absolute steadiness, her iron play and approaching being particularly good.

In 1897 the championship was played at Gullane, there being a record entry of one hundred and two competitors, including thirty-eight Scotch, ten Irish, one Welsh, and the remainder English. It was the first time the event had taken place in Scotland, and the play of the Scotch girls was a revelation to everyone, as was capitally expressed by one old enthusiast, who confided to a friend: "Mon, this is a fair enlichte'ment tull me." The play throughout the meeting was excellent, the best representatives among the Scotch being the Misses Orr, Aitken, Campbell, Titterton, Maxwell, Blanche Anderson, and Aitchison. Most of the crack English players were present, Miss Nevile being a new addition to their ranks, and she proved to be the only English player left in the fourth round. The semifinal lay between Miss E. C. Orr and Miss Titterton, and Miss Orr and Miss Kennedy. Curiously enough, the two sisters were left to fight out the final, the younger of them proving the winner by four up and three to play. Since that time no Scotch girl has held championship honours, partly owing to the fact that the best representatives have never come forth to make good their title.

The record of lovely weather which had been experienced every year was broken at Great Yarmouth in 1898. The links were very much exposed, and as the wind was bitterly cold, the competitors found the conditions somewhat trying. Seventy-eight competitors entered, including one from Scotland and two from Ireland. The great match of the meeting was that between the ex-champion, Miss Pascoe, and Miss Pearson. Miss Pearson led at the turn, but lost several holes coming home, and Miss Pascoe stood in the comfortable position of dormy two. Miss Pearson, however, made a splendid effort, winning the next two holes, and eventually gaining the match on the twentieth green. In the afternoon Miss Pearson had again a tie, but was defeated at the nineteenth hole by Miss E. C. Nevile. In the semifinal round Miss E. C. Nevile defeated Miss Dod and Miss L. Thomson beat Miss A. Barwell. The final thus lay between Miss Thomson and Miss E. C. Nevile, and the former proved successful by six up and five to play. Miss Thomson, now better known as Mrs. Towne, played excellent golf throughout the meeting. She had been silver medallist in 1896, and is very well known in the golfing world. Her opponent, Miss C. Nevile has since that time become very famous, and now ranks as perhaps the best of the

English players. She is an exceedingly powerful player, driving a long ball, and her iron play is also excellent.

Ireland was the scene of the 1899 championship, this being the second time the meeting was held across the water. The meeting proved to be a most successful one, and the chief point noticeable was the wonderfully improved play of the Irish competitors. Since 1895 the number of Irish lady golfers had increased considerably, and there was a marked improvement in their average form. The Council of the Newcastle Club had made every arrangement necessary to the comfort of the visitors, and the course was in splendid condition, the greens being so perfect that bad putting was almost an impossibility. Most of the well-known English players were present, and the entry list was considerably augmented by the large number of Irish competitors, who had been partly attracted by the fact that the Irish championship had been decided the previous week over the Newcastle links. The course ranks as one of the best in Ireland, the special feature being the enormously high sand bunkers which have to be carried from the tee. Long driving is a necessity, as it is fatal to get into the bunkers: they are so high and composed of such heavy sand that once the ball gets embedded in their depths it is almost an impossibility to get it out again. In the semifinal Miss Dod played against Miss May Hezlet but, being a little out of form, was defeated by four up and two to play, while Miss Magill, playing a grand game, defeated Miss Bryan by six up and five to play. Two Irish players were therefore left in to fight out the final, and after a very close match Miss May Hezlet became the winner by two up and one to play, and had the honour of being the first Irish golfer to hold the championship cup and medal. The Countess of Annesley presented the prizes at the conclusion of the meeting, Miss May Hezlet receiving the cup and gold medal, Miss Magill the silver medal, and Miss Dod and Miss Bryan the bronze medals.

In 1900 golfers from far and near travelled to Devonshire to the little village of Westward Ho. This part of the country is of immense interest, as it is the scene of Kingsley's famous book, *Westward Ho*. Within a few miles are Bideford and Clovelly, and the scenery all round the neighbourhood is exquisite. The meeting was a most successful one, and although perhaps not conducive to good play, the golfers thoroughly enjoyed the delicious Devonshire cream with which they were regaled at all meals. On the final days of the meeting the clubhouse presented a most animated scene; tea-tables were spread outside the verandah, and the competitors finished their matches to the strains of a string band. The form shown at this meeting was perhaps the best yet displayed. Great interest was excited by the presence of Miss Rhona Adair, the Irish lady champion, and the Misses Whigham. So many stories had been going the rounds about the play of the latter golfers that wonders were expected, and the spectators had no cause for disappointment, as the Scotch girls certainly played marvellously. They drove beautifully— Miss M. Whigham, in the semifinal, creating a record by driving two successive balls of over two hundred yards each, and this was before Haskell balls were invented—and their iron play was a revelation. The only weak point they displayed was on the green, where their putting was not up to the mark, but this was mainly attributable to nerves. There is very little to choose between the two, but Miss Sybil Whigham is, perhaps, the steadier player. Miss Rhona Adair also played splendid golf, and had the honour of beating both these formidable opponents, as well as many others of note. She is a very powerful player, and is also renowned for her absolute steadiness and her capacity to play up better the more she is pressed. In the semifinal Miss Rhona Adair defeated Miss M. Whigham on the last green, after one of the most exciting matches ever held at a championship meeting. In the other half of the draw Miss Nevile defeated Mrs. Ryder Richardson, who had been one of the bronze medallists in 1895. In the final round Miss Nevile, however, did not play her usual fine game, and Miss Adair had an easy victory, and so gained the well-merited honour of being Open and Irish Lady Champion for the year.

In 1901 the championship meeting for the first time was held in Wales, the scene of the competition being Aberdovey. There were practically no local players, but a large and representative entry of English and Irish players and a few Scotch. Miss Rhona Adair, the champion, was there to defend her title—Miss Whigham, Miss E. C. Nevile, Miss M. Graham, and a host of others were determined to wrest the cup from her, and some exciting struggles took place. Miss Rhona Adair had some difficulty in reaching the final round, as several times she was down most of the way round to her opponents, but somehow she always came to the front at the critical moment, and managed to pull the matches out of the fire. Miss Whigham was opposed to her about the fourth round, and made a great struggle to avenge her defeat of the previous year. Both played capital golf, and at the fourteenth tee Miss Whigham was two up and five to play. Miss Adair, however, managed to reduce the lead, and at the eighteenth hole the match was all square. Amid intense excitement the first tie hole was halved, also the second, and it was only on the twenty-first green that Miss Adair finally gained the victory. Her match against Miss E. C. Nevile in the semifinal was very similar, as the latter had the lead up to the sixteenth tee; but here again Miss Adair's nerve and recuperative powers stood her in good stead, as at the last three holes she made a splendid effort and managed, in the end, to win the match. In the other half of the draw the semifinal heat lay between Mrs. Stanley Stubbs and Mrs. M. Graham. After an exceedingly close match the latter became the winner. After lunch a large crowd assembled to watch the final round between Miss Rhona Adair and Miss M. Graham. The latter player was not so well known as her formidable opponent, and by the majority of spectators it was looked upon as a foregone conclusion that Miss Adair would hold the cup for the second time in succession. Opinions changed very soon after the match started, and it was seen that whatever the final result was to be a close struggle might be expected. Miss Graham obtained the lead in the first few holes, and, what was more important, managed to keep it throughout the round. She played faultless golf, and never gave her opponent a chance, and finally won a well-merited victory on the sixteenth green. It was the first year she had entered for the blue ribbon, and so she came out of the ordeal with flying colours. Miss Graham is a member of the Hoylake Ladies' Club, but ranks herself as a Scotch golfer, as her parents are of that nationality. She has a free, easy swing, is not, perhaps, a particularly long driver, but is most accurate in approaching and putting.

During the week of the meeting the weather had been perfect. The heat was terrific, so much so that most of the golfers were forced to carry sunshades and use them between the strokes; and it was quite a common and amusing sight to see the competitors and referees trying to keep cool by sucking lemons on the way round. Unfortunately, owing to the continued dry weather, the Aberdovey links were not seen at their best; but nothing could have exceeded the friendliness and kindness of the officials of the club. The holes are long and sporting, and afford ample scope for fine play. As there were no regular caddies belonging to the club, the authorities gave the school children a fortnight's holiday; the schoolmaster became caddie-master, and all the little girls and boys caddied indiscriminately. Another unusual feature of the meeting was the beautiful singing of the fishermen in the evenings. They came round to the different houses and sang the old Welsh and English songs in perfect time and tune. The Welsh are renowned for their music, and certainly these fishermen bore witness to the truth of the report.

In 1902 the championship meeting took place over the links of the Deal Golf Club. As the links were within such a short distance of London and were easy to get at, the entry list was a very long one, the total number of players being well over a hundred. The majority of the best-known lady golfers were present, and there were also several new aspirants for championship honours. Notable among these were Miss Glover, the Misses Park, Mrs. Mungo Park, and Miss Buckley. Miss Glover, the Misses Park, and Mrs. Mungo Park were all Scotch representatives, and had the free, easy style characteristic of the players of that country.

The Misses Park had been present at the open meeting at Ranelagh the previous month, and had there given evidence of their fine form. Miss M. Park, although quite young, plays a beautiful game, and with a little more experience in important matches will probably make a successful bid for fame. Miss Glover has an exceedingly graceful swing and is an exceptionally long driver; she successfully overcame her opponents in the first few rounds, but about the fifth met Miss May Hezlet, and, not playing anything like her usual game, sustained defeat. Miss M. Graham, the lady champion, had some very close matches. In the fourth heat she was opposed to Miss M. Park; both played excellent golf, and after an exciting struggle, Miss Graham proved successful by one up. In the fifth round the latter was opposed to Miss E. C. Nevile, and, after a give and take match, was defeated by a putt on the last green. In the fourth round Miss Rhona Adair and Miss May Hezlet were pitted against each other, and somewhat to the surprise of the majority of spectators, Miss May Hezlet won by three up and two to play. In the fifth round the match between Miss Whigham and Miss Dod excited considerable interest. Miss Whigham played absolutely perfect golf, and if she had kept up that form throughout the rest of the meeting, no one could have withstood her, and she would most certainly have carried off the blue ribbon. As it was, in the semifinal heat against Miss E. C. Nevile she did not play quite so perfectly, and Miss E. C. Nevile, who is not a player to give away a chance, and who was also in exceedingly fine form, made the most of her opportunities, and defeated her by four up and two to play. In the other half of the draw Miss May Hezlet overcame Mrs. Mungo Park by six up and five to play. The final round thus lay between Miss E. C. Nevile and Miss May Hezlet. They had a most exciting encounter, in the midst of which a thunderstorm came on, accompanied by torrents of rain, which drenched players and spectators. Miss Hezlet led going out, but coming home Miss E. C. Nevile had the advantage, and at the seventeenth tee they were all square. The seventeenth fell to Miss Nevile, and as at the eighteenth hole Miss Hezlet missed her drive, victory seemed certain to be on the side of the former. One can, however, never be certain of anything in golf. And although Miss Hezlet played two more on to the green, Miss Nevile by an unfortunate stroke got into the bunker and lost the hole. The nineteenth hole resulted in a half in four, and at the twentieth Miss Nevile's ball stopped on the lip for a half, and so she lost a splendid match, and Miss May Hezlet became champion for the second time. The feature of the 1902 championship was the great number of exceedingly close matches which took place; the majority were only decided on the eighteenth green, and several after extra holes had been played. Another point of interest was that it was the first occasion on which Haskell balls were used by the majority of competitors; and to this fact were partly due the exceptionally fine driving and brassey shots displayed by the ladies.

In 1903 the Royal Portrush Golf Club was the scene of the most important event in the year to lady golfers, and for the second time the competition was played on those links. The course had been greatly changed since 1895, and this time the event was played practically over the full men's links. There was, therefore, ample scope for fine play, and the holes proved a thorough test of good golf. The absence of the Misses Whigham and the Misses Park was greatly regretted, but a larger number than usual of Irish players took part.

During the meeting Miss Rhona Adair carried off all the honours and played in superb form. The champion, Miss May

Hezlet, was defeated, after a good match, by Miss M. E. Stuart on the last green. In the semifinal heat the latter came against Miss Rhona Adair, and a terrific encounter took place. At first it seemed to be almost a walk-over for Miss Adair, as she led on the outward holes, and at the tenth was in the comfortable position of four up. From that point, however, Miss Stuart made a splendid effort, and playing perfect golf managed to reduce the score to all square and one to play. Both made good drives at the last hole, but Miss Stuart missed her approach, and so lost the match. It was no mean performance to make such a match and play such an uphill game against so formidable an adversary as Miss Adair, and Miss Stuart is to be congratulated on her plucky fight.

In the other half of the draw Miss Macbeth and Miss Walker Leigh were opposed to each other. The latter is a thoroughly good golfer whose name is very well known in Ireland. The former comes from the Lytham and St Anne's Club, and had entered for the first time. She is a fine player and, with a little more experience, is likely to come well to the front. They had an exciting match, and it was only on the twentieth green that Miss F. Walker Leigh eventually gained the victory.

In the afternoon a large crowd of spectators assembled to watch the final round between Miss Adair and Miss Walker Leigh. The former played faultlessly, never giving her opponent a chance, and eventually won the match, so gaining the honour of being Open Champion for the second time. Miss Adair is far and away the most consistent lady golfer in the world: she never seems to be out of form, and the more she is pressed—which only occasionally happens—the better she plays.

THE STORY OF MY RETURN TO GOLF

J. GORDON McPHERSON

On New Year's Day the writer played golf on the Braids for the first time, and for the first time has touched a club for fifteen years. The day, the place, and the survival had, therefore, an unusual association. During that interval he had been accustomed to look at his old weapons of war, with the same personal fondness that a veteran angler studies his deadly hooks. That mid-spoon—a rare old Hugh—which Major Boothby gave him for its remarkable powers of letting the donor have a chance of holing from its approach stroke! That split-ash-shafted grass-club (also a half-century Hugh), which could jerk a ball out of a cup with a force not unlike that given by the black-headed weapon of Captain Stewart! And so on! The glory of play seemed to have departed by the depressing isolation of a country parish work; and the happy reminiscences of the brilliant work done by the several clubs seemed to be all that would be left to a once very keen player.

However, golf never dies. The player may be for a time in a coma; but let the name be spoken, and once again he revives to the enthusiasm. On Hogmanay it was arranged that a great match be played on the Braids next day between the Rev. Mr. Wood of Blackfriars and Mr. Grinder the Mathematical Master of James's Square, against Mr. Weaver the artist, and the writer. Each was to take his several way to the green. The writer raked up the very obliging M'Ewan of Bruntsfield for a set of clubs, coat, and hat. He got a flat toy-driver compared with his own upright firm swiper, an old Jackson for a mid-spoon, a capital cleek, and the beautiful iron which once did such deadly work in the hands of the late Davie Park at Musselburgh. No coat was to be got; and even the wideawake had to be retained. Little did he know that his sprigless boots would bring him to grief on the icy slopes.

The first forenoon of the year was piercingly cold, and the roads were covered with ice. The Pentlands were streaked with snow, which had gathered in the clefts; the sky was leaden and repulsive; yet the hearts of the warriors were not daunted by Nature's terrors. It is a hard walk of two miles from Bruntsfield; and even after leaving the main road for the scene of action the steep ascents told severely on the soft frame, untrained for much walking. How in the world the old players can get up for a game is a mystery! Yet golf is generally a craze with veteran players.

We met at the temporary Club-house, and chaffed each other into the martial fire. On to the starting-point we went; but alas! there we found a score of balls "teed" to give the players precedence. New Year's Day had brought out a galaxy of golfers. But what a prospect before us! The damper—in the shape of a chill after the brisk walk—was on us; and a slight refresher had to be taken in order to give us patience as well as courage. A good deal of teasing went on among the good-natured players— among whom were competitors of the Thistle Club—as to the handicap absurdity. "A've eicht," said a keen-looking old man, "but that's mair nor A need, ony wye." "The Scratch'll be oot the day, wi' the frost on the grund," remarked a cautious player who had been out a hole or two in the morning. "The thing's mole-skin," another cried; "it'll mak' 's mair even, at ony rate."

A strong sense of justice prevailed on the whole. Good humour blended with anxious keenness. At last, after about an hour's waiting, Messrs Wood and Weaver struck off. Hanging over the ball is not for edification; accordingly the shots were not brilliant. But what was our surprise to find, after we went over the hill, that half a dozen couples were waiting to approach the hole. Two out of these players were taking a swing to keep up the slowly dying heat, and we noticed the easily recognised St Andrews style. Thirty years ago was it when we last saw them at the Madras College, St Andrews; but the swing was equal to the masonic pass-sign to bring us together. Here were actually Bob Harvey and Davie Lynn in the flesh—both playing scratch. To while away the time at the several holes, we had a crack about the days of old:—

> "Oh, through the twilight of autumnal years,
> How sweet the back-look on our first youth-world! "

At length we were allowed to approach. Mr Grinder's practice for some days helped him to make a brilliant cleek-stroke. "Now, Doctor," said Mr Weaver, "there's a chance now to distinguish yourself." Davie Park was taken. But, oh! what a funk! The hand had lost its cunning. The flinty ground sounded like iron with the stroke; but "Ichabod" seemed written on the player's face.

"What a skuttle!" remarked Bob. "What's cum ower ye? Ye've surely been jerkin' wi' Robbie Paterson or Cawnel Young." These and other remarks did not at first tend to mend matters.

But an old golfing hand will die hard. He won't give in. Up the Redan slope of ice he played from the tee. Alas! he has to use a tee now; the day was when he preferred the slightly raised piece of grass. He excused himself, however, by reflecting that the ground was like ice, and he might break M'Ewan's favourite. Off went Weaver; but Wood shouted, "Just wait; you may get the ball back to your foot yet." And true it was; this ball had not reached the top, but tottered down with ever-increasing momentum. Again we wrought away on the putting-green in semi-despair. Even the iron would not hold in the ball. The only advantage of storming the Redan is to test the golfer's head and feet on a New-Year's morning! A few went up with bent legs and in-toes; but there "the sinner cannot stand on slippery paths."

The terrible congestion at the first three or four holes soon opened up, and the play became a little more bearable and safer. At the turning hole, two genial friends were waiting for us. "Just look at the scenery!" cried out Russell, in unrestrained rapture. And true was his remark. For round us lay a stretch of land and sea rarely equalled of its kind in this country. Inchkeith encircled by the deep blue sea, the shores of Fife in the distance, Arthur's Seat so massive in its lion mould, the valley on the right looking gloriously level in wooded beauty from the precipitous height, the colossal buildings of the metropolis, gold-tinged by the rays of the sun that had overcome the clouds, and like a man of god-like mien had stretched himself free from surrounding encumbrances. "Barron," remarked the more logically prosaic Wood, "ask Russell to tell you about the witch that lived in the cave under Blackford Hill—over there—about the third century before our era!" "None of your nonsense," Weaver replied; "why chaff the recognised antiquary? Do you not know that long-forgotten lore has for him a passion far exceeding the golfer's enthusiasm?" "Play on," broke in the practical Grinder; "we'll do for you now! We're all square."

But the ups and downs of the game need not be here recorded. A century afterwards some historian might be anxious to know the feats performed, or the sweet words uttered in a smothered voice as mistakes were made; but this account is not for such as he. One fortunate thing, the artist was not beaten; and he has been since studying for a statue the pose of the writer when he made an unconscious fluke.

The Braids must in the spring-time be a glorious parading ground; but they can never make a golf-course. The Town Council might do something to level the putting-greens here and there; but there is too much of the element of equalising lottery to make the game appreciated by good players. In fact, play there is a caricature of the game. The less we have of the chance element the better. Still, as Musselburgh is becoming honeycombed with bunkers—doubly tormenting and unfair with the present left-handed course—and other greens are not so easily reached, the Braids are useful, especially for the dwellers of the fashionable south-side. If a county hotel were built there, the attraction might increase; for it is hard for some to have their two-mile walk home again, after the fatigue of the ascents and descents of the successive Alma heights, without some little refreshment. Surely Sir Wilfrid Lawson, if a golfer, would stretch a point for that boon to so many thirsty souls!

One never-to-be-forgotten incident must be recorded. That New Year's night was dedicated to a *gaudeamus* in honour of the match. None will fail to remember with glowing delight the brilliant speech which Mr Hamden made when congratulating the victors, in the enthusiastic welcome which he gave to the golfing Ulysses who once more had put on his armour in search of the Golden ("golfing") Helen.

Hemera/Thinkstock

THE STORY OF THE BIRTH OF THE GAME OF GOLF

GARDEN GRANT SMITH

The early history of golf, like that of most other ancient sports, is obscure and fragmentary, while its origin, buried in vague and voiceless prehistoric times, can only be guessed at.

No doubt it all began in a very simple way.

Far back in the dark ages, a warrior was exercising himself with his club one day, in time of peace. Seizing a round stone or block of wood, he hit it so hard and so truly that it flew over the neighbouring trees. After smiling complacently on his club, in pleased astonishment at the result, he hastened round to the other side to search for the missile. Having found it, he repeated the performance, and it is easy to picture him challenging his brother warriors to do the like. Easy also it is to fancy their attempts, the success of some, the failure of others, and the applause or jeers of the onlookers. After the longest hitter had in this manner established his reputation, certain cunning men of the tribe—men who had failed in the far-hitting contests—came to him and said, "Behold! we see that our brother is strong, and that for strength there is none like him. And strength, truly, is a great thing, but so also is judgment, and he that hath strength without judgment is but as the ox that goeth in the furrows. Now, therefore, let our brother hit the stone so that it passes only between these two trees, or that it flies only to a spot which we have marked out behind the trees, and there remains, and lo! we will lay the odds of six to four against him."

In some such manner, doubtless, was the first game of golf initiated, compact of strength and skill, a relaxation for the warrior's mind, "tired with war's alarms," and a method of keeping his body in condition against its renewal.

Seriously speaking, it is difficult to discover which nation may lay claim to the credit of inventing golf. People have been known to affirm that the game was played by the early Italians, and there are others who contend that the Dutch are our true golfing parents, sundry works of art being produced in support of both these contentions. The Italian myth has been exploded, as the drawing on which the theory was founded, was discovered, after all, to be a representation of a man slaying an ox, and not, as was at first enthusiastically supposed, the presentment of an early golfer hitting at a ball. The Dutch pictures remain, but it must be confessed that they are more of a testimony to the Dutchman's skill in art than a proof of his knowledge of golf, for the game, as he depicts it, is a very poor affair indeed. In one case it appears to be a sort of hockey, and in another it bears a strong resemblance to croquet, while it was obviously a matter of complete indifference what sort of ground it was played on. In addition, it must be remembered that, as various ancient records and statutes show, golf was played in Scotland at a much earlier date than the first Dutch pictorial representation of the game. Moreover, the Dutch were an artistic people and the Scotch were not, and it is absurd to argue that because the Dutch were artists and made pictures of the game, that therefore they were the first golfers. As well might it be claimed for them that they invented skating, bowls, and many other pastimes, which are represented in scores of Dutch pictures, but which have been common to many European countries for centuries.

It has been said, in referring to this question, that no trace of a hole, the characteristic feature of the Scottish game, is to be found in any Dutch or Flemish picture. This would have been a useful argument with which to support, if not to settle, the case for the Scottish origin of the game, but unfortunately it is no longer available. In a beautifully illuminated Book of Hours, in the British Museum, executed at Bruges about 1510, there is a representation of four golfers, one of whom is putting at an unmistakable hole. Exception may be taken to the player's costume, his manner of kneeling on the ground, and his grip of the club, but there is no doubt about the hole.

I do not think, however, that the presence of the hole in this early Flemish picture weakens, to any great extent, the case for the Scottish origin of the game. It only proves, what is not surprising, that the hole was also known in the Low Countries. But Dutch and Flemish golfers are depicted playing at many other marks, such as pegs, stones, and church and pot-house doors. This shows, at any rate, that in the Low Countries the hole was not *de rigueur*, as it always has been in Scotland, and that the game of the Hollander was a bastard one, without the purity and simplicity which have always characterised its practice in Scotland. There, the mark has always been the hole, the true hole, and nothing but the hole.

Although it may be impossible, from the facts at our disposal, to arrive at any positive finding, I submit that the balance of probability, and even of evidence, is in favour of the Scottish origin of golf. The game has been practised in Scotland, in all its essential particulars, for many centuries, and that with an ardour and persistency unknown elsewhere. If the Dutch or Flemings played any game akin to ours, it seems more reasonable to suppose, in view of their widely different practice and their feebler enthusiasm, that their game was only a clumsy copy of what they saw at Leith and Musselburgh.

Be these things as they may, golf in these islands has certainly come to stay, and the surprising thing is that, with the firm hold it has so long had in Scotland, it should have taken so long to become popular in England, and that its popularity there should have been so sudden and widespread. Fifty years ago there was but one golf club in England; today there are nearly 1,000, while everywhere, all over the world, where Scotchmen and Englishmen are to be found, golf clubs are springing up and the game is being enthusiastically prosecuted.

Although everybody must admit the fascination of the thing, it is a somewhat curious matter, when one comes to consider it, this hitting of a ball with a bat or club. So universal and clamorous an instinct must have its base somewhere very far down in human nature, for it has manifested itself in all climes, except, perhaps, in the torrid zone, and in all ages, while advancing civilisation seems only to develop and confirm the more primitive, but still inevitable, tendency. What subtle and potent agency working within us is it that hurries us in our thousands to the cricket-ground, regardless of the claims of business and society—not to perform in our own proper persons—but only that we may sit and watch a man hit, with a piece of wood, a round ball hurtled at him by another?

What madness in their blood is it, that causes obese and elderly gentlemen, who ought to be thinking of their latter end, to array themselves in knickerbockers and gaiters, and to take early suburban trains to inland parks, that they may strike with a club, round trees, and over ditches, a sphere of gutta-percha, and babble of their prowess in the family circle? Surely so strange a manifestation, so overwhelming and imperious in the claims it makes on its victims, must be a recrudescence of some primeval habit of the race, the precise nature and purpose of which it is now impossible to divine.

But apart from this mysterious and metaphysical aspect of the fascination of golf, the reasons for its widespread popularity are not far to seek. With the gradual centralisation of our population, and the ever-increasing strain and struggle of city life, physical recreation, both for its own sake and for the rest and healing it brings to the overworked mental energies, has become a necessity of existence. Cricket, tennis, football, and cycling all do their share in meeting this demand, but none of these can compare with golf as a healthful recreation for all ages and conditions of people. For it is not only the overworked city man who has found in golf the health-giving recreation he so much needed. In our country there is a large and increasing leisured class, men who have retired from the active pursuit of their professions, while still in possession of their physical energies. For these men, bilious and bored with the inaction and monotony of town life, broken only by the afternoon rubber at the club, or the yearly shooting or fishing holiday, golf has come as a boon and a blessing indeed.

The healthy surroundings of the game are doubtless another element that go far to make its popularity. Cricket and football are too often played in confined spaces, sometimes in the centre of large towns, surrounded by smoke and bad air. For golf, an open park or common of considerable size is necessary, and of course its original and proper home is the breezy "links" by the seashore.

As a physical training, golf is surpassed by no other form of exercise. No other game develops and strengthens, so evenly and roundly, all the muscles of the body. Here there is no dangerous straining of muscle or organ such as occurs in rowing, running, or football. The nature of the exercise is continuous, and calls into active play all the chief muscles of the body, but without violent strain, and, in consequence, the heart is strengthened in a gradual manner, and the circulation improved, to the manifest advantage of all the other organs.

These characteristics which golf possesses make it the game *par excellence* for all men whose physique, whether from constitutional weakness or from the weight of advancing years, has become impaired, and who are consequently debarred from the more violent forms of exercise. Many a cricketer and football player, whose heart or lungs have gone wrong, has found in the pursuit of golf not only improvement and cure for his body, but equal scope for the satisfaction of his sporting instincts. Many a man past fifty, who has imagined that all outdoor games were henceforward beyond his capacity, has in golf renewed his youth, finding himself under the spell of the game, half cheated of his years and his anxieties. It is quite common to hear such a man declare that golf has added ten years to his life.

The presence of elderly men enjoying themselves on the golf links, however, has led to golf being frequently described as "an old man's game"; and this remark is not intended to convey, what indeed would be cheerfully admitted, that it is capable of being played and enjoyed by our uncles and fathers, but the implication is that it is not a game which any young man should take up, to the neglect of, say, cricket or football, unless he wishes to be set down as a muff. This view of the matter, it need hardly be said, is seldom expressed by those who have ever tried to play the game themselves, and it will probably surprise the irresponsible outsider to learn that no golfer has ever attained first-class form who began golf late in life, or, so far as I am aware, after he was out of the twenties; that, conversely, all the best players who have ever lived or are now alive, have played from their childhood, or at any rate from their teens. As a general rule, experience and history confirm the view that a golfer plays his best game between the ages of twenty and thirty, and usually when he is nearer twenty than thirty. At that age he possesses, in the highest degree, the activity, suppleness, and strength which are essential to a powerful, long game, and a long-sustained call upon his physical energies. At that age, too, he has more confidence in himself, his attitude of mind is simpler, less analytical, than at a later stage, when worldly cares and worries have done their work upon his nervous system.

It is quite true, on the other hand, that, against the decay of his more purely physical forces, the golfer often gains valuable compensation in the judgment and steadiness which come to him from experience and the formation of character. In consequence, many golfers, who have played, and played well, all their lives, only reach their best form comparatively late in life—though this, of course, can only occur before any marked physical deterioration has set in. Mr. Balfour-Melville, who won the Amateur Championship in 1895, is perhaps the most eminent example of this class.

But while golf confers these physical advantages on its votaries, its importance and usefulness as a training for the mind and character cannot be overestimated. In the course of a game of golf, all the strength and weakness of a man's nature come to the surface, and lie bare to the gaze of the most superficial observer. In the ordinary pursuits and intercourse of life, men comport themselves in a more or less conventional manner, so that their strong and weak points are often hidden, even from themselves. On the golf green, under the storm and stress of a tight match, these masks are flung aside, and we see our own and our neighbours' real natures in all their nakedness. Here, as in the greater issues of life, it is the "still, strong man" that endures. Pluck, steadiness, patience, and self-restraint are the qualities that win the day. The sanguine and excitable temperament, though often found in combination with extreme brilliancy, nearly always cracks under the strain of bad luck, or if the struggle be much prolonged. The game thus provides a bloodless arena, where the highest attributes of human character—the qualities of courage, patience and self-restraint—may be studied and cultivated, and where a man may learn his true relation to his environment, and how to comport himself before his fellows.

But there is yet one more aspect of golf which endears it to its votaries, and that is its social aspect. Like its sister game of curling, it is a great leveller, and, on the golf green, social distinctions are ignored, and all men are equal, or separated only by the breadth of their handicaps. No matter how rich, or influential, or talented a man may be, he is judged on the links by his golfing capacity and his good-fellowship, and by nothing else. Here the simple confound the wise, and out of the mouths of babes and sucklings the great ones of the earth extract golfing wisdom. The game thus performs a great and patriotic service, in bringing all classes of the community together on a common basis, where they learn to know and respect each other, finding out, as they inevitably do on the golf green, what a deal of human nature there is about everybody. The golfing snob we of course encounter, but he is a *rara avis* on the golf links and, from his position of splendid isolation, is incapable of doing much to disturb the prevailing harmony of the proceedings.

Now that the ladies have taken up the game in real earnest, and are proving themselves such redoubtable performers, there seems nothing to be added to the completeness of the social side of golf.

Talleyrand has said that he who does not learn to play whist lays up for himself a miserable old age. With equal force the remark may be applied to golf. To enjoy golf, a man may begin at any age. It may be that to become a first-class player a golfer must begin early, and have, besides, a natural aptitude for the game; but be the period of his probation long or short, or his ultimate proficiency what it may, he will never regret the happy days he has spent in pleasant places, and he will be thankful that he has embraced a game which, as time goes on, will not cast him off scornfully, unmindful of his youthful devotion, but which will accompany him gladly, making his failing steps easy and pleasant, down the vale of years.

pocketwiley

THE STORY BEHIND THE BIRTH OF THE RIVALRY BETWEEN JACK NICKLAUS AND ARNOLD PALMER

BY MATTHEW SILVERMAN

There have been great rivalries in professional golf: the amateur Bobby Jones against the pro Walter Hagen in the 1920s—with Gene Sarazen battling both as well; Ben Hogan fought fellow Texan Byron Nelson on the course, and when Lord Byron retired at the top of his game in 1946, Sam Snead became Hogan's top competitor; and in recent years there has been a lot of heat generated by the public and the media about Phil Mickelson against Tiger Woods. But no rivalry has meant as much to golf or its devotees as Arnold Palmer versus Jack Nicklaus.

Their rivalry helped fuel a golf explosion in the United States in the 1960s—and the duo's desire to play in the British Isles helped renew their countrymen's attitudes regarding the Open Championship. (Snead, who won the 1946 British Open and then did not play in the event for 15 years, dismissed the travel and paltry purses: "Any time you leave the U.S.A., you're just camping out.") The Nicklaus-Palmer rivalry changed the way people followed golf, and the way it was covered on television. And their styles could not have been any different.

First came Palmer, the swashbuckling everyman with a loopy swing that would make a pro blush, bringing the masses to the game. Arnie constantly hit into trouble, hit out of trouble, and won and won and won. Nicklaus was more polished, growing up playing at a country club and developing a game that never had him out of place on any golf course against anybody, even as a 17-year-old amateur at the U.S. Open. By the time Nicklaus turned pro in 1961, Jack and Arnie already had a rivalry going. The star-studded, heart-stopping 1960 U.S. Open is where it began.

When he stepped to the first tee for the 1960 U.S. Open at Cherry Hills Country Club, outside Denver, Palmer had been a pro for six years. He had played golf at Wake Forest, dropped out of college, joined the Coast Guard, and after winning the 1954 U.S. Amateur, reluctantly decided to try his hand at playing professionally. Money was a lot harder to come by on the golf circuit in the 1950s, but Palmer proved he'd made the right decision by winning 18 tournaments in his first five years as a professional, including the 1958 and 1960 Masters. He would have won three straight at Augusta had it not been for meltdown on the last seven holes in 1959. Palmer hit two balls in the water at 12 and missed short putts on the last two holes to allow journeyman Art Wall to pass him with a stunning 66. Though gifted and popular, Palmer was not infallible. And he had plenty of competition.

Ben Hogan was a four-time Open winner and a legend. The gruff Texan's idyllic swing could still dissect any given course at age 47, but his putting tormented him. Lucky to have survived a 1949 head-on collision with a bus, Hogan collected six of his nine major triumphs after the accident. He won all four majors at least once, a career Grand Slam achieved only by Gene Sarazen before him—and only Jack Nicklaus, Gary Player, and Tiger Woods managed the feat afterward.

Player, who would win nine majors, 24 PGA tournaments, and 166 professional wins around the world, was considered part of golf's "Big Three" in the 1960s and 1970s along with Palmer and Nicklaus. The South African was 24 in 1960—and he was the defending British Open champion.

Nicklaus was still in college in 1960, but he already had plenty of game. He had overcome a mild case of polio at 13 in 1953, the same year he broke 70 for the first time. The 66 he shot at age 15 was the record at his home course, Scotio Country Club in suburban Columbus, Ohio. He won five straight state junior titles and qualified for the U.S Open for the first time at 17. While at Ohio State he won the 1959 U.S. Amateur by sinking a birdie on the final hole and later that year helped America win the Walker Cup. Pudgy with a blonde crew cut, "Fat Jack" had visions of winning the U.S. Open as an amateur, as his idol Bobby Jones had. Nicklaus planned on becoming a pharmacist, like his father.

The 1960 U.S. Open was Nicklaus's fourth Open, he'd twice missed the cut and tied for 41st in 1959. He shot an even-par 71 in the first round in Denver, a tie for 12th with Ken Venturi and five others. The top amateur behind first-round leader Mike Souchak's 68 wasn't even Nicklaus, it was Don Cherry. No, not the hockey icon of Canadian TV, but the Texas-born singer who crooned out top 10 hits and wrote the jingle for "Mr. Clean." Two pros missing from the first day leader board at Cherry Hills were Palmer, with a 72, and Hogan, whose 75 put him in danger of missing a U.S. Open cut for the first time since 1938.

Hogan got on track with a sizzling 67 on Friday, tying for 11th place with Nicklaus, Player, and Julius Boros. Souchak's lead, in the meantime, grew to three strokes after carding a 67. Palmer shot a 71 and was tied for 15th place with six others. As author Julian I. Grauber relates in his marvelous account of the 1960 U.S. Open, *Golf's Greatest Championship*, Palmer "was barely mentioned in second-round newspaper accounts. In a few articles, writers declared matter-of-factly that the pre-tournament favorite was out of the running."

All was to be decided on Saturday. The U.S. Open still finished with a 36-hole final day, which would be the rule until finally switching to a four-day tournament in 1965. Not only did this make it harder to televise (NBC provided trimmed-down, taped-delay coverage of certain holes), but the drama was also somewhat stifled by the pairing order (11 groups went out for the final round *after* third-round leader Mike Souchak). So in the nation's biggest golf weekend, coverage was hours behind "real time," and players were still coming in from the morning round while others were teeing off for the decisive afternoon round. Oh, but there would be drama in the afternoon.

Palmer's morning 72 left him seven shots behind Souchak and tied for 14th place with eight others. No one had ever come back from more than five strokes to win in the 56 U.S. Opens held since 1898—and since World War II, the biggest comeback had been from three strokes (Jack Fleck, ironically trailing by four after 54 holes in 1960, had made up three strokes in the last round in the 1955 Open to catch Ben Hogan, beating the Hawk the next day in an 18-hole playoff).

Palmer made a comment to a couple of writers in the locker room as he changed shirts and ate a hamburger, "Wonder what a 65 would bring this afternoon?" Palmer got only grins and a dismissive comment from *Pittsburgh Press* reporter Bob Drum, who had long followed the hometown hero from Latrobe, Pennsylvania.

Still angry on the first tee, Palmer got off a booming drive in the thin Colorado air that bounced on the green 355 yards away and started a legendary birdie flurry that turned the leaderboard upside down. Palmer birdied six of the first seven holes, hitting the turn with a score of 30 to tie the lowest nine ever in a U.S. Open (by James B. McHale in 1947). But the guy in the lead wasn't Palmer, or even Souchak—Nicklaus was in front with nine holes left.

Jack shot a 32 for the front nine, including an eagle at the fifth hole, to claim his first of many U.S. Open leads. Ohio State football coaching legend Woody Hayes appointed himself an acting marshal in the Nicklaus gallery and shooshed any who dared stir while OSU star Jack prepared to hit. Playing with stoic Ben Hogan, and battling him for the lead, Nicklaus felt intimidated enough not to ask an official about repairing a ball mark on 13 (which was within the rules). His putt from just a foot and a half away hit the indentation and missed the cup. Suddenly, five players were tied for the lead: Boros, Fleck, Souchak, Nicklaus, and Palmer.

Nicklaus, rattled for the first time all weekend, bogeyed again on 14. Now only Fleck and Palmer were tied at the top. Arnie was separated on the course from Nicklaus and Hogan by Gary Player, who stumbled home with a 76 to knock him to 19th. By for all the young guns shooting for the Open, it was the grizzled Hawk, Ben Hogan, who grabbed a share of the lead even as his agonizing putting threatened to undo an amazing run of 34 consecutive greens reached in regulation. Communication on the course was such—and his concentration so intense—that Hogan did not even know that it was Palmer he was tied with for the lead. When informed as much, Hogan responded, "*He's* not a contender, is he?"

Hogan laid up in two on 17, as did Nicklaus. Hogan went for birdie and the ball landed on the green, but backspin pushed it into the water. He took off his shoe—then put it back on without his sock—and hit out of the drink.

Hogan's bogey—and Nicklaus's par—left the pair thinking they had no shot at winning the tournament. Without updated leaderboards visible, players learned their fate from officials or fans who passed on information, and were not always correct. Both Hogan and Palmer could have birdied 18 and forced Palmer to make birdie on the last two holes. Hogan's tee shot hit the water—this time irretrievable—and he triple bogeyed. Nicklaus bogeyed. Palmer played it safe and sank a short putt on the final hole, firing his sun visor into the crowd in celebration.

Arnie had indeed shot his 65, bringing home a 280 for the tournament to set a U.S. Open record. Nicklaus placed second, his 282 an Open mark for an amateur. Hogan wound up tied for ninth place—the Hawk would never again get this close to his fifth Open title or tenth major.

Nicklaus and Palmer, on the other hand, were just beginning their rivalry. Nicklaus was married shortly after the Open in Cherry Hills, then returned to college, won an NCAA title, captured another U.S. Amateur, and—in an utter reversal of the average recreational golfer's dream—gave up his 9-to-5 ambitions to become a professional golfer. In 1962, in Arnie's backyard at Oakmont, Jack fired a 69 in the final round to catch Palmer, force an 18-hole playoff, and win the first of his record 18 majors. Between 1962 and 1969, Nicklaus posted 29 wins (seven majors, including the career Grand Slam) while Palmer won 28 times (three majors).

The rivalry burned white hot at times, reaching a boiling point when Arnie's Army openly rooted against Nicklaus at Baltusrol in the 1967 U.S. Open, but Jack shot a 65 on the last day to beat Palmer by four strokes. Tom Watson would become far more of a Nicklaus nemesis in the 1970s than Palmer, yet the public always relished the Jack-Arnie rivalry, even as both men moved away from playing and focused on golf-club manufacturing and course design. The respect has remained.

In a 1994 *Golf Magazine* interview with the two legends, Nicklaus said, "Today, because of high tech equipment that minimizes errant shots, if a player hits too many shots offline, there are enough other guys out there hitting the fairways and greens and making putts that someone's gonna pass him. So there really isn't room for a personality like Arnold to show that exciting brand of golf—to come out of trouble and into the winner's circle."

Just like Palmer did at the 1960 Open. Golf hasn't quite been the same since.

AN INTIMATE STORY OF MISS ALEXA STIRLING'S GOLF VICTORIES

H. E. HARMAN

IT is just ten years ago since I built a bungalow opposite the famous East Lake Golf Club, Atlanta, and at that time Dr. A. W. Stirling, father of Miss Alexa, had just finished a picturesque home, only two blocks away. Thus, being near neighbors, the Stirling family and my own became fast friends, and during these ten years I have observed with an ever-growing interest the steady development of the present woman golf champion of this country and Canada.

During the early years of my residence at East Lake, Miss Alexa Stirling began her first work as a golf player. Her home being opposite the links, she dropped into golf playing naturally. Her father and I played a few frames together each week, and even as a girl she used to join us in our rounds. At first there was nothing remarkable about her playing, but as the years went on her game developed rapidly, and "wisehead" golfers used to say, "There's a coming champion; watch her."

When her game commenced to show unusual skill she was taken in hand by the East Lake expert, Stewart Maiden, and a large part of Miss Stirling's success in these after years must be credited to the splendid help given by her teacher. Maiden worked with her over and over the links, with untiring interest, and no doubt did more to develop her game than anything else. The reader can therefore understand the fundamentals of Miss Stirling's success as a golfer—taking up the game in early girlhood, falling into the hands of an interested and competent teacher, and a characteristic determination in the girl to make a success of whatever she undertook to do.

These characteristics stand out boldly in her other achievements. She plays the violin with exquisite touch and ease, partly from talent in that direction, but largely from constant practise. When the war came on she entered, almost as a girl, into war work and became an expert auto driver, in which she still excels.

And yet when we analyze the wonderful record Miss Stirling has made in the golf world we must admit that her unswerving Scotch character has had its big share. Those who have noticed her games during the last year or so, and especially during the three recent matches in Canada, Cleveland, and Philadelphia, know just what that has meant to her. Calmness, poise, and determination go with her from green to green. Bad playing on one hole does not seem to influence her playing on the next. She has learned a self-confidence to such extent that many of her competitors would give anything to possess it themselves.

These are the things which have made Miss Stirling now three times the southern champion, three times the national, and once the Canadian—with many, many other golf honors heaped upon her, besides. Having won about all she can in this country, her friends are now planning a tour abroad for next year in search of foreign championships, provided they can induce the young champion to go.

A remarkable feature about Miss Stirling's golf is the little interest she now takes in the game while at home. The entire fall and winter months pass with rarely a game being played. She is busy with other things and thinks last of golf. A month before the summer games she usually begins to practise at East Lake, and in a few weeks her game is up to its usual standard and she is ready for the fray. This may be accounted for largely from the fact that she started golf right as a little girl, studied the different plays under a real master, learned thoroughly the best methods, and now she needs only to get into practise to make unequalled records. That's easy when one knows it as she does.

The Atlanta Athletic Club is very proud of Miss Stirling's achievements in the golf world, to which club her membership is accredited. For three years she has kept the national championship cup in this clubhouse, to say nothing of the other honors she has won on the links in all parts of the country.

About the Stirling home life there is a simplicity and charm which is exquisite. The whole atmosphere breathes a literary spirit. Dr. Stirling, in addition to being an eminent specialist, has a national reputation as a scholar and a writer. In this home, with its refinement and poise, Miss Alexa has grown up to young womanhood, and it is hardly any wonder that she has gone forth to accomplish real big things in life, with so much in the home to stand back of her and encourage.

Miss Stirling's golf record begins with 1911, when in the Southern Tournament, played at East Lake, she won the low score for approaching and putting, and in a local tournament won the only prize.

In the 1912 Southern Tournament at Nashville, Tennessee, she won, defeating eight; also, the same year, she won the Blount trophy at East Lake.

In the 1914 Southern Tournament played at Knoxville, Tennessee, she played only the last day, on account of illness, winning the handicap gross score and broke the record of the course. This year she contested in the National at Nassau, Long Island, but was put out by Miss Bishop. She also played in the Berthellyn Tournament and won in driving competition.

Miss Stirling won the Southern Championship in 1915 at Birmingham, Alabama, also the low score. This year she also won first flight, Davis & Freeman cup, Atlanta; also other local cups.

In 1916 she won the National Championship at Boston; the Southern Championship at Chattanooga, Tennessee; and the Berthellyn cup at Philadelphia.

During the war years 1917–1918, Miss Stirling through the East and Middle West played in behalf of the Red Cross and thus helped to make thousands of dollars for the cause. She also did a vast amount of war work in the motor corps, from private to lieutenant.

She again won the National Cup in 1919 at Shawnee and also the Southern championship at Memphis, Tennessee, together with many low score records.

The present year, 1920, Miss Stirling has exceeded all her past records by winning three championships on one trip, the Canadian at Hamilton, Ontario, the National at Cleveland, and the Berthellyn at Philadelphia. During this trip she broke three course records, at Hamilton (75), at Cleveland (80), and at Philadelphia (81). During this year she has also broken the records on a number of other courses, especially in the South.

A great many experts have watched Miss Stirling's golfing for a number of years and have been of the one opinion that she stands to lead the world as the woman champion. Her playing up to this year, however, has been far surpassed by her 1920 triumphs. This year she has developed a game of such steadiness that few women see any hope of overcoming. If this improvement continues, as it promises to do from all her past efforts, Miss Stirling stands to hold the world championship among women players, provided she wishes it.

And just here comes the rub. While her American friends in the golf world, and they are legion, would like to see this timid girl hold this title, Miss Stirling seems to be entirely indifferent about it. Her modesty is such that she will not even discuss her past victories, and certainly not the promise of future ones. She has the highest opinion of the foreign women golfers and frankly admits her doubt of winning from them, in case she plays abroad. This indifference to her accomplishment, by the honors heaped upon her, is one of the crowning charms of this clever girl, whose name is a household word in the golf world of today.

PART II

GOLF AMATEURS

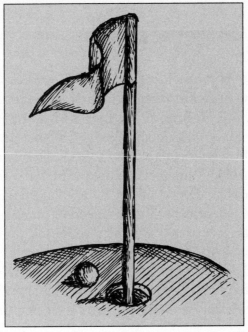

THE STORY OF BEGINNING GOLF

W. PROUDFOOT

An old friend told me the other day he would say, "Don't" to every man who thought of beginning golf. I looked surprised, and paused for an explanation. "It's difficult, it's expensive, it's an acute irritant, it's heart-breaking. By the way, will you play me at Barnton tomorrow?" Rather a comical non-sequitur it seemed to me; yet very eloquent testimony of the irresistible fascination of the game, despite every detraction his lips could utter.

Beginning golf is what someone is doing every day. What the writer did more than thirty years ago. There is nothing he remembers more vividly. He learned to drive with a spooned putter, which was, of course, all wrong; but which did not prevent progress. He would have begun in the orthodox fashion, hereafter to be mentioned, had circumstances permitted. *Res angusta!* The putter was an old castaway of his father's; and necessity being the mother of invention, a liberal reduction of lead and ample spooning of the face soon converted the rejected club into quite a serviceable weapon and made it an unfailing source of juvenile joy. It was a shade upright certainly, but a little humoring as to stance prevented heeling, or what is known in polite circles at St. Andrews as "richt aff the wuppin." There is no trouble with boys in learning golf.

The foregoing personal and, I trust, pardonable reminiscence may not be entirely intelligible to American beginners; but it does not much matter, as they are not likely to experience any such awkward introduction to the sport in a land where dollars are plentiful, and old wooden putters are rare.

What method then of initiation is to be regarded with favor? Consider it well, ye who are about to dedicate a portion of your spare time to this grand game, "this royal, ancient, irritating sport." Whatever be your motive in approaching this pastime— desire of health, conformity to fashion, an excuse for refreshment, the winning of some fair partner in life or only a handicap cruet stand, the prolongation of your days upon the earth, or the pure love of sport—if you attach any value to personal comfort and happiness, give no quarter to your own notions, which are certain to be hopelessly wrong. Assuming that you desire to play a good game, the first thing you must do, and its importance cannot easily be overstated, is to submit with the utmost docility to authority. What a multitude, who are now irredeemable, would have been saved from the pains of dufferdom had this simple condition been frankly accepted! Of course the "natural man" rebels against the uncompromising severity of this fundamental provision. "Why all this fuss about hitting a ball?" he asks himself. "Do they take me for a ninny?" and so on. With exulting breast he grasps the club, and * * * but let us draw a veil over the tragic scene. Or, rather, let us hear General Grant's peculiarly American comment on a similar proceeding—quite inimitable, we think, in the way of criticism. When the General was in Scotland some years ago, he heard a good deal about golf, and on a fine afternoon he asked one of his many admiring friends to explain the use of the bulger in a practical way. Out to the spacious park they went, and the obliging host, who was very much the "natural man" in regard to the game, teed the ball and waggled the club with all due solemnity. The General's expectations were running high, as he carefully observed the impressive preliminaries. Presently there was a heavy thud, a flight of turf, and the little ball still sat on the tee. Again, and yet again a thud, heavier than before, with turf still flying, with ball unmoved, with "natural man" perspiring and perplexed. Whereupon the distinguished guest quietly remarked: "There seems to be a fair amount of exercise in the game, but I fail to guess the use of the ball."

Of course the "natural man" may easily improve on that exhibition. In defiance of all authority, he will be able to hit the ball—in a way—but powerful in build though he be, he cannot shut his eyes to the fact that many a slim golfer, who would at once succumb to his superior strength in a football maul, easily out-distances his most successful drives on the links. How does it happen that a mere stripling so often outdrives a big, strong man? Both are fired with the same laudable ambition, but to compass it, the former submits to authority and succeeds. He keenly watches and loyally imitates an able exponent of the game in every movement. While the latter follows his own delusions and reaps vexation of spirit. His thuds are very grievous to the face of mother earth, he mutters dark sayings, he complains of the total depravity of inanimate nature, and runs up a formidable bill at the clubmaker's.

But let us indicate some of his errors. By a hundred chances to one the "natural man" will have the thumb of his right hand straight and tight down the shaft, instead of placing it loosely across, slanting wise, thereby reducing his driving power by at least 50 yards, and very probably, in a moment of extra press, spraining his thumb. To beginners the position of that thumb is of the utmost importance. It does not drive the ball, and unless it is rightly adjusted, it will very seriously interfere with the fullness and freedom of the swing. In fact, the whole of the right-hand grip should be comparatively loose.

Another common aberration which handicaps the strong man's driving is a certain ugly hitch of the body. You see him rising tiptoe on both feet as the club reaches its altitude, instead of keeping the right foot flat and allowing the left heel gradually to lift in obedience to the backward draw of the club—a perfectly simple and harmonious movement both of the body and foot.

This is well sketched in the October number of Golf page 19, where Willie Dunn is playing the cleek shot, and on page 27, where H. R. Sweeny is driving from the tee. [Editor's Note: page numbers reflect pages in original source.] The correct position of the thumb is also clearly shown on page 19, where you have an excellent representation of Willie Dunn addressing the ball. A careful study of all such useful illustrations might quickly act as a wholesome corrective to false methods and deliver the adult beginner from his own mischievous devices. He requires to be saved from himself, and if he lives, he will bless the man and book that helped to nip his budding fads; for he will have little difficulty in finding a portrait of what, but for timely interference, he might have been in the obdurate duffer who is superior to all counsel.

A candid caddie was not far off the mark in his somewhat caustic comment on one of these incorrigibles. A foursome was just leaving the putting-green of a short hole, when up came a ball with startling velocity over the bunker that fronted the green. The distance would be about 130 yards, and the above-mentioned party naturally looked for the arrival of the second ball. "You needna fash yersels, gentlemen. You're quite safe," said the caddie, who knew the calibre of the player. "He couldna cairy that bunker, though he played a hundred years." The ball fell far short. He was a young man who despised lessons, and who had accordingly acquired a style of his own—incurable, original, and, therefore, not warranted to hurt a full cleek range, even with a bulger.

The probabilities of going wrong at golf are too numerous and too serious to permit of any beginner dispensing with guidance. If a man has not the luck to reckon a really good amateur among his friends, he will find a few dollars given to a reliable professional to be money well spent.

It may also be mentioned that "slow back" and "keep your eye on the ball" are two maxims never to be forgotten. The latter can hardly be misapplied; but the former often suffers misconstruction. It can be too literally obeyed, and then the effect is ludicrous. We have heard more than one beginner alluded to as Mr. Slow Back—the motion of the club being so snail like as to make the most solemn caddie smile, and the frivolous ones go into fits. The point of the maxim is its check to quickness, and not any emphasis on slowness; the object being to obtain ease and grace of style.

In regard to equipment, we think most players will endorse the counsel to be content with few clubs for some little time. A brassie, cleek, and iron—or mashie—will keep you going quite merrily in every department of the game. Many a fine golfer has begun with less; for it is the correct swing, and not the number of clubs, that must engage the attention of the beginner; and once he is able to do fair execution with what he has, he may venture to enlarge the little set.

Avoid heavy clubs, unless you are an oldish man, inclined to corpulence, and incapable of more than a half swing; otherwise, such clubs will play you, and convince you of a too common fallacy. We have heard of a workingman, not an adept in the game but a radical in politics, who dislocated his knee cap in making frantic efforts with a heavy club to outdrive a member of the aristocracy who was playing a good game in front. His ambition was painfully thwarted. He kissed the sod, and was carried home. Avoid supple shafts, if you would drive straight and reduce the chances of topping. The longest drivers I have known use clubs of ordinary weight and steely spring. It was not with a heavy club that Mr. F. G. Tait drove his 359 yards at St. Andrews, but with a club he swung with perfect ease, putting arms, body, and legs into the stroke.

May all beginners in the Great Republic endeavor to emulate the achievements of the mother country, and add new honors to their native land.

THE STORY OF MY FIRST GOLF LESSON

TRIPP BOWDEN

My first official golf lesson takes place in the most unlikely of places on the most unusual of days: the Augusta National Golf Club, the Monday after the Masters.

Talk about your intimidating stages.

I'm riding down Magnolia Lane in my mother's car, brand-new glove on one hand and faded tennis shoes on my feet. Freddie greets us in the members' parking lot, which is packed with cars and people. Milling about and scrambling for tee times are the chosen ones, lucky stiffs who've been granted a once-in-a-lifetime chance to play the most exclusive golf course in the world the day after the conclusion of golf's most coveted major. The tees, the pins, even the scoreboards are all exactly as they were only twenty-four hours ago, when a young Tom Watson shot 67 to clip the great Jack Nicklaus by two.

Much of this is lost on me, however, as I know little of Tom Watson and even less of Nicklaus.

But I do know Jerry Pate, the defending U.S. Open Champion. Just three days ago I watched him hit practice balls in a driving rain, orange Prostaffs soaring into a gunmetal sky, his caddy holding an umbrella over the champion's head after each swing was finished.

I know because I'm standing in the exact same spot.

"Hey, pahds. I'm Mike Shannon. What's the good word?"

He offers a hand and we shake.

"Hi," I say.

"Mike, this is Tripp Bowden. My doctor's son," says Freddie, smiling. "The kid I told you about. Think you can work a little magic on him?"

Magic?

"Shoooot, yeah. He even looks like a player."

I do?

"All right, then. I'll leave you two to have at it." Freddie turns to face me. "Listen to him, man. He might not look like it, but this cat knows his stuff."

My mom is clutching her pocketbook, jangling her keys.

"Any chance I could do a little shopping, Freddie? I need to buy a couple shirts and time just got away from me yesterday. We got so caught up in the excitement we never made it past sixteen."

"Got caught up in the beer tent, too, I bet," says Freddie, in a voice only I can hear, before turning to my mother. "Absolutely,

Mrs. Bowden. Shop till you drop. Tell them I said give you the Charleston discount, okay?"

"You're a dear, Freddie Bennett," says Mom as she hurries into the pro shop.

"All right, pahds. You ready?"

I follow the voice. This Mike guy is young, twenty-five I'm guessing, but he looks like a little kid, not much bigger than me. *He's* gonna teach me golf?

My worries are soon over when Mike launches the first of five towering drives into a big green net at the end of the range. I have no idea how far he's hitting it, but as I look around at the other golfers, no one is coming close. Some have even stopped what they were doing, unable to take their eyes off Mike.

"Freddie says you're the pro here," I say. What I really want to say is, Wow—you can sure knock the shit out of a golf ball!

"*Assistant* pro," says Mike. "Maybe one day I'll run with the big dogs." He props his driver, a big Tony Penna with a blond finish, against my golf bag and looks inside.

"Say, look at what you've got. Real blades. Where'd you get these babies?"

Mike pulls out my 7-iron, grips it, and sends a ball sailing into the distance. The club is a little short for him, but not by much.

"Who cut these down for you? Freddie?"

I shake my head. "They came that way. But yeah, Freddie gave them to me."

"Nice," says Mike. "Birthday gift or something?"

"Just something, I guess. Freddie showed up at the house one day and handed them over. Shag bag and balls and gloves too." I hold up my left hand, show him the brand-new glove with the Augusta National logo embroidered on the strap.

"Look at you," he says. "All logo-ed up like a member." He points to my glove and then my shirt, a pink polo with the Augusta logo in full view. "All you're missing is a Green Jacket!"

I stop laughing when he looks down at my shoes.

"No spikes, eh?"

"Freddie said I had to break fifty before he would get me some. Said he didn't want to hear about my mama buying me a pair or he'd make her take 'em back."

Mike laughs.

"That Freddie's a piece of work, no doubt. But he's a great guy. Good man to have on your team." Mike grips the 7-iron, brushing the grass as he talks. "Freddie tells me you and him do a lot of fishing out here. Down by the Par 3. Says you catch 'em hand over fist."

"I've never seen fish like that in my life," I say.

"Yeah, this place is something, all right. Got the best of everything—even the fishing. Who would think some of the best fishing in the world is at Augusta National?"

Mike hands me the 7-iron. I put it back in the bag.

"No, pahds. I want to see what you got. Freddie said he taught you a few things. Says you got a pretty mean grip. Let's see it."

I pull out the 7-iron, wrap my hands around the tacky rubber handle.

"Whoa, check you out. You look like Ben Hogan holding that thing. Shoot, man. You don't need any of *my* help." He laughs and tosses a ball at my feet. "Freddie teach you that grip?"

I nod. "With a fishing pole."

"A fishing pole?"

"Yep"

"Ain't that something? But with Freddie Bennett, nothing surprises me. Not anymore."

Mike bends down and tees up a Titleist. "All right, pahds. Let's see what you got."

Uh-oh. The last time somebody said that to me the ball went nose-diving into a pond.

I look away. The practice tee at Augusta National is a sea of green. Thick, lush grass as far as the eye can see. Not a drop of water in sight.

I rare back and swing as hard as I can. The ball dribbles off the tee.

Mike quickly bends down and pegs up another, though it's clear he could just take two steps, pick up my shot, and place it back on the tee.

Another fierce swing and another dribbler. Who said tees make things easier?

This goes on for what seems like forever, though in reality only a minute or two, because there are only a few balls at my feet, barely outside the cast of my shadow.

"I see your problem," says Mike. "You're standing too close to the ball."

I look down. Something drips on my shoes. Sweat? Tears?

"I'm standing too close to the ball?"

Mike puts a hand on my shoulder, points to the grouping of balls not six feet away.

"Yeah, pahds. *After* you hit it." He laughs and so do I.

How can I not?

"Don't sweat it, pahds. Golf is a bitch to learn, but it's a beautiful game and you can play it for the rest of your life. You've only been playing for five minutes, man. Don't worry—we'll get you straightened out. This is the Augusta National. Magic happens out here."

I'm thinking it's gonna take a lot more than magic to straighten me out. Breaking 50 suddenly seems a thousand miles away.

"Let's start with your stance," says Mike, positioning my feet shoulder width apart. "And let's bend a little more from the waist, like a basketball player getting ready to guard somebody. Relax those shoulders a little. That's a 7-iron you've got in your hands, not a machete. You're not trying to kill anything with it." Mike tees up another, looks at me, and smiles.

"Now forget everything I just told you and launch that sucker."

I wind up and give my 7-iron a rip, clipping the ball off the tee as neat as you please. It flies like a bell curve onto a green some hundred yards out.

When the ball bounces twice and spins to a stop, I almost fall down.

"Whoa!" I say.

Mike is really smiling now.

"Say, pahds. You ever hear of a guy named Harvey Penick?"

THE STORY OF THE EARLY DAYS ON THE LINKS

BY CECIL LEITCH

JUST beyond Silloth, on the left side of the road that leads to the pretty little village of Skinburness (once a flourishing market town which was washed away by a terrific storm), there used to be a stretch of natural seaside ground remembered by Sillothians as "The Banks"—"used to be," for gradually the encroaching waters of Solway Firth have eaten it away, until little remains of the bonnie "Banks" of my childhood.

Although I love the dear old Solway in all its moods, I can never forgive it for this act of destruction. In devouring "The Banks" it destroyed the actual birthplace of my golf, the spot where I first hit a golf ball, disregarding the sanctity that always attaches to a birthplace. For that, it can never be forgiven.

It was here on this strip of land, about 200 yards wide and stretching away into the distance, intersected by numerous paths made by those who took their daily walks overlooking the Solway Firth, that I, at the age of about nine, in company with my elder sister May, began my golfing career.

Had my family or I known at that time that I should one day be called upon to perpetrate a golfing autobiography, a careful record would, no doubt, have been kept of the year, the day, and the hour when I first struck a golf ball and of all later developments.

Happily we did not know, and memory, though not such an accurate recorder as written memoranda, must be relied upon for the earlier dates and facts.

Going back to my extreme infancy, to the days beyond the reach of my memory, I was, my elders tell me, just the every-day child, with, however, one unusual predilection for a girl: I preferred whips to dolls. Dolls held no attraction for me—my heart's affections ran to whips—and at the mature age of two and a half I insisted on being photographed with a whip in my hands. The imaginative will, of course, see in this the germ of the future golfer!

Between this and the beginnings of my golf, that is between the ages of two and nine, I spent most of my time on the sea-shore at Silloth, my native place. My father was a Scotsman, a doctor by profession, and my mother English, so that I am an Anglo-Scot. Living in England, we had only to look a few miles across the water to see Scotland, a happy blend which seemed to express our Anglo-Scottish descent.

Silloth lies in a remote northwest comer of England, on the coast of Cumberland, 20 miles from Carlisle, the capital of the county, and 320 miles from London. Its residential population is under three thousand, but in the summer it is crowded with visitors, for as a seaside resort Silloth is very popular in the North of England. Fishing, a harbour, and a flour mill represent the industrial activities of the place, with the agriculture, which is the chief interest of the district. From Silloth, the coast of Scotland can always be seen, while on super-bright days the Isle of Man, 60 miles away, is clearly visible. But this latter is an evil omen, greatly feared by golfers; for it augurs rain, much rain, within three days. Quite apart from the natural affection one has for one's birthplace, Silloth is a lovable place, and casts its pleasant spell especially on those who haunt the links. Golfing visitors feel this and return again and again.

My father was the pioneer of golf at Silloth, laying out a nine-hole course on common land and playing there, with his sister, the first game of golf ever played on the shores of the Solway Firth. The natives of the place regarded them as a pair of lunatics. So there were hereditary reasons why I should not only play golf, but become "mad" on the game. And I may say here that never once since I first took a dub in my hand has there been any doubt about my love for golf; my love for it has never faltered; neither victory nor defeat has made any difference; I have just gone on growing fonder and fonder of the game, and nothing in the whole of my golfing career has been harder to bear than my banishment from the links after returning from America, the result of an injured arm.

At the age of nine then, I began my golfing career, on a stretch of ground 200 yards wide and a quarter of a mile long; for this was all we made use of for our primitive nine-hole course. Our fairways were the paths made by pedestrians, our putting greens the good patches on these paths, our holes cut by ourselves and lined with treacle tins, and our "trouble" the bents, sand holes, and wiry grass common to seaside links.

My first club was one of the old-fashioned cleeks, and my first ball—and only one for a long time—a guttie. This was my introduction to the game, and in its independence, it bears a close relationship to the rest of my golfing career. My golf has developed along independent lines; I am entirely self-taught, and I never had a lesson in my life. I watched others of course, and learnt from them, avoiding their faults and, no doubt, assimilating some of the good features of their play. Then I have received many valuable tips from leading players—from Mr. Hilton, who impressed upon me the importance of firmly gripping the ground with my feet; from the late Tom Ball, who taught me a cut shot with an iron; from Arnaud Massy, from whom I learnt an effective approach shot, and from several others, while I know no better corrective for "off one's game" than having a round with a first-class amateur or professional. Watching his even, rhythmical swing, one soon finds oneself falling into his way of doing it. It is a sort of unconscious mimicry.

But though I certainly owe a good deal to others, I am essentially a self-taught golfer. This should encourage, rather than discourage young players.

I think we must have played for about three years on our little makeshift course before joining the Carlisle and Silloth Golf Club. My brother Monie (the family consisted of five girls and two boys) and my sister Edith were already members of the Club, and the former had begun to show himself a player of much promise.

When I say that the ladies' annual subscription at that time was only five shillings, it will be seen that my sisters and I were not very important assets so far as the Club's income was concerned. Nor did we seem to be important in other respects. Ladies and children were a rare sight on the links, and no one appeared to take much notice of us, or to be troubled by our existence.

I well remember that my sister May and I (we usually played together) were too timid to drive off from the first tee, which is in full view of the Clubhouse, for some time after we had every right to do so.

By this time I had been promoted to a bag, and from one club to a set of six, as follows: driver, the favorite and veteran cleek, lofting iron, mashie, niblick and putter.

My sister May, a left-handed player, had begun her golf with a cleek, a club with which she has always been an adept. Great difficulty was experienced in persuading the professional, at that time, to make a left-handed club for a child. He argued that she ought to be made to play in the ordinary right-handed way.

May is undoubtedly left-handed and always has been; she plays tennis with the left hand, and invariably uses the left hand when other people would use the right. Many children want to play in a left-handed manner, but few are actually left-handed. The professional, no doubt, had it in his mind that May was one of these. However, he made her her left-handed clubs and, judging from the way she used them, with just as much care as if they had been right-handed.

It must have been during this very raw stage of our apprenticeship that a male member of the Club witnessed the following incident, which he long after related to us. "I was playing golf at Silloth" (to give it in his own words) "one day many years ago, and, arriving at the 14th, or Heather hole, my partner and I came across two little curly-haired girls dressed alike in white sailor coats, blue serge kilted skirts, white socks and little black patent-leather ankle-strap slippers. One was hacking away in the heather, while the other stood with her legs crossed and looked on. After many fruitless efforts by the smaller to dislodge the ball, she turned round and, in a pathetic voice exclaimed, 'I can't get it out!' To which the other answered, 'No, it needs strength and you lack it.'" This little story certainly has the ring of truth, for Silloth heather is plentiful and thick, terrible stuff to escape from. I paid it frequent visits and also I was not nearly as strong as my sister May.

And here let me say that this constant playing on a course where heather and sand, bents and wind abounded was the best possible education for the young golfer with any grit or gift for the game. The trying conditions might have discouraged some, but never did us. We loved the buffetings of the wind and the high adventure of the difficulties, and these things gave a fibre to our game which easier conditions would never have given. Wind was almost the normal condition at Silloth, and one's game had to be adapted accordingly. Experience teaches the best and most permanent lessons, and even in the earlier and more irresponsible days Silloth was teaching me lessons which have left their mark on my game. Constant battling with the wind gradually evolved in me a means of reducing its resistance, and much familiarity with difficult "lies" on or off the course bred in me, if not exactly a contempt for them, at any rate no great fear of them.

We never allowed either wind or weather to curtail a round once started. We persevered until our balls were at the bottom of the last hole, determined to see the thing through. I am sure this was good for us and developed in us the spirit of fighting to a finish when it came to important match play.

No sooner had I joined the Carlisle and Silloth Club than I began to keep a record of every round or match played. To this day I have kept up that practice.

Had circumstances allowed, we would have played golf every day and all day; but education and its claims forbade this. There is no doubt that education does interfere with a child's golf! I am not sure that it is not a greater nuisance in that way than work in later life!

Everyone knows the story of the ardent golfer who told a friend that golf was interfering with business, and that he would have to give it up. "What! " exclaimed his friend, "give up golf?" "No," replied the other, "business." That was my feeling about golf and education.

As a matter of fact we had little to grumble at. After being started off in our education at home, we went to school in Carlisle for many years. This necessitated an hour's train journey morning and afternoon; but as we got back to Silloth by three o'clock on most days, we had time for a round of golf nearly every day during the summer months. The guard of the train, Mr. Selkirk, an official well known to visitors and golfers, often speaks of the responsibility he felt in looking after the four of us. I think it says a great deal for our sense of duty that we never once missed the train. To have done so would, probably, have meant a day's golf! The temptation was great, and it would have been such a simple matter to succumb to it. A little lagging or imaginary trouble with a boot-lace was all that was necessary. But I must not take all the credit to ourselves for our regular attendance at school. Our friend, the guard, was largely responsible for it. Many were the times he stood at the end of the platform, whistle and flag in hand, beckoning to one, two, three, or even four small figures trailing stationwards. That particular train had not a good reputation for punctuality. It was a very different story coming back; there was only eagerness to get to the station as soon as possible.

Arrived at Silloth, we invariably made for the Club-house and, throwing our school-bags into the locker and our school worries with them, set off from the first tee full of hope that we should play the game of our life.

Not long after it's publication, I became the proud possessor of a copy of Braid's book, *Advanced Golf*. How I used to devour this in the train to and from school. Alas! my zeal for the study of Braid outran my discretion. One day, under cover of the lid of my desk, I was secretly feeding on Braid when my mental diet should have been of a more edifying (!) kind. Detection was followed by confiscation, and *Advanced Golf* spent several unhappy and profitless days in the mistress's desk.

Our keenness for golf was not at all understood by the school-mistresses. On returning to school after the summer holidays, we were, on one occasion, told to write an essay on how we had spent them. We, of course, had spent ours on the links; but the innocent colloquial golfing expression, "Spent my holidays on the links," was taken as a gross exaggeration by the mistress and underlined as such.

One of the questions in a geography examination paper was: "What do you know about the denudation of the earth's surface?" Having no idea what "denudation" meant, I had, perforce, to give this question a miss. But when later I learnt the meaning of denudation, and its geological significance, I felt I had let slip the chance of a lifetime, for my own practical experience of denudation on the Silloth links fitted me to write feelingly on the subject.

I had my favourite subjects at school and worked hard enough at these, which, perhaps fittingly, were mathematics, science, drawing, and physical geography, especially those parts of the last named dealing with the composition of the earth's surface and with climatic conditions. Political geography made no appeal to me. It might have been otherwise had I known that the game I loved would one day take me to many different parts of the world. Though school prizes never fell to my share, I had the satisfaction of always being in a class where I was younger than the average age.

At home we were always encouraged in outdoor games, our mother maintaining that it was far better for our health to forget lessons entirely on leaving school each day. Nor did she believe in too much home-work. For these beliefs we blessed her! Hockey, cricket, and tennis were included in the school curriculum, but, though keen on these, I would willingly have given them all up for golf.

The energy of a child, viewed through adult eyes, is an amazing thing. Many times, in those early days, did I play three rounds of the Silloth course in one day. Remembering the number of shots and the amount of energy I used to expend per round, I wonder

I was not often exhausted. And yet I do not recollect ever feeling even tired. But the bracing air of Silloth must share the credit for this. Limpness is a feeling I, personally, have never experienced at Silloth, though I have played on courses where I hardly had the energy to drag one foot after the other.

In another respect, too, I was very fortunate in having Silloth for my native course. A large-minded and generous Committee allowed children the full privileges of the links. What a blessing this was has often been forcibly brought to my mind when hearing of boys and girls unable to play over their local courses, and unable, therefore, to make an early start at the game.

As I knocked a guttie ball round the Silloth links by the means I found most comfortable, I had no prophetic vision that golf would be the cause of my travelling thousands of miles, playing before thousands of spectators, making multitudes of friends, experiencing countless thrills and excitements, and achieving success in the great big golfing world. I understood as a child, I thought as a child, I played as a child.

Soon after joining the Club, I was taking part in Club matches and competitions. A Leitch usually headed the latter, while in the former the Leitch family furnished the majority of the team. An amusing incident of one of these matches is worth retelling. The Silloth team, largely Leitch in flavour, journeyed to Moffat to play the local Club. After mutual greetings, the Moffat captain, seeing two small children with the team, remarked to the Silloth captain, "Oh, you needn't have brought caddies with you, we have plenty here." Her embarrassment on learning that the "caddies" were members of the team was only second to her amazement when later the little sisters returned to the Clubhouse, bringing with them the scalps of their adult opponents.

During all this time we were quite unconscious of the fact that we played any better than other ordinary mortals in the outside world. And it was not until Mr. Eustace White, the well-known writer on women's sport, paid a chance visit to Silloth in

1907, that we were led to believe we were anything more than beginners.

The great names in ladies' golf were known to us, and we read with keen interest of the doings of Rhona Adair, Lottie Dod and the Hezlets. But they were just names to us, golfing goddesses, too far above us to make us either envious or ambitious. A story I was told about Rhona Adair impressed me. She was playing on a course laid out over rocky ground. Before using a spoon for which she had great affection, she would pull a hatpin from her hat and test the ground with it, in case a hidden rock should damage her pet club.

When not playing myself, I loved nothing so much as "carrying" for my brother, especially when he was taking part in a Club match or competition. He used very few clubs: brassie, driving iron, jigger, mashie and putter. He would never have these cleaned and became known as the boy with the "bronze set of clubs." Though he was not exceptionally long, his short game was the most marvellous thing imaginable. I have yet to see its equal. He never had a handicap worse than scratch, and on winning with ease the first competition he took part in as a full member, he was made plus 2, a handicap he retained till his early death in 1907, at the age of twenty-two.

We all learned our golf with the old guttie ball, and I am glad of it. That old solid ball had to be hit in the proper manner before it would go. There was no running bunkers with it, and a "top" meant an ugly gash that made one realize the fault must not be repeated. One great advantage it had over the rubber-cored ball was that it could be re-made. Often on hitting one hard on the head, I found consolation in the fact that it was a 27½ and that Renouf, who was the professional at the time, would give me a re-made for it, together with sixpence. I never remember experiencing the drudgery stage, through which most players have to pass. All being self-taught, our styles were quite different. Of the sisters, Edith, the eldest, was always looked up to by the others, as she was, undoubtedly, the most capable performer. My allotted place was No. 3. The wind and the guttie ball together had an influence on our style, and produced in us our powerful and rather manlike swings.

Since success has come my way, two or three professionals claim to have taught me my golf. But surely no professional would allow a pupil to adopt, to the extent to which I do, the palm grip, flat swing, and bent knee at the top of the swing. Such an unorthodox combination should be condemned and disowned by the professional teacher!

There is a famous hole at Silloth called the "Duffer's Bunker." A very wide and deep sand pit has to be carried from the tee. This used to be the dread of lady (and many men) players, especially in a medal round, as it came near the end (formerly the 16th, now the 17th). To this day I can remember the exquisite thrill of pleasure at my first successful "crack" over this trouble.

The improvement in my play came gradually, and I was encouraged by friends interested in my efforts to keep on improving my "best round." The day I broke 100 by one stroke was a red-letter day. Slowly and surely I improved this, until at the age of seventeen (the year of my first championship), my average match-play round was between 80 and 84 from the men's tees, bogey at that time being about 78.

In the summer of 1907 Mrs. Archbold Smith, a moving spirit in Yorkshire golf, paid a golfing visit to Silloth. She tried hard to make us believe that we played better than most of the competitors in the ladies' open championship. But we did not share this flattering opinion of our own play, and would certainly have gasped had anyone predicted that one of us would come within measurable distance of winning the open championship in less than a year.

THE STORY BEHIND MY FIRST "BIG" MATCH, AND OTHER LESSONS FROM MY YOUTH: AN EXCERPT FROM *GOLF FACTS FOR YOUNG PEOPLE*

FRANCIS OUIMET

It was as a school-boy golfer that I first had that feeling of satisfaction which comes in winning a tournament, and it was as a school-boy golfer that I learned a few things which perhaps may be useful to some boys who are pupils in school now and who are interested in golf. It was in 1908 that I took part for the first time in an interscholastic tournament, at the Wollaston Golf Club, and I may as well say, right here, that I did not win the title; the fact is that I barely qualified, my 85 being only one stroke better than the worst score in the championship qualifying division. The best score was 74, which I must say was extraordinarily good for such a course as that on which the event was played. It is a fine score there today for any golfer, even in the ranks of the men. In my first round of match play, fortune favored me, only to make me the victim of its caprices in the second round, when I was defeated two up and one to play by the eventual winner of the championship title, Carl Anderson. It was inability to run down putts of about three feet in length which cost me that match, and, to my sorrow, I have passed through that same experience more than once since leaving school. But what I recollect distinctly about that match, aside from my troubles on the putting-greens, was that I felt nervous from the start, for it was my first "big" match. I mention this because it has its own little lesson, which is that the chances of winning are less when the thought of winning is so much on the mind as to affect the nerves.

In 1909 I won the championship of the Greater Boston Interscholastic Golf Association, the tournament being played at the Commonwealth Country Club, Newton, Massachusetts. Only one match was at all close, that one going to the sixteenth green. The final, at thirty-six holes, I won by ten up and nine to play. In that tournament I learned a lesson invaluable, which was to avoid trying to play every shot equally well with my opponent. In other words, there were boys in that tournament who were vastly my superiors in long hitting. Frequently they were reaching the green in two shots where I required three, or else they were getting there with a drive and a mashie shot where I required two long shots. But, fortunately, I was of a tempera ment at that time which enabled me to go along my own way, never trying to hit the ball beyond my natural strength in order to go as far as my opponent, and making up for lack of distance by accuracy of direction and better putting. My advice to any boy is to play his own game, irrespective of what his opponent does. This does not mean, of course, that a boy should lose his ambition to improve his game, or that he should be content with moderate distance when he might be able to do better. But the time for striving to do better is not when ambition is aroused merely through the desire to win some one match or to outhit some opponent. The average boy or man who strives in some one match to hit the ball harder than he does normally generally finds that, instead of getting greater distance, he is only spoiling his natural game. Then, the harder he tries, the worse he gets. Greater distance on the drive, as well as accuracy in all departments of the game, comes through practice and natural development, rather than through the extra efforts of some one round.

In that tournament at the Commonwealth Country Club, which gave me the first championship title which I ever held in golf, there were a number of players who subsequently have achieved successes in athletic lines, several of them having become prominent for their skill in golf. Among these was Heinrich Schmidt, of Worcester, Massachusetts, who in the spring of 1913, made such a great showing in the British amateur championship. Even at that time, "Heinie," as we called him, was a more than ordinarily good golfer, and he was looked upon as one of the possible winners of the championship. It was one of his Worcester team-mates, Arthur Knight, who put him out of the running, in a match that went two extra holes. "Heinie's" twin brother, Karl, who looked so much like him that it was difficult to tell the two apart, also was in the tournament, and among others were the late Dana Wingate, afterwards captain of the Harvard varsity baseball nine; Forrester Ainsworth, halfback on the Yale football eleven in 1913; and Fletcher Gill, who later played on the Williams College golf team.

The following year, 1910, I was honored with election to the presidency of the Greater Boston Interscholastic Golf Association, which did not, however, help me to retain the championship title, for that year the winner was Arthur Knight, of Worcester.

This interesting tournament was played on the links of the Woodland Golf Club at Auburndale, Massachusetts, and in the qualifying round I was medalist, with a score of 77. Singularly enough, I had that same score in winning my match of the first round, and also had a 77 in the second round; but on that occasion it was not good enough to win; for Francis Mahan, one of my team-mates from Brookline High School, was around with a brilliant 73, whereby he won by three up and two to play. It was beautiful golf for a boy (for a man, either, as far as that goes), and the loss of the title, under such circumstances, left nothing for me to regret. It always has struck me that for any one who truly loves the game of golf, there is even a pleasure in being defeated when you have played first-class golf yourself, and have been beaten only because your opponent has played even better. It certainly was so in that case, and I was sorry that Mahan could not keep up the gait in his other matches. He was beaten by the eventual winner of the tournament, Arthur Knight, in the semi-final round, Knight winning the thirty-six-hole final by two up and one to play from R. W. Gleason, later a member of the Williams College team.

From my own experiences in school-boy golf, I should be an enthusiastic supporter of any movement tending to make the game a greater factor in the athletic life of school-boys or, for that matter, in the colleges. I do think, however, that it should come under more direct supervision of older heads, and that boys should be taught not only how to play the game, but that they should have impressed upon them the fact that it is a game that demands absolute honesty.

I have known instances where, in school-boy tournaments, scores have been returned which were surprisingly low, and there have been occasions when such scores, appearing in print, have brought a tinge of suspicion upon the boys returning them. Such instances would be rare if proper methods were taken to explain to the boys that golf is a game which puts them strictly on their honor. They should be taught to realize that winning is not everything in the game; that a prize won through trickery, either in turning in a wrong score or moving the ball to give it a more desirable position, gives no lasting pleasure. Any boy winning a prize by such methods would in later life want to have it out of sight. Every time he looked at it, he would have a feeling of contempt for himself for having adopted dishonest methods. Under proper supervision, golf can be made a great agency in the schools for the development of character; a game which will teach the boy to be honest with himself and with others.

THE STORY OF MY FIRST NATIONAL CHAMPIONSHIP: ANOTHER EXCERPT FROM *GOLF FACTS FOR YOUNG PEOPLE*

BY FRANCIS OUIMET

The 1910 Amateur Championship at The Country Club, Brookline, where I saw Mr. Herreshoff make the drive above mentioned, was the first national event I ever entered, my age at the time being seventeen years. I did not qualify, but my failure did not make me feel very badly, considering all the circumstances. My total of 169 in the qualifying rounds was only one stroke worse than the top qualifying figure; and among those who, like myself, failed to get in the match play were such noted golfers as Robert A. Gardner, then the national amateur champion, and H. Chandler Egan, a former champion.

Furthermore, I played under circumstances that were a handicap in themselves. The championship field was inordinately large, and I was among the late starters for the first round, getting away from the first tee at 2:44 in the afternoon. This would have been ample time to get around before dark, had it not been for an extraordinary congestion at the third tee. Some one of the earlier starters was exceedingly slow, not to mention the time taken to search for a ball, and other little things that helped to cause delay and hold the players back. When my partner and I arrived at the third tee, there were ten pairs then waiting for an opportunity to play that hole, and there was nothing to do but wait. An hour and ten minutes of waiting at one tee in a championship is not conducive to best efforts; at any rate, it was not in my case.

While waiting at this tee, I remember having watched W. C. Chick take eight for the sixth hole, and, while mentally sympathizing with him, I did not dream that I would get a similar figure for my own card, when I finally did play the third hole, for I had started most satisfactorily with four for the first hole, and the same figure for the second. When it came my turn to drive from the third tee, I drove into a trap, lost a stroke getting out, put my third in the woods, was back on the fair green in four, on the green in five, and then took three putts for an eight. But from that point, I was forty-four strokes for the first nine holes. By this time, the afternoon was pretty well gone, and my partner and I had to stop playing at the fourteenth, because of darkness. As my card showed even fours for the first five holes of the inward half, I was beginning to feel better, and had I been able to complete the round that day, I think I might have been around in seventy-nine or eighty.

Along with several other pairs who were caught in the same dilemma, I had to go out the following morning to play the remaining four holes, and the best I could get for them was a total of nineteen strokes, whereas I would do those same holes ordinarily in sixteen strokes, at most. My score of eighty-three for the first round was not bad, however, and a similar round the second day would have put me in the match play.

But I had made one serious mistake, as I learned in the course of the second round. My supposition had been that, after playing the last four holes of the first round on the morning of the second day, I would have ample time to go home to breakfast and then return for the second round, my home being in close proximity to the grounds. What actually happened was that, after completing the four holes of the first round, I was told to report immediately at the first tee for my second round, in which I was to have the pleasure of being partnered with the then president of the United States Golf Association, Robert C. Watson. For the first nine holes I had reason to feel satisfied, doing them in forty-one strokes, with every prospect of doing even better in the scoring for the last nine, which are less difficult. But by this time the pangs of hunger had taken a firm hold, and I could feel myself weakening physically, which was the result both of my failure to get breakfast, and the strain of a week of hard practising. The consequence was that I made a poor finish, took forty-five for the last nine, eighty-six for the round, and had one hundred and sixty-nine for my thirty-six-hole total, or just out of the match-play running. The moral is to be properly prepared for competition.

About that "week of hard practising" I would like to add a little. My experiences of practising for the championship of 1910 taught me a good lesson, which is that practising may easily be overdone. My idea of practising for that event was to get in at least thirty-six holes a day for the week prior to the championship. This was based partly on the idea that, with so much play, the game could be brought to such a point of mechanical precision that it would be second nature to hit the ball properly. The thought of "going stale" from so much play never occurred to me. Probably one reason was that I never had had a feeling of physical staleness in any sport up to that time. I always had been keen for golf, from the time of becoming interested in the game, and could not imagine a state of feeling that would mean even the slightest repugnance for play.

This is, perhaps, an error natural to youth and inexperience. It was not for me to know that a growing youth of seventeen years is not likely to have such a robust constitution that he can stand thirty-six holes of golf a day for a week, not to mention fairly steady play for weeks in advance of that, and still be on edge for a championship tournament.

It was not only on the Saturday previous to the championship (which began Monday) that I noticed this feeling of staleness. It did not come on all at once, by any means, and I did not realize what was the trouble, for on the day that I first noticed that I was not so keen for play as usual, I made a particularly good score. That day I was playing in company with H. H. Wilder, R. R. Freeman, and W. R. Tuckerman. This round was more or less of a tryout for places on the Massachusetts State team and I was fortunate enough to get in the best round, a seventy-six. Incidentally, I might add that this performance did not land me the coveted place on the State team, for Mr. Tuckerman reached the semifinals of the championship the succeeding week, which gave him precedence. That year I did play one match for the State team, however. It was in the match against Rhode Island, when the Massachusetts team found itself one man shy on the day set for play, which also was at The Country Club. Somebody discovered that I was in the vicinity, looked me up, and I played with a set of borrowed clubs, and also won my match.

To revert to the physical strain of too much practice, I found that on Saturday of the practice week my hands were sore, and that I was playing with unwonted effort, though not getting any better results that when hitting the ball with normal ease. It was my first lesson in the knowledge that when the game becomes a task, rather than a pleasure, something is wrong physically.

My advice to any golfer preparing for a championship is, therefore, not to overdo the practice end. To my mind, the wise thing is to play thirty-six holes a day for perhaps two days a week in advance of the championship. Then spend a morning in practising shots with the irons, the mashie, and putting, followed by a round of the course in the afternoon. This might be done for two or three days, with special attention given to the club which perhaps is not getting satisfactory results. One round of golf, without special exertion, the day before the tournament, after such a program, ought to put the player in good shape for the real competition. As for the superstition of some golfers that a particularly fine round in practice means so much less chance of duplicating it in tournament play, I hold a different view, which is that an especially good round gives an inspiration to equal it when the real test comes. I always feel after such a round that if I can do it once, there is no reason why I cannot again.

Elimination from the championship, in the qualifying round, had its compensations. It gave me the opportunity to watch the championship play for the remainder of the week, to see in action those golfers of whom I had heard so much. That in itself was a treat. Some of the matches, moreover, gave me some new ideas about golf as played in competition by men in the foremost ranks. For one thing, it was rather startling, if such a word can apply, to see a golfer like Mr. Herreshoff literally "swamped" in his match with Mr. Evans. Mr. Herreshoff had made the lowest score of the entire field in the qualifying round, yet here was the same man unable to put up anything but the most feeble opposition to the young Chicago golfer. Such a match only goes to show that the best of golfers occasionally have their bad days, days on which they find it seemingly impossible to play satisfactorily. That is a good thing to bear in mind—no match is lost before it is played. When a golfer possessed of such ability as had Mr. Herreshoff can be defeated eleven up and nine to play, it simply shows that golf is a game of uncertainties, after all; that, in fact, is one of its great charms.

In that same championship, the uncertainties of the game were shown in another match, and again Mr. Evans was one of the factors, though this time on the losing side. He had been playing in form which made him a distinctive favorite for the title, and, in the semifinal round, he came to the sixteenth hole two up on W. C. Fownes, Jr., of Pittsburgh. The sixteenth is a short hole, just a mashie pitch. Mr. Evans reached the edge of the green with his tee shot, whereas Mr. Fownes made a poor effort, and put his ball in a sand-trap.

The match appeared to be over, then and there. But a match in golf never is over until one player has a lead of more holes than there are holes to play, a fact which was demonstrated anew in this match. Mr. Fownes played out of the trap, and holed a long putt for a three, while Mr. Evans, using his mid-iron instead of his putter from the edge of the green, was well past the hole on his second shot, and failed to get the putt coming back. Hence, instead of winning the hole and the match, as he seemed bound to do, he lost the hole. Then, as so often happens when a man apparently has a match absolutely in hand and loses an opening to clinch it, Mr. Evans lost the seventeenth, likewise the home hole, and, with the loss of the eighteenth, he also lost the match. Instead of winning the match and the championship, as nearly everybody figured he would, he only got to the semi-finals. It is true that Mr. Fownes made a wonderful recovery at the sixteenth, to get his three; he played a remarkable shot at the seventeenth, too; but a man is apt to do that after recovering from an almost hopeless situation.

It was in that championship that I was astonished to see such a great golfer as Mr. Evans using his mid-iron instead of his putter most of the time on the greens. He was then following the same practice that was true of his play in the middle west, notwithstanding that the putter is a much superior club for greens such as are found at The Country Club. He could not be expected, of course, to come east and learn to get the best results from the putter in such a short time as he had for practice.

To see him use the mid-iron on the greens, and then practically lose his semifinal round match, and possibly the title, because he could not lay a mid-iron approach-putt dead at the sixteenth, helped me to form one resolution for which I since have been thankful. That was to use my putter from any point on the green, provided there was no special reason for doing otherwise. Of course, there are circumstances when the mid-iron is better for an approach-putt than the putter, as, for example, when there is a little piece of dirt on or in front of the ball, casual water, or uneven surface to go over. But under normal conditions, nowadays, I would rather use my putter and take three putts, than take a mid-iron or another club. By adhering to that policy, I think I have gained more confidence in my putting, and confidence is a wonderful asset in this branch of the game. Watching the good players in that championship gave me one distinct ambition, which was to try to steady my game down to a point where I would not play four holes well, say, and then have two or three poor ones before getting another three-or four-hole streak of satisfactory play. The steadily good game is better than the combination of brilliant and erratic. It is something like the hare and the tortoise.

Man vyi

THE STORY OF MY BEGINNINGS AS A GOLFER, FROM ONE MEMBER OF THE "GREAT TRIUMVIRATE"

HARRY VARDON

I have sometimes heard good golfers sigh regretfully, after holing out on the eighteenth green, that in the best of circumstances as to health and duration of life they cannot hope for more than another twenty, or thirty, or forty years of golf, and they are then very likely inclined to be a little bitter about the good years of their youth that they may have "wasted" at some other less fascinating sport. When the golfer's mind turns to reflections such as these, you may depend upon it that it has been one of those days when everything has gone right and nothing wrong, and the supreme joy of life has been experienced on the links. The little white ball has seemed possessed of a soul—a soul full of kindness and the desire for doing good. The clubs have seemed endowed with some subtle qualities that had rarely been discovered in them before. Their lie, their balance, their whip, have appeared to reach the ideal, and such command has been felt over them as over a dissecting instrument in the hands of a skilful surgeon. The sun has been shining and the atmosphere has sparkled when, flicked cleanly from the tee, the rubber-cored ball has been sent singing through the air. The drives have all been long and straight, the brassy shots well up, the approaches mostly dead, and the putts have taken the true line to the tin. Hole after hole has been done in bogey, and here and there the common enemy has been beaten by a stroke. Perhaps the result is a record round, and, so great is the enthusiasm for the game at this moment, that it is regarded as a great misfortune that the sun has set and there is no more light left for play. These are the times when the golfer's pulse beats strong, and he feels the remorse of the man with the misspent youth because he was grown up and his limbs were setting before ever he teed a ball.

Well, at least I can say that I have not missed much of the game that I love with a great fondness, for I played a kind of prehistoric golf when I was a bad boy of seven, and off and on I have played it ever since. It was fortunate for me that the common land at Jersey was years ago the ideal thing for a golfing links, and that golfers from abroad found out its secret, as they always do. If they had failed to do so in this case, I might still have been spending my life in horticultural pursuits. For I was born (on May 9, 1870) and bred in Jersey, at that little place called Grouville, which is no more than a

collection of scattered cottages and farmhouses a few miles
from St. Heliers. Both my parents were natives of Jersey, and
my father, who was seventy-four on the 5th of last November,
has been a gardener there all his life, holding the proud record
of having changed his place of employment only once during the whole period. There was a big family of us—six boys
and two girls—and all, except one of my sisters, are still alive.
My brothers were George, Phil, Edward, Tom, and Fred, and
I came fourth down the list, after Edward. As most golfers
know, my brother Tom, to whom I owe very much, is now
the professional at the Royal St George's Club at Sandwich,
while Fred is a professional in the Isle of Man. In due course
we all went to the little village school; but I fear, from all that
I can remember, and from what I have been told, that knowledge had little attraction for me in those days, and I know
that I very often played truant, sometimes for three weeks at a
stretch. Consequently my old schoolmaster, Mr. Boomer, had
no particular reason to be proud of me at that time, as he seems
to have become since. He never enjoys a holiday so much in
these days as when he comes over from Jersey to see me play
for the Open Championship, as he does whenever the meeting is held at Sandwich. But when I did win a Championship
on that course, he was so nervous and excited about my play
and my prospects that he felt himself unequal to watching me,
and during most of the time that I was doing my four rounds
he was sitting in a fretful state upon the seashore. I was a thin
and rather delicate boy with not much physical strength, but I
was as enthusiastic as the others in the games that were played
at that time, and my first ambition was to excel at cricket. A
while afterwards I became attached to football, and I retained
some fondness for this game long after I took up golf. Even
after my golfing tour in America a few years ago, when quite
at my best, I captained the Ganton football team and played
regularly in its matches.

One day, when I was about seven years of age, a very shocking thing happened at Grouville. All the people there lived a quiet, undisturbed life, and had a very wholesome respect for the sanctity of the Sabbath day. But of all days of the week it was a Sunday when a small party of strange gentlemen made their appearance on the common land, and began to survey and to mark out places for greens and tees. Then the story went about that they were making preparations to play a game called golf. That was enough to excite the wrathful indignation of all the tenant-farmers round about, and without delay they began to think out means for expelling these trespassers from the common land. A tale of indignation spread through Grouville, and these golfers, of whom I remember that Mr. Brewster was one, were not at first regarded in the light of friendship. But they soon made their position secure by obtaining all necessary authority and permission for what they were about to do from the constable of the parish, and from that day we had to resign ourselves to the fact that a new feature had entered into the quiet life of Jersey. The little party went ahead with the marking out of their course, though indeed the natural state of the place was so perfect from the golfer's point of view that very little work was necessary, and no first-class golf links was ever made more easily. There were sand and other natural hazards everywhere, the grass was short and springy just as it is on all good sea-coast links, and all that it was necessary to do was to put a flag down where each hole was going to be, and run the mower and the roller over the space selected for the putting green. Rooms were rented at a little inn hard by, which was forthwith rechristened the Golf Inn, and the headquarters of the Jersey golfers are still at the same place, though a large club-room has been added. That was the beginning of the Royal Jersey Golf Club. The links as they were when they were first completed were really excellent—much better than they are today, for since then, in order to prevent the sand being blown all over the course by the strong winds which sweep across the island, the bunkers have in most cases been filled with clay, which has to a great extent spoiled them.

When everything was ready, more of these golfers came across from England to play this new game which we had never seen before, and all the youngsters of the locality were enticed into their service to carry their clubs. I was among the number, and that was my first introduction to the game. We did not think much of it upon our first experience; but after we had carried for a few rounds we came to see that it contained more than we had imagined. Then we were seized with a desire to play it ourselves, and discover what we could do. But we had no links to play upon, no clubs, no balls, and no money. However, we surmounted all these difficulties. To begin with, we laid out a special course of our very own. It consisted of only four holes, and each one of them was only about fifty yards long, but for boys of seven that was quite enough. We made our teeing grounds, smoothed out the greens, and, so far as this part of the business was concerned, were soon ready for play. There was no difficulty about balls, for we decided at once that the most suitable article for us, in the absence of real gutties, was the big white marble which we called a taw, and which was about half the size of an ordinary golf ball, or perhaps a little less than that. But there was some anxiety in our juvenile minds when the question of clubs came to be considered, and I think we deserved credit for the manner in which we disposed of it. It was apparent that nothing would be satisfactory except a club fashioned on the lines of a real golf club, and that to procure anything of the sort, we should have to make it ourselves. Therefore, after several experiments, we decided that we would use for the purpose the hard wood of the tree which we called the lady oak. To make a club we cut a thick branch from the tree, sawed off a few inches from it, and then trimmed this piece so that it had a faint resemblance to the heads of the drivers we had seen used on the links. Any elaborate splicing operations were out of the question, so we agreed that we must bore a hole in the centre of the head. The shaft sticks that we chose and trimmed were made of good thorn, white or black, and when we had prepared them to our satisfaction we put the poker in the fire and made it red hot, then bored a hole with it through the head, and tightened the shaft with wedges until the club was complete. With this primitive driver we could get what was for our diminutive limbs a really long ball, or a long taw as one should say. In these later days a patent has been taken out for drivers with the shaft let into the head, which are to all intents and purposes the same in principle as those which we used to make at Grouville.

By and by some of us became quite expert at the making of these clubs, and we set ourselves to discover ways and means of improving them. The greater elaboration of such brassies as we had seen impressed us, and we also found some trouble with our oak heads in that, being green, they were rather inclined to chip and crack. Ultimately we decided to sheathe the heads entirely with tin. It was not an easy thing to make a good job of this, and we were further troubled by the circumstance that our respective fathers had no sympathy with us, and declined upon any account to lend us their tools. Consequently we had no option but to wait until the coast was clear and then surreptitiously borrow the tools for an hour or two. We called these tin-plated drivers our brassies, and they were certainly an improvement on our original clubs. Occasionally a club was made in this manner which exhibited properties superior to those possessed by any other, as clubs will do even today. Forthwith the reputation of the maker of this club went up by leaps and bounds, and he was petitioned by others to make clubs for them, a heavy price in taws and marbles being offered for the service. The club that had created all this stir would change hands two or three times at an increasing price until it required the payment of four or five dozen marbles to become possessed of it. But the boy who owned the treasure was looked upon as the lord of the manor, and odds were demanded of him in the matches that we played.

We practised our very elementary kind of golf whenever we could, and were soon enthusiastic. I remember particularly that many of our best matches were played in the moonlight. The moon seemed to shine more clearly at Jersey than in England, and we could see splendidly. Four of us would go out together on a moonlight night to play, and our little competition was arranged on the medal system by scores. Usually a few marbles were at stake. To prevent the loss of taws one of us was sent ahead to watch for their coming and listen for the faint thud of their fall, while the other three drove from the tee. Then the three came forward while the watcher went back to drive, and I am sorry to say that our keenness in those days led us to disregard certain principles of the sportsman's code of honour, which we appreciated better as we grew up. What I mean is that the watcher was often handicapped in a way that he little suspected, for when he went back to the tee, and we went forward and found that our balls were not always so well up as we had hoped, we gave them a gentle kick forwards; for in the dim light we were able to do this unknown to each other. But in legitimate play we often got a 3 at these fifty-yard holes, and with our home-made clubs, our little white taws, our lack of knowledge, and our physical feebleness all taken into consideration, I say we have often done less creditable things since then.

After such beginnings, we progressed very well. We began to carry more and more for the golfers who came to Grouville; we found or were given real balls that took the place of the taws, and then a damaged club occasionally came our way, and was repaired and brought into our own service. Usually it was necessary to put in new shafts, and so we burnt holes in the heads and put in the sticks, as we did with clubs of our own make; but these converted clubs were disappointing in the matter of durability. It happened once or twice that golfers for whom we had been carrying gave us an undamaged club as a reward for our enthusiasm, and we were greatly excited and encouraged when such a thing happened. I used to carry clubs about twice a week. I remember that Mr. Molesworth and Dr. Purves, both well known in the golfing world, were two players for whom I very often carried, and only the other day when I saw the former at the Professional Tournament at Richmond, watching the play, I was able to remind him of those times and of a particular shot he once played. We young caddies were very eager to learn the game thoroughly, and we were in the habit of watching these golfers very closely, comparing their styles, and then copying anything from them that seemed to take our fancy. I may say at once, in reply to a question that I am often asked, and which perhaps my present readers may themselves be inclined to put, that I have never in my life taken a single golfing lesson from anyone, and that whatever style I may possess is purely the result of watching others play and copying them when I thought they made a stroke in a particularly easy and satisfactory manner. It was my habit for very many years after these early days, until in fact I had won the Open Championship, to study the methods of good golfers in this way, and there are few from whom one is not able to learn something. I cannot say that the play of any one man particularly impressed me; I cannot point to any player, past or present, and declare that I modelled my style on his. It seemed to me that I took a little from one and a little from another until my swing was a composition of the swings of several players, and my approach shots likewise were of a very mixed parentage. Of course when I took a hint from the play of anyone I had been watching it required much subsequent practice properly to weld it into my own system; but I think that this close watching of good players, and the borrowing from their styles of all information that you think is good, and then constantly practising the new idea yourself, is an excellent method of improving your golf, though I do not recommend it as the sole method of learning, despite the success which I personally have achieved. However, this is a matter for later consideration.

As we were such a large family and my father's means were very limited, there was the necessity which is common in such cases for all of the boys to turn out early in life and do something towards helping the others, and accordingly I went to work when I was thirteen. Some time afterwards I became gardener to the late Major Spofforth of Beauview, who was himself a very keen golfer, and who occasionally gave me some of his old clubs. Now and then, when he was in want of a partner, he used to take me out to play with him, and I shall never forget the words he spoke to me one day after we had played one of these matches. "Henry, my boy," he said, "take my advice, and never give up golf. It may be very useful to you some day." Certainly his words came true. I can only remember about these games that I was in the habit of getting very nervous over them, much more so than I did later on when I played matches of far more consequence. I joined a working men's golf club that had been formed, and it was through this agency that I won my first prize. A vase was offered for competition among the members, the conditions being that six medal rounds were to be played at the rate of one a month. When we had played five, I was leading by so very many strokes that it was next to impossible for any of the others to catch me up, and as just then my time came for leaving home and going out into the greater world of golf, the committee kindly gave me permission to play my last round two or three weeks before the proper time. It removed all doubt as to the destination of the prize, which has still one of the most honoured places on my mantelpiece. At that time my handicap for this club was plus 3, but that did not mean that I would have been plus 3 anywhere else. As a matter of fact, I should think I must have been about 8 or 10.

By this time my younger brother Tom had already gone away to learn club-making from Lowe at St. Anne's-on-Sea. He played very much the same game of golf as I did at that time, and it was his venture and the success that waited upon it that made me determine to strike out. While Tom was at St. Anne's he went on a journey north to take part in a tournament at Musselburgh, where he captured the second prize. Thereupon I came to the conclusion that, if Tom could do that, then I too with a little patience might do the same. Indeed, I was a very keen golfer just then. At last Lowe was summoned to Lord Ripon's place at Ripon, near Harrogate, to lay out a new nine-holes course, and Tom wrote to me saying that they would be wanting a professional there, and if I desired such an appointment I had better apply for it without delay. I did so, and was engaged. I was twenty years of age when I left home to assume these duties.

ronnie leask

THE STORY OF MY LIFE AS AN AMATEUR GOLFER, FROM A MEMBER OF THE "GREAT TRIUMVIRATE"

JAMES BRAID

They say that I was just like the average Earlsferry boy, but that I was a little more precocious than some of the others in golfing matters. My first dim recollections of anything at all in this world were of some vague happenings about the time when I was five or six years of age, and they are of my always being about with a miniature golf club in my hand, and running about outside my parents' house knocking a ball with it at every chance that presented itself. The tendency towards golf, therefore, seemed strong, and the natural result of it, seeing what were my parents' circumstances in life, was that I should be a caddie—during school holidays only. I went to school in the usual way, and filled up my spare time in carrying clubs for the visitors; but when there were no visitors I spent the odd hours in practising all manner of shots; and thus when I was a very small boy I had already begun to take the game seriously and was starting on the right lines, since I was watching a good deal and then practising with just an odd club—which very likely was all that I possessed at the time, so there was not much self-sacrifice really in this kind of practice. My driver generally consisted of an old wooden head that I had picked up somewhere after it had been discarded as worthless, and to this was attached a shaft that had been found somewhere else in the same way. People nowadays talk about the modern system of socketing the shafts of wooden clubs on to the heads, as if it were a recent invention, whereas the caddies of my generation certainly socketed the shafts of the clubs that they made for themselves in this way, the method being the simplest possible, namely, boring a hole through the head and fastening the shaft in it as tightly as possible. As for iron clubs, we had never more than one, and that one was usually a cleek with a long and well-lofted head. We had no such things as putters and niblicks in those days. The cleek had to do all the work, and, with the practice we had with it, we made it do it very well. Reflecting on the practice got in this way by boys who have no money to spend on clubs, one cannot but think, however hard their lot may have appeared to them at the time, that it was exceedingly valuable, very likely more so than it would have been if a set of clubs had been available.

I never had any lessons; I simply watched and copied. The Earlsferry course was not quite the same then as it is now. At that time it was made up of nine good holes, and besides these there were three others in Melon Park, which were taken in whenever it was thought desirable to do so. By the time I was seven or eight years of age I began to show pretty good form for a boy such as I was, and I was apparently a little better than the other youngsters of my age. The visitors to the place gave prizes every year for a competition among the caddies, and some of the boys who took part in these contests achieved considerable distinction afterwards. Among them were the Simpsons, who were, of course, much older than I was. I was only eight years old when I first entered in one of these competitions, and they put me to play in the junior section that time, and the test was score play over nine holes, these nine being the three in Melon Park played over three times. I won with twenty strokes to spare, and thus came out a winner in the first competition that I ever played in, which was encouraging. My score on that occasion was 54, which, all things considered, was not at all bad. I found in those early days that I could reach the green in three shots at the long holes, and nobody could get there in less than two. In the next competition that I took part in, Archie Simpson, who was four years older than I was, had to give me eight strokes start, and he beat me by two for first place; but in the two following competitions, in which I had to play from scratch, I won the first prize each time, so that I won three times out of four, and I should add that in the last three competitions I played with the senior caddies over the full nine-holes course. This brought me to about the end of my schooldays, and the beginning of another important period in my life.

I was naturally very keen on golf at this time, and was full of dreams and ambitions as to what I might do in the future. Jamie Anderson, the famous champion of a generation that has passed, had something to do with the stimulation of this ambition, and I shall never forget the encouragement that he gave to me on one occasion when I was only a little boy of about nine years of age. What he said was in its way rather remarkable—to my mind, at least—in view of the things that have happened since then. He was taking part in a match between amateurs and professionals at Earlsferry, and, being Open Champion at the time, his play naturally attracted a great deal of attention. As for us boys, we were, of course, inclined to look upon him as not much less than an idol, and he fascinated me in particular to such an extent that I followed him round the links in a very doglike way, thought it a great thing to touch his clubs, and listened intently to the most trivial remarks that he made, so that I could repeat them to the other boys. Then I hit a shot or two myself to show him what I could do, and he took particular notice of the way that I played them, and asked me to do one or two over again, so that he might make another examination of my style, if such it was to be called. He seemed really to mean what he said, when at last he patted me on the shoulder and told me to go in for as much golf as I could, and practise as thoroughly as possible, and that if I did that I should be Open Champion myself one day. Another incident of these caddie days that I remember very well, was a challenge that was sent by the caddies at Earlsferry to play the caddies at Leven. There was great rivalry between the boys of the two places as to which could put the strongest team on the links, and one day a couple came along from Leven in a boastful manner and declared that if we played them we should not see the way they went. We felt offended, and after consultation among ourselves we sent a formal challenge to the Leven caddies, which, alas! they did not see their way to accept.

Having left school at the age of thirteen, the usual question arose as to what was to be made of me. For my own part I was, as might be imagined, very anxious to keep to the links in some capacity or other; but my parents had a very strong prejudice against the game. No doubt they were right in their reasons, for golf then in many respects was not what it is now, but their attitude upset me very much. However, they would not hear of my having any more to do with the game except as a recreation in my spare time, and to settle the matter finally I was apprenticed to a joiner in a little village three miles from Earlsferry. Having to walk forwards and backwards between my home and the village every morning and night, and, having a long working day in the joiner's shop, I had very little time left for play, except in the summer time, when I usually managed to get in an evening round, and on Saturday afternoons. I joined the local Thistle Golf Club when I was fifteen years of age and won several prizes in its competitions, and generally did fairly well when representing it in the team matches that were played against the St. Andrews Club. By the time I was sixteen I was playing a very useful game, for I was not only down to scratch, but I won a scratch medal and broke the record of the course, which now consisted of eleven holes. This record stood to my credit for two or three years. I might mention that at this time I was playing with heavy clubs, which were also rather longer in the shaft than usual—longer, in fact, than those with which I play now. My style, I suppose, was pretty well what it is now, except that my swing was certainly much shorter; in fact it was a very short swing, and this was a matter that worried me rather, because I felt that I should never do much good in the long game until I let the swing out more. I tried to lengthen it gradually, and, while it was at its shortest when I was about fourteen, I managed to improve it considerably during the next two years. However, it made no material difference to the length of my drive, and it was an unpleasant fact for me at the time that though strong physically, and tall, I was an unusually short driver. I could get no length at all, and almost everybody who could golf respectably could get a longer ball than I could. I tried every known alternative to my system, but to no purpose, and I felt I must resign myself to being a short driver. My driving had, however, the merit of being both steady and straight, and this helped me a good deal. Besides this, my game suffered seriously in another respect, for, as is generally known, I was quite a bad putter until recent years, and during all the years when I was coming on at the game my putting was at its very worst. For my short driving I could make up a great deal in the rest of the play through the green, for I was good with my irons; but I could not save my matches when I was putting in the shocking fashion that I so generally did, and whenever I lost it was nearly all due to this weakness—with the short putts. I was always fairly good at the long ones. It was not until many years afterwards that I overcame this weakness, and did so as the result of hours and days and years of hard practice.

How I came to be cured of my weakness in driving I really do not know, but the cure in this department came long before the other, in fact I was still in my teens when I got to driving a long ball nearly every time. I am not conscious that I made any difference whatever in my style or methods. I was simply going on in the same old way when suddenly I found myself driving farther and farther, and the complete conversion from short to long was effected within a week. As I have often said, it was just the same as if I went to bed a short driver one night and got up a long driver in the morning. It was then, and is still, the greatest golfing mystery that I have ever come across; but the happy result of it was that, while at one time certain rivals were getting twenty yards past me almost every time, at the end of that week I was getting that much past them, and, except for brief lapses, I have never been a very short driver since those days, the long balls not going away again in the same mysterious manner that they came, as so often happens in this tantalising game.

When I was nineteen I left home for the first time and went to work as a joiner at St. Andrews, and as by that time I was playing a very good game, it naturally happened that I got many good matches with the best players there, which served to pull me out and to improve my own game considerably. Thus I had many fine games with Andrew Kirkaldy, and also with his brother Hugh, now dead. I found that I could hold my own in these matches in almost every department of the game except on the putting greens. Even now, when time was getting on, I had no idea of ever adopting golf as a career, and very soon after my arrival at St. Andrews there came an interruption in my game, for my employers sent me to work in different parts of the country, and during that time I had very little play, and did not get the opportunity to keep myself in any sort of form. This lasted for two or three years; but in 1891 I left St. Andrews and went to Edinburgh, and there, with the fine course on the Braid Hills available for everybody, I soon got very keen again, and joined the Edinburgh Thistle Club without delay. My best form came back to me immediately, and I won the scratch medal of the club for two years in succession, besides which I gained a few prizes in the club tournaments. Of course, all this time I was an amateur. I had a handicap of plus 2 or 3, and was generally chosen to represent the Thistle Club in the competition for the *Dispatch and Glasgow Evening Times* trophies. As most people who are acquainted with general golfing matters know, these are important competitions in Scotland, and arouse great interest in the Edinburgh and Glasgow districts. Both are by foursome, two pairs representing each club in the one case and one in the other. The first year that I played for the Thistle we were knocked out in the final for the *Dispatch* trophy, while we were beaten in the semifinal for the other by the club that eventually secured the trophy. The most important success that I achieved so far came my way in 1892, when I won the Braid Hills Tournament, open to members of the Edinburgh and Leith clubs. The competition was very keen, for there were a hundred and forty players entered. One round, by strokes, had to be played, and I started from scratch, broke the record of the course, and won the first prize. This was my top achievement as an amateur. I look back on a very pleasant time spent in Edinburgh.

THE STORY OF CHILDREN'S GOLF

BERNARD DARWIN

When I was about ten, and so a golfer of some two years' standing, I was one day off my infantile game and the professional was asked to look at my swing. He looked and said that there was nothing much the matter except that at the top of the swing I bent my knees rather too much. No doubt he was right, and the horrid proof of it is this, that though at this present day I am subject to many superficially different diseases at golf, yet the cause of them all is the same, a tendency to too loose and florid a movement of the knees, which sends my whole body sprawling. I rid myself of it for a while, but it is always lying in wait for me. In a certain camp in Macedonia we had some men of an Egyptian Labour Corps, and attached to them an interpreter. He had one stock phrase to describe general debility. "This man," he said, "bends at the kneels." Well, that is my stock disease—I bend at the kneels; and though I was warned against it at ten, I shall suffer from it at eighty. I suppose I was not caught early or warned impressively enough.

The moral is that we must look out for bad habits even in the youngest golfers. When we find them we must be very sparing in our good advice, for a boy has a facility for exaggeration. One whom I know well was waving his mashie round his head like a driver. I insinuated that this was too long a swing, and the next moment he was taking the club no further back than a putter and giving the ball nothing but a little poke or prod. If you tell him to be less like an eel, he stiffens up into a statue: if you as much as whisper "follow-through," he spins twice round after his stroke like a hammer-thrower. Therefore, though we may have to say the same thing many times, we must not say it at too frequent intervals, and must rather understate our case. What we have to say will generally be in the nature of a restriction. A grown-up beginner may be urged to greater freedom. Not so, as a rule, a boy. He is lissom and fearless enough; his errors will nearly always tend towards a swing too long and florid: a body movement that is too free. And however loose and slashing his style we dare only check it ever so slightly, because really to cramp him would be fatal. The best of young golfers have some wild oats that they must sow. I remember once, on a tour of the Oxford and Cambridge Golfing Society in Lancashire, that an undergraduate member of our side played against Mr. John Ball. He played a very good, sound, steady game, going very straight and taking plenty of pains, making no outrageous errors and no great shots. Mr. Ball's verdict (he does not often give one, but it is worth hearing when he does) was that he "did not like to see a youngster too careful." And so, let us beware lest the boy's game becomes lifeless: let him take his wooden club and go gallantly for the impossible carry: he has plenty of time in which to learn to play short.

Besides this pusillanimous wisdom, which children to begin with will do better without, grown-up golfers have also many tiresome habits which children will do better without both now and for all eternity. Of such are the habits of waggling or of growing fussy over the slightest sound or movement in the neighbourhood. The natural child has only the most rudimentary waggle, if any, and he swings the club with only too little thought of anyone being near him, so as to be in fact rather dangerous. Soon, however, he adopts the grown-up weaknesses, has many and ornate waggles, looks angrily out of the tail of his eye at some object moving in the distance, and peremptorily orders his own mother not to talk on the stroke. In this case, if we cannot set a good example we can at least try to counteract the effect of a bad one, and there is a good deal to be done by not too unkind laughter. The professional's play makes an excellent object lesson. It is hard work taking a child to see a professional match: it is necessary to run like a lamp-lighter in order that the small, eager person may be squeezed into the front rank, but it is worth doing. The rapidity of the play makes a deep impression, and the child is an imitative animal. The game of pretending is one to be played conscientiously, and no one can enact the part of a champion with any degree of artistic satisfaction if he fidget and waggle overmuch.

I always think that the watching and copying of a good model is more vital to education in iron play than in any other part of the game. A good driving style seems to come more easily and naturally to a boy "agile as a young opossum." Driving with its dash and go is, besides, the most superficially fascinating part of the game, and he will be more inclined to take pains to acquire it. Iron play is not so attractive to the young. It does not give so much scope for the boast that clamours for recognition—"Look how far I hit that one! Look, oh *do* look!" There is or should be a certain restraint about it. Restraint is unnatural in the young player, and the stroke which is perhaps the crown of the golfer's skill, the half-iron shot, is not quite a natural one and demands more control of the club than any other. It is in the iron shots that the professional and the "professionally moulded" amateur, as he has been called, is most unmistakably recognisable. Let others strive as they will, they cannot acquire that formidable, downward thrust of the club that sends the ball and the divot flying. So let our hypothetical boy be encouraged, above everything else, to watch good iron play and to observe wherein its merits lie. He must not, it is true, try to run before he can walk. The first thing to do is to learn to hit a straight-forward shot simply and truly. But, I think, granted the good model, the sequence of his shots may largely be left to nature. The more masterful, punching iron shots will come naturally with the growing strength of hand and wrist.

As to the form which a boy's games should take, if a boy is keen enough to enjoy it—and he generally is—I doubt if there is anything better for him than playing by himself. He must play some matches, of course, and that if possible with a rival of his own age. This will not only break him into match-playing: it will, as the saying is, "keep him in his proper place." There is nobody whose company is in the long run so salutary for us as a contemporary, for he stands no nonsense from us. Elders grant us little indulgences if only in the matter of losing our tempers and throwing our clubs about, which we come to expect as a right. An occasional match then, but otherwise the solitary round is excellent, for the boy will not grow slack over it as the grown-up would do. If he misses a particular shot he will try it over and over again till he gets it right. When he comes home, the account that he gives of his score will probably be inaccurate. The most honest little boys are often bad counters, but at worst this is a very lovable weakness and will disappear too soon.

If there be a grown-up good-natured enough to sacrifice himself, it is a good plan for him and the boy to play a solitary ball between them as if in a foursome. In the summer evenings at Felixstowe my father and I used to play one ball thus for a whole round of nine holes. I don't think we had any imaginary foe—it was before the days of Bogey—but we counted our score. I can still recall the thrill when we did the nine holes in 56, though it does not sound a very good score today. Those rounds made the culminating joy of the day, and I hope it is not even now too late to express my gratitude for them.

This form of game will of course be excellent practice for a real foursome. A family foursome is very good fun, granted an empty course, so that there is not that paralysing sensation of people waiting behind us. So is an inter-family foursome, though in this case the feeling may run almost too high. One word of advice may be given to the elders in a family foursome, and that is that they observe, to a reasonable degree at any rate, the rigour of the game. I would not have them too relentless. For instance, I have known a foursome, in which some of the players are very young, played under the rule that "air shots do not count." Perhaps this is immoral, but it is disheartening to the son to walk after a long tee shot of the father's, miss the globe himself, and then stand aside for another vast paternal drive. It must seem to him that he is not getting his money's worth. In the case of a complete miss, then, some relaxation may be allowable so long as there is a definitely understood rule on the point, and not merely an occasional concession from motives of pity. On the other hand, into whatever bunker or other horribly bad place the ball finds its way, there it should be played. It seems cruel to insist on a small creature of ten struggling with a patch of rushes that would test Braid and his heaviest niblick. There is a natural temptation to bid the young player lift into some lie rather less hopeless, both because we are sorry for him and because we want to get on a little faster. But not only is this unwise, but to the credit of the young be it said, it is unpopular. They like to play the strict game, and twelve strokes or so per hole do not strike them in the light of a tragedy nor even as a weariness of the flesh. Twelve is only two over an average of tens, and on a long course tens take some getting.

I have written hitherto about real children, the eight- and nine- and ten-year-olds. because so many children have today the chance of beginning very young, and the younger the better. But I think most of what I have said is applicable also to older children, to the fourteens and fifteens. Certainly a boy of fourteen, generally a most hero-worshipping age at a public school, should be encouraged to observe good players as much as he can, and if he is a strong, well-grown boy, he should soon be a good player himself. We have lately seen young Bocatzou, the French boy of fourteen, playing with Abe Mitchell on his own course, and that in a competition, and finishing in one round within three strokes of the great man. Young Tommy Morris was Open Champion at seventeen; America is full of infant prodigies of fifteen and sixteen. There are heaps of Bobby Joneses in embryo. There is no reason why a boy of sixteen with good opportunities should not be a very good golfer. When I hear a boy of that age remarked on by his adoring relations as wonderful because he has a handicap of eight or nine, I feel inclined to be thoroughly crabbed and unpleasant and say he ought to have a much lower one. Of course he will still have a great deal to learn, but he ought to be able to hit the ball in a way that may be ignorant but is the despair of many of his elders. He will not know enough to know what is the matter with him when he is "off," and generally he will have a good deal of hard thinking about the game before him if he is to make the best of himself as a golfer. Some young players play very well by instinct till they come to the almost inevitable thinking stage: then they lose confidence and never quite get over it. Others will not be bothered to think and remain instinctive players all their lives, good, but not so good as they might have been, with some weak joints in their harness. Perhaps they are the happier ones and the wiser. There is certainly such a thing as thinking too much about golf for our general well-being. But it is certain that nobody, young or old, will make the best of himself as a golfer if he does not think hard about the game and think intelligently. Whether it is worth the golfer's while to do so is a matter of taste and temperament which only he can decide.

PART III
MAJOR
TOURNAMENTS

iStockphoto/Thinkstock

THE STORY OF BEN HOGAN'S FIRST MAJOR CHAMPIONSHIP

JEFF MILLER

Ben Hogan had one final chance to cap his stellar 1946 season with his first major championship. The P.G.A. Championship would be played in late August at Oregon's Portland Golf Club, the course Hogan had personally annexed during the 1945 Portland Open with the record-sheering 27-under-par 261. Yet Byron Nelson came into the tournament considered at least the co-favorite, despite a sore back, on the basis of being the event's defending champion along with the fact that he'd won three of his last five starts. As Hogan and Nelson reached the quarterfinals, Nelson had little to worry about other than his sacroiliac. He eliminated Frank Rodia 8-and-7 (playing twenty-seven holes in 10-under-par), host pro Larry Lamberger (3-and-2), and his 1943 New York City tour guide, Herman Barron, (3-and-2). Hogan's victories to reach the three 18-hole rounds began somewhat tight but became progressively easier. He downed Charles Weisner (2-and-1), Bill Heinlein (4-and-3), and Arthur Bell (5-and-4).

In the quarterfinals that started 36-hole play, Nelson was pitted against "Porky" Oliver while Hogan's foe was Frank Moore. Nelson owned a two-hole lead with five holes to play but couldn't put Oliver away. The match was square going to the thirty-sixth hole, when Nelson yanked his second shot into the woods. That left him needing to convert a 25-foot putt to save par and extend the match beyond regulation; the putt didn't fall, and the defending champion was shockingly out in the quarterfinals. There had been talk earlier in the tournament that Nelson was hampered by a bad back, but after being eliminated he denied that. "My back never bothered me at all," Nelson said, sipping a Coke and chewing on some ice. "I lost to a man who shot better golf. Ed's a great guy and a fine competitor."

Meanwhile, the Hogan express continued to pick up steam. He defeated Moore 5-and-4, then routed his pal, Jimmy Demaret, 10-and-9. "Sunny Jim" actually built a lead of 2-up through the match's first three holes, but that only seemed to inject life into Hogan's game. He birdied three of the next four holes to swipe the lead as he completed the morning round 6-up. Afternoon competition wasn't much different. The match was over at twenty-seven holes. The drastic margin of victory prompted reporters to see if the normally jovial Demaret was provoked by Hogan's killer instinct. It was after this round that Demaret contributed to the legion of quotes pertaining to how little Hogan would say while playing. Asked if Hogan talked to him during the one-sided day, Demaret said, "Yes. 'You're away.'"

The final provided a contrast in silhouettes, Hogan at 137 and the somewhat slimmed-down Oliver at about 220. Hogan fell behind by three holes during the morning round because of—naturally—putting predicaments. But he immediately made amends with a 30 on the front nine of his afternoon play, taking a two-hole lead into the back nine. Hogan played the final fourteen holes in 8-under-par and defeated Oliver 6-and-4 to win the Wanamaker Trophy. Henny Bogan had won a major championship. "The only time I was sure of winning was when 'Porky' walked over and shook my hand," Hogan said. "No one gets as many birdies as I did without being lucky, and, boy, was I tickled when those long putts started to drop. It's impossible to explain how much this means to me, so I'll just say, 'Thank you,' to the P.G.A. and my wife, Valerie." The path to a first major championship was so much more of an odyssey, a test of will and skill and guile for Hogan, than it appeared to be for Nelson. Whereas Nelson won the 1937 Masters in only his third season of week-in, week-out Tour competition, Hogan's path covered the better part of eight seasons—which followed the fits and starts that began eight years before that, when he first teed it up as a professional at Brackenridge in San Antonio at the 1930 Texas Open.

iStockphoto/Thinkstock

THE STORY OF BEN HOGAN AND THE 1950 U.S. OPEN

DAVID BARRETT

It was well into evening by the time Ben Hogan returned to the Barclay Hotel in Philadelphia after the double round on Saturday. A late room-service dinner became even later because Hogan had to sit in a hot bath for an hour to soak his legs. He told a writer six months later that his legs swelled so much that day that it took a hectic evening of massage and bathing to get them in a condition where he might be able to play the next day.

His wife, Valerie, later recalled that she "had given up on his being able to tee off in the playoff, but I couldn't tell him that."

Meanwhile, back in Fort Worth, Ben's brother Royal was frantically trying to figure out how to send a putter to Pennsylvania for morning arrival. He heard a radio report about Ben's putting woes in the final round, and thought about the brass putter that Ben left in his garage at home in favor of a blade model he had been using for the last three months since picking it up during an exhibition in Memphis. Royal reached his brother by telephone at the hotel and said he could send the putter to New York with an airline pilot friend. But Ben didn't think he had anyone who could pick up the putter for him, so he told Royal to forget it. Instead, Royal went to work on arranging for a messenger to take the putter from New York directly to Merion.

Valerie Hogan said that during the night she woke up to the noise of jackhammers in the street below, but Ben was sleeping so soundly he never heard them. In the morning, Valerie recalled, he was "fresh as a daisy."

"Isn't it a nice day?" he said.

Hogan got a break because the playoff didn't start until 2 PM, due to Pennsylvania blue laws governing events on Sundays. That gave him more time to recover from Saturday's 36-hole ordeal, and meant he did not have to wake up exceptionally early to go through his morning soaking routine.

It also meant there was no chance of a second straight 36-hole day if there was a tie. (That's what happened in the 1946 Open at Canterbury, where Lloyd Mangrum, Byron Nelson, and Vic Ghezzi tied in an 18-hole playoff in the morning and went 18 more in the afternoon, Mangrum winning.)

When the Hogans reached the lobby of the hotel on their way to Merion, they received a surprise—a group of newsmen was waiting for Ben. They had probably gathered to be able to check Hogan's condition and get a comment from him if it turned out he was unable to play in the playoff. Seeing that he would not only play, but was moving well and in good spirits, they cheered him and some said, "Go get 'em, Ben."

Newspaper estimates of the playoff gallery ranged from 6,000 to 10,000, but again that was high. Daily tickets were offered at $3.00, but only 1,440 were sold (compared to 6,088 the previous day). Weekly tournament tickets remained good for the playoff. If all the 3,865 people who purchased tournament tickets attended the playoff, it would have brought the number to above 5,000, but some of those people undoubtedly had other commitments.

Still, several thousand people following one threesome represented a formidable challenge for the marshals. The players had to wait on every hole for the gallery to settle into place, which Championship Committee chairman John D. Ames later estimated took five minutes per hole. There was a photo in the next day's paper of Hogan, George Fazio, and Mangrum on the 14th tee, with the caption noting they were "taking a rest." Hogan is taking a drag on a cigarette while sitting on what appears to be a "shooting stick" type of chair that presumably was being carried in his golf bag, Fazio is sitting on a folding chair that he may have borrowed from a gallery member. Mangrum is standing, looking impatient. They must have been waiting on an "all clear" signal from the marshals.

Not *everyone* was rooting for Hogan in the playoff. Fazio not only had a group of family and friends watching, he was also being cheered on by a contingent of some 150 members of his club, Woodmont, who had arrived from Washington, D.C., by car, plane, and train, according to the *Washington Post*.

"Win or lose, we're going to have a big 'Welcome Home' banquet and reception for him Tuesday night," said Woodmont President Arthur Sundlun.

Other than that, though, Hogan had the gallery in the palm of his hand. Mangrum had to settle for only polite applause when he hit a good shot or made a birdie.

Shirley Povich wrote in the *Washington Post* that, unlike in the past, the usually dour and aloof competitor Hogan was actually feeding off the gallery.

"Hogan was the least tense of any of the three men in the playoff," Povich wrote. "He was gallery-conscious, and they liked it. For the first time in his career, he was probably trying to win for the gallery as well as for Hogan."

Povich had observed a changed Hogan the previous week at the National Celebrities Tournament in Washington. Admittedly it was more of a fun event than a serious competition, but still Hogan's friends noted that it was the first time they remembered seeing him smile on the first tee of a tournament. "He found himself even manning the loudspeaker during the antics of Danny Kaye and Milton Berle and Bob Hope and [Arthur] Godfrey, and having fun," according to Povich.

"Hogan didn't know that things like this could ever happen on a golf course," said one of his friends. "It is loosening him up, and I hope he keeps this mood the next week at the Open."

Hogan certainly appeared to be in a good mood as he arrived at the course on Sunday. "I feel fine," he stated while sitting in the locker room—an assertion he was liable to make in any case, but it really did seem to be true.

It is likely that with only three competitors they were allowed to warm up by hitting shots into the 14th fairway instead of having to go to the West Course, followed by some strokes on the practice green. Just before tee time, Hogan's brass putter arrived by messenger.

A scriptwriter would have Hogan delightedly grab his old familiar weapon and go on a putting spree that netted him the Open title. Unfortunately, Royal's best efforts were for naught.

The club arrived too late for Ben to even try it on the practice green, so he stuck with the one he had warmed up with.

Fazio was a big underdog, but looking back on it he said he felt he had a chance to win. He told Al Barkow in *Gettin' to the Dance Floor* that the only player he ever felt he couldn't beat was Byron Nelson. "With everybody else I felt I might be able to out luck them, they might get a bad bounce or I might hit a lucky shot or something—even Hogan. Like in that playoff for the '50 Open. I was first up on the first tee, and when I went to put it down I was shaking. When Ben went I was looking at him tee it up and he was shaking, too, so I said, 'This is not too bad.' Mangrum liked to play the cool cat, but he was shaking, too."

Mangrum at least had one thing going for him. He had been in a three-way U.S. Open playoff before, and had won.

Mangrum had a prickly relationship with Hogan, however. In a *Sport* magazine profile of Hogan in 1953, Bob Brumby wrote that there was a long-standing personal feud between the two, though each had a healthy respect for the others' ability. At the time of the article, Mangrum had just been quoted with a remark that was seen as disparaging Hogan. When it was related to Hogan that Mangrum said he was misquoted, Hogan responded, "He has never liked me and the feeling is mutual." Mangrum, on the other hand, said the two had gotten along fine until a couple of years before.

In truth, it was probably just a lack of mutual understanding by two men who were difficult to get to know. They had little to say to each other, and each may have misinterpreted the sometimes blunt comments both were liable to make in the press.

Fazio and Hogan got along well; indeed, George had joined Ben for his first practice round at the Los Angeles Open when he returned to the tour after an 11-month absence. Fazio was the only gregarious member of the trio, but he knew there would be little conversation that day, which was fine. "Hogan is the most perfect gentleman on the golf course that I ever played with," he told Barkow. "I mean, he's not going to do anything *for* you, but he's not going to do anything against you. You play your game, he plays his."

The first hole was a short par four of 360 yards, but it was no pushover at the Open, playing as the seventh toughest hole. Hogan and Mangrum calmed their nerves and made routine pars, while Fazio showed signs of an inability to control his adrenaline. For the first of three times on the front nine, his approach shot went over the green, and it resulted in a bogey.

Fazio got the stroke back with a birdie from 20 feet on the par-five second, while Mangrum moved in front by planting his approach three feet from the hole and making a birdie to go one under. Hogan was still getting his bearings. His drive was on the fringe of the right rough, and his second shot with an iron found the left rough. Still, he hit his next one on the green and made a par.

Mangrum pulled his tee shot on the par-three third. While it found the fringe instead of the deep rough, he was unable to get up and down, his par putt catching the lip and staying out. With regulation pars by Hogan and Fazio, all three were now at even par after three holes. They remained that way after the par-five fourth, where Hogan and Fazio hit into the rough with their second shots. Hogan hit the green from there to join Mangrum in two-putting for pars, while Fazio missed the putting surface but chipped close and made his par putt. All three emerged unscathed from the dangerous par-four fifth, with Fazio again one-putting for a par while the other two both hit the green. All three players were even par through five holes.

Things began to unravel for Fazio on the par-four sixth, where his approach shot went long into a bunker. This time he couldn't get up and down, and made a bogey.

The par-four seventh and eighth holes were birdie opportunities—if you could keep your tee shot in the fairway. But Fazio was wild off the tee on the seventh, hitting it out of bounds to the right and making a bogey. The winner of only two tour events in his career seemed to be succumbing in the pressure-cooker of a playoff for the national championship.

In that out-of-bounds area to the right of the seventh, hundreds of spectators perched on the framework of a house being built near the green. The ground slopes down sharply to the left of that green and the eighth tee is immediately behind the putting surface, making viewing impossible from either spot, so enterprising fans utilized the partially built home as a chance to see the action on an otherwise difficult spectator hole. Fortunately for both the spectators and the property owner, the frame did not collapse under the fans' weight.

Hogan took the lead for the first time in the playoff by hitting his short-iron approach to within four feet and making the birdie putt on the seventh, after missing a birdie try from a similar distance on the previous hole. Mangrum, after a routine par on the sixth, caught a bunker with his approach on the seventh. He avoided losing two strokes to Hogan, coming out of the sand to within four feet and making the putt to save par.

On the eighth hole, Hogan hit what was to be his only poor shot of the round, finding a fairway bunker with his tee shot. Even then, it wasn't so much a poor swing as a poor club selection.

"I made a mistake," Hogan said after the round. "We couldn't feel the wind there, and I used a No. 1 iron when I should have hit a brassie [three-wood]."

Wait a minute! A one-iron? Didn't Hogan later say his one-iron had been stolen after the fourth round?

Hogan missed the green on his shot from the fairway bunker and ended up with a bogey, dropping back to even par. Meanwhile, Mangrum had another solid par, while Fazio bounced back from his two consecutive bogeys with a birdie on the eighth, holing a nine-foot putt.

On the par-three ninth, Fazio missed the green yet again, finishing in a bunker, but escaped with a par. It completed a scrambling nine where he hit a scant three greens in regulation, but one-putted five holes to keep himself in the thick of things with a one-over 37, just a stroke behind his companions.

"I was too keyed up for that playoff," Fazio recalled. "I usually drove even with Hogan for length, and that day I was 10 and 15 yards ahead of him. But I'd forget I was keyed up and knock the approach shots over the greens."

Hogan and Mangrum, in contrast, were solid on the front nine, Hogan hitting eight greens and Mangrum seven. Both shot even-par 36s with one birdie and one bogey, the birdies coming on short putts.

The back nine would be a different story, at least for Mangrum. While Hogan continued his relentless, error-free play, knocking it down the fairway and onto the green hole after hole, Mangrum had one of the wilder nine-hole rides ever seen in a U.S. Open playoff. Over the next seven holes, Mangrum made only one par, and became involved in a pair of strange incidents that turned the tide in Hogan's favor.

The yo-yo act started on the 10th hole, where Mangrum's tee shot ended up in the same bunker that had caught Middlecoff and Hogan in the fourth round. The USGA's Richard Tufts, who had suggested the bunker, must have been smiling.

Mangrum missed the green and made a bogey on the 10th, but he came right back on the 11th with an approach to five feet and a holed birdie putt. He walked to the 12th tee tied with Hogan, while Fazio was still one stroke back. Mangrum hit his drive into the 12th fairway and then entered the Twilight Zone. Mangrum's second shot flew over the heads of the amazed gallery, past Ardmore Avenue, and came to rest in the rough just past the 13th tee, at least 30 yards over the 12th green.

There was some question whether the ball was out of bounds. It had crossed over an out-of-bounds road, but was sitting on the property of the golf course, which could have allowed for an interpretation that it was in bounds. USGA rules chairman Isaac Grainger ruled that it was out.

In truth, that was a break for Mangrum, especially with the distance-only penalty. He would have faced an exceptionally difficult shot from where his ball lay near the 13th tee, back across the road to a hard and fast green sloping away from him. Making par from there would have been almost impossible, while double bogey was a definite possibility. Instead, he dropped one in the fairway and, using the correct club this time, found the green and walked off with a bogey.

This extraordinary turn of events was glossed over in the newspaper accounts. The *New York Times* said that Mangrum hit a five-iron "too strongly as the breeze faded and the ball flew over the crowd." While mentioning the out-of-bounds approach shot, all of the reports simply state that Mangrum made a five on the hole without any further description. But a fading breeze could hardly explain the ball flying that far past its target. In an interview with Merion historian John Capers in 1986, Grainger offered a more plausible explanation. Mangrum, he said, asked his caddie for a nine-iron. The caddie handed him a six-iron instead, and Lloyd somehow didn't notice.

It's hard to imagine a player escaping scrutiny for such a gaffe today. But the playoff wasn't televised and post-round press interviews were more perfunctory than they are now. Also, an even more unusual incident on the 16th hole would overshadow this one, and that's what reporters asked Mangrum about after the round.

Hogan, meanwhile, pounded out routine pars on the 10th, 11th, and 12th, as did Fazio, who was getting his ball-striking (and nerves) under control. Through 12 holes, Hogan was even par, with Mangrum and Fazio a stroke behind. Still tight. It remained that way through the 13th, where they all hit the green off the tee and two-putted that par three.

Hogan found himself with a little bit of breathing room after the par-four 14th. Continuing to play like a machine, he drove in the fairway and hit the green for yet another par. His long game straightened out, Fazio's putting now began to go sour as he three-putted for a bogey. An erratic Mangrum hit his second shot into a greenside bunker and also bogeyed the hole. Hogan pulled two strokes ahead of both of his fellow competitors.

Mangrum cut Hogan's lead to one on the 15th. His drive nearly went out of bounds, but he hit an outstanding shot from the rough to within 12 feet of the cup and sank the birdie putt. Fazio, however, fell three behind with his second consecutive three-putt. Either his new putting method let him down at the end, or he reverted to old habits under pressure.

The feared 16th hole claimed Mangrum as a victim in the playoff, but in truth it was Lloyd who did himself in. Or perhaps some blame should be placed on what Mangrum described as a "bug fly" that landed on his ball while he was about to putt it.

Mangrum, his Achilles heel (shaky driving) continuing to haunt him, sprayed his drive into the right rough. With a not-so-good lie in the deep stuff and some trees in the way, Mangrum made his one smart decision on the back nine by laying up short of the quarry.

He figured he could still make a par with a nice third shot and a one-putt. He hit a decent shot to the green, leaving himself with a 15-foot putt to salvage a four. Mangrum marked his ball because it was in the line of Fazio, who was on his way to a third straight bogey after missing the green. Mangrum then replaced his ball, and here is how Associated Press writer Gayle Talbot described the scene:

"He addressed his ball carefully several times, bobbed his head back and forth the way golfers are supposed to do, and then stopped dead still. He planted his putter in front of the pellet to 'mark' it, lifted the sphere and blew upon it gently to dislodge the unwelcome guest [the 'bug fly'], then replaced it as the gallery laughed."

The USGA's Grainger wasn't laughing, though. He knew that Mangrum had just incurred a two-stroke penalty for lifting his ball. Not until 1960 were players allowed to lift and clean their ball on the green. In 1950, they were allowed to mark and lift their ball on the green in stroke play only if it interfered with or might assist another player.

Mangrum rolled in the putt for what nearly everyone thought was a par. Hogan had a birdie putt from 10 feet, but he missed. It was high drama, with Mangrum apparently managing to stay right on Hogan's heels just when it looked like he was going to lose one or two strokes.

Mangrum strode confidently to the 17th tee, and prepared to tee off (he had the honor from his birdie on the 15th.) Then Grainger appeared on the tee and the drama was drained from the event, replaced by confusion and an altered scoreboard that showed Hogan's lead grow from one stroke to three.

Grainger later said in a USGA oral history that he had trouble getting to the 17th tee to inform Mangrum of the penalty because of the rush of the gallery. When he arrived, he delivered the bad news. "Lloyd, I'm sorry to tell you, but I have to enact a penalty of two strokes because you lifted and cleaned your ball on the previous hole."

As Grainger recalled, "He immediately realized that he had done that, and put the club back into the bag and made the statement, 'Well, I guess I can still feed the children,' or something like that."

For Mangrum, it was a matter of Ike Grainger giveth and Ike Grainger taketh away. In the 1946 U.S. Open, Grainger had been the one to levy a one-stroke penalty on Byron Nelson when his caddie inadvertently kicked his ball in the fairway after emerging from under a gallery rope. The penalty dropped Nelson into a playoff, which Mangrum won.

Knowledgeable spectators knew something was up when they saw that Mangrum wasn't going to play first. Everyone quickly became aware of the penalty—though not necessarily what it was for—when the chalkboard showing the standing of the players was changed, with Mangrum going from one over to three over.

It was a shame it had to happen coming down the stretch of a U.S. Open playoff that was so closely contested, especially on the heels of Mangrum making a great scrambling par that would have kept the pressure on Hogan. Mangrum's absentminded move still ranks as one of the all-time golf blunders.

It has been suggested that cleaning the ball on the green was allowed as a local rule at PGA tournaments at the time, so Mangrum might simply have let instinct take over and forgotten that he couldn't pick up the ball at a USGA event. But the PGA had stopped using this local rule. A pro named Pete Cooper lost a tournament just two months after the U.S. Open because he missed a short putt due to having a piece of chewing gum on his ball (ironically, in that case Cooper would have been allowed to remove the gum because it was a man-made object).

Mangrum's comments after the round show that it wasn't a PGA vs. USGA issue. The problem didn't arise because he temporarily forgot he was in a U.S. Open, it was because he thought blowing off a fly was OK.

"I had the idea you could get off anything like a bug or snake," he said, admitting that he didn't know the rule.

He was wrong, but in a way he was ahead of his time. According to the USGA's current Decisions on the Rules of Golf, a live insect can be removed from a ball in play because it is not considered to be adhering to the ball. But in 1950, the interpretation was different. At that time, a live insect *was* considered to be adhering, so he wouldn't even have been allowed to remove it without touching the ball. Thus, Mangrum breached the rules twice, once for lifting and once for cleaning, but there was no double jeopardy so he incurred only a single two-stroke penalty.

Mangrum earned praise for the equanimity with which he accepted the ruling that practically destroyed his hopes for a second Open championship. His only flash of annoyance came at the awards ceremony, where USGA President James Standish referred to the club as Merion Cricket Club instead of Merion Golf Club. When called to the podium to accept his runner-up medal, Mangrum said, "Well, the brass might not know where they are, but they sure know the rules."

Mangrum didn't hold a grudge. A photographer had taken a picture of Mangrum and Grainger walking down a fairway at Merion during the Open, and Lloyd later sent it to Grainger with this inscription:

To Ike
May we never have
bugs again—Love & kisses
Lloyd Mangrum

Back on the 17th tee, everyone, probably even including Hogan, could agree that this was no good way to determine the Open champion. On this hole, Ben would do his best to make sure the two-stroke penalty wasn't the deciding factor. Or maybe Hogan was happy to have a three-stroke lead any way he could get it. *Life* ran a second U.S. Open spread a week after Peskin's famous 18th-hole photo, and a shot of Hogan walking toward the 17th green in the playoff showed him with a big smile, a rarity during competition.

Minutes later, Hogan would have even more reason to smile. Facing a 50-foot uphill putt from the front level of the 17th green, Hogan hit it perfectly and watched it go into the hole for a birdie, the longest putt he made all week. Another *Life* photo shows Hogan in an uncharacteristically demonstrative gesture, doffing his cap and bowing to the crowd. The fans responded with a loud and prolonged cheer.

Just like later Arnold Palmer roars at the Masters, you didn't have to be on the scene to know who the cheering was for and what it was all about. Those sitting by the 18th green or the club-house knew that Hogan had done something great and that he must have clinched the U.S. Open.

With routine pars on the final two holes, Mangrum finished with a 73, Fazio parred 17, but ended with his fourth bogey on the last five holes as he overshot the green yet again on the 18th and limped in with a 75. After earning his way into the playoff with spectacular back nines of 32 and 33 on Saturday, Fazio gave away his chances on Sunday by stumbling home in four-over 38.

Hogan hit his drive in the fairway—where else?—on 18. He was only a little bit beyond his drive of the previous day, but this time he hit a five-iron. Years later, he explained to Hogan Company vice president Doug McGrath that the breeze was behind him and he felt his adrenaline running. Pumped up instead of leg-weary, Hogan's five-iron bounced over the green.

Standing behind Hogan, a photographer named Alex Bremner reprised Peskin's shot of the previous day. Never printed in a national magazine, the shot appears in Merion's club history, right under Peskin's famous photo. Bremner's photo also shows Hogan frozen in his follow-through, this time wearing a sweater on a day that was not so warm. The crowd is smaller, and has not encroached on the field of play as it did on Saturday. Instead of forming a line on the fairway side of the bunker ahead of Hogan, the gallery has politely stayed to the outside of it.

Hogan finished in style, chipping to seven feet and holing the putt for a par and a one-under 69. An enthusiastic crowd rushed in like they wanted to raise Hogan onto their shoulders the way the gallery did with amateur Francis Ouimet when he won the Open in a major upset in 1913. The Haverford Township police were having none of that.

"There was a mad crush and several persons were knocked down in the melee," the *New York Times* reported. "A cordon of police saved Hogan from the happy jam of well-wishers."

On the clubhouse porch, Valerie Hogan celebrated in a more quiet fashion. Just as she had done the previous three days, she sat sipping iced tea for the entirety of Ben's round. Valerie heard the cheer from the 18th green and heard somebody say, "Ben Hogan won."

She began to cry. The couple at the next table came over and asked, "Is there anything we can do for you?"

"I'm all right," she replied. "I'm just happy for my husband. I'm crying with joy."

Hogan's storybook return from his auto accident and Mangrum's unfortunate blunder attracted most of the attention in the aftermath of the playoff. What got lost in the shuffle was the exceptional round that Hogan played to earn the title. The day after 104 rounds had been posted on the East Course with only one of them under par, Hogan produced a 69 with the U.S. Open title on the line. He did it with an impressive display of controlled golf. The accident may have humanized him, but he played the playoff with almost robotic precision.

His lone mistake, the tee shot into the bunker on the eighth, was the result of misreading the wind and hitting the wrong club. Over the next eight holes, with Mangrum and Fazio nipping at his heels, Hogan methodically hit every fairway and every green, grinding his foes down with eight straight pars. It was effective on the scorecard, and also mentally. As his opponents watched Hogan's relentlessly efficient play, they sensed he wasn't going to make any mistakes or give them any openings. Perhaps that led them into trying to force the issue on the back nine, where Mangrum was wildly up-and-down and Fazio fell apart after holding things together with baling wire on the first nine.

That eight-hole stretch of regulation pars was broken by Hogan's clinching birdie on the 17th. He ended up hitting 16 of 18 greens in regulation, including a meaningless miss on the finishing hole. Hogan's putting held up, too. The blade putter that had served him poorly the previous afternoon was a worthy companion on Sunday. The playoff was his only round without a three-putt, he showed a good touch in getting his long putts close to the hole on Merion's tricky greens, and missed only one short putt (the birdie try on the sixth), finishing the round with 33 putts.

Hogan had told reporters in the hotel lobby before the playoff round, "The trouble with Merion is that it always has you on the defensive. There's no way you can take the offensive against it."

He said it with a tone of frustration, because he preferred to be able to attack. But, like a smart quarterback, Hogan knew to take what the defense gave him. Taking few chances, Hogan played for the center of greens and walked away with the U.S. Open trophy.

Hemera/Thinkstock

THE STORY OF MY OPEN CHAMPIONSHIP VICTORY AGAINST MY FELLOW MEMBERS OF THE "GREAT TRIUMVIRATE"

JOHN HENRY TAYLOR

It was fair golfing weather, although a strong breeze on the first day bothered some of the competitors considerably. Prior to the start Mr. H. H. Hilton, Harry Vardon, James Braid, and myself were favourites for the premier honours, but on the first round I think Vardon was followed by the largest "gallery." This did not disturb him in the slightest, and at one period it appeared probable that he would play a remarkably good round. This did not exactly happen, for his half round in was marred by a 6 at the eleventh green. He finished in 77, Braid's figures being 79 and mine the same.

In the second round Braid played a much better game, or, possibly, his strokes were not dogged by ill-fortune, and his 76 was the result of really sound, indeed wonderfully good golf, the score he returned being only four strokes above the record of the green which, considering the adverse circumstances, was a grand performance. Only one big hole, a 6, was played, and that was the second on the outward journey.

Vardon, though, had not quite maintained his earlier form, his round being accomplished in 78, which, however, placed him upon an equality with the ultimate winner. It was on the home green that he lost his chance of securing the lead, for a moderately easy putt was missed. As for myself, I will be contented by simply stating that my round totalled up to 83.

This being the condition of affairs as far as the leaders were concerned, excitement ran desperately high when the final day arrived. The weather was good, the crowd better, and superior to all was the play. Braid never lost his nerve, his driving was as strong as ever, and his short game remarkably good.

That he still remained favourite for first place was proved by the crowd that followed him when he started on his third round. He made no mistake, neither did he display any signs of weakness, for his first shot from the tee well-nigh carried the ball to the edge of the first green. Handling his wooden putter capitally, he ran up with the greatest accuracy, and the first hole fell to him in a 3.

His attack upon the second hole was not so successful, for slightly pulling his drive from the tee, he had a heavy lie from which to play. This made just a little difference, despite a capital stroke away to the right of the green, and as he failed to get down his putt, this hole required the playing of 5. Again going to the third hole, Braid overshot the mark and got into the rougher ground beyond the green. It was a somewhat difficult position to be in, but he extricated himself, pitched the ball dead, and got the hole in a 4.

At the fourth hole it looked as though Braid possessed a great chance for a 3, but it was spoilt by his failure to hole out, the ball just missing its objective by a hair's breadth. But he made no mistake with his next stroke, and another 4 was returned.

The long hole came next, and here Braid's mastery over the driver stood him in good stead at first, but his second shot planted him to the right of the bunker, not in the best of positions. It cost him an additional stroke, and he could do no better than 5, although the sixth hole was taken in 4. Indeed, he was well up in 2, but his third proved too strong, it being necessary to hole a long putt with his next.

More bad luck was experienced at the seventh, for after Braid had driven a long ball from the tee, everything pointed to the probability of a 3 being the result It was not to be, however; the ball trembled, but lay on the edge of the hole, and yet another 4 remained to be written up. His fortune was the same at the eighth hole, for although his approach put him into a position to secure a long putt, again he failed to catch the edge of the hole by the merest shave, and so missed his 3.

At the ninth hole his ball stopped within an inch of the hole, but despite these drawbacks, his first half-round was finished in 37. Going to the tenth hole, had he succeeded in a moderately difficult putt, he would have had a 3 in place of a 4, but his 4 for the eleventh was quite above the average merit. Had Braid been a less powerful driver, he could not have got so near the green with his second, while his third carried him almost to the edge of the hole, and the final putt was all that remained to finish what was a splendid performance.

Braid's approach to the twelfth hole was of a somewhat too vigorous nature, and he had to pay the penalty, despite the best of his skill, with a 5. He almost succeeded in recovering himself, but not quite, and his putt for the hole did not travel the full distance necessary. At the thirteenth he found himself in a far-from-favourable lie after his drive from the tee, and although a good approach shot was seen on this occasion, it was a difficult putt that remained. Still, he succeeded in negotiating it successfully, while the same may be said concerning the short hole.

The hope of the Scotsman was indeed playing at the very top of his game. Going to this last-named hole, he played wide of the green and also overran the hole with the next stroke. Again it was a good putt that saved him, a fact that supports my contention that in the majority of instances a game is lost or won upon the greens. I have treated this in a far more exhaustive manner in another portion of the book, hence I have but mentioned it in a cursory manner here. It is not altogether in the driving that a player wins or loses; he requires a sure eye and a steady hand when he takes up his putter. Too much attention cannot be paid to this particular department of the game, for it was through his improvement in this phase of play that Braid succeeded in taking the Championship back across the Border.

At the fifteenth hole he secured a 4, and narrowly escaped a similar return at the long sixteenth, the ball overhanging the edge of the hole. Then he obtained a couple of additional 4s and so finished the round in 74, his aggregate total for the three rounds being 229.

Meanwhile Harry Vardon and myself were battling along. Vardon was not doing himself justice, his driving being continually at fault; but I did much better in this round than at my previous attempts, finishing in 74, my aggregate, however, being at this stage 236.

But it was during the final round that the battle royal was witnessed. The crowd, whose sympathies were very naturally with the leader, were asking themselves one question—"Could he maintain his form, or would he lose his nerve?" As after events proved, in this three-ball contest Braid *did* maintain the greater portion of his form; and although both Vardon and I each returned a better round, the earlier advantage proved far too great for either of us to wipe off.

To tell the story of the final round, it is only necessary for me to say that Braid did not commence too well, for after getting close to the first hole he succeeded in missing a putt that should have been well within his compass, and so took 4 to hole out instead of a 3. This did not tend to unsettle him in the slightest, for at the second hole he played a great iron approach shot, and was finally faced by a three-yard putt. There was a sigh of suppressed excitement as he prepared to play the stroke. Slowly the ball rolled up to the edge of the hole, wavered just for a moment, and then disappeared from view. It was one of Braid's best putts, and it deserved the applause bestowed upon it.

He was slightly off his game again at the next hole, which is a not difficult 4. A short iron shot was responsible for his failure in this instance, and he exceeded the figure I have named by a stroke.

A far better recovery, after being short, was witnessed at the fourth hole, but at the next the prospective champion made what was really his first mistake of any magnitude. It is a long hole, but he got very near to it in 4—within a couple of feet, as a matter of fact. A putt of this distance is as near becoming a certainty as is possible, but by some unaccountable means Braid managed to miss it, and he had to return a 6. At the next he did nothing better than a 5, although it must be pleaded as an excuse for this figure that he was left with a very awkward lie after his iron shot. Accidents will happen, even in the best-regulated families, and it was but the fortune of war after all.

So he was not a whit dismayed, and at the seventh narrowly escaped a 3 (a performance he repeated at the eighth), while with a 4 for the ninth he turned in 40—three strokes above his figures in the earlier portion of the day.

Turning for the return, Braid certainly did not reproduce the initial steadiness of his game, but, on the other hand, there were occasional flashes of brilliance. His first hole when coming in cost 4, and at the eleventh (another long hole) he was well-nigh up in a couple of shots. Then he fell away badly, proved terribly weak on the green, and finally could accomplish nothing better than a 6—a great disappointment to those who were anticipating his success. Again, at the next hole he displayed weakness in putting, just where he had failed to do himself justice on previous occasions, and when he failed to discover the way to the hole, his score had reached seven above 4s.

Then it was that the fighting qualities of the man reasserted themselves. Braid knew that one man at least (Vardon) might run him desperately close, and he succeeded in steadying himself, a fact rendered patent to all by his getting down a difficult putt at his next attempt. At the fourteenth he made a still better showing, for he had the hole in 3; and although he discovered the bunker by his drive to the fifteenth, he made a grand recovery from a deeply indented hollow, and his ball rested within ten yards of the hole. It was a possible 3, but there was nothing disturbing in the fact that he took 4, for that is the par value of this hole.

Braid dropped another stroke two holes later, for again he missed what appeared to be a certainty, his putt of a yard's distance not being sufficiently well calculated. But with an aggregate of 80, Braid finished his four rounds in 309, and then attention was turned to Vardon.

He had not done too well when he started, his tee shot for the first hole going into the wood; but he recovered himself magnificently, and 4 represented the hole. At the second hole I succeeded in securing an advantage of a stroke by means of a four-yard putt, but at the fourth and fifth Vardon recovered himself.

At the turn his total was 39 and mine 40, and when we had reached the fifteenth we learnt what Braid had done. To maintain the English hold upon the Championship Vardon would need to play a round of 75—a big task at the best of times, but a doubly difficult one now.

Excitement became intense, for the Ganton man had played such absolutely wonderful games on other occasions that there was no knowing what he might do now; but going to the sixteenth hole he missed his approach by some means, and found himself badly bunkered. This was not encouraging certainly, for the hole cost 6, and it was a necessity for Vardon to take the last couple in 3 apiece in order to make a tie.

That this was almost impossible of accomplishment was recognised to the full, and the seventeenth taking 4, the hopes of the English brigade fell considerably below zero. Then, in approaching the last hole, Vardon had more bad luck, for he sliced his second shot into the crowd, and his full round amounted to 78, giving a complete aggregate of 312, Braid thus winning by three strokes upon the full four rounds. My round cost me 77, and my aggregate for the complete contest was 313.

So the Scot trounced the Saxon, and as I said at the start of the chapter, Braid deserved to win upon the game he played. He is a native of Elie, Fifeshire, learnt his golf at Earlsferry and the Braids course at Edinburgh, came southward to the golfing department of one of the principal London stores, and then secured the position of resident professional to the Romford Club.

US Mint design: Obverse-Don Everhart Reverse-Phebe Hemphill

THE STORY OF MASTERS WEEK
AT AUGUSTA NATIONAL

TRIPP BOWDEN

It's the first full week in April, Masters Week, and I'm sitting on a bench in the caddy house, lacing up a pair of fresh out of the box green and white FootJoys. The shoes are custom-made for Augusta National, caddies in particular.

This is the first year someone who's not a caddy gets the privilege of slipping them on.

That someone is me. Me and two others, a veteran Augusta caddy named Tip Lite and another kid who is a couple years older than me. I figure he must have some pull, though I never get around to asking how much.

Outside I retrace the cart steps from my ride with Freddie, and twenty minutes later I'm slipping under the yellow ropes and taking my position behind the 2nd green. The one Freddie drove onto from the Bobby Jones sundial wearing bedroom slippers.

It's a different sort of job, this forecaddying. My assignment is to fix players' ball marks and sweep sand off the green with a fiberglass pole after they blast out of the bunker. Sounds dull as Parcheesi at first glance, but I feel like the guy who feeds the dolphins at Sea World. It's a menial job, but once you're on stage you get as many eyes on you as the Golden Bear himself.

There's no feeling quite like it, being not two feet from the likes of Nicklaus, Palmer, Player, and Watson, fixing their ball marks as they approach the green to raucous applause. Some players seem to appreciate us, some act as if we're not even there.

Palmer always says thank you.

Two years ago I had no idea who he was. Today I know him as the King. And the King just acknowledged one of his court jesters.

Good stuff, this. But as good as this is, it's not nearly as good as what awaits me after my job is done for the day.

Freddie's office.

Freddie's invited me to come by after I'm done, but only if I want to. My forecaddy ID gives me all-day and all-week access to Augusta National, the most revered golf course in the world. And to the Masters, the most elusive ticket in all of sports.

I understand if you want to take a rain check.

Rain check, my ass.

An invitation to Freddie's office blows everything else out of the water in ways you could never imagine. When the last group putts out I tell my fellow forecaddies I'll see 'em tomorrow. Walking towards the clubhouse, I repeat Freddie's words like a mantra.

Walk up to the pro shop like you belong. Push back your hat so the Pinkerton can see your eyes. Look dead into his and say, "I'm here to see Freddie." Don't miss a beat and don't slow down. Walk in like you own the place.

I do as I'm told, only to later realize all I ever need to do to access almost anything at Augusta is mention five simple words: *I'm here to see Freddie.*

After thanking the Pinkerton, I walk down the short path around the side of the pro shop, squeak open the door to Freddie's office. A tall, good-looking Spaniard is standing over Freddie's desk, talking in broken English. He would win the Masters that year, after a rain delay that pushed the tournament to Monday, beginning his final round 3, 3, 3.

Birdie, eagle, birdie.

Freddie sees me, nods, and flicks his wrist, the sign to come in. He gets up from his chair and gestures to it with an open hand and so I sit down. The Spaniard looks at me like I just walked on water. He turns to Freddie, asks about changing out his grips. Had Freddie ever done that before?

Freddie nods and says, "Yes, sir. All day long."

Under his breath I hear something else, but I can't quite make it out.

The Spaniard shakes Freddie's hand, thanks him, and leaves.

When the door bounces shut, Freddie opens his hand and a five-dollar bill falls onto the floor. He laughs.

"Ain't that something? That sonofabitch wants me to re-grip his clubs and he gives me five bucks—*five bucks* to make sure they're ready for tomorrow!" He's really laughing now. "But I'll do it. Ain't no doubt about that." Freddie reaches into the

Spaniard's bag and pulls out his driver. "Hey, this feels pretty good. Got it balanced just right."

The fiver is still lying on the floor.

He hands me the driver. I stand up, grip it, and waggle. I'm in awe as much as I am dumbfounded, but Freddie's right. This club feels great.

"So, how'd it go, man? You make out all right?"

"It was awesome," I say, and then I tell him how Chi Chi Rodriguez poked me with his putter and asked if I was Frank Beard's son (I had no idea who Frank Beard was) and how Arnold Palmer thanked me for fixing his ball mark. Looked me right in the eye.

"You mean this guy?" asks Freddie, in a voice only I can hear.

In walks the King himself.

"Hey, Freddie," says Palmer as the two men shake hands. "Always good to see you."

"Always good to be seen," says Freddie, "especially at my age." Palmer laughs, and they talk about things that don't pertain to me, don't pertain to golf. I stand there in pure disbelief, not three feet from the man who, through television and his amazing charisma, changed the game of golf forever.

Just like with the Spaniard, I can feel Arnie's eyes on me, wondering who I must be, given access to this mother of all backstage passes.

"This here's my doctor's son," says Freddie, as if reading Arnie's mind.

The look on his face says he has a vague memory of me, but nothing clicks. He smiles a hello, turns to Freddie, back to me, then Freddie again. He says something about him and his 4-iron no longer being friends, then pulls the iron out of the bag and grips it.

What a grip! If God had hands they would be Arnie's. Wrapped around a golf club they look like something off a wall in the Sistine Chapel. No wonder they call him the King.

Arnie slips the 4-iron back in the bag, tells Freddie he'll see him tomorrow, and walks out, waving as he goes.

"Check this out," says Freddie as the door shuts. He hands me Arnie's 4-iron. The clubface has his name on it. "Grip it, see what you think."

Are you kidding me? Grip Arnold Palmer's 4-iron?

But grip it I do, and the leather grip feels sticky and smells like earth. Not dirt, but the big ball you're standing on.

"This is real golf here, man. How the game was meant to be played. Leather grips, iron shafts, and a ball that won't fly to hell and gone." Freddie looks at me, looks through me, comes back to himself, and reaches for the 4-iron. "Come over here," he says. "Got something I want you to see."

What could possibly top this?

Comstock/Thinkstock

THE STORY OF BEN HOGAN'S ULTIMATE TEST

JEFF MILLER

After Lloyd Mangrum christened the 1949 P.G.A. Tour season with a victory at the Los Angeles Open, Ben Hogan and Jimmy Demaret did their best to turn the rest of the month's schedule into a match race. Hogan won the Bing Crosby Pro-Am. Then they finished in a tie at Long Beach with Hogan taking the playoff 67 to 69. On to Phoenix and another playoff between them, won this time by Demaret 67-70. There was no reason to believe things would be any different at the Tour's next stop, the Tucson Open, except that Hogan was headed back to Texas for a break before resuming play in San Antonio following a week's break.

If the Hogan-Demaret heroics weren't enough to gain the attention of golf fans across the country, Hogan was the cover story of the January 10, 1949 edition of *Time* magazine. The cover display offered the advice on which he based his career: "If you can't outplay them, outwork them." The extensive profile was written by Marshall Smith, who gave Hogan a taste of his own medicine while interviewing him. When Hogan was made aware of something that would be in the story that he wasn't enthusiastic about, he confronted Smith: "You're not going to say *that* in your story." To which the writer replied, "Look. Your game is golf. This story is my business. Let me handle it my way."

As January gave way to February, post-war tensions between the United States and the Soviet Union reached a new milepost. Soviet Premier Josef Stalin had offered President Harry S. Truman the opportunity to engage in disarmament talks—but only at a location behind the Iron Curtain because of his health. The administration recoiled; the new Secretary of State, Dean Acheson, replied in a news conference that the United States wasn't interested in such a summit. Stalin, Acheson said while referring to voluminous notes, had previously rejected invitations from the Americans to meet in Washington. Plus, Acheson added, such talks would involve many other countries and shouldn't be confined to simply the two well-armed superpowers.

Everything was going Hogan's way until the Greyhound bus coming at him in far west Texas knocked his Cadillac off the road, nearly killing him and his wife. Hogan skipped the Tucson tournament and left Phoenix on Tuesday, February 1 bound for

Fort Worth, where that night "Jug" McSpaden was giving a golfing lecture at TCU's auditorium. The Hogans nearly covered half the distance in driving about seventy-five miles beyond El Paso. They reached the small town of Van Horn and called it a day, stopping at the El Capitan Motel. The following morning was frigidly cold across much of the Lone Star State, with snow covering parts of Waco and Austin. In Fort Worth, Oscar the Groundhog saw his shadow. Out in far west Texas, there was early morning fog and at least a slight glaze of ice on U.S. Highway 80, the main route between El Paso and Dallas-Fort Worth. The Hogans were back on the road at eight looking at almost another full day's drive before arriving home. They had not gone far when Hogan told his wife, "I think we've got a flat tire." He pulled off the two-lane road, determined there was nothing wrong with the tires, and continued driving. Having noticed ice on the road for the first time that morning, he told Valerie that he'd drive slightly slower.

Only a few minutes after the Hogans were rolling again, the glow of headlights—right in front of their Cadillac—came seeping through the fog. It was a bus in their lane, the driver in the midst of passing a truck. The driver, Alvin Logan, had spent about six miles behind the truck and decided this stretch of winding, dipping road was suitable for trying to make the pass. As the Cadillac and Greyhound bore down on each other, the Hogans were crossing over a culvert with a concrete barrier that prevented Hogan from swerving to the right. Valerie screamed, "Honey, he's going to hit us!" Hogan instinctively threw himself over his wife's lap to shield her from the impending collision. Had he remained in the driver's seat, the impact of the steering column being thrust back into him surely would have killed him. The car was knocked well off the road and into the ditch. Hogan was concerned the Cadillac would catch fire and yelled for Valerie to get out of the car. As they both managed to escape the vehicle, passersby began to come to their aid. With people frantically concerned for the

Hogans' welfare, it somehow took about an hour for someone to summon an ambulance. Hogan tried to assure people that he was fine, though it was already obvious that he'd suffered at the very least a broken ankle and an injured left leg. While they were waiting to make the trip to the Hotel Dieu Hospital back in El Paso, Hogan kept asking about his golf clubs, which were in the trunk of the Cadillac. Valerie asked police on the scene to please get the clubs and send them along with them. It turned out Hogan had sustained a double fracture of the pelvis, a fractured collar bone and a chipped rib in addition to the leg and foot issues. As for Valerie, her injuries were limited to some bruises and a black eye thanks to her husband's quick thinking.

Hogan initially recovered at an encouraging pace in El Paso. Royal Hogan, who rushed there upon hearing the news, indicated to hometown reporters that his brother would be transferred home within a matter of days. But the timetable soon changed when Hogan suffered a significant setback; blood clots worked their way from his injured left leg into his lungs. For the first time since the initial aftermath of the crash, there was legitimate concern for Hogan's life. A specialist in vascular surgery was contacted in New Orleans, but he couldn't immediately get a seat on a commercial plane bound for El Paso because of the ongoing Mardi Gras celebration. Valerie then recalled one of the visitors in Hogan's first days in the hospital was a brigadier general stationed nearby. She contacted him at midnight and, with his help, a plane was sent to bring Dr. Alton Ochsner to Hotel Dieu. The operation was a success, but Hogan remained hospitalized in El Paso for two months and never fully recovered from the leg injuries. They would require daily attention—massages, baths and extensive leg wrappings—for years to come. The Hogans were overwhelmed with well-wishers and expressions of people's concern for Ben while in El Paso. Valerie told the *Fort Worth Star-Telegram* the episode had made her husband realize how much people cared for him.

By the time the Hogans rode a train to Fort Worth in early April, no one was possibly considering Hogan would play P.G.A. Tour golf again—except for Hogan himself. Maybe he doubted he could do it or maybe he was building his own target for motivation when he told reporters, "Don't waste your time writing about me. People are tired of hearing about Ben Hogan. They're interested in the guys who are playing now. It won't be long until they forget all about me." His return to golf came as captain of the United States' 1949 Ryder Cup team, which retained the trophy with a 7-to-5 victory at the Ganton Golf Club in Scarborough, England. By that autumn, he was prepared to take steps to return to the game. In early November, he was on the practice range at Colonial. About a month later, Hogan played his first round of golf, with the aid of a cart, since the playoff in Phoenix about eleven months earlier. News of the Saturday afternoon jaunt around Colonial on a chilly, cloudy day appeared in the next day's *Star-Telegram* without a writer's byline and beneath a headline that began with the word FLASH! "I didn't hit them very well," Hogan allowed. His playing partner, Ridglea pro Raymond Gafford, offered that Hogan hit them "well enough." That following day's *Press* noted Hogan played another eighteen holes at Colonial that Sunday, shot 71 and 72 for the weekend and complained of being "a little tired."

His next step—literally—was to complete a round while walking, which he did a week later. His goal was to enter the first event of the 1950 season, the $15,000 Los Angeles Open scheduled for Friday through Monday, January 6–9. About the same time that Hogan was first playing eighteen holes without a cart, representatives of the L.A. event asked him if he could come out to the tournament and serve as the honorary starter. A few days later, the Hogans were on a train headed to California. He piqued the interest of reporters at the station in Fort Worth by indicating he was interested in actually playing at Riviera Country Club, where he won the 1948 National Open. At least one Hogan fan was certain he would return to tournament play—Alton Ochsner, the surgeon who saved his life. "Ben has the kind of determination that leaves no doubt as to the ultimate outcome," Ochsner was quoted in the *Star-Telegram* during the Los Angeles tournament. "Doctors not infrequently recognize this will in patients, but in few people has it ever been more evident than in Hogan."

Oh, Hogan indeed played; his performance at the 1950 Los Angeles Open would have been the story of the year on the Tour were it not for his later heroics on a grander stage. The four practice rounds that he played totaled three shots less than Mangrum's winning score a year earlier, though he brought along a chair for resting between holes. "It's all a question of my legs," he said after a practice round. "They've been tiring in the latter parts of rounds." Among those who played practice rounds with Hogan was Cary Middlecoff, the defending U.S. Open champion. "He pinned our ears back," reported Middlecoff, the former dentist who gave up his practice to play professional golf. At one point, Hogan told his playing partners that his legs hurt like hell and then deposited his next shot twenty feet from the pin.

Hogan opened with a 2-over-par 73 that left him five shots behind leader Ed Furgol. As per his fears, his play withered along with his legs on the back nine. Hogan also appeared unusually distracted by things that previously didn't affect him, like noises from a construction crew working on a home site above the seventh green. But he then incredibly fired off three consecutive rounds of 69 on Saturday, Monday, and Tuesday (with Sunday's play rained out) and no longer seemed impacted by potential agitations such as an amateur photographer facing down his putting line. Hogan tied for first place at 4-under 280 with Sam Snead, who required a 15-foot birdie putt on his seventy-second hole to force the playoff. An exhausted Hogan obviously didn't welcome the prospect of another grueling eighteen holes. "I'm awfully tired," he told reporters. "I wish I didn't have to play tomorrow."

Hogan didn't have to play tomorrow. More rain washed out the Wednesday playoff and, with the popular Bing Crosby Pro-Am scheduled to start up the coast on Friday, the decision was made to re-schedule the L.A. playoff until *after* the Crosby event. Hogan played at the three-round Pebble Beach tournament, where he was the defending champion. He didn't experience the same success that he enjoyed at Riviera. His best round there was "only" a par-72—still remarkable given what had happened to him in the previous year—and finished in a tie for nineteenth place. Byron Nelson, playing in a Tour event for the first time since the previous May, shot 4-over 148 for two rounds and withdrew.

Snead was among four players who tied for first at the Crosby—missing an eight-foot putt that would have claimed the championship—and tournament officials didn't bother with a playoff; all four were declared winners. Hogan was glad to be leaving chilly northern California, but the forecast on Monday called for showers in Los Angeles on Wednesday. The rain held off, but the combatants were greeted at Riviera by low fog. The proceedings began with a dismal omen for Hogan when his initial tee shot went hooking out of bounds. Snead led by two shots after two holes and maintained that edge through the front nine. He did the same coming home, holding even par while Hogan shot 2-over to win 72 to 76. "I was lousy," Hogan growled afterward. Snead countered: "He was terrific. He's the same old Hogan. He scares you to death." There was an awkward episode on no. 13 when Snead became impatient with the amount of time that Hogan was taking on putts and walked off the green while Hogan was putting. Years later, Snead told the *Los Angeles Times* that he thought Hogan purposely took that much time, trying to drain his opponent's momentum. For those in Dallas–Fort Worth who wished to watch a delayed telecast of the playoff, WBAP-TV provided that opportunity the following Sunday night—sponsored by Royal Hogan's office supply store.

Hogan skipped the Long Beach tournament but played in Phoenix, where organizers renamed the 1950 event the Ben Hogan Open; following a first-round 65, he faded and finished in a tie for twentieth place. Hogan didn't make another start for almost two months, appearing in the non-Tour Seminole Pro-Am in Palm Beach, Florida, in mid-March. He was working out of a hole opening with a 79 and could manage only a tie for twenty-fourth place. Then it was on to a triumphant return to Augusta. Incredibly, Hogan stood only two shots out of the lead heading to the final round. But he closed with a 4-over 76 leaving him in fourth place, five shots behind three-time Masters winner Demaret.

If there was any animosity between Hogan and Snead given the events of the Los Angeles Open, it didn't prevent Hogan from showing up for Snead's Greenbriar Open a few weeks later. The event featured only twenty-five players, and Hogan shot a 21-under 259 to beat the host pro by ten shots. Hogan's plan had been to follow the West Virginia stop with a trip to the Western Open, but he decided against that. Next up would be another emotional experience—as if any appearance at this stage wouldn't be—returning to Marvin Leonard's course. It appeared the Colonial National Invitational Tournament couldn't be played without Bantam Ben; the 1949 event that was scheduled while Hogan was convalescing was cancelled because of flooding. At Hogan's homecoming in May 1950, Snead gained a measure of revenge by winning on Hogan's home layout. Hogan was hardly a disappointment, though, placing third. The following day, he caught a train for Philadelphia to play in two weeks in the U.S. Open at Merion Golf Club, where he would be required to play thirty-six holes in a single day for the first time in his return.

In the days leading up to the National Open, Snead acknowledged to the *Richmond News Leader* that Hogan was on his mind—either that or he was writing another chapter of gamesmanship.

"The man who wins it will have to beat me," Snead said. "I'm not playing sensationally, but I'm playing well. I actually think Hogan is the man who might make some trouble. He's the man I've got to beat." During Hogan's practice rounds at Merion, he made the decision to replace his usual 7-iron with a 1-iron after determining there were no 7-iron shots on the historic East Course. Like it was at Riviera, the issue of Hogan's durability seemed to be the most popular topic of pre-tournament repartee. Gene Sarazen, the 1934 Open winner, was forthright if not polite in his assessment: "If they were going to play it without walking—just hitting the shots—I would pick Ben without hesitation. But, unfortunately, he will have to walk."

For at least a day, events pushed the story of the historic Hogan comeback to the back pages. Lee Mackey, Jr., a 26-year-old from Birmingham, Alabama, with no professional wins, broke both the course record and the National Open one-round mark in Thursday's first round by one-putting ten holes and firing a 6-under-par 64. Hogan opened with a 2-over-par 72, recovering from a rickety start shooting 39 on the front nine. When reporters sought an explanation from Mackey for his implausible taming of Merion, he replied, "I guess I just got lucky." Alas, he failed to pack luck into his bag the next day; he stumbled through an 11-over 81 that took him out of contention. Hogan's second-day score of 1-under 69 was shot with a mid-morning tee time that enabled him to miss the most scorching portion of a Philadelphia day that reached a humid 95 degrees, though he did experience some cramping at the no. 12 hole. His overall 1-over 141 placed him only two shots behind leader "Dutch" Harrison in fifth place.

For Saturday's 36-hole finale viewed by a National Open record 12,500 spectators, Hogan was paired with Middlecoff going off at 9:30 a.m. and 2 p.m. As would be the case for the rest of Hogan's career, early starting times were problematic because the hours of preparation required for getting his legs ready for competition. He completed the morning round in 2-over 72, putting him two behind Mangrum and one behind Harrison. On the twelfth hole of the afternoon round, owning a three-stroke advantage, Hogan suffered through more than cramping this time around; he grimaced after striking his tee shot and began to stagger, grabbing onto a friend to prevent himself from falling and went on to bogey the hole. Years later, Hogan told the *Star-Telegram* that his legs had turned to stone and he wasn't certain he could finish. For the balance of the round, Hogan's putts were extracted from the cups by either his caddie or Middlecoff's. And then after playing the thirteenth, according to separate interviews that Hogan gave years later, the pain was so great he was resigned to the fact that he couldn't finish—only to have his caddie insist on meeting him at the no. 14 tee box.

Suffering bogeys on nos. 15 and 17 because of putting issues, Hogan trudged to the par-4, 458-yard eighteenth having lost a three-shot lead over six holes. He needed a par to force a three-way playoff with Mangrum and George Fazio, the latter a hometown boy whose two Tour triumphs consisted of the 1946 Canadian Open and the '47 Crosby. After a tee shot that nestled in the middle of the fairway more than 200 yards from the pin, he called upon the 1-iron that he'd subbed into his bag just before play began. His approach, captured in the renowned photograph shot by Hy Peskin for *Life,* carried the treacherous rough lurking right of the fairway and in front of the green and landed just short of the green but carried up onto the putting surface about forty feet from the flag stick. His first putt rolled four feet past the hole; he quickly struck the return putt to earn his par for the hole—a 4-over 74 for the round—and another day's play. (Hogan told long-time golf writer Charles Price that he struck the putt hastily because his legs hurt so much he was eager to end the round and get off his feet. On the way back to his hotel afterward, Hogan became sick to his stomach.) In the chaos of excitement in the aftermath of the drama, the club that

Hogan used to reach the eighteenth green—years later, debate raged over whether it was his 1-iron or 2-iron—was absconded from his golf bag. If it *wasn't* the 1-iron, the granite marker placed in the fairway to honor the achievement is in error.

Valerie Hogan feared her husband couldn't endure another eighteen holes that Sunday. Wasn't she pleasantly surprised, as she recalled for Dave Anderson, when Ben awoke that morning and exclaimed, "Isn't it a nice day?" In the lobby of the Barclay Hotel, reporters diligently checked on Hogan's condition—and some all but rooted him on as he and Valerie left for the 30-minute drive to Merion. Hogan's day would ordinarily have started much earlier with a morning tee time for the playoff, but state blue laws prohibited starting before 1 p.m. In the three-way battle, Hogan took his first lead on the par-4 seventh when his approach landed only four feet from the pin and he converted the birdie putt. He gave back the stroke with a bogey on the eighth hole, and Hogan and Mangrum stood even following nine holes. Hogan was back on top through twelve holes, his even-par round providing him a one-shot lead over both of his competitors. When Fazio and Mangrum each bogeyed the par-4 fourteenth, Hogan enjoyed a two-stroke cushion with four holes to play. Mangrum managed to birdie no. 15 to get back within one.

Then came the infamous turn of events at no. 16. With Mangrum preparing to putt, he unwittingly committed a rules violation when he addressed his ball, then picked it up to blow a bug off it. He was assessed a two-stroke penalty; prior to 1960, U.S.G.A. rules allowed players to mark and pick up their ball on the green only when the ball interfered with another player. Mangrum later stated he was initially unaware of the ruling, thinking he'd putted for a par. It was only in the tee area on no. 17 that U.S.G.A. official Ike Grainger explained to him what happened. Hogan was ahead by three shots with two holes to play but played like a man needing to shoot a birdie. Which he did on no. 17, thanks to a 50-foot uphill putt. On no. 18, missing the club that he used for his second shot on Saturday afternoon, Hogan played a 5-iron—and sent the ball over the green. His chip back came to rest seven feet from the cup, and a one-putt gave him a 1-under 69 to Mangrum's 73 and Fazio's 75. The crowd around the green was prepared to hoist the victorious Hogan on their shoulders but was halted by the local constabulary. Hogan admitted to reporters that winning the 1950 Open topped even his first Open victory in Los Angeles two years earlier: "This was my biggest thrill. And I'm awfully glad that those two strokes Lloyd lost on the sixteenth green penalty didn't make the difference." One of the wags later mentioned something about retirement. "Retire?" Hogan replied with a laugh. "I love golf, and I'll never quit it competitively."

Pixland/Thinkstock

THE STORY OF THE 18 HOLES AT AUGUSTA NATIONAL

TRIPP BOWDEN

During my sophomore year of high school, my golf game stalls. I get no better, I get no worse. I'm breaking 80 more often than not, but throwing way too many 84s into the mix.

I don't know much about life on the PGA Tour, but I know it doesn't include many rounds in the 80s.

Freddie's voice is in my head: ~~Two things that don't last, man:~~
~~dogs that chase cars and pros that putt for pars.~~

But as he does for everything, Freddie has an answer for my
golf game. His name is Mike Shannon, the former Augusta
National assistant who gave me my first real golf lesson. A player
in his own right, Shannon can also count as a claim to fame a
certain college roommate who won the Masters on his first try—
Frank Urban Zoeller. You know him as Fuzzy.

The summer of '81 finds me in the sleepy little town of Tupelo,
Mississippi. Elvis was born here, and looking around I see little
has changed since he first donned the blue suede shoes. I don't
really want to go (who wants to go to Tupelo?), but Freddie
insists.

"If you ever hope to realize your potential, Mike is the man.
Can't nobody lay your cards on the table like him. Not big as a
minute but can knock the ball into next week. Trained under a
cat named Harvey Penick, who just so happened to teach the
game to a couple young bucks named Ben and Tom. Last names
Crenshaw and Kite. Mike knows his stuff. Listen to him, okay?"

Do I ever.

Mike Shannon is a big believer in practice, but not just any
practice. Mike calls it perfect practice, the theory being that
when you're faced with a similar situation on the golf course, you
expect to be successful.

I like this theory. But not at first.

With the Mississippi sun beating down like a boxer, I spend
my summer on a baked-out putting green, rolling three-footers
until I can make fifty in a row. Miss one and start over, even if
it's number forty-nine.

Grass dies under my feet until I get it right.

Three-footers are just the beginning. Make ten putts in a row
from five feet. Two in a row from ten. Hole a twenty-footer
before you can move on to the next level. Dig down into the
bunker, the sun's reflection like a fun house mirror. No escaping

until you've holed one out. Might be on the first swing, might not be until sunset.

Might not be at all.

Matters not. Only thing that does is getting back into that sweltering pit at 7:00 AM the next day, hitting bunker shot after bunker shot until one finally disappears.

It's a pain in the ass sometimes, but by week's end there is no denying perfect practice works perfectly. My putting and sand play are now the best parts of my game, the last to leave when the others fly south for the winter.

The night before my flight back to Augusta, I call Freddie with fingers so swollen I can hardly punch the numbers. The line rings twice, then a third time before Freddie answers. I'd rather tell him in person, but I know I won't be able to sleep if I don't tell him now.

"Hey, Freddie. It's Tripp."

"Hey, man. What's shakin'? You learning a lot, ain'tcha? Things about the game you never knew existed, I bet. Told you Mike knew his stuff."

"Mike's great," I say, and I go on to tell Freddie all about perfect practice, not knowing he's heard it all before.

Freddie lets me talk.

"You sitting down?" I ask.

"I am now."

"I shot 74 today! Best round ever. I hit 14 greens. Can you believe it?"

"That's great, man. How many birdies?"

"Four," I say. "Three on the back nine. One I made after my second shot bounced off a tree and onto the green. It almost rolled in for an eagle!" I'm so excited I can hardly breathe. "I mean, what are the odds of *that* happening?"

There's a short pause on the other end.

"Apparently, they're pretty good," says Freddie, laughing. "Come see me when you get home, all right, man?"

I tell him I will, of course I will. Then I do something I should've done long ago.

"Freddie?"

"Yeah, man?"

"Thanks."

"For what?"

"For everything."

"Don't thank me. Thank Mike. And fly safe, all right?"

I promise I will and we say our goodbyes. I hang up the phone and stare at fingers so swollen I can't close my hand. I have calluses on my calluses, the sun's fist print on my face. Every muscle in my body aches and I could sleep standing up if given half a chance.

Man, do I feel great.

THE STORY OF THE 1897 OPEN CHAMPIONSHIP

GARDEN GRANT SMITH

Lovely summer-like weather prevailed at Hoylake, in the month of May, for the week in which, for the first time on this course, the Open Championship was played. Cloudless skies overhead, and the hot sun tempered by a gentle easterly breeze, that eased the outward journey and did not seriously impede the homeward, made the weather conditions perfect, for players and spectators alike. The course was in first-rate order, if a trifle on the hard side, and the putting greens, especially, would have been much improved by a day's rain.

For a few days previous to the event, the combatants had been gathering from near and from far. Professional competitions, organised during the previous week by the neighbouring clubs at Wallasey and Southport, helped to relieve the monotony of practice at Hoylake, and the results of these were eagerly scanned, as affording some index of the prevalent form of the players.

The championship fell to be played on the Wednesday and Thursday, but by the Sunday previous, almost all the competitors, of whom there were 88, were at Hoylake, and all day long—there being no Sunday play at Hoylake—the links were dotted over with little groups of golfers, inspecting the course, and discussing the probabilities of the coming event. At the "Old Alps," quite early, was a group comprised of Mr. J. E. Laidlay, Mr. C. Hutchings, Mr. H. H. Hilton, Andrew Kirkaldy, J. H. Taylor, W. Auchterlonie, J. Kay, the two Simpsons, and Willie Park—a pretty strong galaxy of golfers. Andrew Kirkaldy, though he had not yet played over the course, expressed the opinion that the putting greens "were jist the kin' that he liked"; and how accurately he had diagnosed their suitability for himself, he proved, next morning, by going round in 76. Taylor had done a 73 the previous week, but he now seemed a bit off-colour, and ascribed that marvellous performance to luck on the greens. He and the other professionals seemed to fancy most the chances of Harry Vardon, last year's champion, who had been first at Southport, the previous day, and who was in magnificent form. Mr. Hilton, who knows Hoylake and its possibilities better perhaps than any other player, gave it as his opinion that two 79s and two 80s would win, and that while an individual score of 76 might be returned, two rounds of 75 would not be done throughout the competition. Little he recked, as he stood there, that he was to prove, in his own proper person, the falsity of his predictions in each particular. But we must not anticipate. Willie Park and Mr. Laidlay were engaged in an animated discussion on putting, in which department of the game they both found themselves, for the moment, out of form, and were administering to each other sundry hints and pre-scriptions for their respective varieties of this distressing malady. Elsewhere were to be seen the two Vardons, with their finely cut features and fists like legs of mutton, and the stalwart form of Braid, towering above a group in which were cheery Ben Sayers from North Berwick, and Davie Brown and Willie Fernie, two former champions. With the exception of Mr. H. Hutchinson and Douglas Rolland no golfing figure of note was absent. In the club-house, the chances of the amateurs were favourably enter-tained. With Mr. Ball and Mr. Hilton playing on their own green, with Mr. Tait, Mr. Laidlay, and Mr. Mure Fergusson all to the fore, it was felt that the professionals would not have things all their own way, as had so often previously been the case.

Monday and Tuesday were again glorious days, though Jack Morris's prayers for rain remained unanswered, and the putting greens became more and more fiery. From morning till night the air was alive with the crack of clean-hit balls, and some excellent scores were made in practice, though Andrew Kirkaldy's score of 76 on Monday morning, was not beaten before Wednesday, when the competition opened.

The first round produced nothing sensational in the way of scores. Mr. John Ball and A. Herd returned cards of 78 each; Mr. Tait and Davie Brown 79 each; and Mr. Hilton, J. Braid, and G. Pulford took 80. Mr. Laidlay and J. H. Taylor were 82 each, Harry Vardon 84, while Willie Park put himself completely out of the running with a 91.

The afternoon saw the best all-round play of the competi-tion. Mr. Hilton returned a magnificent card of 75, which was immediately surpassed by a 74—an absolutely perfect score—by J. Braid. Ben Sayers greatly improved his position with a 78. Mr. Tait again did 79, a score which was equalled by G. Pulford, Peter McEwan, and T. Renouf.

The results of the first day's play left the competition a very open one, and was remarkable in that three amateurs were to be found in the first six. The following list shows the respective scores of the first six:—

J. Braid	80 ...	74 = 154
Mr. H. H. Hilton	80 ...	75 = 155
Mr. F. G. Tait	79 ...	79 = 158
G. Pulford	80 ...	79 = 159
Mr. John Ball	78 ...	81 = 159
A. Herd	78 ...	81 = 159

The first round on Thursday—another perfect day—seemed to be, on the face of it, a disastrous one for the two leaders, for Mr. Hilton took 84, and J. Braid 82. Mr. Ball spoiled his chance with an 88. Pulford, Herd, and Mr. Tait improved their positions with two 79's and an 80, respectively, so that, at the completion of the third round, the position of the leaders was as follows:—

	1st Day's Score.	
J. Braid	154 ...	82 = 236
Mr. F. G. Tait	158 ...	80 = 238
G. Pulford	159 ...	79 = 238
A. Herd	159 ...	79 = 238
Mr. H. H. Hilton	155 ...	84 = 239

All this promised a close and exciting finish, and the onlookers were not disappointed in this respect. Mr. Tait was the first of the likely ones to finish his fourth round. By steady and beautiful golf, he handed in another score of 79, bringing his grand aggregate to 317; and this score, in the opinion of many, gave him a very strong position. This fine score, however, was not long allowed to go unchallenged. It was soon reported that Mr. Hilton was playing in surprising form. Starting in the most sensational way, with 18 for the first five holes, he accomplished the outward journey in 38 strokes—a performance which he even excelled coming homewards, and he finished, full of running, in 75, making his grand aggregate 314, or three better than Mr. Tait's. This brilliant effort completely altered the aspect of events, and all interest was now transferred to the doings of Braid, who, with Pulford and A. Herd alone, had any chance of beating Mr. Hilton's total. When Mr. Hilton finished, Braid was at the "Rushes" hole, and hither, helter-skelter, sped Mr. Hilton's crowd, all agog with excitement. They learned that Braid's score to the 13th hole was 55, so that he only required to complete the remaining five holes in 22 strokes, or three under fives, to beat Mr. Hilton. Holing out in magnificent style at the "Field" hole in four, he still further improved his chance, and 18 to win, or 19 to tie, was now the comparatively easy task he had before him. The "Lake" hole he played steadily in five, leaving one five and two fours for the remaining three holes. But alas! the "Dun" hole proved disastrous to his chances. A raking tee shot, followed by a superb brassy, in which he crossed the corner of the field and lay about 30 yards short of the green, seemed to make a five certain. The approach to this green, however, is of the most tricky description, and Braid's ball, though beautifully struck, got a bad fall on the hard green, and shot past the hole, some 10 yards, into the rough ground beyond the green. He failed to get his long putt dead, and took six to hole out. Even yet, two fours would enable him to tie—a three and a four seemed too much to hope for—but owing to weakness on the green at the 17th hole, he took five, so that even to tie with Mr. Hilton, he had to do the last hole in three. His second shot to the hole-side with his cleek was a beauty, and looked as if it were going to lie dead. It rolled some yards past, however, and as he failed to hole the long putt, he lost the championship by two strokes, finishing one stroke behind Mr. Hilton. Pulford and Herd, though again returning good scores of 79 and 80, had to be content with third and fourth places, Pulford tieing with Mr. Tait for third place. The final scores were as follows:—

	1st Day's Score.		2nd Day's Score.				
Mr. H. H. Hilton	155	...	84	75	= 159	= 314
J. Braid	154	...	82	79	= 161	= 315
Mr. F. G. Tait ...	158	...	80	79	= 159	= 317
G. Pulford	159	...	79	79	= 158	= 317
A. Herd	159	...	79	80	= 159	= 318
H. Vardon... ...	164	...	80	76	= 156	= 320

As will be seen, H. Vardon, the holder, had the distinction of having the best aggregate on the second day of the competition, and though defeated on this occasion, he worthily upheld his reputation.

Mr. Hilton's win—his second in the open championship—was warmly received, and there can be no question that his was a magnificent performance. The advantage of knowing the course as he does, no doubt counts for something, and though, in receiving the trophy, he modestly, in view of this fact, gave the greater merit to Braid, it seems probable that this advantage is much overestimated. A man may know a course too well. Mr. Hilton himself took 84 to his third round, and the fact that Braid returned a 74 in the competition, and H. Vardon a 76, is sufficient to show that, in the few days at their disposal, these players, at any rate, had managed to master a good deal of Hoylake's peculiarities.

Braid's play throughout was a treat to witness, and indeed more superb golf it would be difficult to conceive. He drives an exceedingly long and low ball, that keeps very straight, and the ball leaves the club as if shot from a cannon. His second stroke for the "Dun" hole in the final round, in which he successfully carried the corner of the field, straight on the hole, was, under the circumstances, a magnificent effort, and one that will live in the memory of all golfers who witnessed it.

Perhaps the most satisfying player to watch, however, was Mr. F. G. Tait. Mr. Tait's style is particularly fascinating, by reason of its quietness, and the suggestion it conveys of reserves of power.

Here, there is nothing of the exuberant waggle of the professional, no wide straddle, or other strongly accented peculiarity. Nor is any trace of "side" temper, or playing to the gallery to be seen in Mr. Tait's play. His demeanour, playing before a crowd of 3,000, is like that of the soldier on parade. But after dinner, "Freddy," as he is known to his friends, can unbend, and whether blowing the bagpipes or proposing a toast, he takes, as he does at golf, a deal of beating.

Mr. Ryder Richardson, the club secretary, Mr. Harold Janion, and the rest of the club committee did much to make the meeting one of the most successful gatherings of golfers that has ever been held.

iStockphoto/Thinkstock

THE STORY OF THE 1959 BRITISH OPEN

GARY PLAYER

The first one is always hard, and so it was for me, purely because I had worked myself to the bone to get to this point of winning my first Major.

There are degrees of success, and I arrived at Muirfield in Scotland having fulfilled most of these as a tournament winner around the world. But that was never going to be enough for me. I had to win Majors, to say I had beaten the best in the world at the game's highest level.

It's safe to say I made a disastrous start to this one, opening with a 75 that left me seven shots off the first round lead.

I battled my way through the next rounds, but was still in no great shape going into the final day.

That evening I attended a dinner which the president of Slazenger, Humphrey McMaster, also attended. I remember walking up to his table and saying, "Mr. McMaster, tomorrow I am going to win the Open." He looked at me in disbelief and replied, "Young man, at your age? And besides, you're six shots back."

Willie Auchterlonie was 21 when he won the 1893 Open. Young Tom Morris was 17 when he won the Open in 1868. And here I was, 23 years old, six shots back, and saying I was going to win. Why not?

Then the moment came. I was playing the final hole, and all I needed was a par four to win the tournament. It would've given me the 66 I had set for myself as a target at the start of the round. The 66 I knew would win me the Open and change my life forever.

I made six.

My whole world collapsed on me right there. There is a famous photograph of me with my head in my hands and my wife, Vivienne, trying to console me. It took all of my resolve just to sign my scorecard.

Because I was so far behind at the start of the round, I finished much earlier than the rest of the field. So I left the golf course and headed straight for my hotel, convinced that I had thrown away the Open Championship.

I didn't choke on that last hole. The weather was terrible and the wind was howling. That 18th fairway was very narrow, and I hit a drive that just crept into the bunker. I hit it out and hit the third on the front edge of the green, because the wind was blowing so hard, and then I three-putted.

But I had shot 284 in those conditions, and it proved too much for the rest of the field to match. I received a phone call from the course to inform me that I had won the Open, and could come and collect the Claret Jug at the official prize giving.

At last, I was the Open champion. I had broken through with my first Major.

THE CHOKE CHALLENGE

Breaking through for the first time brings with it a whole different set of pressures. I understood the pressure of Major championship golf. A year before Muirfield I had finished second in the US Open, and I'd had top-ten finishes in the Open in 1958 and the Masters in 1959. But this was new in terms of dealing with the pressure of trying to become a Major championship winner for the first time in my career.

It's a case of dealing with the nerves of realising a dream for the first time. That can be a major obstacle when you want something so badly and have worked all your life to be at that point. The secret is not to focus on the pressure of the situation, but rather on the blessing of being in a position to go for your dream. And often, at the moment when it looks as if that dream has fallen to pieces right in front of your eyes, that's when the phone call comes.

THE STORY OF THE 1965 U.S. OPEN

BY GARY PLAYER

Foreigners just didn't win the US Open in the modern era. Harry Vardon did it in 1900, becoming the first non-American to win. Ted Ray also achieved the feat in 1920. But it eluded South Africa's Bobby Locke, and he told me it was the one thing missing from his amazing career.

Of course, I wasn't immune to the aura of the US Open either. It had long been in my mind to win the US Open. But let's face it, American golfers dominated their national Open.

And of course, there was another not so small matter hanging in the balance here as well. The "Big Three"—the collective term for the dominance of myself, Arnold Palmer, and Jack Nicklaus—was now an established fact in the game. Between us we have won nearly sixty Majors on both the PGA and Senior (now Champions) Tours. This has never happened before by any three players and may never happen again.

By 1965, each of us had won three of the four Majors in the game. For Arnold, the PGA Championship was proving the elusive title. For Jack, it was the British Open. And for me, the US Open. I'd come close in 1958, finishing as runner-up four strokes behind Tommy Bolt.

So it came to pass that on a sweltering week in Missouri, in what is considered one of the most searching and demanding tests of golf established by the United States Golf Association (USGA), the Grand Slam was beckoning. And for a foreigner on top of it.

As always, I did my homework. Ben Hogan was a master of the US Open, and he always arrived well before the tournament to get used to the local conditions. Like Hogan, I made sure I had my daily routine running smoothly, down to the finest detail. I didn't go out for dinner and stayed in my hotel room at night. I'm not a superstitious person, but I washed my same black golf shirt after every round and wore the same outfit every day.

Then I studied the golf course. It was a monster. At 7,190 yards it was the longest of any US Open golf course in history at that time, and was made even longer by the lousy equipment and balls we had. During the practice rounds, I made copious notes and sketches of the course and greens, and would then study them in my hotel room in the evenings.

I started off well by shooting an opening round 70 and was two shots off the lead of Australian Kel Nagle. I added another 70 in the second round, and led Nagle by one stroke. A 71 in the third round kept me in front. It came down to the final nine holes, and what was now just a battle between Nagle and me. I was three strokes ahead of him to start the round.

Kel played superbly over those closing holes, cutting my lead down to only one stroke before I again opened up a three-stroke lead with three holes to play.

I stepped onto the tee at the par-three 16th. It's a long hole, and I had a three wood in my hands. But then the wind died suddenly. I changed to a four wood, but in my mind I had this thought that I need to hit it quickly before the next gust of wind came up again. It was a classic example of how impatience can cost you.

My ball finished in a plugged lie in the greenside bunker, and I made five. Kel had made three, cutting my lead to one again. And when Kel birdied the 17th, it vanished completely. We ended regulation play tied for the lead, setting up an 18-hole playoff on Monday.

I putted superbly in that playoff, and was five up through the first eight holes on my way to winning the tournament with a 71 to Nagle's 74.

I had finally done it. I had won the US Open. I had won my first Major in a playoff. I had won the Grand Slam. I had become only the third person in history to win all four Majors, at the age of 29. I had followed in the footsteps of Gene Sarazen and Ben Hogan. And more significantly, I was the first foreigner to accomplish the feat. Forty-five years later, I remain the only one to do so.

I was also the first of "The Big Three" to reach this milestone. I particularly wanted to beat Jack Nicklaus to winning the Grand Slam. And Jack was a great sport about it. He urged me to practice with him the week before this Major rather than play in another tournament in St Louis. I told him I couldn't because I needed the money from another tournament in Greensboro, North Carolina, but he persisted and played a part in me winning the Grand Slam before him.

From a young age, when I first turned professional, winning the Grand Slam was something I always wanted to achieve. I'd read about Sarazen and Hogan having done it, and Bobby Jones winning his own amateur Grand Slam.

It was a great moment in my life, and I'm honored and grateful to have achieved it. No man does this on his own. It is merely a talent that is loaned to you. We have seen this talent taken away from many golfers whether permanently or for a while; Ian Baker-Finch, Tom Watson, David Duval, to name a few.

PART IV

GOLF IN FICTION

THE STORY OF ARCHIBALD'S BENEFIT

P. G. WODEHOUSE

Archibald Mealing was one of those golfers in whom desire outruns performance. Nobody could have been more willing than Archibald. He tried, and tried hard. Every morning before he took his bath he would stand in front of his mirror and practise swings. Every night before he went to bed he would read the golden words of some master on the subject of putting, driving, or approaching. Yet on the links most of his time was spent in retrieving lost balls or replacing America. Whether it was that Archibald pressed too much or pressed too little, whether it was that his club deviated from the dotted line which joined the two points A and B in the illustrated plate of the man making the brassy shot in the Hints on Golf book, or whether it was that he was pursued by some malignant fate, I do not know. Archibald rather favoured the last theory.

The important point is that, in his thirty-first year, after six seasons of untiring effort, Archibald went in for a championship, and won it.

Archibald, mark you, whose golf was a kind of blend of hockey, Swedish drill, and buck-and-wing dancing.

I know the ordeal I must face when I make such a statement. I see clearly before me the solid phalanx of men from Missouri, some urging me to tell it to the King of Denmark, others insisting that I produce my Eskimos. Nevertheless, I do not shrink. I state once more that in his thirty-first year Archibald Mealing went in for a golf championship, and won it.

* * * * *

Archibald belonged to a select little golf club, the members of which lived and worked in New York, but played in Jersey. Men of substance, financially as well as physically, they had combined their superfluous cash and with it purchased a strip of land close to the sea. This land had been drained—to the huge discomfort of a colony of mosquitoes which had come to look on the place as their private property—and converted into links, which had become a sort of refuge for incompetent golfers. The members of the Cape Pleasant Club were easygoing refugees from other and more exacting clubs, men who pottered rather than raced round the links; men, in short, who had grown tired of having to stop their game and stand aside in order to allow perspiring experts to whiz past them. The Cape Pleasant golfers did not make themselves slaves to the game. Their language, when they foozled, was gently regretful rather than sulphurous. The moment in the day's play which they enjoyed most was when they were saying: "Well, here's luck!" in the club-house.

It will, therefore, be readily understood that Archibald's inability to do a hole in single figures did not handicap him at Cape Pleasant as it might have done at St. Andrews. His kindly club-mates took him to their bosoms to a man, and looked on him as a brother. Archibald's was one of those admirable natures which prompt their possessor frequently to remark: "These are on me!" and his fellow golfers were not slow to appreciate the fact. They all loved Archibald.

Archibald was on the floor of his bedroom one afternoon, picking up the fragments of his mirror—a friend had advised him to practise the Walter J. Travis lofting shot—when the telephone bell rang. He took up the receiver, and was hailed by the comfortable voice of McCay, the club secretary.

"Is that Mealing?" asked McCay. "Say, Archie, I'm putting your name down for our championship competition. That's right, isn't it?"

"Sure," said Archibald. "When does it start?"

"Next Saturday."

"That's me."

"Good for you. Oh, Archie."

"Hello?"

"A man I met today told me you were engaged. Is that a fact?"

"Sure," murmured Archibald, blushfully.

The wire hummed with McCay's congratulations.

"Thanks," said Archibald. "Thanks, old man. What? Oh, yes. Milsom's her name. By the way, her family have taken a cottage at Cape Pleasant for the summer. Some distance from the links. Yes, very convenient, isn't it? Good-bye."

He hung up the receiver and resumed his task of gathering up the fragments. Now McCay happened to be of a romantic and sentimental nature. He was by profession a chartered accountant, and inclined to be stout; and all rather stout chartered accountants are sentimental. McCay was the sort of man who keeps old ball programmes and bundles of letters tied round with lilac ribbon. At country houses, where they lingered in the porch after dinner to watch the moonlight flooding the quiet garden, it was McCay and his colleague who lingered longest. McCay knew Ella Wheeler Wilcox by heart, and could take Browning without anaesthetics. It is not to be wondered at, therefore, that Archibald's remark about his fiancee coming to live at Cape Pleasant should give him food for thought. It appealed to him.

He reflected on it a good deal during the day, and, running across Sigsbee, a fellow Cape Pleasanter, after dinner that night at the Sybarites' Club, he spoke of the matter to him. It so happened that both had dined excellently, and were looking on the world with a sort of cosy benevolence. They were in the mood when men pat small boys on the head and ask them if they mean to be President when they grow up.

"I called up Archie Mealing today," said McCay. "Did you know he was engaged?"

"I did hear something about it. Girl of the name of Wilson, or –

"Milsom. She's going to spend the summer at Cape Pleasant, Archie tells me."

"Then she'll have a chance of seeing him play in the championship competition."

McCay sucked his cigar in silence for a while, watching with dreamy eyes the blue smoke as it curled ceiling-ward. When he spoke his voice was singularly soft.

"Do you know, Sigsbee," he said, sipping his Maraschino with a gentle melancholy—"do you know, there is something wonderfully pathetic to me in this business. I see the whole thing so clearly. There was a kind of quiver in the poor old chap's voice when he said: 'She is coming to Cape Pleasant,' which told me more than any words could have done. It is a tragedy in its way, Sigsbee. We may smile at it, think it trivial; but it is none the less a tragedy. That warm-hearted, enthusiastic girl, all eagerness to see the man she loves do well—Archie, poor old Archie, all on fire to prove to her that her trust in him is not misplaced, and the end—Disillusionment, Disappointment, Unhappiness."

"He ought to keep his eye on the ball," said the more practical Sigsbee.

"Quite possibly," continued McCay, "he has told her that he will win this championship."

"If Archie's mutt enough to have told her that," said Sigsbee decidedly, "he deserves all he gets. Waiter, two Scotch highballs."

McCay was in no mood to subscribe to this stony-hearted view.

"I tell you," he said, "I'm sorry for Archie! I'm sorry for the poor old chap. And I'm more than sorry for the girl."

"Well, I don't see what we can do," said Sigsbee. "We can hardly be expected to foozle on purpose, just to let Archie show off before his girl."

McCay paused in the act of lighting his cigar, as one smitten with a great thought.

"Why not?" he said. "Why not, Sigsbee? Sigsbee, you've hit it."

"Eh?"

"You have! I tell you, Sigsbee, you've solved the whole thing. Archie's such a bully good fellow, why not give him a benefit? Why not let him win this championship? You aren't going to tell me that you care whether you win a tin medal or not?"

Sigsbee's benevolence was expanding under the influence of the Scotch highball and his cigar. Little acts of kindness on Archie's part, here a cigar, there a lunch, at another time seats for the theatre, began to rise to the surface of his memory like rainbow-coloured bubbles. He wavered.

"Yes, but what about the rest of the men?" he said. "There will be a dozen or more in for the medal."

"We can square them," said McCay confidently. "We will broach the matter to them at a series of dinners at which we will be joint hosts. They are white men who will be charmed to do a little thing like that for a sport like Archie."

"How about Gossett?" said Sigsbee.

McCay's face clouded. Gossett was an unpopular subject with members of the Cape Pleasant Golf Club. He was the serpent in their Eden. Nobody seemed quite to know how he had got in, but there, unfortunately, he was. Gossett had introduced into Cape Pleasant golf a cheerless atmosphere of the rigour of the game. It was to enable them to avoid just such golfers as Gossett that the Cape Pleasanters had founded their club. Genial courtesy rather than strict attention to the rules had been the leading charac-teristics of their play till his arrival. Up to that time it had been looked on as rather bad form to exact a penalty. A cheery give-and-take system had prevailed. Then Gossett had come, full of strange rules, and created about the same stir in the community which a hawk would create in a gathering of middle-aged doves.

"You can't square Gossett," said Sigsbee.

McCay looked unhappy.

"I forgot him," he said. "Of course, nothing will stop him try-ing to win. I wish we could think of something. I would almost as soon see him lose as Archie win. But, after all, he does have off days sometimes."

"You need to have a very off day to be as bad as Archie."

They sat and smoked in silence.

"I've got it," said Sigsbee suddenly. "Gossett is a fine golfer, but nervous. If we upset his nerves enough, he will go right off his stroke. Couldn't we think of some way?"

McCay reached out for his glass.

"Yours is a noble nature, Sigsbee," he said.

"Oh, no," said the paragon modestly. "Have another cigar?"

* * * * *

In order that the render may get the mental half-Nelson on the plot of this narrative which is so essential if a short story is to charm, elevate, and instruct, it is necessary now, for the nonce (but only for the nonce), to inspect Archibald's past life.

Archibald, as he had stated to McCay, was engaged to a Miss Milsom—Miss Margaret Milsom. How few men, dear reader, are engaged to girls with svelte figures, brown hair, and large blue eyes, now sparkling and vivacious, now dreamy and soulful, but always large and blue! How few, I say. You are, dear reader, and so am I, but who else? Archibald was one of the few who happened to be.

He was happy. It is true that Margaret's mother was not, as it were, wrapped up in him. She exhibited none of that effervescent joy at his appearance which we like to see in our mothers-in-law elect. On the contrary, she generally cried bitterly whenever she saw him, and at the end of ten minutes was apt to retire sobbing to her room, where she remained in a state of semi-coma till an advanced hour. She was by way of being a confirmed invalid, and something about Archibald seemed to get right in among her nerve centres, reducing them for the time being to a complicated hash. She did not like Archibald. She said she liked big, manly men. Behind his back she not infrequently referred to him as a "gaby"; sometimes even as that "guffin".

She did not do this to Margaret, for Margaret, besides being blue-eyed, was also a shade quick-tempered. Whenever she discussed Archibald, it was with her son Stuyvesant. Stuyvesant Milsom, who thought Archibald a bit of an ass, was always ready to sit and listen to his mother on the subject, it being, however, an understood thing that at the conclusion of the seance she yielded one or two saffron-coloured bills towards his racing debts. For Stuyvesant, having developed a habit of backing horses which either did not start at all or else sat down and thought in the middle of the race, could always do with ten dollars or so. His prices for these interviews worked out, as a rule, at about three cents a word.

In these circumstances it was perhaps natural that Archibald and Margaret should prefer to meet, when they did meet, at some other spot than the Milsom home. It suited them both better that they should arrange a secret tryst on these occasions. Archibald preferred it because being in the same room as Mrs Milsom always made him feel like a murderer with particularly large feet; and Margaret preferred it because, as she told Archibald, these secret meetings lent a touch of poetry to what might otherwise have been a commonplace engagement.

Archibald thought this charming; but at the same time he could not conceal from himself the fact that Margaret's passion for the poetic cut, so to speak, both ways. He admired and loved the loftiness of her soul, but, on the other hand, it was a tough job having to live up to it. For Archibald was a very ordinary young man. They had tried to inoculate him with a love of poetry at school, but it had not taken. Until he was thirty he had been satisfied to class all poetry (except that of Mr George Cohan) under the general heading of punk. Then he met Margaret, and the trouble began. On the day he first met her, at a picnic, she had looked so soulful, so aloof from this world, that he had felt instinctively that here was a girl who expected more from a man than a mere statement that the weather was great. It so chanced that he knew just one quotation from the classics, to wit, Tennyson's critique of the Island-Valley of Avilion. He knew this because he had had the passage to write out one hundred and fifty times at school, on the occasion of his being caught smoking by one of the faculty who happened to be a passionate admirer of the "Idylls of the King".

A remark of Margaret's that it was a splendid day for a picnic and that the country looked nice gave him his opportunity.

"It reminds me," he said, "it reminds me strongly of the Island-Valley of Avilion, where falls not hail, or rain, or any snow, nor ever wind blows loudly; but it lies deep-meadow'd, happy, fair, with orchard lawns...."

He broke off here to squash a hornet; but Margaret had heard enough. "Are you fond of the poets, Mr Mealing?" she said, with a far-off look.

"Me?" said Archibald fervently. "Me? Why, I eat 'em alive!"

* * * * *

And that was how all the trouble had started. It had meant unremitting toil for Archibald. He felt that he had set himself a standard from which he must not fall. He bought every new volume of poetry which was praised in the press, and learned the reviews by heart. Every evening he read painfully a portion of the classics. He plodded through the poetry sections of Bartlett's Familiar Quotations. Margaret's devotion to the various bards was so enthusiastic, and her reading so wide, that there were times when Archibald wondered if he could endure the strain. But he persevered heroically, and so far had not been found wanting. But the strain was fearful.

* * * * *

The early stages of the Cape Pleasant golf tournament need no detailed description. The rules of match play governed the contests, and Archibald disposed of his first three opponents before the twelfth hole. He had been diffident when he teed off with McCay in the first round, but, finding that he defeated the secretary with ease, he met one Butler in the second round with more confidence. Butler, too, he routed; with the result that, by the time he faced Sigsbee in round three, he was practically the conquering hero. Fortune seemed to be beaming upon him with almost insipid sweetness. When he was trapped in the bunker at the seventh hole, Sigsbee became trapped as well. When he sliced at the sixth tee, Sigsbee pulled. And Archibald, striking a brilliant vein, did the next three holes in eleven, nine, and twelve; and, romping home, qualified for the final.

Gossett, that serpent, meanwhile, had beaten each of his three opponents without much difficulty.

The final was fixed for the following Thursday morning. Gossett, who was a broker, had made some frivolous objection about the difficulty of absenting himself from Wall Street, but had been overruled. When Sigsbee pointed out that he could easily defeat Archibald and get to the city by lunch-time if he wished, and that in any case his partner would be looking after things, he allowed himself to be persuaded, though reluctantly. It was a well-known fact that Gossett was in the midst of some rather sizeable deals at that time.

Thursday morning suited Archibald admirably. It had occurred to him that he could bring off a double event. Margaret had arrived at Cape Pleasant on the previous evening, and he had arranged by telephone to meet her at the end of the board-walk, which was about a mile from the links, at one o'clock, supply her with lunch, and spend the afternoon with her on the water. If he started his match with Gossett at eleven-thirty, he would have plenty of time to have his game and be at the end of the board-walk at the appointed hour. He had no delusions about the respective merits of Gossett and himself as golfers. He knew that Gossett would win the necessary ten holes off the reel. It was saddening, but it was a scientific fact. There was no avoiding it. One simply had to face it.

Having laid these plans, he caught the train on the Thursday morning with the consoling feeling that, however sadly the morning might begin, it was bound to end well.

The day was fine, the sun warm, but tempered with a light breeze. One or two of the club had come to watch the match, among them Sigsbee.

Sigsbee drew Gossett aside.

"You must let me caddie for you, old man," he said. "I know your temperament so exactly. I know how little it takes to put you off your stroke. In an ordinary game you might take one of these boys, I know, but on an important occasion like this you must not risk it. A grubby boy, probably with a squint, would almost certainly get on your nerves. He might even make comments on the game, or whistle. But I understand you. You must let me carry your clubs."

"It's very good of you," said Gossett.

"Not at all," said Sigsbee.

* * * * *

Archibald was now preparing to drive off from the first tee. He did this with great care. Everyone who has seen Archibald Mealing play golf knows that his teeing off is one of the most impressive sights ever witnessed on the links. He tilted his cap over his eyes, waggled his club a little, shifted his feet, waggled his club some more, gazed keenly towards the horizon for a moment, waggled his club again, and finally, with the air of a Strong Man lifting a bar of iron, raised it slowly above his head. Then, bringing it down with a sweep, he drove the ball with a lofty slice some fifty yards. It was rarely that he failed either to slice or pull his ball. His progress from hole to hole was generally a majestic zigzag.

Gossett's drive took him well on the way to the green. He holed out in five. Archibald, mournful but not surprised, made his way to the second tee.

The second hole was shorter. Gossett won it in three. The third he took in six, the fourth in four. Archibald began to feel that he might just as well not be there. He was practically a spectator.

At this point he reached in his pocket for his tobacco-pouch, to console himself with smoke. To his dismay he found it was not there. He had had it in the train, but now it had vanished. This added to his gloom, for the pouch had been given to him by Margaret, and he had always thought it one more proof of the way her nature towered over the natures of other girls that she had not woven a monogram on it in forget-me-nots. This record pouch was missing, and Archibald mourned for the loss.

His sorrows were not alleviated by the fact that Gossett won the fifth and sixth holes.

It was now a quarter past twelve, and Archibald reflected with moody satisfaction that the massacre must soon be over, and that he would then be able to forget it in the society of Margaret.

As Gossett was about to drive off from the seventh tee, a telegraph boy approached the little group.

"Mr Gossett," he said.

Gossett lowered his driver, and wheeled round, but Sigsbee had snatched the envelope from the boy's hand.

"It's all right, old man," he said. "Go right ahead. I'll keep it safe for you."

"Give it to me," said Gossett anxiously. "It may be from the office. Something may have happened to the market. I may be needed."

"No, no," said Sigsbee, soothingly. "Don't you worry about it. Better not open it. It might have something in it that would put you off your stroke. Wait till the end of the game."

"Give it to me. I want to see it."

Sigsbee was firm.

"No," he said. "I'm here to see you win this championship and I won't have you taking any risks. Besides, even if it was important, a few minutes won't make any difference."

"Well, at any rate, open it and read it."

"It is probably in cipher," said Sigsbee. "I wouldn't understand it. Play on, old man. You've only a few more holes to win."

Gossett turned and addressed his ball again. Then he swung. The club tipped the ball, and it rolled sluggishly for a couple of feet. Archibald approached the tee. Now there were moments when Archibald could drive quite decently. He always applied a considerable amount of muscular force to his efforts. It was in that direction, as a rule, he erred. On this occasion, whether inspired by his rival's failure or merely favoured by chance, he connected with his ball at precisely the right moment. It flew from the tee, straight, hard, and low, struck the ground near the green, bounded on and finally rocked to within a foot of the hole. No such long ball had been driven on the Cape Pleasant links since their foundation.

That it should have taken him three strokes to hole out from this promising position was unfortunate, but not fatal, for Gossett, who seemed suddenly to have fallen off his game, only reached the green in seven. A moment later a murmur of approval signified the fact that Archibald had won his first hole.

"Mr Gossett," said a voice.

Those murmuring approval observed that the telegraph boy was once more in their midst. This time he bore two missives. Sigsbee dexterously impounded both.

"No," he said with decision. "I absolutely refuse to let you look at them till the game is over. I know your temperament."

Gossett gesticulated.

"But they must be important. They must come from my office. Where else would I get a stream of telegrams? Something has gone wrong. I am urgently needed."

Sigsbee nodded gravely.

"That is what I fear," he said. "That is why I cannot risk having you upset. Time enough, Gossett, for bad news after the game. Play on, man, and dismiss it from your mind. Besides, you couldn't get back to New York just yet, in any case. There are no trains. Dismiss the whole thing from your mind and just play your usual, and you're sure to win."

Archibald had driven off during this conversation, but without his previous success. This time he had pulled his ball into some long grass. Gossett's drive was, however, worse; and the subsequent movement of the pair to the hole resembled more than anything else the manoeuvres of two men rolling peanuts with toothpicks as the result of an election bet. Archibald finally took the hole in twelve after Gossett had played his fourteenth.

When Archibald won the next in eleven and the tenth in nine, hope began to flicker feebly in his bosom. But when he won two more holes, bringing the score to like-as-we-lie, it flamed up within him like a beacon.

The ordinary golfer, whose scores per hole seldom exceed those of Colonel Bogey, does not understand the whirl of mixed sensations which the really incompetent performer experiences on the rare occasions when he does strike a winning vein. As stroke follows stroke, and he continues to hold his opponent, a wild exhilaration surges through him, followed by a sort of awe, as if he were doing something wrong, even irreligious. Then all these yeasty emotions subside and are blended into one glorious sensation of grandeur and majesty, as of a giant among pygmies.

By the time that Archibald, putting with the care of one brushing flies off a sleeping Venus, had holed out and won the thirteenth, he was in the full grip of this feeling. And as he walked to the fifteenth tee, after winning the fourteenth, he felt that this was Life, that till now he had been a mere mollusc.

Just at that moment he happened to look at his watch, and the sight was like a douche of cold water. The hands stood at five minutes to one.

* * * * *

Let us pause and ponder on this point for a while. Let us not dismiss it as if it were some mere trivial, everyday difficulty. You, dear reader, play an accurate, scientific game and beat your opponent with ease every time you go the links, and so do I; but Archibald was not like us. This was the first occasion on which he had ever felt that he was playing well enough to give him a chance of defeating a really good man. True, he had beaten McCay, Sigsbee, and Butler in the earlier rounds; but they were ignoble rivals compared with Gossett. To defeat Gossett, however, meant the championship. On the other hand, he was passionately devoted to Margaret Milsom, whom he was due to meet at the end of the board-walk at one sharp. It was now five minutes to one, and the end of the board-walk still a mile away.

The mental struggle was brief but keen. A sharp pang, and his mind was made up. Cost what it might, he must stay on the links. If Margaret broke off the engagement—well, it might be that Time would heal the wound, and that after many years he would find some other girl for whom he might come to care in a wrecked, broken sort of way. But a chance like this could never come again. What is Love compared with holing out before your opponent?

The excitement now had become so intense that a small boy, following with the crowd, swallowed his chewing-gum; for a slight improvement had become noticeable in Gossett's play, and a slight improvement in the play of almost anyone meant that it became vastly superior to Archibald's. At the next hole the improvement was not marked enough to have its full effect, and Archibald contrived to halve. This made him two up and three to play. What the average golfer would consider a commanding lead. But Archibald was no average golfer. A commanding lead for him would have been two up and one to play.

To give the public of his best, your golfer should have his mind cool and intent upon the game. Inasmuch as Gossett was worrying about the telegrams, while Archibald, strive as he might to dismiss it, was haunted by a vision of Margaret standing alone and deserted on the board-walk, play became, as it were, ragged. Fine putting enabled Gossett to do the sixteenth hole in twelve, and when, winning the seventeenth in nine, he brought his score level with Archibald's the match seemed over. But just then –

"Mr Gossett!" said a familiar voice.

Once more was the much-enduring telegraph boy among those present.

"T'ree dis time!" he observed.

Gossett sprang, but again the watchful Sigsbee was too swift.

"Be brave, Gossett—be brave," he said. "This is a crisis in the game. Keep your nerve. Play just as if nothing existed outside the links. To look at these telegrams now would be fatal."

Eye-witnesses of that great encounter will tell the story of the last hole to their dying day. It was one of those Titanic struggles which Time cannot efface from the memory. Archibald was fortunate in getting a good start. He only missed twice before he struck his ball on the tee. Gossett had four strokes ere he achieved the feat. Nor did Archibald's luck desert him in the journey to the green. He was out of the bunker in eleven.

Gossett emerged only after sixteen. Finally, when Archibald's twenty-first stroke sent the ball trickling into the hole, Gossett had played his thirtieth.

The ball had hardly rested on the bottom of the hole before Gossett had begun to tear the telegrams from their envelopes. As he read, his eyes bulged in their sockets.

"Not bad news, I hope," said a sympathetic bystander.

Sigsbee took the sheaf of telegrams.

The first ran: "Good luck. Hope you win. McCay." The second also ran: "Good luck. Hope you win. McCay." So, singularly enough, did the third, fourth, fifth, sixth, and seventh.

"Great Scott!" said Sigsbee. "He seems to have been pretty anxious not to run any risk of missing you, Gossett."

As he spoke, Archibald, close beside him, was looking at his watch. The hands stood at a quarter to two.

Margaret and her mother were seated in the parlour when Archibald arrived. Mrs Milsom, who had elicited the fact that Archibald had not kept his appointment, had been saying "I told you so" for some time, and this had not improved Margaret's temper. When, therefore, Archibald, damp and dishevelled, was shown in, the chill in the air nearly gave him frost-bite. Mrs Milsom did her celebrated imitation of the Gorgon, while Margaret, lightly humming an air, picked up a weekly paper and became absorbed in it.

"Margaret, let me explain," panted Archibald. Mrs Milsom was understood to remark that she dared say. Margaret's attention was riveted by a fashion plate.

"Driving in a taximeter to the ferry this morning," resumed Archibald, "I had an accident."

This was the result of some rather feverish brainwork on the way from the links to the cottage.

The periodical flopped to the floor.

"Oh, Archie, are you hurt?"

"A few scratches, nothing more; but it made me miss my train."

"What train did you catch?" asked Mrs Milsom sepulchrally.

"The one o'clock. I came straight on here from the station."

"Why," said Margaret, "Stuyvesant was coming home on the one o'clock train. Did you see him?"

Archibald's jaw dropped slightly.

"Er—no," he said.

"How curious," said Margaret.

"Very curious," said Archibald.

"Most curious," said Mrs Milsom.

They were still reflecting on the singularity of this fact when the door opened, and the son of the house entered in person.

"Thought I should find you here, Mealing," he said. "They gave me this at the station to give to you; you dropped it this morning when you got out of the train."

He handed Archibald the missing pouch.

"Thanks," said the latter huskily. "When you say this morning, of course you mean this afternoon, but thanks all the same —thanks—thanks."

"No, Archibald Mealing, he does not mean this afternoon," said Mrs Milsom. "Stuyvesant, speak! From what train did that guf—did Mr Mealing alight when he dropped the tobacco-pouch?"

* * * * *

"The ten o'clock, the fellow told me. Said he would have given it back to him then only he sprinted off in the deuce of a hurry."

Six eyes focused themselves upon Archibald.

"Margaret," he said, "I will not try to deceive you – "

"You may try," observed Mrs Milsom, "but you will not succeed."

"Well, Archibald?"

Archibald fingered his collar.

"There was no taximeter accident."

"Ah!" said Mrs Milsom.

"The fact is, I have been playing in a golf tournament."

Margaret uttered an exclamation of surprise.

"Playing golf!"

Archibald bowed his head with manly resignation.

"Why didn't you tell me? Why didn't you arrange for us to meet on the links? I should have loved it."

Archibald was amazed.

"You take an interest in golf, Margaret? You! I thought you scorned it, considered it an unintellectual game. I thought you considered all games unintellectual."

"Why, I play golf myself. Not very well."

"Margaret! Why didn't you tell me?"

"I thought you might not like it. You were so spiritual, so poetic. I feared you would despise me."

Archibald took a step forward. His voice was tense and trembling.

"Margaret," he said, "this is no time for misunderstandings. We must be open with one another. Our happiness is at stake. Tell me honestly, do you like poetry really?"

Margaret hesitated, then answered bravely:

"No, Archibald," she said, "it is as you suspect. I am not worthy of you. I do not like poetry. Ah, you shudder! You turn away! Your face grows hard and scornful!"

"I don't!" yelled Archibald. "It doesn't! It doesn't do anything of the sort! You've made me another man!"

She stared, wild-eyed, astonished.

"What! Do you mean that you, too—"

"I should just say I do. I tell you I hate the beastly stuff. I only pretended to like it because I thought you did. The hours I've spent learning it up! I wonder I've not got brain fever."

"Archie! Used you to read it up, too? Oh, if I'd only known!"

"And you forgive me—this morning, I mean?"

"Of course. You couldn't leave a golf tournament. By the way, how did you get on?"

Archibald coughed.

"Rather well," he said modestly. "Pretty decently. In fact, not badly. As a matter of fact, I won the championship."

"The championship!" whispered Margaret. "Of America?"

"Well, not absolutely of America," said Archibald. "But all the same, a championship."

"My hero."

"You won't be wanting me for a while, I guess?" said Stuyvesant nonchalantly. "Think I'll smoke a cigarette on the porch."

And sobs from the stairs told that Mrs. Milsom was already on her way to her room.

THE STORY OF STRAIGHT GOLF

ANNA ALICE CHAPIN

"Beastly of you, Pritchard, to keep us in town a day like this!" puffed Darragh, the fattest and fussiest of the directors, as he plumped into a chair near the window, and mopped his face on one of the three clean handkerchiefs with which he provided himself in sultry weather.

"Too bad, Darragh!—How are you, Kent?—I fancy we are all in the same boat, as to not liking the city today."

"I wish I *were* in a boat!" said McGlade, mournfully. He was a brown, quiet man, thin but muscular, with a veiled sparkle in his eye. Kent was obviously in a bad humor, and responded curtly to the greetings of his fellow-directors.

The president's room, at the back of the Cosmopolitan Bank, was cool by comparison with the baking streets outside; but all the men, including Pritchard, the bank president, himself, were chafing to be out of town. It was far from being a full meeting, as most of the bank's officers were off investing great fortunes in summer rest and coolness. But half a dozen were still in town, and Kent had motored down from Ardsley in response to a telephone message from the president. Pritchard had simply explained that he was obliged to call a directors' meeting on short notice, because of an unexpected and, he thought, important situation in the bank.

"Well, what is wrong?" demanded stout Darragh. "Somebody embezzled a million? I don't believe you would have been heathenish enough to call us together for less."

"No," said Pritchard, smiling, but with a certain gravity, "it's quite a small matter so far as money goes. There is only a thousand involved."

"A thousand!" growled Kent. "You did this for the sake of a thousand? Pritchard, you're in your dotage! I'd pay a thousand, gladly to be on my way to St. Andrews this minute."

"I could have done thirty-six holes before dinner," lamented the gloomy McGlade. "Did you have your pocket picked, Pritchard?"

"Why," asked Darragh, bitterly, "didn't you call the cop on the corner?"

"He wants to take up a subscription," suggested Atkinson, who had just come in.

"Well," said Pritchard, quietly, "it doesn't happen to be the quantity of the money that is important; it's one small point about it, which I thought was worth our while taking up. The money has been stolen."

"Stolen!" the men repeated, in varying keys of surprise, incredulity, and increasing seriousness. "Stolen, Pritchard—from *this* bank?"

"Yes, gentlemen." Pritchard had in some subtle way become official as he addressed them. "There is a leakage in our bank. Small or large, it is all the same. A crack big enough to let out a little water will, in time, let out a great deal. And it is a menace. Gentlemen, the Cosmopolitan is so big a bank that it cannot afford to lose a thousand dollars by leakage."

Darragh volunteered rather ineptly that "a chain is no stronger than its weakest link," and the president sighed a shade impatiently. Darragh, fat and platitudinous, tried his patience.

"There's no question about it," said Kent, who was dry and businesslike. "You've done the right thing in bringing us here, Pritchard. If we have a hole being drilled in our vaults, it's time we knew it."

"I wish I had had my game first," murmured McGlade, regretfully, "but"—

"Oh, confound your game, McGlade!" put in Atkinson, crisply. "This is business."

"*But,*" proceeded McGlade, "I can see an excuse,—some very faint, small, trifling excuse,—for poor Pritchard: naturally he couldn't handle this thing alone." He grinned maliciously.

Atkinson went on: "Now, Pritchard, what are the facts?"

"The facts are so simple that, for me at least, they complicate the situation. Our first paying teller is one thousand short on his cash for yesterday."

"First paying teller. Isn't that Teddy Thornton?" said McGlade.

"Yes. A good boy, I've always thought."

"Who O.K.'d his cash for the day?" said Atkinson.

"Green, the cashier. No question about old Green!"

"No shortage *then?*"

"No."

"Did the paying teller put them into the safe himself?" asked Kent.

"Yes. Murdock, the man on the second desk, was with him. The notes were tied up and docketed in the usual way. Thornton closed the safe, set the combination, and said good night to Green. This morning one bundle of notes, just one thousand dollars, was missing."

"It lies then," said Atkinson, "between Thornton and Murdock?"

"Unless some one robbed the safe in the night, in which case they would hardly let it go at a thousand. No, I am not quite fair in that. Strictly speaking, it hardly does lie between them. Thornton is responsible for the money that goes into that safe, and both he and Murdock declare that the latter never touched any of the notes."

"So the proposition," said Kent, "is that Thornton had his notes O.K.'d by Green, and then held out on one package while he deposited the others, trusting to the small sum being overlooked."

The bank president shrugged his shoulders.

"One does not care for the assumption," he said. "Thornton is a simple, pleasant lad enough; it seems too bad. But there it is. Who else could it be? I understand the boy has been hard up lately. And no one else touched the money after it left Green's hands."

"Did Murdock stay after Thornton?"

"No; it is absolutely certain that Murdock left first. Green saw Thornton go, some minutes after Murdock had gotten his hat and said good night."

There was a brief pause.

"Want to question any one?" asked Pritchard.

"Yes," said McGlade, who had made no comment. "I want a look at Murdock."

"Why, certainly," said the president, clearly surprised. He rang a bell, and it was Murdock himself who came to the door,—a slender young man, with a narrow chest, and hollows in his temples. He wore a look of anxiety and concern. So, for that matter, did every one about the branch office that day. "What!" each man seemed secretly and stealthily asking himself, "an untrustworthy among these trusted employees of finance?" Each man looked askance at his fellows.

The impression made by Murdock was wholly creditable. To the few inquiries put to him by the directors he responded frankly and respectfully. There was of course no implied reflection upon Mr. Thornton, the first paying teller, either in questions or in answers, but the result of the interview was merely an accentuation and crystallization of the first general impression: Thornton was the only conceivable suspect.

"Do you know the combination of the safe, Mr. Murdock?" Kent asked in his clipping way.

"No, sir,—not the present one," the young man answered civilly. "Mr. Thornton changes the combination from time to time."

"And was he the only person who knew it?" said Atkinson.

"Why, sir," Murdock returned, "I presume Mr. Green knew it. I suppose Mr. Thornton would hardly have been given so much responsibility as *that.*"

It was said so simply that there was no suggestion of a sneer.

Murdock was just leaving the room when McGlade, who had asked to see him, but who as yet had not addressed him, said kindly, "You look pulled down, Mr. Murdock."

The clerk gave him a puzzled glance. "I imagine it's the heat, sir," he said. "It has been very trying."

"You should get out into the fresh air and play some good healthy game, golf or tennis," pursued McGlade, to the astonishment of his fellow-directors. "Do you ever play golf, Mr. Murdock?"

"Never, sir," returned young Murdock, quietly. "I do not care for sports."

He waited a moment at the door, and then, seeing that they were through with him, bowed just a fraction too humbly, and withdrew.

"Nice, civil young fellow," said Darragh, approvingly. "Pritchard, I wish this highly esthetic private room of yours had a few five-cent palm-leaf fans."

"I'll send out and buy you some in a minute," said Pritchard, disgustedly. "Are you sure you don't want a soda lemonade, too? Well, gentlemen?"

"He's a good man, isn't he?" said Kent, seriously.

"Murdock? Excellent. A deserving case, too. Worked his way up from nothing in particular."

"Wasn't Teddy Thornton promoted in his stead?" said McGlade.

"Yes, over his head, as it were. But they have always seemed friendly, in spite of it, and—well, it's rather a pity now."

"I wonder!" remarked McGlade, and lapsed into silence.

"Just as a matter of form, I think we should speak to Thornton himself," said Atkinson. "Will you have him in, Pritchard?"

The president sighed as he touched the bell a second time. "I hate facing the lad," he said frankly. "I've known him since he was a child."

"So have I," said McGlade.

"His father and I were friends at Harvard," said Pritchard. "And Teddy—oh, ask Mr. Thornton to come here a moment, please. You know, gentlemen, one must not let the past influence one's judgment of the present."

"And I'm not so sure of *that*, either," muttered McGlade, half to himself.

And just then Teddy Thornton came in.

He was, to look at, quite a commonplace type, just the usual clean, well-set-up young American turned out by our big universities in increasing thousands every year. He was sandy-haired and fairskinned, wide of shoulder and narrow of hip and thigh, and he had a pair of clear, green-gray eyes with a twinkle in them. There was nothing else about him that would lend itself to description. Teddy Thornton was a hopelessly every-day sort of person. The older men looked at him with mixed feelings, chiefly those of regret. Most of them had known his father.

"How do you do, Thornton?" said Kent, gruffly.

"Oh, how are you, Mr. Kent?" said the boy, eagerly.

"Hello, Teddy!" remarked McGlade, unofficially.

"How are you, sir?" said the first paying teller, with a faint, boyish grin. Then his face fell once more into the worried mold which was the order of the day. He turned toward the president with a squaring of his shoulders.

"You wanted me, sir?"

"See here, Thornton," said Pritchard, "there's no use beating about the bush. We've always liked you, and we want you to have a decent deal. We—" He paused.

"Yes, sir," said Teddy Thornton. He was a little pale, and the twinkle had gone out of the green-gray eyes, but they looked clearer than ever.

"You know,—well," said the president, desperately, "you know it looks queer about that thousand."

"Yes, sir." The answer came prompt and steady.

"We thought you might care to tell us how it happened."

Teddy shook his head, but he looked straight at the president. "Nothing to tell, sir. I took the money from Mr. Green, and counted it again myself, just for luck, before I put it in the safe. Then I set the combination, and followed Murdock out. I meant to catch up with him, and walk uptown with him, but I think he must have caught the car ahead of me. This morning the money wasn't there. That's all."

"What was your combination?" asked McGlade.

"The same as for the past week, sir." Teddy gave the numbers.

"No one knew it?"

"Just the office, sir."

"We understood from Mr. Murdock that he did not know it."

"That's funny! Probably Murdock thought it had been changed again."

"Mr. Thornton," said Pritchard, "are you prepared to swear that yours were the last hands, to your knowledge, that touched those notes last night?"

"Yes, sir, absolutely."

"And that you yourself put them into the safe, shut and locked it personally, and left the bank after Mr. Murdock?"

"Yes, sir."

"You must realize that this is rather a serious admission, and makes the entire responsibility rest with you?"

"I suppose so, sir."

A pause. "That's all, Mr. Thornton."

"Very well, sir."

"Teddy!" said McGlade.

The boy turned and looked at him. Then a faint smile showed on his white face.

"I didn't take it, Mr. McGlade," he said, and left the room with his head up.

McGlade leaned slowly back in his chair, and breathed a long, inaudible sigh that might have been relief.

"Well—and now?" said the president.

"Well," said Kent, curtly, "it looks as though we had to fix it on some one, and"—

"Maybe," suggested Atkinson, humanely, "we could just let the young man resign, without pressing any charge?"

"It will mean the end of his career anyway," said McGlade.

The president turned upon him. "Hang it, man, I know it will!" he exclaimed testily. "But we can't consider his career. We're here to take care of our bank."

"But suppose he didn't do it, after all?" said Darragh.

"Can't help it; not our concern," said Pritchard. "We can't keep any one we're doubtful about, whether he's guilty or not. This isn't brutality, you know, it's just business."

"Sane and safe, like the New Fourth," murmured McGlade. "You're right, Pritchard, of course. Business is business. Only—sometimes a very unbusinesslike little thing will throw a light on a business proposition. Now, for instance"—he hesitated.

"Go ahead, McGlade," said Pritchard, resignedly. "You've something on your mind; get rid of it!"

"It's just a story," said McGlade, lighting a cigar. "Not much of a story in itself, but it shows,—well, let us say that I think it will serve to illustrate my point, and we'll let it go at that. It's"—he puffed a second to establish his light—"it's a golf-story. We are all golfers here, I know,—except that poor benighted idiot of an Atkinson, who is a lazy brute, and prefers yachting. You others all play golf"—

"When we can," put in Darragh, blinking reproachfully.

"And you'll appreciate my little anecdote. If necessary," added McGlade, "we'll fix up a chart for Atkinson.

"You know the little coast town in New Jersey where I go in the summer? Jolly little place; quiet and informal, but lots of nice people, and a fine feeling of comradeship. And first-class golf. Best little links for its size that I know and a bully crowd in the club, men who are clean-bred sportsmen from their cradles, and that it's a privilege to play with. You know just what all that sort of thing means in a place.

"Well, we've always been keen about the game, and have got up cups and medals out of all proportion to the size and importance of our golf club. We've held some cracking good tournaments, too, and had some of the lowest-handicapped men in our parts down to compete. The time I want to tell you about was a cup day, some few years back, when there were all sorts of entries and all sorts of handicaps. I was one of the greens committee, and there was a lot of interest taken all around.

"The finals came on a fine, open day, and there were a raft of pretty girls at the club-house, and tea, and pleasant fool things of that sort. Green turf, blue sky, motors at the portico within view of the first tee,—you know, the approved setting. There were a lot of young chaps down from college,—it was in June, just after Class Day. A few of them played corking good games,—especially one freckle-faced boy of nineteen, a freshman at Harvard. I knew his people, and he was a thoroughbred little chap, who played all his games very hard.

"He came through his half of the tournament splendidly, and met Crane in the finals for the cup,—Frank Crane of Garden City. You know Crane, a six man in the Metropolitan, and a crackajack good golfer. We were all there to see them play off, and a corking good match it was. Crane was giving him five strokes, and it was nip and tuck between them. The freckle-faced boy played a splendid game, and it was anybody's match right up to the end. At the sixteenth, the lad ran down a long putt, and a half at the seventeenth put him one up, playing the home hole. I want you to fully appreciate this situation, I mean as it affects the boy. It was a great day for him, with his father looking on, and, for all I know, a girl in the background somewhere. It seemed as if he simply *had* to win that cup! And I must say he played like one possessed.

"Now the eighteenth, at Wampsted, is an easy hole. It's a drive and a pitch for anybody,—about two hundred and fifty yards, with a big rolling green and nothing in the way. The lie of the ground is a sort of punch-bowl effect, so that every one around the club-house had a clear view of the putting-green.

"The boy had the honor,—Atkinson, that means that he drove off first. He got a good long ball, with a little slice; it fell into the long grass on the right of the course. Crane drove a beauty straight down the center and a good distance. The boy was away,—that means he was farther from the hole than the other fellow, Atkinson,—so he played first. He made a clean approach, and Crane, too, played on to the green.

"Every one watched the putting breathlessly, for if they took the same number of puts it would mean a victory for the boy, as he was already one ahead. And he was popular with every one,— being the best possible sort, who could 'play the game.' So, when each of them holed out in two more, there was a sort of general deep breath from all the lookers-on; for it looked as if the boy had won.

"Crane stretched out his hand to him across the hole.

"'Congratulations!' he said. 'You played a splendid game!'

"The boy shook hands heartily enough, but he said right away: 'Why, that wasn't a half, Mr. Crane. You won that hole.'

"'How do you make that out?' said Crane.

"'Why,' said the boy, 'while I was addressing my ball down there in the grass, I moved it. That counts one, you know.'

"The man looked at him. 'I didn't see it,' he said a little oddly.

"'I know you didn't,' said the frecklefaced boy, rather impatiently; 'that's why I'm telling you.'

"It happened that Crane won the extra hole when they played it off later. So, you see, because the boy wouldn't keep his mouth shut about something which no one could have seen but himself, and because not even the thought of his people looking on could *make* him keep it shut, he—he didn't win the cup," ended McGlade.

There was a short silence. Then President Pritchard brought his hand down upon the table so that the wood echoed.

"I'd rather have had such a lad for my son," he said, "than the winner of forty cups!"

"That's what I thought," said McGlade, quietly, as he threw away his dead cigar and lighted a fresh one. "He's out there waiting to be fired for dishonesty."

There was a quick ripple of exclamations. "Teddy Thornton?" McGlade nodded.

Then came a sort of explosion. They were all golfers, and they loved a good sportsman.

"By the Lord Harry," cried fat Darragh, who was a golf enthusiast despite his flesh, "a boy that's good enough to do that is good enough for the Cosmopolitan Bank!"

Pritchard, his face working a little, turned to Kent: "You, too?"

"I guess his word will stand," said the business man, shortly. He, too, was a devotee.

"Atkinson, you're not a golfer, but"—

"Sounds all right to me," said the renegade. "It isn't in that chap to lie."

Pritchard rang the bell.

There was complete silence in the room until Teddy Thornton once more stood before them.

The president cleared his throat and became unwontedly formal: "Mr. Thornton, the directors are satisfied that—that no blame attaches to you in the matter of—in the recent matter." He cleared his throat again.

"I—I am very glad, Mr. Pritchard." The fair, slightly freckled face glowed. "Would you tell me—what—"

"We have obtained"—the president coughed—"information —which makes your word entirely satisfactory."

"Thank you!"

Just as he was turning to go, Teddy once more wheeled, frowning a little with a lingering anxiety. "Mr. Green asked me to tell you, sir, that Mur—that Mr. Murdock has gone."

"Gone!"

"Yes, disappeared, just now."

They looked at one another. Teddy proceeded:

"He just cleared out ten minutes ago without a word to any one. Mr. Green thought you ought to know."

After a short pause, the president remarked dryly, "Yes, we ought to know."

"Sure!" said McGlade, smoking with calm joy.

Teddy Thornton departed.

The president regarded his colleagues with a lurking smile. "How about it, gentlemen?" he said.

They chuckled gladly.

"No man can play straight golf and live crooked," declared McGlade, wisely. "Atkinson, you don't play; what do you think of it?"

"I never thought much of the fool game," said Atkinson, solemnly; "but I'm going to a professional next week to learn it."

THE STORY OF THE GREAT CHALLENGE: AN EXCERPT FROM *THE ENCHANTED GOLF CLUBS*

ROBERT MARSHALL

One warm, delicious evening late in July I was dining at Lowchester House. It was almost my last dinner engagement for the season, as all the world and his wife had suddenly got sick of the baking pavements and dusty trees of the great city, and were making in shoals for green fields or briny sea.

The ladies had just left us, and we men were preparing to enjoy the heavenly hour that brings cigarettes, coffee, and liqueurs in its wake. Through the wide-open French windows of the dining-room (which look out over St. James's Park) came softened sounds of busy traffic; a ravishing odour of sweet peas stole in from the garden, and the moon gave to the trees and shrubs without those strange, grave tints that are her wonderful gifts to the night.

As a rule such an environment impresses and invigorates me pleasurably. I enjoy the journeys of the eye as it travels lightly over polished mahogany, glittering silver, and gleaming glass, noting here the deep red of the wine and roses, there the sunset-like effulgence of the hanginglamps, the vague outlines of the pictured oak walls, and the clearer groups of well-groomed men that sit in easy comfort under a blue canopy of lazily curling smoke. Or, as the glance passes to the scented garden without, noting the blue-green and silver wonderlands that the moon creates in the most commonplace and probably grimy of trees, and the quiver that the soft July wind gives to branch, leaf, and flower.

But tonight, somehow, such things had no charm for me.

And yet Lady Lowchester's dinner had been good. The cutlets, perhaps, a trifle uninteresting and the wine somewhat overiced; but, on the whole, distinctly good.

How, then, account for my mood?

Katherine was of the party, but at the other end of the table from mine. A tall, well-built, massive man, good-looking, and possessed of an attractive smile, had taken her in to dinner, and I have rarely seen two people so completely absorbed in each other.

Therein lay the sting of the evening.

I had eaten and drunk mechanically with eyes riveted, as far as good breeding would permit, on Katherine and her neighbour.

Who was he?

I know everybody that one meets in London, either personally or by sight, yet I had never before come across this good-looking Hercules. I must find out.

He was talking to Lowchester as, leaving my chair, I carelessly joined the group at the other end of the table.

"Yes, I first held the Open Championship five years ago," I heard him say.

I pricked my ears. Of what championship was he speaking?

"And again last year, I think?" asked Lowchester.

"Yes," replied Hercules.

I quickly inquired of my neighbour as to what championship was under discussion.

"Why golf, of course," was the response. "That's Jim Lindsay, the finest player living."

So that was it. No wonder Katherine was so deeply absorbed during dinner.

I hated the man at once. I lost not a moment. I darted my eyes across the table, caught his, and stabbed him with one of those withering knife-like glances that only the descendants of the great can inflict.

Then I discovered that he wasn't looking at me at all, but at one of my shirt studs which had escaped from its buttonhole. He drew my attention to it. I grunted out an ungrateful "Thanks!" and hated him the more.

Now, as a rule, after dinner—wherever I may be—I manage to hold the conversation. So much a habit has this become with me, that I can scarcely endure to hear another man similarly exploiting himself. Not, I am bound to say, that Lindsay was belauding his own prowess. But, what was worse, he appeared a centre of enormous interest to the men around him. They drew him out. They hung on his words. They gaped at him with reverential admiration. Truly golf must have made many converts during the last three years I had been in India. Bah! And I knew it to be such a childish game.

"I've taken a house close to the links at St. Magnus for the summer, Lindsay," Lowchester presently observed. "And as you tell me you're going there next month, you must let me put you up. There's lots of room, and Mrs. Gunter will be with us during August and September."

"I shall be delighted; it will suit me exactly," replied Lindsay.

So Lowchester too had become a golfer! Lowchester—who used to live for hunting and cricket! Lowchester—the President of the Board of Education! Good heavens!

Presently we were all in the hideous gilded and damasked drawing-room; for Lowchester House is a sort of museum of the tawdry vulgarities of the early fifties.

The rooms were hot. That no doubt was the reason why presently Mrs. Gunter and the champion were to be seen hanging over the railing of a flower-laden balcony; but the heat could in no way account for their gazing into each other's eyes so frequently, or so raptly.

I seized on a slip of a girl in pink, led her close to the window, and in tones that I knew must be overheard by the occupants of the balcony, began to relate how I won the Lahore Polo Cup for my team in '92.

I was well under way and just reaching a stirring description of the magnificent goal I scored by taking the ball the whole length of the ground, on a pony that had suddenly gone lame, when Katherine and the champion pointedly left the window and proceeded to another and more distant one.

So! My reminiscences bored them! Polo was nothing if golf were in the air!

It was enough. I could stand no more. I peevishly bade my hostess good night, and passed through the rooms.

As I entered the great hall, which was but dimly lit, my eyes encountered a portrait of the famous (or infamous) Cardinal Smeaton, one of Lowchester's proudest pictorial possessions. The great Scotch prelate, I could have sworn, winked at me.

I was moving on, when suddenly, close to my shoulder, I heard the words, "I will meet ye at St. Magnus!"

I started and turned. There was no one near. I gazed fixedly at the portrait, but never was marble more immovable. I was about to investigate a recess and some pillars, near me, when I observed a footman at the hall door eyeing me with mild but interested scrutiny. He came forward with my coat and hat, and putting them on I passed listlessly into the courtyard and thence to St. James's Street, where I mechanically entered the doors of the Racing Club.

I rang the bell and ordered a brandy-and-soda.

* * * * *

The Racing Club, as the reader knows, is the smartest sporting club in London, and the Inner Temple of the popular game of "Bridge." But tonight cards held no temptation for me; and I sat alone in the reading-room, chewing the cud of a humiliation that was quite novel to my experience.

The incident of the Cardinal's wink and the unknown voice had already escaped my memory, and I was rapt in rankling memories of the unsatisfactory evening I had spent.

To me, it was inconceivable that even the finest exponent of a wretched game like golf could oust an all-round sportsman like myself from the circle of interest at a dinner table. It was not so much that I had not been afforded an opportunity to talk, as that when I did I was listened to with a wandering and simulated attention, suggesting that the listeners were only waiting for me to stop. The moment I paused between two anecdotes, someone precipitately led the conversation away to a channel that had no possible interest for me.

Then Katherine had indubitably avoided and ignored me.

It has always been understood between us that if I am in a room with her, mine is the first claim on her attention. Yet, to-night, there was, if not an open rebellion, at least a new departure.

It was extremely galling, and I ordered a second brandy-and-soda.

Must I, then, take to golf in self-defence?

Of course I could pick it up easily. There is no minor game that I have not mastered with ease, after about a week's hard application; and to acquire the art of striking a ball from a certain distance into a hole presents no alarming difficulties to the adroit cricketer and practised polo player. Still, to go over, as it were, to the camp of the enemy, to apply myself to a game that I have openly and avowedly sneered at, was not altogether a pleasing prospect.

How it would tickle my pals at Hurlingham, Ranelagh, the Oval, and Lord's!

I took from the bookshelves the Badminton volume on Golf, and with a third brandy-and-soda applied myself to a rapid study of its contents. I admit that I was somewhat dismayed at the mass of printed matter and numerous diagrams that confronted me, but reflecting that I had often seen voluminous books on such trivial games as croquet or tennis, I concluded that the principle of sporting journalism is to make the maximum of bricks out of the minimum of straw.

I had not read more than three chapters when half a dozen men, including Lowchester and Lindsay, entered the room.

"My dear Jacky," said the former, "you left us very early tonight."

"Yes," I replied. "I found the atmosphere indoors a bit oppressive; and I'm not as yet a convert to golf, your sole topic of discussion during the evening."

"You ought to try the game," said Lindsay. "There's more in it than outsiders imagine."

"'Outsiders' in what sense?" I inquired, with an obvious courtship of a wordy wrangle.

"Oh! only as regards golf, of course. For aught I know you may be a celebrity in many other branches of sport."

"I am" was on the tip of my tongue, but I repressed it.

I felt strangely antagonistic towards this man. A sort of magnetic antipathy (if I may be allowed such a seeming contradiction in terms) warned me that we should influence each other's lives in the future, and that to the detriment of one, if not both of us. In fact, I felt myself being drawn irresistibly towards the vulgar vortex of a "row" with him.

"Golf," I suddenly found myself asserting after one of those deadly pauses that give an altogether exaggerated significance to any casual remark that may break the silence, "Golf is a game for one's dotage."

"A period that sets in quite early in the lives of many of us," retorted Lindsay.

There was another pause. Lowchester was chuckling quietly. A club waiter with thin lips was grinning faintly.

"Which means?" I asked, with an affectation of bored inattention.

"Well, it means," was the reply, "that to stigmatise as only suitable for one's dotage a fine, healthy, outdoor sport, that employs skill and science, and exercises one's patience and temper as few other games do, suggests to my mind incipient dotage in common perception."

I did not understand this at first, so merely remarked, "Really," an ambiguous and useful word, which commits one to nothing.

But as I reflected on Lindsay's words, I perceived a deadly stab at my authority as a judge of sport. My blood tingled. I seized a fourth brandy-and-soda and drank it. It was Lowchester's, but I was only aware of this when the glass was empty. My lips compressed themselves. I recalled Katherine and the champion hanging over the balcony. The thin-lipped club waiter was loitering with an evident desire to overhear what else was to be said. Lowchester looked at me with gently humorous inquiry in his eyes. The others regarded me with the sphinxlike calm that is the ordinary expression of the average Englishman when he is thinking hard but not lucidly. I had, in fact, an audience, always to me an overpowering temptation.

"I'll tell you what I'll do," I said, in the calm, deep tones born of a great determination. "After one week's practice on the St. Magnus links I'll play you a match on even terms, and I dare to hope lick your head off at your own game."

There was a pause of a moment. Then, as if to clear the oppressive air, a chorus of "Bravo, Old Jacky!" broke out from the bystanders.

Only Lindsay was silent, barring, of course, the waiters.

"Well?" I asked.

"I accept, of course," said he; "you leave me no alternative. But the whole scheme is absolutely childish, and, as I fear you will find, quite futile."

"I'll take my chance of that," I replied. "I can reach St. Magnus by August eighth, and on the fifteenth I'll play you."

"It's a match," cried Lowchester, and proceeded to enter it in a notebook. "Any stakes?"

"I will privately suggest to Mr. Lindsay the stakes to be played for," I answered. "May I ask you to come with me for a moment?"

Lindsay assented, and I led him to an adjoining room that was empty.

"The stake I suggest—and it must be known to none but ourselves—is this: The winner of the match shall have the first right to propose matrimony to a certain lady. I mention no names. It is enough if we agree that neither of us shall propose to any lady whatsoever on or before August fifteenth, and that the loser shall further abstain from any such proposal till August twenty-second. This will give the winner a clear week's start, which really constitutes the stake. The subject is a delicate one," I hastily added, as I saw his surprise and evident desire to go further into the matter, "and I shall be obliged if you merely signify your assent or dissent, as the case may be."

With a certain bewildered yet half-amused air he replied, "I assent, of course, but—"

"There is nothing more that need be said," hurriedly interrupted, "except that I shall be glad if you will join me at supper."

For at one of my own clubs, when a stranger is introduced, even by another member, I trust I can ever play the host with tact and grace. I asked Lowchester and Grimsby to join us, and during supper I was able to recount the chief exploits of my life to the attentive audience that a host can always rely on.

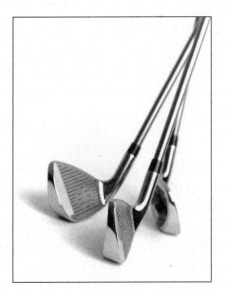

iStockphoto/Thinkstock

THE STORY OF AN EXCITING FINISH: A SECOND EXCERPT FROM *THE ENCHANTED GOLF CLUBS*

ROBERT MARSHALL

Editor's Note: The following chapter appears several chapters after the chapter about the Great Challenge in Marshall's original book. At this point, Marshall has described most of the match, and the opponents are about to finish playing the last hole.

My ball was duly fished out of the burn and dropped behind my shoulder. I returned my own faithless driver to Kirkintulloch, and once again took hold of the Cardinal's. As I did so a telepathic throb of excitement passed through the bystanders.

I played the shot.

It eclipsed all my former efforts. I never have seen, nor shall I ever see again, such a hard-hit ball. With a trajectory scarcely higher than that of a rifle bullet at a medium range, it winged its way straight to the hole, dropping eventually within a yard or so of His Eminence. And then, straining my eyes, I saw a sight that startled me into a sudden realisation of the latter's purpose. He had, so to speak, fielded the ball—that is to say, he had dashed towards it as it fell; and now, by a series of nervous but skilful kicks, he was directing its course straight to the hole! The red skirts were held high in his hands, and the white bony legs flashed to and fro as he sped in the wake of the running globe. I could not, of course, actually see the ball, but, by an intuition that admitted of no doubt whatever, I knew what he was up to. I held my breath in an agony of suspense as nearer and nearer to the red flag flew the gaunt figure of the Cardinal. I swear my heart stopped beating, and the paralysed crowd seemed similarly affected, though the sight that I saw was mercifully denied to its eyes. There was no doubt about it. The Cardinal had so manipulated the ball that I had holed out in three.

But the match was not yet over.

What Lindsay's feelings at the moment were I know not, but he managed to play a clever second stroke that landed him on the green, some seven feet from the hole.

And now came the supreme moment.

If Lindsay holed his put we halved the match, if he failed I won the day.

Such was the pressure of the excited crowd that only the most strenuous efforts enabled the rope holders to maintain a clear circular space round the hole. It measured about fifteen yards in diameter, and within this charmed circle stood Lindsay and his caddie, Wetherby and Kirkintulloch, old Jock Johnson (the keeper of the green), Hanbury-Smith (the captain of the golf club), and myself. All other spectators were without the pale, with the important exception of the Cardinal.

I looked about me. My part in the game was over. I had but to watch and wait. I was thankful the final shot was Lindsay's and not mine.

The faces of my betting friends had changed again in expression, and become drawn and strained. The unfortunate gentlemen no longer chattered and chuckled. The magnet of luck was again slowly but surely attracting golden coins from the depths of their purses, and such pangs could only be borne with dumb fortitude.

The crowd was so terribly congested that two women fainted. I looked anxiously at Mrs. Gunter, but—thank Heaven!—the rich carmine still glowed on her cheeks.

At length, putter in hand, Lindsay approached his ball, and even the breathing of the crowd seemed to be suspended.

I moved to a spot some six feet from the hole, on the opposite side to Lindsay. As I did so my eyes fell on the ground, and I saw a startling and curious sight.

My terrible ally, the Cardinal, had stretched himself at full length, face downward, on the turf, so that his ghastly head was directly over the hole and his shadowy feet close to mine.

A sense of faintness crept over me.

As in a red mist I saw Lindsay strike the ball. I saw it travelling straight and sure to the hole!

And then—heavens above us!—I saw the Cardinal take a quick and gulping breath, and blow with might and main against the skilfully directed ball! It reached the edge of the hole, trembled a moment on the brink, and then ran off at an angle and lay still on the turf a couple of inches from the hole!

I had won the match.

A tumult sounded in my ears, the sky turned a blazing scarlet, the crowd swam before my eyes, and of a sudden I fell prone on the turf with my nose plunged in the fateful hole!

* * * * *

When I came to myself I found kind friends grouped about me, and my head resting luxuriously in Mrs. Gunter's lap. I think I should have been perfectly happy and content with this state of things, had I not unfortunately just at that moment caught a glimpse of the ubiquitous Cardinal standing ridiculously on his head and kicking his heels in mid air in an ecstasy of frenzied glee.

The sight so upset me that I went off a second time into a dead faint.

Dynamic Graphics/Thinkstock

THE STORY OF HOW THE QUAKERS BECAME RECONCILED TO THE GOLFERS

SARAH GUNDERSON

"Rachel, Rachel, my child, why dost thou not come and finish this sewing?"

"In half a second, grandmother; only do come and see all these men in red coats. Wouldn't it be fun if Farmer Jenkins's bull got loose! But I wonder who they are, and what those funny looking sticks are for," and the young girl sighed with curiosity.

"Thy usual curiosity. Probably they are those town people who bought the Peterson farm. They are to use all those good fields for some foolish game—golf, I think they call it. I was reading about it this morning," replied the old Quaker lady, with a sweet smile at her pretty granddaughter.

"Well, I wish I knew about a game that takes up so much land. But now to that hateful sewing;" and then, in an undertone, "I wish it were in the mill pond, and Alfred Bitterson with it."

Alfred Bitterson was a quiet, homely man; a Quaker. He was about 28 or so, but one who frowned on anything frivolus; a man not likely to attract a young girl's fancy. Mrs. Littleby, Rachel's grandmother, had set her heart on having Alfred for a grandson, but Rachel wished otherwise.

Within a month the passing of the golfers was no longer remarked on, only Rachel from her curtained bedroom window watched the busloads of prettily dressed women and red-coated men. By June numerous small cottages had been leased by these people, and gay parties more often passed the little white house. Mrs. Littleby supplied a few of them with fresh butter and eggs. One day Jonathan, the hired man, hurt his foot, and so could not deliver these things. The task fell on Rachel, who was only too glad to get a nearer glimpse of these fascinating people.

Golf must indeed be an attractive game, for they played all day long. Even the most delicate-looking women could be seen on the hottest days with a long stick in their hands, hitting a small ball around the large farm. They wore dark-brown veils and short check skirts, which showed off to a great advantage their pretty ankles.

The horse being hitched, Rachel set out and drove to a small house, where people by the name of Hackett-Jones were living. Mrs. Jones was a tall, attractive-looking blonde, known as one of the best players in S_____. Rachel jumped out with the butter and rang the front doorbell. A neat maid came to the door and she handed her the butter, when a sweet voice from within the house said: What is it Anne?"

"The young lady with the butter, ma'am."

"Ask her to come here."

The maid ushered Rachel into a small sitting-room, where Mrs. Jones was seated at a desk, writing.

"Are you Mrs. Littleby's granddaughter?" she asked.

"Yes, Mrs. Jones—I mean, Mrs. Hackett-Jones," answered the embarrassed Rachel.

The woman laughed and said, "No, only Mrs. Jones; but are you a Quaker, like your grandmother? Yes? I wanted so much to speak to you, as I once knew your mother very well, and often I have thought of you. You are very like her, my dear. But now, I want you to come here a great deal. Will you? I am expecting a niece to visit me, who is about your age—19—and when she comes I want you to know her."

"Oh, I would love to, if grandmother is willing."

"Well, come and lunch with us on Monday, and we will go to the club and try to teach Louise and you a bit of golf. I will come and see your grandmother; but don't mention it to her until I have my little say first. Good-by, dear."

"Goodbye," said happy Rachel, who could think of nothing else but her invitation. "Oh, if grandmother is only willing; and Alfred will be worse than ever," she thought.

The Monday came, as also did numerous other days, when she went to the club and proved herself quite a little sport, in spite of her Quaker ways. Young Jack Carrington found that an especially attractive way of spending his time was in giving Miss Littleby pointers. He is a very nice man, thought Rachel, and so kind to help me improve my game.

All this, you may be sure, was not going on under Mrs. Littleby's eyes, but under those of the gracious Mrs. Jones, who thought that they would make a good match, and did all in her power to throw them together and appreciate one another. What woman is not a matchmaker? One day, while on the links, Carrington gave some pointers to Rachel about the state of his heart, and told her a story that made her very happy; but if a Quaker gentleman that we know could have heard, he would have been angry. Then she thought of her grandmother, and of Alfred, whom she hated, and her heart grew sick.

When she arrived home she told her grandmother, who at once said that Rachel was crazy to even think of marrying one of those wild golf men, when there was honest Alfred that wanted her so much. One of those red-coated fools, as well as wicked! She forbade her granddaughter to go any more to the old ball club. Then she went and gave Mrs. Jones a piece of her mind, indeed, such a piece that Mrs. Jones no longer came to the house.

Days passed and poor Rachel only heard from Jack by mail, as she was forbidden to see him, and was accustomed to obey. Alfred came to the house more often than ever. One night he offered to kiss her as he left, whereupon he received a slap in the face, which made him highly furious; but was also told that the door was open for him to leave, and not come back again. The next day Mrs. Littleby got a letter from him, saying that he did not care to have such a spitfire as her granddaughter for a wife. Mrs. Littleby asked Rachel what she had done, but she would not tell. Later, when Rachel began to grow pale and unhappy, Mrs. Littleby gave her consent to have Jack come and call. Jack made himself especially attractive to the old lady, who thought him a charming young fellow, even if he did play golf.

The following winter there was a marriage between one of the golf coterie and one of the Quakers. Thus the Quakers were reconciled to golf.

Comstock/Thinkstock

THE STORY OF HOW RANKIN PLAYS "GOLF"

MILES BANTOCK, Ed.

Those who knew Mr. Rankin before his marriage would never have deemed it possible that he could so radically change. Those who knew him downtown during business hours felt that they had a pretty good conception of his character, and that they could decide to a nicety what he would be likely to do, but even they had reckoned without taking into consideration the great influence of the future Mrs. Rankin. Lofty superiority had been the keynote of Mr. Rankin's own position as far as regards life away from the city. Brooklyn, if you had been so indiscreet as to mention it to him as a desirable place of residence, Brooklyn would have been met with a sneer. Jersey City, Hoboken—the sneer would have been changed to a snort. The suburbs—withering sarcasm would have been in order. So that, considering this narrow-mindedness of attitude, it is no wonder that a little start of surprise went the rounds when the news of Mr. Rankin's marriage was followed by the intelligence that he had taken the lease of a "little place in Jersey" with the privilege of buying it for himself if he should so wish at the end of a year.

The prophecies varied. Some said two months; others gave him six months in which to pine for town; but all agreed that he'd be tired of country life long before the end of the year, and that that privilege of buying the small estate was a good joke, at which they all smiled widely.

It was early in the fall when the place in Jersey first welcomed the Rankins. Two months passed, and instead of wearing into town the jaded, worried look of a commuter, Mr. Rankin had the audacity to appear perfectly happy, smooth and smiling. The gibes and sneers with which his old associates tried to make his life a dream of bliss fell from him without so much as marring his equanimity, till at last his old associates were obliged to take refuge in the decision that the country isn't so bad after all in the fall, but that winter is the time!

To be sure, it was rather an open winter when it came, and on that account hardly a fair test by which to try his staying qualities, but at any rate the winter passed without forcing so much as a murmur from the newly-fledged commuter.

The snowy days were few and far between and rarely stormy enough to prevent Mrs. Rankin's walk to the station to see Mr. Rankin depart. At times the frivolous would ask him if he had been snowed in over Sunday, and how he had managed to get out. Sometimes, as if in search of information, they would ask how many times during the night he had to go down and stoke the furnace. But to all such queries Mr. Rankin turned a bland and smiling face that showed he really pitied the ignorance behind them.

By spring patience had its own reward. The aggressive attitude of the confirmed New Yorkers began to change slightly. Mr. Rankin still looked happy, and besides every now and then he let out an alluring hint about the fine games he had on his grounds.

"Old Rankin seems to have a pretty good thing of it out there. Plays golf."

That sort of remark going the rounds had much to do with the way his downtown friends viewed his suburban venture. The rumor grew on its way so that, as it happened, without making more than a few modest allusions to the successful games he had played on Saturday afternoon, his reputation as a golf player built itself up.

"Mrs. Rankin plays too, I suppose," some one might ask him.

"Oh, yes, fine player," would be the reply, followed by the generous invitation to come out some Saturday and have a game. Mr. Rankin was hospitable. Mrs. Rankin was also hospitable.

One Friday night when Mr. Rankin went home he carried some news to his wife. Four of his downtown friends were coming out the next day. Mrs. Rankin was pleased.

"We must show them what good times we have out here. I know they've laughed at you for living in the country, poor old boy."

Mr. Rankin admitted that they had tried to be funny about it; but let them laugh, he didn't care, they were only jealous.

And then Mrs. Rankin smoothed Mr. Rankin's hair and Mr. Rankin kissed Mrs. Rankin's hand, and they were both very foolish and very happy.

"Of course they will stay to dinner," said Mrs. Rankin. "You will bring them out when you come and we'll have time for a few good games in the afternoon, and I'll have such a good dinner.

I guess they won't feel so sorry for you after tomorrow." In which sentiment Mr. Rankin evidently agreed with all his heart.

The next day the country was on the best of its usual good behavior. The very youthful tree in front of the Rankin's abode spread itself in an attempt to seem grown up and shady. The little plot of grass that lay between the tree and the neat front steps strove to look velvety and soft in spite of its sparseness. The air was mild and sweet with the scent of magnolias.

When Mrs. Rankin came to greet her guests she found that only two of them had come out with her husband; the other two were coming on the next train.

"You see, they had to go home to get their things," one of those who did come explained.

"We're not much of sportsmen so we just intend to look on."

"Yes," said Mrs. Rankin, and she wondered just what he meant.

A sudden realizing sense of what it all meant came an hour later when the two tardy guests arrived in full golf outfit. Mrs. Rankin felt surprised and Mr. Rankin seemed embarrassed, but only for a moment.

The conversation had drifted along smoothly for a short time when Mr. Rankin broached the subject.

"My dear," he said, "shall we take our guests out and teach them how to play?"

In answer to this mild pleasantry Mrs. Rankin thought it might be a good idea. And Mr. Rankin led the way out of doors.

That evening when the last train drew into the suburban station it found four men waiting to be taken back to town, two of them carried bundles of golf sticks. In silence, they tramped into the almost empty car and settled down for the ride. Finally the smaller of the two who carried golf sticks spoke up.

"Croquet, by Jove," he said.

"Yes, by Jove, croquet," ejaculated another of the party.

"Poor old Rankin!" said a third.

"Poor Rankin!" they all sighed together.

They never laughed at him after that. They pitied him instead.

THE STORY OF THE LONG HOLE

P. G. WODEHOUSE

The young man, as he sat filling his pipe in the clubhouse smoking room, was inclined to be bitter.

"If there's one thing that gives me a pain squarely in the centre of the gizzard," he burst out, breaking a silence that had lasted for some minutes, "it's a golf-lawyer. They oughtn't to be allowed on the links."

The Oldest Member, who had been meditatively putting himself outside a cup of tea and a slice of seed-cake, raised his white eyebrows.

"The Law," he said, "is an honourable profession. Why should its practitioners be restrained from indulgence in the game of games?"

"I don't mean actual lawyers," said the young man, his acerbity mellowing a trifle under the influence of tobacco. "I mean the blighters whose best club is the book of rules. You know the sort of excrescences. Every time you think you've won a hole, they dig out Rule 853, section two, sub-section four, to prove that you've disqualified yourself by having an ingrowing toe nail. Well, take my case." The young man's voice was high and plaintive. "I go out with that man Hemmingway to play an ordinary friendly round—nothing depending on it except a measly ball—and on the seventh he pulls me up and claims the hole simply because I happened to drop my niblick in the bunker. Oh, well, a tick's a tick, and there's nothing more to say, I suppose."

The Sage shook his head.

"Rules are rules, my boy, and must be kept. It is odd that you should have brought up this subject, for only a moment before you came in I was thinking of a somewhat curious match which ultimately turned upon a question of the rule-book. It is true that, as far as the actual prize was concerned, it made little difference. But perhaps I had better tell you the whole story from the beginning."

The young man shifted uneasily in his chair.

"Well, you know, I've had a pretty rotten time this afternoon already—"

"I will call my story," said the Sage, tranquilly, "'The Long Hole', for it involved the playing of what I am inclined to think must be the longest hole in the history of golf. In its beginnings the story may remind you of one I once told you about Peter Willard and James Todd, but you will find that it develops in quite a different manner. Ralph Bingham. . . ."

"I half promised to go and see a man—"

"But I will begin at the beginning," said the Sage. "I see that you are all impatience to hear the full details."

* * * * *

Ralph Bingham and Arthur Jukes (said the Oldest Member) had never been friends—their rivalry was too keen to admit of that—but it was not till Amanda Trivett came to stay here that a smouldering distaste for each other burst out into the flames of actual enmity. It is ever so. One of the poets, whose name I cannot recall, has a passage, which I am unable at the moment to remember, in one of his works, which for the time being has slipped my mind, which hits off admirably this age-old situation. The gist of his remarks is that lovely woman rarely fails to start something. In the weeks that followed her arrival, being in the same room with the two men was like dropping in on a reunion of Capulets and Montagues.

You see, Ralph and Arthur were so exactly equal in their skill on the links that life for them had for sometime past resolved itself into a silent, bitter struggle in which first one, then the other, gained some slight advantage. If Ralph won the May medal by a stroke, Arthur would be one ahead in the June competition, only to be nosed out again in July. It was a state of affairs which, had they been men of a more generous stamp, would have bred a mutual respect, esteem, and even love. But I am sorry to say that, apart from their golf, which was in a class of its own as far as this neighbourhood was concerned, Ralph Bingham and Arthur Jukes were a sorry pair—and yet, mark you, far from lacking in mere superficial good looks. They were handsome fellows, both of them, and well aware of the fact; and when Amanda Trivett came to stay they simply straightened their ties, twirled their moustaches, and expected her to do the rest.

But there they were disappointed. Perfectly friendly though she was to both of them, the lovelight was conspicuously absent from her beautiful eyes. And it was not long before each had come independently to a solution of this mystery. It was plain to them that the whole trouble lay in the fact that each neutralized the other's attractions. Arthur felt that, if he could only have a clear field, all would be over except the sending out of the wedding invitations; and Ralph was of the opinion that, if he could just call on the girl one evening without finding the place all littered up with Arthur, his natural charms would swiftly bring home the bacon. And, indeed, it was true that they had no rivals except themselves. It happened at the moment that Woodhaven was very short of eligible bachelors. We marry young in this delightful spot, and all the likely men were already paired off. It seemed that, if Amanda Trivett intended to get married, she would have to select either Ralph Bingham or Arthur Jukes. A dreadful choice.

* * * * *

It had not occurred to me at the outset that my position in the affair would be anything closer than that of a detached and mildly interested spectator. Yet it was to me that Ralph came in his hour of need. When I returned home one evening, I found that my man had brought him in and laid him on the mat in my sitting-room.

I offered him a chair and a cigar, and he came to the point with commendable rapidity.

"Leigh," he said, directly he had lighted his cigar, "is too small for Arthur Jukes and myself."

"Ah, you have been talking it over and decided to move?" I said, delighted. "I think you are perfectly right. Leigh is over-built. Men like you and Jukes need a lot of space. Where do you think of going?"

"I'm not going."

"But I thought you said—"

"What I meant was that the time has come when one of us must leave."

"Oh, only one of you?" It was something, of course, but I confess I was disappointed, and I think my disappointment must have shown in my voice; for he looked at me, surprised.

"Surely you wouldn't mind Jukes going?" he said.

"Why, certainly not. He really is going, is he?"

A look of saturnine determination came into Ralph's face.

"He is. He thinks he isn't, but he is."

I failed to understand him, and said so. He looked cautiously about the room, as if to reassure himself that he could not be overheard.

"I suppose you've noticed," he said, "the disgusting way that man Jukes has been hanging round Miss Trivett, boring her to death?"

"I have seen them together sometimes."

"I love Amanda Trivett!" said Ralph.

"Poor girl!" I sighed.

"I beg your pardon?"

"Poor girl!" I said. "I mean, to have Arthur Jukes hanging round her."

"That's just what I think," said Ralph Bingham. "And that's why we're going to play this match."

"What match?"

"This match we've decided to play. I want you to act as one of the judges, to go along with Jukes and see that he doesn't play any of his tricks. You know what he is! And in a vital match like this—"

"How much are you playing for?"

"The whole world!"

"I beg your pardon?"

"The whole world. It amounts to that. The loser is to leave Leigh for good, and the winner stays on and marries Amanda

Trivett. We have arranged all the details. Rupert Bailey will accompany me, acting as the other judge."

"And you want me to go round with Jukes?"

"Not round," said Ralph Bingham. "Along."

"What is the distinction?"

"We are not going to play a round. Only one hole."

"Sudden death, eh?"

"Not so very sudden. It's a longish hole. We start on the first tee here and hole out in the town in the doorway of the Majestic Hotel in Royal Square. A distance, I imagine, of about sixteen miles."

I was revolted. About that time a perfect epidemic of freak matches had broken out in the club, and I had strongly opposed them from the start. George Willis had begun it by playing a medal round with the pro, George's first nine against the pro's complete eighteen. After that came the contest between Herbert Widgeon and Montague Brown, the latter, a twenty-four handicap man, being entitled to shout "Boo!" three times during the round at moments selected by himself. There had been many more of these degrading travesties on the sacred game, and I had writhed to see them. Playing freak golf-matches is to my mind like ragging a great classical melody. But of the whole collection this one, considering the sentimental interest and the magnitude of the stakes, seemed to me the most terrible. My face, I imagine, betrayed my disgust, for Bingham attempted extenuation.

"It's the only way," he said. "You know how Jukes and I are on the links. We are as level as two men can be. This, of course is due to his extraordinary luck. Everybody knows that he is the world's champion fluker. I, on the other hand, invariably have the worst luck. The consequence is that in an ordinary round it is always a toss-up which of us wins. The test we propose will eliminate luck. After sixteen miles of give-and-take play, I am certain—that is to say, the better man is certain to be ahead. That is what I meant when I said that Arthur Jukes would shortly be leaving Leigh. Well, may I take it that you will consent to act as one of the judges?"

I considered. After all, the match was likely to be historic, and one always feels tempted to hand one's name down to posterity.

"Very well," I said.

"Excellent. You will have to keep a sharp eye on Jukes, I need scarcely remind you. You will, of course, carry a book of the rules in your pocket and refer to them when you wish to refresh your memory. We start at daybreak, for, if we put it off till later, the course at the other end might be somewhat congested when we reached it. We want to avoid publicity as far as possible. If I took a full iron and hit a policeman, it would excite a remark."

"It would. I can tell you the exact remark which it would excite."

"We will take bicycles with us, to minimize the fatigue of covering the distance. Well, I am glad that we have your co-operation. At daybreak tomorrow on the first tee, and don't forget to bring your rule-book."

* * * * *

The atmosphere brooding over the first tee when I reached it on the following morning, somewhat resembled that of a duelling-ground in the days when these affairs were sealed with rapiers or pistols. Rupert Bailey, an old friend of mine, was the only cheerful member of the party. I am never at my best in the early morning, and the two rivals glared at each other with silent sneers. I had never supposed till that moment that men ever really sneered at one another outside the movies, but these two were indisputably doing so. They were in the mood when men say "Pshaw!"

They tossed for the honour, and Arthur Jukes, having won, drove off with a fine ball that landed well down the course. Ralph Bingham, having teed up, turned to Rupert Bailey.

"Go down on to the fairway of the seventeenth," he said. "I want you to mark my ball."

Rupert stared.

"The seventeenth!"

"I am going to take that direction," said Ralph, pointing over the trees.

"But that will land your second or third shot in the lake."

"I have provided for that. I have a fiat-bottomed boat moored close by the sixteenth green. I shall use a mashie-niblick and chip my ball aboard, row across to the other side, chip it ashore, and carry on. I propose to go across country as far as Woodfield. I think it will save me a stroke or two."

I gasped. I had never before realized the man's devilish cunning. His tactics gave him a flying start. Arthur, who had driven straight down the course, had as his objective the high road, which adjoins the waste ground beyond the first green. Once there, he would play the orthodox game by driving his ball along till he reached the bridge. While Arthur was winding along the high road, Ralph would have cut off practically two sides of a triangle. And it was hopeless for Arthur to imitate his enemy's tactics now. From where his ball lay he would have to cross a wide tract of marsh in order to reach the seventeenth fairway—an impossible feat. And, even if it had been feasible, he had no boat to take him across the water.

He uttered a violent protest. He was an unpleasant young man, almost—it seems absurd to say so, but almost as unpleasant as Ralph Bingham; yet at the moment I am bound to say I sympathized with him.

"What are you doing?" he demanded. "You can't play fast and loose with the rules like that."

"To what rule do you refer?" said Ralph, coldly.

"Well, that bally boat of yours is a hazard, isn't it? And you can't row a hazard about all over the place."

"Why not?"

The simple question seemed to take Arthur Jukes aback.

"Why not?" he repeated. "Why not? Well, you can't. That's why."

"There is nothing in the rules," said Ralph Bingham, "against moving a hazard. If a hazard can be moved without disturbing the ball, you are at liberty, I gather, to move it wherever you please. Besides, what is all this about moving hazards? I have a perfect right to go for a morning row, haven't I? If I were to ask my doctor, he would probably actually recommend it. I am going to row my boat across the sound. If it happens to have my ball on board, that is not my affair. I shall not disturb my ball, and I shall play it from where it lies. Am I right in saying that the rules enact that the ball shall be played from where it lies?"

We admitted that it was.

"Very well, then," said Ralph Bingham. "Don't let us waste any more time. We will wait for you at Woodfield."

He addressed his ball, and drove a beauty over the trees. It flashed out of sight in the direction of the seventeenth tee. Arthur and I made our way down the hill to play our second.

* * * * *

It is a curious trait of the human mind that, however little personal interest one may have in the result, it is impossible to prevent oneself taking sides in any event of a competitive nature. I had embarked on this affair in a purely neutral spirit, not caring which of the two won and only sorry that both could not lose. Yet, as the morning wore on, I found myself almost unconsciously becoming distinctly pro-Jukes. I did not like the man. I objected to his face, his manners, and the colour of his tie. Yet there was something in the dogged way in which he struggled against adversity which touched me and won my grudging support. Many men, I felt, having been so outmanoeuvred at the start, would have given up the contest in despair; but Arthur Jukes, for all his defects, had the soul of a true golfer. He declined to give up. In grim silence he hacked his ball through the rough till he reached the high road; and then, having played twenty-seven, set himself resolutely to propel it on its long journey.

It was a lovely morning, and, as I bicycled along, keeping a fatherly eye on Arthur's activities, I realized for the first time in my life the full meaning of that exquisite phrase of Coleridge: "Clothing the palpable and familiar/With golden exhalations of the dawn." For in the pellucid air everything seemed weirdly beautiful, even Arthur Juke's heather-mixture knickerbockers, of which hitherto I had never approved. The sun gleamed on their seat, as he bent to make his shots, in a cheerful and almost a poetic way. The birds were singing gaily in the hedgerows, and such was my uplifted state that I, too, burst into song, until Arthur petulantly desired me to refrain, on the plea that, though he yielded to no man in his enjoyment of farmyard imitations in their proper place, I put him off his stroke. And so we passed through Bayside in silence and started to cover that long stretch of road which ends in the railway bridge and the gentle descent into Woodfield.

Arthur was not doing badly. He was at least keeping them straight. And in the circumstances straightness was to be preferred to distance. Soon after leaving Little Hadley he had become ambitious and had used his brassey with disastrous results, slicing his fifty-third into the rough on the right of the road. It had taken him ten with the niblick to get back on to the car tracks, and this had taught him prudence.

He was now using his putter for every shot, and, except when he got trapped in the cross-lines at the top of the hill just before reaching Bayside, he had been in no serious difficulties. He was playing a nice easy game, getting the full face of the putter on to each shot.

At the top of the slope that drops down into Woodfield High Street he paused.

"I think I might try my brassey again here," he said. "I have a nice lie."

"Is it wise?" I said.

He looked down the hill.

"What I was thinking," he said, "was that with it I might wing that man Bingham. I see he is standing right out in the middle of the fairway."

I followed his gaze. It was perfectly true. Ralph Bingham was leaning on his bicycle in the roadway, smoking a cigarette. Even at this distance one could detect the man's disgustingly complacent expression. Rupert Bailey was sitting with his back against the door of the Woodfield Garage, looking rather used up. He was a man who liked to keep himself clean and tidy, and it was plain that the cross-country trip had done him no good. He seemed to be scraping mud off his face. I learned later that he had had the misfortune to fall into a ditch just beyond Bayside.

"No," said Arthur. "On second thoughts, the safe game is the one to play. I'll stick to the putter."

We dropped down the hill, and presently came up with the opposition. I had not been mistaken in thinking that Ralph Bingham looked complacent. The man was smirking.

"Playing three hundred and ninety-six," he said, as we drew near. "How are you?"

I consulted my score-card.

"We have played a snappy seven hundred and eleven." I said.

Ralph exulted openly. Rupert Bailey made no comment. He was too busy with the alluvial deposits on his person.

"Perhaps you would like to give up the match?" said Ralph to Arthur.

"Tchah!" said Arthur.

"Might just as well."

"Pah!" said Arthur.

"You can't win now."

"Pshaw!" said Arthur.

I am aware that Arthur's dialogue might have been brighter, but he had been through a trying time.

Rupert Bailey sidled up to me.

"I'm going home," he said.

"Nonsense!" I replied. "You are in an official capacity. You must stick to your post. Besides, what could be nicer than a pleasant morning ramble?"

"Pleasant morning ramble my number nine foot!" he replied, peevishly. "I want to get back to civilization and set an excavating party with pickaxes to work on me."

"You take too gloomy a view of the matter. You are a little dusty. Nothing more."

"And it's not only the being buried alive that I mind. I cannot stick Ralph Bingham much longer."

"You have found him trying?"

"Trying! Why, after I had fallen into that ditch and was coming up for the third time, all the man did was simply to call to me to admire an infernal iron shot he had just made. No sympathy, mind you! Wrapped up in himself. Why don't you make your man give up the match? He can't win."

"I refuse to admit it. Much may happen between here and Royal Square."

I have seldom known a prophecy more swiftly fulfilled. At this moment the doors of the Woodfield Garage opened and a small car rolled out with a grimy young man in a sweater at the wheel. He brought the machine out into the road, and alighted and went back into the garage, where we heard him shouting unintelligibly to someone in the rear premises. The car remained puffing and panting against the kerb.

Engaged in conversation with Rupert Bailey, I was paying little attention to this evidence of an awakening world, when suddenly I heard a hoarse, triumphant cry from Arthur Jukes, and, turned, I perceived his ball dropping neatly into the car's interior. Arthur himself, brandishing a niblick, was dancing about in the fairway.

"Now what about your moving hazards?" he cried.

At this moment the man in the sweater returned, carrying a spanner. Arthur Jukes sprang towards him.

"I'll give you five pounds to drive me to Royal Square," he said.

I do not know what the sweater-clad young man's engagements for the morning had been originally, but nothing could have been more obliging than the ready way in which he consented to revise them at a moment's notice. I dare say you have noticed that the sturdy peasantry of our beloved land respond to an offer of five pounds as to a bugle-call.

"You're on," said the youth.

"Good!" said Arthur Jukes.

"You think you're darned clever," said Ralph Bingham.

"I know it," said Arthur.

"Well, then," said Ralph, "perhaps you will tell us how you propose to get the ball out of the car when you reach Royal Square?"

"Certainly," replied Arthur. "You will observe on the side of the vehicle a convenient handle which, when turned, opens the door. The door thus opened, I shall chip my ball out!"

"I see," said Ralph. "Yes, I never thought of that."

There was something in the way the man spoke that I did not like. His mildness seemed to me suspicious. He had the air of a man who has something up his sleeve. I was still musing on this when Arthur called to me impatiently to get in. I did so, and we drove off. Arthur was in great spirits. He had ascertained from the young man at the wheel that there was no chance of the opposition being able to hire another car at the garage. This machine was his own property, and the only other one at present in the shop was suffering from complicated trouble of the oiling-system and would not be able to be moved for at least another day.

I, however, shook my head when he pointed out the advantages of his position. I was still wondering about Ralph.

"I don't like it," I said.

"Don't like what?"

"Ralph Bingham's manner."

"Of course not," said Arthur. "Nobody does. There have been complaints on all sides."

"I mean, when you told him how you intended to get the ball out of the car."

"What was the matter with him?"

"He was too—ha!"

"How do you mean he was too—ha?"

"I have it!"

"What?"

"I see the trap he was laying for you. It has just dawned on me. No wonder he didn't object to your opening the door and chipping the ball out. By doing so you would forfeit the match."

"Nonsense! Why?"

"Because," I said, "it is against the rules to tamper with a hazard. If you had got into a sand-bunker, would you smooth away the sand? If you had put your shot under a tree, could your caddie hold up the branches to give you a clear shot? Obviously you would disqualify yourself if you touched that door."

Arthur's jaw dropped.

"What! Then how the deuce am I to get it out?"

"That," I said, gravely, "is a question between you and your Maker."

It was here that Arthur Jukes forfeited the sympathy which I had begun to feel for him. A crafty, sinister look came into his eyes.

"Listen!" he said. "It'll take them an hour to catch up with us. Suppose, during that time, that door happened to open accidentally, as it were, and close again? You wouldn't think it necessary to mention the fact, eh? You would be a good fellow and keep your mouth shut, yes? You might even see your way to go so far as to back me up in a statement to the effect that I hooked it out with my—?"

I was revolted.

"I am a golfer," I said, coldly, "and I obey the rules."

"Yes, but—"

"Those rules were drawn up by—"I bared my head reverently. "By the Committee of the Royal and Ancient at St. Andrews. I have always respected them, and I shall not deviate on this occasion from the policy of a lifetime."

Arthur Jukes relapsed into a moody silence. He broke it once, crossing the West Street Bridge, to observe that he would like to know if I called myself a friend of his—a question which I was able to answer with a whole-hearted negative. After that he did not speak till the car drew up in front of the Majestic Hotel in Royal Square.

Early as the hour was, a certain bustle and animation already prevailed in that centre of the city, and the spectacle of a man in a golf-coat and plus-four knickerbockers hacking with a niblick at the floor of a car was not long in collecting a crowd of some dimensions. Three messenger-boys, four typists, and a gentleman in full evening-dress, who obviously possessed or was friendly with someone who possessed a large cellar, formed the nucleus of it; and they were joined about the time when Arthur addressed the ball in order to play his nine hundred and fifteenth by six news-boys, eleven charladies, and perhaps a dozen assorted loafers, all speculating with the liveliest interest as to which particular asylum had had the honour of sheltering Arthur before he had contrived to elude the vigilance of his custodians.

Arthur had prepared for some such contingency. He suspended his activities with the niblick, and drew from his pocket a large poster, which he proceeded to hang over the side of the car. It read:

COME
TO
McCLURG AND MACDONALD,
18, WEST STREET,
FOR
ALL GOLFING SUPPLIES.

His knowledge of psychology had not misled him. Directly they gathered that he was advertising something, the crowd declined to look at it; they melted away, and Arthur returned to his work in solitude.

He was taking a well-earned rest after playing his eleven hundred and fifth, a nice niblick shot with lots of wrist behind it, when out of Bridle Street there trickled a weary-looking golf-ball, followed in the order named by Ralph Bingham, resolute but going a trifle at the knees, and Rupert Bailey on a bicycle. The latter, on whose face and limbs the mud had dried, made an arresting spectacle.

"What are you playing?" I inquired.

"Eleven hundred," said Rupert. "We got into a casual dog."

"A casual dog?"

"Yes, just before the bridge. We were coming along nicely, when a stray dog grabbed our nine hundred and ninety-eighth and took it nearly back to Woodfield, and we had to start all over again. How are you getting on?"

"We have just played our eleven hundred and fifth. A nice even game." I looked at Ralph's ball, which was lying close to the kerb. "You are farther from the hole, I think. Your shot, Bingham."

Rupert Bailey suggested breakfast. He was a man who was altogether too fond of creature comforts. He had not the true golfing spirit.

"Breakfast!" I exclaimed.

"Breakfast," said Rupert, firmly. "If you don't know what it is, I can teach you in half a minute. You play it with a pot of coffee, a knife and fork, and about a hundred-weight of scrambled eggs. Try it. It's a pastime that grows on you."

I was surprised when Ralph Bingham supported the suggestion. He was so near holing out that I should have supposed that nothing would have kept him from finishing the match. But he agreed heartily.

"Breakfast," he said, "is an excellent idea. You go along in. I'll follow in a moment. I want to buy a paper."

We went into the hotel, and a few minutes later he joined us. Now that we were actually at the table, I confess that the idea of breakfast was by no means repugnant to me. The keen air and the exercise had given me an appetite, and it was some little time before I was able to assure the waiter definitely that he could cease bringing orders of scrambled eggs. The others having finished also, I suggested a move. I was anxious to get the match over and be free to go home.

We filed out of the hotel, Arthur Jukes leading. When I had passed through the swing-doors, I found him gazing perplexedly up and down the street.

"What is the matter?" I asked.

"It's gone!"

"What has gone?"

"The car!"

"Oh, the car?" said Ralph Bingham. "That's all right. Didn't I tell you about that? I bought it just now and engaged the driver as my chauffeur, I've been meaning to buy a car for a long time. A man ought to have a car."

"Where is it?" said Arthur, blankly. The man seemed dazed.

"I couldn't tell you to a mile or two," replied Ralph. "I told the man to drive to Glasgow. Why? Had you any message for him?"

"But my ball was inside it!"

"Now that," said Ralph, "is really unfortunate! Do you mean to tell me you hadn't managed to get it out yet? Yes, that is a little awkward for you. I'm afraid it means that you lose the match."

"Lose the match?"

"Certainly. The rules are perfectly definite on that point. A period of five minutes is allowed for each stroke. The player who fails to make his stroke within that time loses the hole. Unfortunate, but there it is!"

Arthur Jukes sank down on the path and buried his face in his hands. He had the appearance of a broken man. Once more, I am bound to say, I felt a certain pity for him. He had certainly struggled gamely, and it was hard to be beaten like this on the post.

"Playing eleven hundred and one," said Ralph Bingham, in his odiously self-satisfied voice, as he addressed his ball. He laughed jovially. A messenger-boy had paused close by and was watching the proceedings gravely. Ralph Bingham patted him on the head.

"Well, sonny," he said, "what club would *you* use here?"

"I claim the match!" cried Arthur Jukes, springing up. Ralph Bingham regarded him coldly.

"I beg your pardon?"

"I claim the match!" repeated Arthur Jukes. "The rules say that a player who asks advice from any person other than his caddie shall lose the hole."

"This is absurd!" said Ralph, but I noticed that he had turned pale.

"I appeal to the judges."

"We sustain the appeal," I said, after a brief consultation with Rupert Bailey. "The rule is perfectly clear."

"But you had lost the match already by not playing within five minutes," said Ralph, vehemently.

"It was not my turn to play. You were farther from the pin."

"Well, play now. Go on! Let's see you make your shot."

"There is no necessity," said Arthur, frigidly. "Why should I play when you have already disqualified yourself?"

"I claim a draw!"

"I deny the claim."

"I appeal to the judges."

"Very well. We will leave it to the judges."

I consulted with Rupert Bailey. It seemed to me that Arthur Jukes was entitled to the verdict. Rupert, who, though an amiable and delightful companion, had always been one of Nature's fat-heads, could not see it. We had to go back to our principals and announce that we had been unable to agree.

"This is ridiculous," said Ralph Bingham. "We ought to have had a third judge."

At this moment, who should come out of the hotel but Amanda Trivett! A veritable goddess from the machine.

"It seems to me," I said, "that you would both be well advised to leave the decision to Miss Trivett. You could have no better referee."

"I'm game," said Arthur Jukes.

"Suits me," said Ralph Bingham.

"Why, whatever are you all doing here with your golf clubs?" asked the girl, wonderingly.

"These two gentlemen," I explained, "have been playing a match, and a point has arisen on which the judges do not find themselves in agreement. We need an unbiased outside opinion, and we should like to put it up to you. The facts are as follows: . . ."

Amanda Trivett listened attentively, but, when I had finished, she shook her head.

"I'm afraid I don't know enough about the game to be able to decide a question like that," she said.

"Then we must consult St. Andrews," said Rupert Bailey.

"I'll tell you who might know," said Amanda Trivett, after a moment's thought.

"Who is that?" I asked.

"My fiancé. He has just come back from a golfing holiday. That's why I'm in town this morning. I've been to meet him. He is very good at golf. He won a medal at Little-Mudbury-in-the-Wold the day before he left."

There was a tense silence. I had the delicacy not to look at Ralph or Arthur. Then the silence was broken by a sharp crack. Ralph Bingham had broken his mashie-niblick across his knee. From the direction where Arthur Jukes was standing there came a muffled gulp.

"Shall I ask him?" said Amanda Trivett.

"Don't bother," said Ralph Bingham.

"It doesn't matter," said Arthur Jukes.

THE STORY OF THE GOLF VS. FOOTBALL DEBATE: AN EXCERPT FROM *THE HALFBACK*

RALPH HENRY BARBOUR

"How's craps, Country?"

"Shut up, Bart! he may hear you."

"What if he does, ninny? I want him to. Say, Spinach!"

"Do you suppose he's going to try and play football, Bart?"

"Not he. He's looking for a rake. Thinks this is a hayfield, Wall."

The speakers were lying on the turf back of the north goal on the campus at Hillton Academy. The elder and larger of the two was a rather coarse-looking youth of seventeen. His name was Bartlett Cloud, shortened by his acquaintances to "Bart" for the sake of that brevity beloved of the schoolboy. His companion, Wallace Clausen, was a handsome though rather frail-looking boy, a year his junior. The two were roommates and friends.

"He'd better rake his hair," responded the latter youth jeeringly. "I'll bet there's lots of hayseed in it!"

The subject of their derisive remarks, although standing but a scant distance away, apparently heard none of them.

"Hi, West!" shouted Bartlett Cloud as a youth, attired in a finely fitting golf costume, and swinging a brassie, approached. The newcomer hesitated, then joined the two friends.

"Hello! you fellows. What's up? Thought it was golf, from the crowd over here." He stretched himself beside them on the grass.

"Golf!" answered Bartlett Cloud contemptuously. "I don't believe you ever think of anything except golf, Out! Do you ever wake up in the middle of the night trying to drive the pillow out of the window with a bed-slat?"

"Oh, sometimes," answered Outfield West smilingly. "There's a heap more sense in being daft over a decent game like golf than in going crazy about football. It's just a kid's game."

"Oh, is it?" growled Bartlett Cloud. "I'd just like to have you opposite me in a good stiff game for about five minutes. I'd show you something about the kid's game!"

"Well, I don't say you couldn't knock me down a few times and walk over me, but who wants to play such games—except a lot of bullies like yourself?"

"Plenty of fellows, apparently," answered the third member of the group, Wallace Clausen, hastening to avert the threatening quarrel. "Just look around you. I've never seen more fellows turn out at the beginning of the season than are here today. There must be sixty here."

"More like a hundred," grunted "Bart" Cloud, not yet won over to good temper. "Every little freshman thinks he can buy a pair of moleskins and be a football man. Look at that fellow over yonder, the one with the baggy trousers and straw hat. The idea of that fellow coming down here just out of the hayfield and having the cheek to report for football practice! What do you suppose he would do if some one threw a ball at him?"

"Catch it in his hat," suggested Wallace Clausen.

"He does look a bit—er—rural," said Outfield West, eying the youth in question. "I fear he doesn't know a bulger from a baffy," he added sorrowfully.

"What's more to the subject," said Wallace Clausen, "is that he probably doesn't know a touch-down from a referee. There's where the fun will come in."

"Well, I'm no judge of football, thank goodness!" answered West, "but from the length of that chap I'll bet he's a bully kicker."

"Nonsense. That's what a fellow always thinks who doesn't know anything about the game. It takes something more than long legs to make a good punter."

"Perhaps; but there's one thing sure, Bart: that hayseed will be a better player than you at the end of two months—that is, if he gets taken on."

"I'll bet you he won't be able to catch a punt," growled Cloud. "A fool like him can no more learn football than—than——"

"Than you could learn golf," continued West sweetly.

"Oh, shut up! I know a mule that plays golf better than you do."

"Well, I sha'n't attempt to compete with your friends, Bart."

"There you both go, quarreling again," cried Clausen. "If you don't shut up, I'll have to whip the pair of you."

Wallace Clausen was about two thirds the size of Cloud, and lacked both the height and breadth of shoulder that made West's popular nickname of "Out" West seem so appropriate. Clausen's threat was so absurd that Cloud came back to good humor with a laugh, and even West grinned.

"Come on, Wall—there's Blair," said Cloud. "You'd better come too, Out, and learn something about a decent game." West shook his head, and the other two arose and hurried away to where the captain of the school eleven was standing beneath the west goal, surrounded by a crowd of variously attired football aspirants. West, left to himself, sighed lazily and fell to digging holes in the turf with his brassie. Tiring of this amusement in a trice, he arose and sauntered over to the side-line and watched the operations. Some sixty boys, varying in age from fifteen to nineteen, some clothed in full football rig, some wearing the ordinary dress in which they had stepped from the school rooms an hour before, all laughing or talking with the high spirits produced upon healthy youth by the tonic breezes of late September, were standing about the gridiron. I have said that all were laughing or talking. This is not true; one among them was silent.

For standing near by was the youth who had aroused the merriment of Cloud and Clausen, and who West had shortly before dubbed "rural." And rural he looked. His gray and rather wrinkled trousers and his black coat and vest of cheap goods were in the cut of two seasons gone, and his discolored straw hat looked sadly out of place among so many warm caps. But as he watched the scene with intent and earnest face there was that about him that held West's attention. He looked to be about seventeen. His height was above the ordinary, and in the broad shoulders and hips lay promise of great strength and vigor.

But it was the face that attracted West most. So earnest, honest, and fearless was it that West unconsciously wished to know it better, and found himself drawing nearer to the straw hat and baggy gray trousers. But their owner appeared to be unconscious of his presence and West paused.

"I don't believe that chap knows golf from Puss-in-the-Comer," mused West, "but I'll bet a dozen Silvertowns that he could learn; and that's more than most chaps here can. I almost believe that I'd loan him my new dogwood driver!"

Wesley Blair, captain of the eleven, was bringing order out of chaos. Blair was one of the leaders in school life at Hillton, a strongly built, manly fellow, beloved of the higher class boys, adored from a distance by the youngsters. Blair was serving his second term as football captain, having been elected to succeed himself the previous fall. At this moment, attired in the crimson sweater, moleskin trousers, and black and crimson stockings that made up the school uniform, he looked every inch the commander of the motley array that surrounded him.

"Warren, you take a dozen or so of these fellows over there out of the way and pass the ball awhile. Get their names first—Christie, you take another dozen farther down the field."

The crowd began to melt away, squad after squad moving off down the field to take position and learn the rudiments of the game. Blair assembled the experienced players about him and, dividing them into two groups, put them to work at passing and falling. The youth with the straw hat still stood unnoticed on the side-line. When the last of the squads had moved away he stepped forward and addressed the captain:

"Where do you want me?"

Blair, suppressing a smile of amusement as he looked the applicant over, asked:

"Ever played any?"

"Some; I was right end on the Felton Grammar School team last year."

"Where's Felton Grammar School, please?"

"Maine, near Auburn."

"Oh! What's your name?"

"Joel March."

"Can you kick?"

"Pretty fair."

"Well, show me what you consider pretty fair." He turned to the nearest squad. "Toss me the ball a minute, Ned. Here's a chap who wants to try a kick."

Ned Post threw the ball, and his squad of veterans turned to observe the odd-looking country boy toe the pigskin. Several audible remarks were made, none of them at all flattering to the subject of them; but if the latter heard them he made no sign, but accepted the ball from Blair without fumbling it, much to the surprise of the onlookers. Among these were Clausen and Cloud, their mouths prepared for the burst of ironical laughter that was expected to follow the country boy's effort.

"Drop or punt?" asked the latter, as he settled the oval in a rather ample hand.

"Which can you kick best?" questioned Blair. The youth considered a moment.

"I guess I can punt best." He stepped back, balancing the ball in his right hand, took a long stride forward, swung his right leg in a wide arc, dropped the ball, and sent it sailing down the field toward the distant goal. A murmur of applause took the place of the derisive laugh, and Blair glanced curiously at the former right end-rush of the Felton Grammar School.

"Yes, that's pretty fair. Some day with hard practice you may make a kicker." Several of the older fellows smiled knowingly. It was Blair's way of nipping conceit in the bud. "What class are you in?"

"Upper middle," replied the youth under the straw hat, displaying no disappointment at the scant praise.

"Well, March, kindly go down the field to that last squad and tell Tom Warren that I sent you. And say," he continued, as the candidate started off, and he was struck anew with the oddity of the straw hat and wrinkled trousers, "you had better tell him that you are the man that punted that ball."

"That chap has got to learn golf," said Outfield West to himself as he turned away after witnessing the incident, "even if I have to hog-tie him and teach it to him. What did he say his name was? February? March? That was it. It's kind of a chilly name. I'll make it a point to scrape acquaintance with him. He's a born golfer. His calm indifference when Blair tried to 'take him down' was beautiful to see. He's the sort of fellow that would smile if he made a foozle in a medal play."

West drew a golf ball from his pocket and, throwing it on the turf, gave it a half-shot off toward the river, following leisurely after it and pondering on the possibility of making a crack golfer out of a country lad in a straw hat.

Over on the gridiron, meanwhile, the candidates for football honors were limbering up in a way that greatly surprised not a few of the inexperienced. It is one thing to watch the game from the grand stand or side-lines and another to have an awkward, wobbly, elusive spheroid tossed to the ground a few feet from you and be required to straightway throw yourself upon it in such manner that when it stops rolling it will be snugly stowed between you and the ground. If the reader has played football he will know what this means. If he has not—well, there is no use trying to explain it to him. He must get a ball and try it for himself.

But even this exercise may lose its terrors after a while, and when at the end of an hour or more the lads were dismissed, there were many among them who limped back to their rooms sore and bruised, but proudly elated over their first day with the pigskin. Even to the youth in the straw hat it was tiresome work, although not new to him, and after practice was over, instead of joining in the little stream that eddied back to the academy grounds, he struck off to where a long straggling row of cedars and firs marked the course of the river. Once there he found himself standing on a bluff with the broad, placid stream stretching away to the north and south at his feet. The bank was some twenty feet high and covered sparsely with grass and weeds; and a few feet below him a granite bowlder stuck its lichened head outward from the cliff, forming an inviting seat from which to view the sunset across the lowland opposite. The boy half scrambled, half fell the short distance, and, settling himself in comfort on the ledge, became at once absorbed in his thoughts.

Perhaps he was thinking a trifle sadly of the home which he had left back there among the Maine hills, and which must have seemed a very long way off; or perhaps he was dwelling in awe upon the erudition of that excellent Greek gentleman, Mr. Xenophon, whose acquaintance, by means of the Anabasis, he was just making; or perhaps he was thinking of no more serious a subject than football and the intricate art of punting. But, whatever his thoughts may have been, they were doomed to speedy interruption, as will be seen.

Outfield West left the campus behind and, with the little white ball soaring ahead, took his way leisurely to the woods that bordered the tiny lake. Here he spent a quarter of an hour amid the tall grass and bushes, fighting his way patiently out of awkward lies, and finally driving off by the river bank, where a stretch of close, hard sod offered excellent chances for long shots. Again and again the ball flew singing on its way, till at last the campus was at hand again, and Stony Bunker intervened between West and Home.

Stony Bunker lay close to the river bluff and was the terror of all Hillton golfers, for, while a too short stroke was likely to leave you in the sand pit, a too vigorous one was just as likely to land you in the river. West knew Stony Bunker well by reason of former meetings, and he knew equally well what amount of swing was necessary to land just over the hazard, but well short of the bluff.

Perhaps it was the brassie that was to blame—for a full-length, supple-shafted, wooden driver would have been what you or I would have chosen for that stroke—or perhaps West himself was to blame. That as it may be, the fact remains that that provoking ball flew clear over the bunker as though possessed of wings and disappeared over the bluff!

With an exclamation of disgust West hurried after, for when they cost thirty-five cents apiece golf balls are not willingly lost even by lads who, like Outfield West, possess allowances far in excess of their needs. But the first glance down the bank reassured him, for there was the runaway ball snugly ensconced on the tiny strip of sandy beach that intervened between the bank and the water. West grasped an overhanging fir branch and swung himself over the ledge.

Now, that particular branch was no longer youthful and strong, and consequently when it felt the full weight of West's one hundred and thirty-five pounds it simply broke in his hand, and the boy started down the steep slope with a rapidity that rather unnerved him and brought an involuntary cry of alarm to his lips. It was the cry that was the means of saving him from painful results, since at the bottom of the bank lay a bed of good-sized rocks that would have caused many an ugly bruise had he fallen among them.

But suddenly, as he went falling, slipping, clutching wildly at the elusive weeds, he was brought up with a suddenness that drove the breath from his body. Weak and panting, he struggled up to the top of the jutting ledge, assisted by two strong arms, and throwing himself upon it looked wonderingly around for his rescuer.

Above him towered the boy in the straw hat.

THE STORY OF THE GOLF TOURNAMENT: ANOTHER EXCERPT FROM *THE HALFBACK*

RALPH HENRY BARBOUR

It was Saturday afternoon. The day was bright and sunny, and in the shelter of the grand stand on the campus, where the little east wind could not rustle, it was comfortably warm. The grass still held much of its summer verdancy, and the sky overhead was as deeply blue as on the mildest spring day. After a week of dull or stormy weather yesterday and today, with their fair skies, were as welcome as flowers in May, and gladness and light-heartedness were in the very air.

On the gridiron Westvale Grammar School and Hillton Academy were trying conclusions. On the grand stand all Hillton, academy and village, was assembled, and here and there a bright dress or wrap indicated the presence of a mother or sister in the throng. The Westvale team had arrived, accompanied by a coterie of enthusiastic supporters, armed with tin horns, maroon-colored banners, and mighty voices, which, with small hopes of winning on the field, were resolved to accomplish a notable victory of sound. On the side-line, with a dozen other substitutes whose greatest desire was to be taken on the first eleven, sat Joel. Outfield West was sprawled beside him with his caddie bag clutched to his breast, and the two boys were discussing the game. West had arrived upon the scene but a moment before.

"We'll beat them by about a dozen points, I guess," Joel was prophesying. "They say the score was twenty to nothing last year, but Remsen declares the first isn't nearly as far advanced as it was this time last season. Just hear the racket those fellows are making! You ought to have seen Blair kick down the field a while ago. I thought the ball never would come down, and I guess Westvale thought so too. Their full-back nearly killed himself running backward, and finally caught it on their five-yard line, and had it down there. Then Greer walked through, lugging Andrews for a touch-down, after Westvale had tried three times to move the ball. There's the whistle; half's up. How is the golf getting along?"

"Somers and Whipple were at Look Off when I came away. I asked Billy Jones to come over and call me when they got to The Hill. I think Whipple will win by a couple of strokes. Somers is too nervous. I wish they'd hurry up. We'll not get through the last round before dark if they don't finish soon. You'll go round with me, won't you?"

"If the game's over. They're playing twenty-minute halves, you know; so I guess it will be. I hope Blair will let me on this half. Have you seen Cloud?"

"Yes; he's over on the seats. Who has his place?"

"Ned Post; and Clausen's playing at right. I'm glad that Blair is doing such good work today. I think he was rather cut up about getting beaten this morning."

"Yes; wasn't that hard luck? To think of his being downed by a cub of a junior! Though that same junior is going to be a fine player some day. He drives just grand. He had too much handicap, he did. Remsen didn't know anything about him, and allowed him ten. Here they come again."

The two elevens were trotting out on the field once more, and Joel stood up in the hope that Blair might see him and decide to take him on. But Joel was doomed to disappointment, for the second half of the game began with practically the same line-up. The score stood six to nothing in favor of Hillton. The playing had been decidedly ragged on both sides; and Remsen, as he left the team after administering a severe lecture, walked past with a slight frown on his face.

" Well, I guess I'll go over and see if I can hurry those chumps up some." West swung his bag over his shoulder and turned away. "When the game's done, hurry over, March. You'll find us somewhere on the course." Joel nodded, and West sauntered away toward the links. The second half of the game was similar to the first, save in that Remsen's scolding had accomplished an awakening, and the first put more snap into its playing. Six more points were scored from a touch-down by the Hillton right end, after a thirty-yard run, followed by a difficult goal by Blair. But the Westvale rooters kept up their cheering bravely to the end, and took defeat with smiling faces and upraised voices; and long after the coach containing them had passed from sight their cheers could still be heard in the distance toward the station.

The bulk of the spectators turned at the conclusion of the match toward the links, and Joel followed in his football togs. At Home Hole he found Whipple and West preparing for the deciding round of the tournament, and the latter greeted him with a shout, and put his clubs into his keeping. Then Whipple went to the tee and led off with a long drive for the first hole, and the round began. West followed with a shorter shot and the march was taken up.

The links at Hillton consists of nine holes, five out and four in. The entire length of the course is a trifle over one and a half mile, and although the land is upland meadow and given to growing long grass, yet the course is generally conceded to be excellent. The holes are short, allowing the round to be accomplished by a capable player in thirty-two strokes. The course has thirteen bunkers of varying sizes, besides two water hazards at the inlet and outlet of the lake. The lake itself is spoiled as a hazard by the thick grove of trees on the side nearest the Academy. Sometimes a poor drive lands a ball in that same grove, and there is much trial and tribulation ere the player has succeeded in dislodging it from the underbrush.

While generally level, the course is diversified by slight elevations, upon which are the putting greens, their red and white flags visible from all parts of the links. As has been said, the holes are short, the longest, Lake Hole, being four hundred and ninety-six yards, and the shortest, the first, but one hundred and thirty-three. Outfield West once spent the better part of two weeks, at great cost to his class standing, in making a plan of the links, and, while it is not warranted accurate as to distances, it is reproduced here with his permission as giving a clearer idea of the ground than any verbal description.

Play had begun this morning at nine o'clock, and by noon only Somers, Whipple, and West had been left in the match. Blair had encountered defeat most unexpectedly at the hands of Greene, a junior, of whose prowess but little had been known by the handicapper; for, although Blair had done the round in three strokes less than his adversary's gross score, the latter's allowance of six strokes had placed him an easy winner. But Blair had been avenged later by West, who had defeated the youngster by three strokes in the net. In the afternoon Somers and Whipple had met, and, as West had predicted, the latter won by two strokes.

And now West and Whipple, both excellent players, and sworn enemies of the links, were fighting it out, and on this round depended the possession of the title of champion and the ownership for one year of the handicap cup, a modest but highly prized pewter tankard. Medal Play rules governed today, and the scoring was by strokes.

Whipple reached the first green in one stroke, but used two more to hole-out. West took two short drives to reach a lie, from which he dropped his ball into the hole in one try. And the honors were even. The next hole was forty yards longer, and was played either in two short drives or one long drive and an approach shot. It contained two hazards, Track Bunker and High Bunker, the latter alone being formidable. Whipple led off with a long shot that went soaring up against the blue and then settled down as gently as a bird just a few yards in front of High Bunker. He had reversed his play of the last hole, and was now relying on his approach shot for position. West played a rather short drive off an iron which left his ball midway between the two bunkers. Whipple's next stroke took him neatly out of danger and on to the putting green, but West had fared not so well.

There was a great deal of noise from the younger boys who were looking on, much discussion of the methods of play, and much loud boasting of what someone else would have done under existing circumstances. West glanced up once and glared at one offending junior, and an admonitory "Hush!" was heard. But he was plainly disturbed, and when the little white sphere made its flight it went sadly aglee and dropped to earth far to the right of the green, and where rough and cuppy ground made exact putting well-nigh impossible. Professor Beck promptly laid down a command of absolute silence during shots, and some of the smaller youths left the course in favor of another portion of the campus, where a boy's right to make all the noise he likes could not be disputed. But the harm was done, and when play for the third hole began the score was: Whipple 7, West 8.

Even to one of such intense ignorance of the science of golf as Joel March, there was a perceptible difference in the style of the two competitors. Outfield West was a great stickler for form, and imitated the full St. Andrews swing to the best of his ability. In addressing the ball he stood as squarely to it as was possible, without the use of a measuring tape, and drove off the right leg, as the expression is. Despite an almost exaggerated adherence to nicety of style, West's play had an ease and grace much envied by other golf disciples in the school, and his shots were nearly always successful.

Whipple's manner of driving was very different from his opponent's. His swing was short and often stopped too soon. His stance was rather awkward, after West's, and even his hold on the club was not according to established precedent. Yet, notwithstanding all this, it must be acknowledged that Whipple's drives had a way of carrying straight and far and landing well.

Joel followed the play with much interest if small appreciation of its intricacies, and carried West's bag, and hoped all the time that that youth would win, knowing how greatly he had set his heart upon so doing.

There is no bunker between second and third holes, but the brook which supplies the lake runs across the course and is about six yards wide from bank to bank. But it has no terrors for a long drive, and both the players went safely over and won Academy Hole in three strokes. West still held the odd. Two long strokes carried Whipple a scant distance from Railroad Bunker, which fronts Ditch Hole, a dangerous lie, since Railroad Bunker is high and the putting green is on an elevation, almost meriting the title of hill, directly back of it. But if Whipple erred in judgment or skill, West found himself in even a sorrier plight when two more strokes had been laid to his score. His first drive with a brassie had fallen rather short, and for the second he had chosen an iron. The ball sailed off on a long flight that brought words of delight from the spectators, but which caused Joel to look glum and West to grind the turf under his heel in anger. For, like a thing possessed, that ball fell straight into the very middle of the bunker, and when it was found lay up to its middle in gravel.

West groaned as he lifted the ball, replaced it loosely in its cup, and carefully selected a club. Whipple meanwhile cleared the bunker in the best of style, and landed on the green in a good position to hole out in two shots. "Great Gobble!" muttered West as he swung his club, and fixed his eye on a point an inch and a half back of the imbedded ball, "if I don't get this out of here on this shot, I'm a gone goose!" March grinned sympathetically but anxiously, and the onlookers held their breath. Then back went the club—there was a scattering of sand and gravel, and the ball dropped dead on the green, four yards from the hole.

"Excellent!" shouted Professor Beck, and Joel jumped in the air from sheer delight. "Good for you, Out!" yelled Dave Somers; and the rest of the watchers echoed the sentiment in various ways, even those who desired to see Whipple triumphant yielding their meed of praise for the performance. And, "I guess, Out," said Whipple ruefully, "you might as well take the cup." But Outfield West only smiled silently in response, and followed his ball with businesslike attention to the game.

Whipple was weak on putting, and his first stroke with an iron failed to carry his ball to the hole. West, on the contrary, was a sure player on the green, and now with his ball but four yards from the hole he had just the opportunity he desired to better his score. The green was level and clean, and West selected a small iron putter, and addressed the ball with all the attention to form that the oldest St. Andrews veteran might desire. Playing on the principle that it is better to go too far than not far enough, since the hole is larger than the ball, West gave a long stroke, and the gutta-percha disappeared from view. Whipple holed out on his next try, adopting a wooden putter this time, and the score stood fifteen strokes each.

The honor was West's, and he led off for End Hole with a beautiful brassie drive that cleared the first two bunkers with room to spare. Whipple, for the first time in the round, drove poorly, toeing his ball badly, and dropping it almost off of the course and just short of the second bunker. West's second drive was a loft over Halfway Bunker that fell fairly on the green and rolled within ten feet of the hole. From there, on the next shot, he holed out very neatly in eighteen. Whipple meanwhile had redeemed himself with a high lofting stroke that carried past the threatening dangers of Masters Bunker and back on to the course within a few yards of West's lie. But again skill on the putting green was wanting, and he required two strokes to make the hole. Once more the honor was West's, and that youth turned toward home with a short and high stroke. The subsequent hole left the score "the like" at 22, and the seventh gave Whipple, 25, West 26.

"But here's where Mr. West takes the lead," confided that young gentleman to Joel as they walked to the teeing ground. "From here to Lake Hole is four hundred and ninety-six yards, and I'm going to do it in three shots on to the green. You watch!"

Four hundred and ninety-odd yards is nothing out of the ordinary for an older player, but to a lad of seventeen it is a creditable distance to do in three drives. Yet that is what West did it in; and strange to relate, and greatly to that young gentleman's surprise, Whipple duplicated the performance, and amid the excited whispers of the onlookers the two youths holed out on their next strokes; and the score still gave the odd to West—29 to 30.

"I didn't think he could do it," whispered West to Joel, "and that makes it look bad for your uncle Out. But never mind, my lad, there's still Rocky Bunker ahead of us, and——" West did not complete his remark, but his face took on a very determined look as he teed his ball. The last hole was in sight, and victory hovered overhead.

Now, the distance from Lake Hole to the Home Hole is but a few yards over three hundred, and it can be accomplished comfortably in two long brassie drives. Midway lies The Hill, a small elevation rising from about the middle of the course to the river bluff, and there falling off sheer to the beach below. It is perhaps thirty yards across, and if the ball reaches it safely it forms an excellent place from which to make the second drive. So both boys tried for The Hill. Whipple landed at the foot of it, while West came plump upon the side some five yards from the summit, and his next drive took him cleanly over Rocky Bunker and to the right of the Home Green. But Whipple summoned discretion to his aid, and instead of trying to make the green on the next drive, played short, and landed far to the right of the Bunker. This necessitated a short approach, and by the time he had gained the green and was "made" within holing distance of the flag, the score was once more even, and the end was in sight.

And now the watchers moved about restlessly, and Joel found his heart in his throat. But West gripped his wooden putter firmly and studied the situation. It was quite possible for a skillful player to hole out on the next stroke from Whipple's lie. West, on the contrary, was too far distant to possess more than one chance in ten of winning the hole in one play. Whether to take that one chance or to use his next play in bettering his lie was the question. Whipple, West knew, was weak on putting, but it is ever risky to rely on your opponent's weakness. While West pondered, Whipple studied the lay of the green with eyes that strove to show no triumph, and the little throng kept silence save for an occasional nervous whisper.

Then West leaned down and cleared a pebble from before his ball. It was the veriest atom of a pebble that ever showed on a putting green, but West was willing to take no chances beyond those that already confronted him. His mind was made up. Gripping his iron putter firmly rather low on the shaft and bending far over, West slowly, cautiously swung the club above the gutty, glancing once and only once as he did so at the distant goal. Then there was a pause. Whipple no longer studied his own play; his eyes were on that other sphere that nestled there so innocently against the grass. Joel leaned breathlessly forward. Professor Beck muttered under his breath, and then cried "S—sh!" to himself in an angry whisper. And then West's club swung back gently, easily, paused an instant—and—forward sped the ball—on and on—slower—slower—but straight as an arrow—and then—Presto! it was gone from sight!

A moment of silence followed ere the applause broke out, and in that moment Professor Beck announced:

"The odd to Whipple. Thirty-two to thirty-three." Then the group became silent again. Whipple addressed his ball. It was yet possible to tie the score. His face was pale, and for the first time during the tournament he felt nervous. A better player could scarce have missed the hole from Whipple's lie, but for once that youth's nerve forsook him and he hit too short; the ball stopped a foot from the hole. The game was decided. Professor Beck again announced the score:

"The two more to Whipple. Thirty-two to thirty-four." Again Whipple addressed his ball, and this time, but too late to win the victory, the tiny sphere dropped neatly into the hole, and the throng broke silence. And as West and Whipple, victor and vanquished, shook hands over the Home Hole, Professor Beck announced:

"Thirty-two to thirty-five. West wins the Cup!"

iStockphoto/Thinkstock

THE STORY OF SIMPSON AND HIS DECISION TO TAKE UP GOLF

A. A. MILNE

"Well," said Dahlia, "what do you think of it?"

I knocked the ashes out of my after-breakfast pipe, arranged the cushions of my deck-chair, and let my eyes wander lazily over the house and its surroundings. After a year of hotels and other people's houses, Dahlia and Archie had come into their own.

"I've no complaints," I said, happily.

A vision of white and gold appeared in the doorway and glided over the lawn toward us—Myra with a jug.

"None at all," said Simpson, sitting up eagerly.

"But Thomas isn't quite satisfied with one of the bathrooms, I'm afraid. I heard him saying something in the passage about it this morning when I was inside."

"I asked if you'd gone to sleep in the bath," explained Thomas.

"I hadn't. It is practically impossible, Thomas, to go to sleep in a cold bath."

"Except, perhaps, for a Civil Servant," said Blair.

"Exactly. Of the practice in the Admiralty, Thomas can tell us later on. For myself I was at the window looking at the beautiful view."

"Why can't you look at it from your own window instead of keeping people out of the bathroom?" grunted Thomas.

"Because the view from my room is an entirely different one."

"There is no stint in this house," Dahlia pointed out.

"No," said Simpson, jumping up excitedly.

Myra put the jug of cider down in front of us.

"There!" she said. "Please count it, and see that I haven't drunk any on the way."

"'Tis awfully nice of you, Myra. And a complete surprise to all of us except Simpson. We shall probably be here again tomorrow about the same time."

There was a long silence, broken only by the extremely jolly sound of liquid falling from a height.

Just as it was coming to an end Archie appeared suddenly among us and dropped on the grass by the side of Dahlia. Simpson looked guiltily at the empty jug, and then leant down to his host.

"*Tomorrow!*" he said in a stage whisper. "About the same time."

"I doubt it," said Archie.

"I know it for a fact," protested Simpson.

"I'm afraid Myra and Samuel made an assignation for this morning," said Dahlia.

"There's nothing in it, really," said Myra. "He's only trifling with me. He doesn't mean anything."

Simpson buried his confused head in his glass, and proceeded to change the subject.

"We all like your house, Archie," he said.

"We do," I agreed, "and we think it's very nice of you to ask us down to open it."

"It is rather," said Archie.

"We are determined, therefore, to do all we can to give the house a homey appearance. I did what I could for the bathroom this morning. I flatter myself that the taint of newness has now been dispelled."

"I was sure it was you," said Myra. "How do you get the water right up the walls?"

"Easily. Further, Archie, if you want any suggestions as to how to improve the place, our ideas are at your disposal."

"For instance," said Thomas, "where do we play cricket?"

"By the way, you fellows," announced Simpson, "I've given up playing cricket."

We all looked at him in consternation.

"Do you mean you've given up bowling?" said Dahlia, with wide-open eyes.

"Aren't you ever going to walk to the wicket again?" asked Blair.

"Aren't you ever going to walk back to the pavilion again?" asked Archie.

"What will Montgomeryshire say?" wondered Myra in tones of awe.

"May I have your belt and your sand-shoes?" I begged.

"It's the cider," said Thomas. "I knew he was overdoing it."

Simpson fixed his glasses firmly on his nose and looked round at us benignly.

"I've given it up for golf," he observed.

"Traitor," said every one.

"And the Triangular Tournament arranged for, and every-thing," added Myra.

"You could make a jolly little course round here," went on the infatuated victim. "If you like, Archie, I'll—"

Archie stood up and made a speech.

"Ladies and gentlemen," he said, "at 11:30 tomorrow precisely I invite you to the paddock beyond the kitchen-garden."

"Myra and I have an appointment," put in Simpson hastily.

"A net will be erected," Archie went on, ignoring him, "and Mr. Simpson will take his stand therein, while we all bowl at him—or, if any prefer it, at the wicket—for five minutes. He will then bowl at us for an hour, after which he will have another hour's smart fielding practice. If he is still alive and still talks about golf, why, then, I won't say but what he mightn't be allowed to plan out a little course—or, at any rate, to do a little preliminary weeding."

"Good man," said Simpson.

"And if anybody else thinks he has given up cricket for ludo or croquet or oranges and lemons, then he can devote him-self to planning out a little course for that too—or anyhow to removing a few plantains in preparation for it. In fact, ladies and gentlemen, all I want is for you to make yourselves as happy and as useful as you can."

"It's what you're here for," said Dahlia.

A GALA PERFORMANCE

The sun came into my room early next morning and woke me up. It was followed immediately by a large blue-bottle which set-tled down to play with me. We adopted the usual formation, the blue-bottle keeping mostly to the back of the court whilst I waited at the net for a kill. After two sets I decided to change my tactics. I looked up at the ceiling and pretended I wasn't playing. The blue-bottle settled on my nose and walked up my forehead. "Heavens!"

I cried, "I've forgotten my toothbrush!" This took it completely by surprise, and I removed its corpse into the candlestick.

Then Simpson came in with a golf club in his hand.

"Great Scott," he shouted, "you're not still in bed?"

"I am not. This is telepathic suggestion. You think I'm in bed; I appear to be in bed; in reality there is no bed here. Do go away— I haven't had a wink of sleep yet."

"But, man, look at the lovely morning!"

"Simpson," I said sternly, rolling up the sleeves of my pyjamas with great deliberation, "I have had one visitor already today. His corpse is now in the candlestick. It is an omen, Simpson."

"I thought you'd like to come outside with me, and I'd show you my swing."

"Yes, yes, I shall like to see that, but after breakfast, Simpson. I suppose one of the gardeners put it up for you? You must show me your box of soldiers and your tricycle horse, too. But run away now, there's a good boy."

"My golf swing, idiot."

I sat up in bed and stared at him in sheer amazement. For a long time words wouldn't come to me. Simpson backed nervously to the door.

"I saw the Coronation," I said at last, and I dropped back on my pillow and went to sleep.

* * * * *

"I feel very important," said Archie, coming on to the lawn where Myra and I were playing a quiet game of bowls with the croquet balls. "I've been paying the wages."

"Archie and I do hate it so," said Dahlia. "I'm luckier, because I only pay mine once a month."

"It would be much nicer if they did it for love," said Archie, "and just accepted a tie-pin occasionally. I never know what to say when I hand a man eighteen-and-six."

"Here's eighteen-and-six," I suggested, "and don't bite the half-sovereign, because it may be bad."

"You should shake his hand," said Myra, "and say, 'Thank you very much for the azaleas.'"

"Or you might wrap the money up in paper and leave it for him in one of the beds."

"And then you'd know whether he had made it properly."

"Well, you're all very helpful," said Archie "Thank you extremely. Where are the others? It's a pity that they should be left out of this."

"Simpson disappeared after breakfast with his golf clubs. He is in high dudgeon—which is the surname of a small fish—because no one wanted to see his swing."

"Oh, but I do!" said Dahlia, eagerly. "Where is he?"

"We will track him down," announced Archie. "I will go to the stables, unchain the truffle-hounds, and show them one of his reversible cuffs."

We found Simpson in the pigsty. The third hole, as he was planning it out for Archie, necessitated the carrying of the farm buildings, which he described as a natural hazard. Unfortunately, his ball had fallen into a casual pigsty. It had not yet been decided whether the ball could be picked out without penalty—the more immediate need being to find the blessed thing. So Simpson was in the pigsty, searching.

"If you're looking for the old sow," I said, "there she is, just behind you."

"What's the local rule about loose pigs blown on to the course?" asked Archie.

"Oh, you fellows, there you are!" said Simpson rapidly." I'm getting on first-rate. This is the third hole, Archie. It will be rather good, I think; the green is just the other side of the pond I can make a very sporting little course."

"We've come to see your swing, Samuel," said Myra. "Can you do it in there, or is it too crowded?"

"I'll come out. This ball's lost, I'm afraid."

"One of the little pigs will eat it," complained Archie, "and we shall have india-rubber crackling."

Simpson came out and proceeded to give his display. Fortunately the weather kept fine, the conditions indeed being all that could be desired. The sun shone brightly, and there was a slight breeze from the south which tempered the heat and in no way militated against the general enjoyment. The performance was divided into two parts. The first part consisted of Mr. Simpson's swing without the ball, the second part being dovoted to Mr. Simpson's swing with the ball.

"This is my swing," said Simpson.

He settled himself ostentatiously into his stance, and placed his club-head stiffly on the ground three feet away from him.

"Middle," said Archie.

Simpson frowned and began to waggle his club. He waggled it carefully a dozen times.

"It's a very nice swing," said Myra, at the end of the ninth movement," but isn't it rather short?"

Simpson said nothing, but drew his club slowly and jerkily back, twisting his body and keeping his eye fixed on an imaginary ball until the back of his neck hid it from sight.

"You can see it better round this side now," suggested Archie.

"He'll split if he goes on," said Thomas, anxiously. "Watch this," I warned Myra. "He's going to pick a pin out of the back of his calf with his teeth."

Then Simpson let himself go, finishing up in a very creditable knot indeed.

"That's quite good," said Dahlia. "Does it do as well when there's a ball?"

"Well, I miss it sometimes, of course."

"We all do that," said Thomas.

Thus encouraged, Simpson put down a ball and began to address it. It was apparent at once that the last address had been only his telegraphic one; this was the genuine affair. After what seemed to be four or five minutes there was a general feeling that some apology was necessary. Simpson recognized this himself.

"I'm a little nervous," he said.

"Not so nervous as the pigs are," said Archie.

Simpson finished his address and got on to his swing. He swung. He hit the ball. The ball, which seemed to have too much left-hand side on it, whizzed off and disappeared into the pond. It sank. . . .

Luckily the weather had held up till the last.

"Well, well," said Archie, "It's time for lunch. We have had a riotous morning. Let's all take it easy this afternoon."

THE STORY OF GOLF AND
SOCIAL ACCOUNTS

JOHN KENDRICK BANGS

"It's rather strange, I think," observed Mrs. Idiot one evening, as she and the Idiot sat down to dine, "that the Dawkinses haven't been here for three or four months."

"I've noticed it myself," said the Idiot. "We used to see 'em every day about. What's up? You and Polly Dawkins had a fight?"

"Not that I know of," said Mrs. Idiot. "The last time we met she was very cordial, and asked most affectionately after you and the children. I presumed that possibly you and Dick had had some kind of a falling out."

"Not a bit of it. Dick and I couldn't quarrel any more than you and Polly could. Perhaps as we grow older our ideals differ. Polly's rather anthropological in her talks, isn't she?"

"A trifle," said Mrs. Idiot. "And musical and literary and scientific."

"While you?" queried the Idiot.

"Well, I'm fond of golf and—ah— well—"

"Golf again," laughed the Idiot. "I guess that's it, Bess. When a woman wants to talk about the origin of the species and has to hear about a splendid putt, and her observations upon the sonata are invariably interrupted by animadversions upon the morals of caddies, and her criticisms of Browning end in a discussion of the St. Andrew's Rules, she's apt to shy off into a more congenial atmosphere, don't you think?"

"I am sure," retorted Mrs. Idiot, "that while I admit I am more interested in golf than in anything else outside of you and the children, I can and do talk sometimes of other things than caddies, and beautiful drives, and stymies. You are very much mistaken if you think otherwise."

"That is very true, my dear," said the Idiot. "And nobody knows it better than I do. I've heard you talk charmingly about lots of things besides stymies, and foozles, and putts, and drives, but you don't know anything about the men of the Stone Age, and you couldn't tell the difference between a sonata and a fugue any more than I. Furthermore, you have no patience with Browning, so that when Polly Dawkins asks if you like *Sordello*, you are more likely than not to say that you never ate any, but on the whole for small fish prefer whitebait."

Mrs. Idiot laughed.

"No, indeed," she replied. "I'd fall back on golf if Polly mentioned *Sordello* to me. You may remember that you sent it to me when we were engaged, and I loved you so much—then—that I read it. If I hadn't loved you I couldn't have done it."

"Well," smiled the Idiot, "what did you think of it?"

"I think Browning had a good lie, but he foozled," said Mrs. Idiot, with her eyes atwinkle, and the Idiot subsided for at least ten seconds.

"I wish you'd say that to Polly some time," he observed. "It's so very true, and put with an originality which cannot but appeal to the most hardened of literary women."

"I will if I ever get the chance," said Mrs. Idiot.

"Suppose we make the chance?" suggested the Idiot. "Let's go down there and call tonight. I'll work the conversation up so that you can get that off as an impromptu."

"No," said Mrs. Idiot. "I don't think we'd better. In the first place, Mrs. Whalker told me yesterday that Polly is to read a paper on Balzac before the S. F. M. E. tomorrow evening, and on Friday morning she is to discuss the 'Influence of Mozart on De Koven' before the Musical Mothers' Meeting, and on Saturday afternoon she is going to have an anthropological tea at her house, which she is to open with some speculations as to whether in the Glacial Period dudes were addicted to the use of cigarettes."

"Great Scott!" said the Idiot. "This is her busy week."

"Tolerably so," said Mrs. Idiot. "She has probably reserved this evening to read up on Balzac for tomorrow's essay, so I think, my dear, we'd better not go."

"Right as usual," said the Idiot. And then he added, "Poor Dawkins, who is taking care of him now?"

"I think," said Mrs. Idiot, "that possibly Mrs. Dawkins has sublet the contract for looking after her husband and children to the United States Housekeeping Company Limited."

The Idiot gazed blankly at his wife, and awaited an explanation.

"An organization, my dear," she continued, "formed by a number of well-meaning and remorseful widows who, having lost their husbands, begin to appreciate their virtues, and who, finding themselves sympathetic when it is too late, are devoting themselves to the husbands of others who are neglected. A subscription of five hundred dollars will secure the supervision of all the domestic arrangements of a home—marketing, engagement and discharge of domestics, house-cleaning, buttons sewed on, darning done, care of flowers, wifely duties generally; for one thousand dollars they will bring up the children, and see that the baby is rocked to sleep every night, and suitably interested in elevating narratives and poems like Joseph's coat of many colors, and Tom, Tom the Piper's Son. This enables an advanced woman like Mrs. Dawkins to devote her mornings to the encyclopedias, her afternoons to the public libraries, and her evenings to the functions whereat she may read the papers which her devotion to the encyclopedias and the libraries has brought forth."

"Excuse me, my dear Bess," said the Idiot, rising. "I wish to telephone Dr. Simmons."

"For what—for whom?" demanded the lady.

"You, of course," returned the Idiot. "You are developing alarming symptoms. You give every indication of a bad attack of professional humor. Your 'International Widows Company for the Protection and Amelioration of Neglected Husbandry' proves that!"

Mrs. Idiot laughed again.

"Oh, I didn't say that there really is such an institution!" she cried. "I said that I supposed there was, for if there isn't, poor Dick Dawkins isn't taken care of at all."

"Well, I'm sorry for it all, anyhow," said the Idiot, seriously. "They're both of 'em good friends of ours, and I hate to see two families that have been so close drawing apart."

Just then Mollie and Tommy came in. "Mamma, Willie Dawkins says he can't come to our party because his ma won't let him," said Mollie. "She says we don't never go down there."

"That's it," said the Idiot. "Mrs. Dawkins has got so many irons in the fire she's begun to keep social books. I'll bet you she's got a ledger and a full set of double-entry account-books charging up calls payable and calls receivable."

"I don't see how she can get along unless she has," replied Mrs. Idiot. "With all her clubs and church societies and varied social obligations she needs an expert accountant to keep track of them all."

"I suppose a promise to read a paper on Balzac," put in the Idiot, "is something like a three-months' note. It's easy to promise to pay, with three months in which to prepare, but you've got to keep track of the date and meet the obligation when it falls due. As for me, I'd rather meet the note."

"That is about it," said Mrs. Idiot. "If a woman goes into society properly she's got to make a business of it. For instance, there are about ten dances given at the club here every year. Polly is patroness for every one of 'em. There are twenty-five teas during the spring and summer months. Polly assists at half of them, and gives a fifth of them. She's president of the King's Daughters, corresponding secretary of the Dorcas, treasurer of the Red Cross Society, and goodness knows what all!"

"I can quite understand why she needs to keep accounts—social accounts," said the Idiot. "But it's rather queer, don't you think, that she has the children on her books? The idea of saying that Jimmie and Gladys can't come to Mollie's party because Mollie hasn't been down there—why, it's nonsense!"

"No," said Mrs. Idiot, "it is merely logical. Whatever Polly Dawkins does she tries to do thoroughly. I've no doubt she'll do Balzac up completely. If she keeps social books showing call balances in her favor or against herself she might as well go the whole thing and write the children in—only she's made a mistake, as far as we are concerned, unless she means to write us off without squaring up."

"You talk like a financier," said the Idiot, admiringly. "What do you know about writing off?"

"I used to help my father with his accounts, occasionally," said Mrs. Idiot. "Polly Dawkins's books ought to show a balance of one call in our favor. That's really the reason I'm not willing to call there tonight. She's so queer about it all, and, as a matter of fact, she owes me a call. I'm not going to overwhelm her with an added obligation."

"Ho!" smiled the Idiot. "You keep books yourself, eh?"

"I keep score," said Mrs. Idiot. "I learned that playing golf."

"It's a bad thing to keep score in golf," said the Idiot.

"So they say, but I find it amusing," she replied.

"And how many calls does Mrs. Wilkins owe you?" demanded the Idiot.

"I don't know," returned the wife. "And I don't care. When I want to see Mrs. Wilkins I call on her whether she owes me a call or not, but with Polly Dawkins it's different. She began the book-keeping, and as long as she likes it I must try to live up to her ideas. If social intercourse develops into a business, business requirements must be observed."

"It's a good idea in a way," said the Idiot, reflectively. "But if you make a business of society, why don't you carry it to a logical conclusion? Balance your books, if you mean business, every month, and send your debtors a statement of their account."

"Well, I will if you wish me to," said Mrs. Idiot. "Suppose they don't pay?"

"Dun 'em," said the Idiot. And then the matter dropped.

On the fifth of the following month Mr. and Mrs. Idiot were seated comfortably in their library. The children had gone to bed, and they were enjoying the bliss of a quiet evening at home, when the door-bell rang, and in a moment or two the maid ushered in Mr. and Mrs. Richard Dawkins, preceded, of course, by their cards. The young householders were delighted, and Polly Dawkins was never more charming. She looked well, and she talked well, and there was not a symptom of any diminution of the old-time friendship perceptible—only she did appear to be tired and care-worn.

The evening wore away pleasantly. The chat reverted to old times, and by degrees Mrs. Dawkins seemed to grow less tired.

About ten o'clock the Idiot invited his neighbor to adjourn to the smoking-room, where they each lit a cigar and indulged in a companionable glass.

"Idiot," said Dawkins, when his wife called out to him that it was time to go home, "your wife is a wonder. I've been trying for three months to make Polly come up here and she wouldn't. Keeps books, you know—now. Has to—so much to do. Thought you owed us a call, but received your bill Wednesday—looked it up—questioned servants—found you were right."

"Bill," cried the Idiot. "What bill?"

"Why, the one Mrs. Idiot sent—this," said Dawkins, taking a piece of paper out of his pocket. "Confoundedly good joke."

The Idiot took up the piece of paper. It was type-written—on Tommy's machine—and read as follows:

		November 1, 1898	
MR. AND MRS. RICHARD DAWKINS			
To Mr. and Mrs. Idiot Dr.			
September 20	Evening call	1	
	Account overdue. Please remit.		

"Great Scott!" laughed the Idiot.

"My dear," said the Idiot after the Dawkinses had gone, "that bill of yours was a great idea."

"It wasn't my idea at all—it was yours," said Mrs. Idiot, laughing. "You said we ought to be business-like to the last and send out a statement on the first of the month. I sent it. And they paid up."

"Richard," said Mrs. Dawkins, as they drove home, "did you get a receipt?"

Comstock/Thinkstock

THE STORY OF THE CURSE OF IMAGINATION

BERNARD DARWIN

S ome years ago there was an unfortunate gentleman who finished eighteen holes down in a team match. As the match
was only one of eighteen holes, it was felt that in a record-break-
ing age there was at least one feat that was very unlikely to be

beaten, and several comments appeared upon it in the newspapers. Thereupon the gentleman wrote a most pathetic letter, in which he complained, if I remember rightly, that two mitigating circumstances had not been mentioned: first, that he was playing with a strange set of clubs; and secondly, that he had only just recovered from a severe attack of influenza. Now here were two unimpeachable excuses. They were much better than most excuses, and yet it is hardly open to doubt that the gentleman would have done better to keep silence. It is a hard lesson—so hard that scarcely any of us learn it thoroughly—that not only do other people not care about our excuses, but they do not even believe them.

To all our adversary's excuses we make, if we are wise, one and the same answer, "Hard luck!" but in our own minds we do in a measure differentiate between them. The one to which we mentally extend the very smallest possible amount of sympathy is the excuse that the enemy's hand slipped or, as it is sometimes stated with wholly unconvincing exaggeration, that "the club flew clean out of my hand." The proper answer to that remark is clearly, "Then why the dickens did you not hold tighter?" Everybody thinks it, though few are brutal enough to say it. The statement that the player's foot slipped is not looked upon with such scorn, because no doubt the best regulated feet will slip sometimes. Not infrequently, however, our feet slip just because they are not well regulated; because, in fact, we overswing ourselves in a very outrageous manner.

Then there is, of course, that enormous race of excuses that may be classed under the head of diseases. Now there is only one imperative piece of advice about diseases; we must remember to mention them before the game begins. There is everything to gain by this honest policy and nothing to lose, except, indeed, the character for suffering in Spartan silence, and that we have as a rule irretrievably lost long ago. A disease clearly announced on the first tee may possibly be believed in; and it may actually mitigate the shame of defeat or enhance the glories of a victory. The chances of a victory are always worth considering, because it is a common knowledge that a splitting headache, or, still better, a severe cold in the head, will sometimes lead to incredible brilliancy. On the other hand, a disease bottled up to begin with, and only brought out as a last resource when we are four down at the sixth hole is worse than useless. It will do no good if we lose, while if by some miracle we pull ourselves together and win, it will add an unspeakable bitterness to our enemy's ordinary discomfiture. He will probably not forget to mention to a few friends our mendacious and contemptible tactics.

There are numerous things which are recognised as being reasonably good excuses. Under this head come dogs, people standing or moving immediately behind us, and, commonest of all perhaps, caddies suffering from the hiccups. These are, as it were, excuses by Act of Parliament. Nobody would think of arguing about them, and we shall be quite safe in using them. The only question is whether it would not be better, after all, to refrain from doing all that the law allows. When all is said, however, I think that by far the best excuse is a photographer. He stands and aims at us from a portion that would in the cricket field be known as "silly point," and he keeps us on tenterhooks as to the exact moment at which he will apply the fuse to his infernal machine. As a rule, it is our classical follow-through that he desires to photograph, and so we can, at least, go through the subsidiary performance of hitting the ball in some kind of peace, but sometimes a not-unjustifiable fear seizes him that we are not going to follow through at all. Then, to make quite sure of bagging something, he fires just as we are coming down to the ball.

Never was any one so plagued with cameras as was Miss Leitch in her historic match against Mr. Hilton at Walton Heath. Pale, but courageous, she had to play nearly every shot under a heavy fire. When she got into difficulties the fusillade was worst of all, snapping fiends posting themselves actually on the very ramparts of the bunker. Mr. Hilton did not have nearly such a trying time of it in this respect. He is, I suppose, regularly kept in stock. His follow-through, his cap tumbling off, his cigarette—all have been part of golfing history so long that a good reliable picture can always be obtained at a moment's notice. Through his many battles on the links, he has been, as it were, inoculated against photographers and enjoys a measure of immunity.

Differing slightly in kind from those excuses with which he plagues his adversary are the consolations which the golfer administers to himself; consolations founded as a rule upon a train of reasoning that will not for a moment bear searching analysis. For instance, what can be commoner than the following scene: A. and B. are on the tee about to drive off to a short hole. A. has the honour, and foozles the shot so egregiously that the ball topples into a bunker in front of his nose. Thereupon B. lays his ball about a yard from the pin. But a moment ago A. was furious and miserable, but now he picks up his ball, quite serene and happy, and remarks: "Ah well—it doesn't matter. I could never have done any good against a two." If he is playing in a single he cheers himself by this reflection; if in a foursome he expects to cheer his partner by it.

How angry he would be, if his foursome partner were to address him in some such words as these: "Do not talk such arrant nonsense. If you had hit your ball over the bunker, not only would B. not have put his ball dead, but I think it highly probable that he would not have put it even on the green." A player who should make such an observation would be neither a popular nor a successful foursome player, but he would have the barren satisfaction of feeling that he had, as nearly as possible, spoken the truth. It is a truth that one seldom hears openly acknowledged. Most golfers dislike it, because to admit that the good or bad shots of other people so often depend on circumstances that may be called mental is also to admit a certain nervous weakness in themselves. Therefore, we all join in a general conspiracy to deny the obvious fact that we are all much more likely to play a good shot when our adversary is in a bunker than when he is lying dead at the hole.

I remember one honest man who declined to be a party to this conspiracy. He was complaining of his bad play, and in particular of how he had lost a certain hole in spite of having received a stroke there. I murmured that I had been very lucky at that hole, and got down a very long putt for a three. My friend refused to be consoled. "Yes, sir," he said, and his manner was worthy of Dr. Johnson, "but if I had put my third dead, as I ought, you would not have holed your long putt."

This kind of spurious consolation at any rate does little harm. It is rather contemptible, but it may stop us from getting angry. There is, however, another kind which is sometimes administered by an adversary which quite justifies us in striking him to the earth with a niblick. We are, let us imagine, playing a hole which, with a favouring breeze, we can reach very easily with a drive and an iron shot. We ought, therefore, to do a four, but, in fact, we do a five, a result with which we express ourselves as dissatisfied. Thereupon our offensive beast of an opponent says, "Oh well, it is a Bogey five." If I were on the jury in a trial for murder, and it was proved that this provocation had been given, nothing should induce me to find the prisoner guilty. What more deadly insult can there be than to insinuate that we cannot form our own estimate of the score in which we ought to do a hole; that we have to be instructed on that point by a half a dozen old gentlemen sitting in committee and imagining what an imaginary old gentleman would do.

A form of consolation, which has a substratum of sense underlying it, is often expressed in the words, "Well, anyhow, I hit the ball." True, the ball is at the bottom of the deepest bunker on the course, and the hole is hopelessly lost, but still. In this case there is a distinction to be drawn as to the spirit in which we say the words. If we are merely arrogant, puffed up with the fact of hitting the ball farther than our opponent, although his ball is lying on the turf and ours in a bunker, then we are also silly, because the object of the game is to get into the hole in the smallest possible number of shots. If, on the other hand, we rejoice only because that cleanly hit shot gives promise of future shots, which shall be hit not only clean but straight, then we are being moderately sensible. On this second ground it is sometimes almost cheering to begin a match with a fine long hit in the direction of long-on. A long hook generally means that we are at any rate getting well through with the shot. When we have warmed to our work, and the early morning stiffness has disappeared, we may reasonably hope that the length and the follow-through will remain and the hook disappear. In the same way it is endurable to start a round with a long putt in which the ball races past the hole, far out of holing distance. It is bad if it is going to frighten us and make us short for the rest of the round. It is good if we accept it merely as evidence that we are doing that most difficult thing, hitting the ball a fine, free blow with the middle of the putter.

Doubtless all these are but the idlest fancies, and we should do well to cast them from us. But there are few who have the strength of mind to light their battles without some support, however illusory. There are at golf so many horrible things that we know are going to happen, and that do happen. There is the really appalling way in which history repeats itself in the matter of hazards. I do not know who originally remarked that "familiarity breeds contempt," but I do not believe he was a golfer. Rather does it too often breed an intolerable measure of respect. A year ago I spent a most delightful month at Ashdown Forest, and at the end of it I knew exactly what I was going to do at nearly every hole. I knew that I should push my first tee shot into the heather, and at the fourth hole hit my second far too gently and off the heel of the iron. At the dreaded "island" hole I should give a horrible lurch of my body, resulting either in an ineffectual sort fluff or else in a half-topped skimmer which raced far over the green. At the twelfth I should hit the ball beautifully clean, and my follow-through would be much admired by anybody seeing me from afar off, but the ball would fly away to the left with the accuracy of a homing pigeon, ultimately to repose in a particular patch of bracken. Finally, at the fifteenth, I should pitch just too far; the ball would run down the sloping green into a rut, while I called gods and men to witness that it was a grossly unfair shot. Much as I loved Ashdown, I began to long for a course where the doctrine of predestination should not oppress me quite so heavily: where to get into a hazard should be an unpleasant surprise instead of being merely part of a daily routine. It is, of course, a dreadful mistake to be a fatalist at golf, but it is one dreadfully difficult to avoid. Consider the case of our match with Jones, whom for some reason we are particularly anxious to beat. We are both on the green in the same number of strokes. Jones plays the odd; he makes an execrable putt and runs some three or four yards past the hole. We feel practically certain that we have only to get dead in the like in order to win the hole. Let our ball be within two feet of the hole, and we will bet anything in reason that Jones makes a most miserable attempt for the half. We play, and we do not lay our ball dead. We do not make such a vile putt as he did, but we are several feet away from the hole. Nobody could possibly give us that putt; certainly not Jones, who is an ungenerous fellow, and likes his pound of flesh. The worst of it is that *now* it is absolutely certain that he will hole his four-yard putt. We may shut our eyes and buoy ourselves up by murmuring *sotto voce*, "He is sure to miss it." The rattle of his ball against the tin will soon undeceive us; not that we ever really were deceived, the thing was and is a certainty. Moreover, a similar tragedy befalls us in respect to bunkers. Jones puts his ball into a bunker. "We've got you this time," we say to ourselves, and, removing the eye too impetuously, deposit the ball in the very identical bunker.

As we approach the bunker we observe that one ball is lying teed on a little pinnacle of sand; the other, what there is visible of it, is in a deep footmark in close proximity to a perpendicular black board. There is no need to inquire which ball is which. Of course, Jones is on the pinnacle. We knew he would be.

Golf is a horribly unforgiving game. We are told that "the cards never forgive," but the experience of a lamentable bridge player is that they are not half so relentless as golf clubs and balls. I was once upon a time playing in the semifinal of a certain handicap tournament.

Going to the last hole, which was an easy one, I was dormy one down; my opponent had to receive a stroke, and he hit a good tee shot. A more depressing predicament from my point of view could not be conceived. As we were walking up to our respective balls the enemy remarked that he hoped his favourite driver, which had some ailment or other, would hold out for the final. At those words the fire of hope, which had almost gone out, absolutely flared up in my breast. Surely the golfing fates could never forgive a speech that flouted them so impudently. Nor did they forgive, for the rash man's second shot went plump into a bunker, he took three putts on the green, and neither he nor his driver played any part in the final of that tournament.

PART V

ADDITIONAL
GOLF MUSINGS

IF I WERE A GOLF INSTRUCTOR

JEROME DUNSTAN TRAVERS

If I were a golf instructor it would be some little time before my pupil were allowed to go round the links. Starting with the wooden clubs, driver and brassie, I would have him learn each club separately. I would place him on the tee with a peck of golf balls beside him and a caddie on the fair green ahead to chase them. For an hour at a time I would instruct him in the art of driving alone, striving to correct his mistakes before they became habit, showing him how to grip his club, how to address the ball, how to follow through properly. At the end of an hour, if he were an apt pupil, he would know something about driving whereas, if he had devoted the time to play over the links with six different clubs, he would have learned nothing of value about any one of them.

Then I would take him out on the fair green, place a brassie in his hand and have him put in another hour learning how to use this club. I would explain to him the difference between a good brassie lie and a poor one, laying particular stress upon the fact that a poor lie usually means a poor shot and that one of the first things to learn about this club is when *not* to use it.

If, after an hour of driving and another hour of brassie play, the novice felt the need of something less strenuous, I would then have him devote another hour to putting. I would show him the proper stance and how to grip the club and at the end of his first long lesson he would know more about putting than the average beginner knows after he has played the entire course a dozen times with all the clubs.

In the same manner I would instruct him in the use of the cleek, mid-iron, and mashie, assigning from half an hour to an hour to each club, and when he had gained a fair working knowledge concerning the manipulation of these clubs and the driver, brassie and putter, I would turn him loose upon the links for an entire round of the eighteen holes. When, in response to different needs, he was compelled to play one club after another, each club would not be a comparative stranger but an old friend with which he was already familiar through hours of practice. I do not carry a cleek myself because I get better results with a driving iron, but I would not advise a novice to follow this example. Also, unlike many players, I do not use a spoon because I found that it shortened my game and that I was playing it when I should have relied upon the mid-iron.

I have laid particular stress upon the necessity for long practice with each club because it is difficult for a beginner to learn the game if he only plays eighteen holes once or twice a week and contents himself with that. Walter J. Travis, who learned to play golf after he was 35, is probably the most remarkable example of what can be accomplished by constant, patient, untiring practice. No man in America ever worked so hard to become a great golfer as he did, and as his reward he has won the amateur championship of the United States three times and the British amateur championship once. Furthermore, he is the only American amateur who ever succeeded in winning the British championship.

When Travis is "off his game" and is not driving, approaching, or putting as he should, he goes out on the links alone and plays with one club or another for hours, practicing the same shot over and over until he has recovered his very best form.

I have done the same thing myself on many occasions. I have played the same shot fifty times. I have putted for two hours at a stretch, placing my ball at varying distances from the hole, trying for short putts, long putts, up hill and down hill putts and putts across a side hill green where the ball must follow a crescent-like course if it is to be holed out or go "dead to the hole." During the afternoon round of my match against Harold H. Hilton, the British champion, at the national amateur championship on the Apawamis links in 1911, I had before me what my own club's champion declared was an "impossible" putt. Of the two thousand people following the match, most of those near the green no doubt shared his opinion. I was not very hopeful myself. My ball was at least twenty feet from the hole, the green was of the undulating, billowy type and it was a down hill putt.

Remembering the old adage, "Never up, never in," I struck the ball a bit too hard, but it raced down the green as if drawn by a magnet, struck the opposite side of the cup, leaped into the air an inch or two and dropped safely into the hole.

"If you hadn't hit the hole exactly square, Travers, you would have been out of bounds," was Oswald Kirkby's humorous description of the shot after the game.

A putt of this sort is usually called a "lucky" putt, and no doubt there is a certain element of luck about it. Yet hours and hours of practice produced the skill and judgment that sank that "impossible" putt.

When I was playing for the championship at Wheaton in 1912, I got into a very high and formidable bunker on an approach shot. The ball was at the very base of the bunker, close up, and the situation was such a difficult one that I had little hope of getting over with one shot. However, I took my mashie niblick, got well under the ball with it and much to my gratification the ball crawled up the steep side of the bunker, moved slowly across its top, struck the putting green, and rolled up dead to the hole. A putt gave me a four and captured the hole.

Many a time I have thrown a dozen balls into a bunker and practiced for an hour endeavoring to discover the most successful method of getting out of this difficult hazard. As in the case of the "impossible" putt, the Chicago bunker shot was successful because hours of faithful study had been devoted to learning the way to do it.

Many beginners do a great deal of unnecessary fussing about their clubs, discarding this one or that one as of no value when lack of skill and proper practice are more responsible for bad play than lack of merit in the clubs. A novice should buy good clubs and should be largely guided in their selection by a capable professional or amateur. Clubs with whippy shafts are to be avoided and the purchase of every new freak club that is placed on the market is a foolish expenditure of money.

In taking up the game the beginner should familiarize himself thoroughly with the etiquette and the rules. Playing the wrong ball, failing to let the pair behind go through when his ball is lost, playing into the pair ahead, or upon the putting green before they have holed out, talking or moving about when an opponent is making a shot, cutting across the course and endeavoring to get in ahead of other players who are going round the entire links—these and other simple infractions of rules and etiquette make the careless beginner unpopular and are the cause of many unpleasant experiences.

Not long ago I heard of a very prominent man who made all sorts of fun of golf and for years refused to try to play. It was a simple, foolish, easy game, he said, and he knew it would not interest him. Finally a friend dragged him to the links, teed a ball for him and told him to drive. When he had struck four times at the ball without even touching it, he became so exasperated that he bought a set of clubs that very day and started with determination to conquer the little white ball.

A month later the friend who had dragged him to the links met him hurrying toward the golf club although his left arm was in a sling.

"What are you going to do?" asked the friend.

"Oh, I broke my arm," was the enthusiastic reply, "but I'm going down to play with one hand!"

TongRo Images/Thinkstock

STORIES OF PROPER GOLF ETIQUETTE

JOSEPH WALKER McSPADDEN, Ed.

In connection with the game of golf there are certain points of etiquette which, though not of such a nature as to fall within the jurisdiction of written law, are pretty accurately defined by the sanction of custom. Breach of these observances is not punished by the loss of the hole or of a stroke, but rather by the loss of social status in the golfing world. You do not exact an immediate penalty from him who thus outrages *les convenances;* but in your heart of hearts you propose to yourself the severest of all forms of punishment,—never to play with him again.

Of all delinquents against the unwritten code, the grossest offender is perhaps he who stands over you, with, triumph spiced with derision, as you labor in a bunker, and aggressively counts your score aloud. The act of coming ostentatiously out of his own path to look at you is, of itself, almost on the boundary line between good and bad form. Apart from the indecent gloating over your misfortunes which such conduct on his part would seem to imply, it also contains the infinitely more offensive suggestion of a suspicion of your possible unfair dealing when shielded by the bunker's cliff from his espionage. But when he goes the length of audibly counting up your unhappy efforts/ with undisguised satisfaction as the sum increases, you can scarcely look upon it otherwise than as an impugnment either of your arithmetic or of your honesty.

There are, indeed, certain circumstances which may almost, in a medal competition, justify such a proceeding; for in a medal competition, in the absence of markers, each player is responsible for the correctness of the score, as returned, of the other, and, setting the question of honesty—as it is to be hoped we may—on one side, there are medal-players whose arithmetic, as a matter of fact, is *not* above suspicion. It is, moreover, far more difficult than is generally recognized to keep exact account of the strokes at those unfortunate holes where the total approaches the two figures. It is scarcely possible for a man to be in honest doubt as to whether he has played four strokes or five; but it is a very different thing where a question arises as to whether he has played eight or nine. One among so many is a small item easily forgotten. Nevertheless, unless the player for whom one is scoring is known to be what is called a "bad counter"—which not a few perfectly honorable gentlemen and golfers unquestionably are—there is no justification for the *audible* enumeration, one by one, of his strokes. One's duty to one's neighbor—in this case, to all the others engaged in the competition—can be adequately performed, without offense to the sufferer, by silently marking off on the card each stroke as it is played. Should the player think fit to contest the accuracy of this marking, each stroke may for the future be audibly impressed upon him, as it is played, without any regard to the sufferings which he will then have deservedly brought upon himself.

But all such espionage can only be justified by a sense of your responsibility to the other competitors. In a match there is no conceivable excuse for it. If it be a friendly match, to start with, it cannot long continue such if either subject the other to such indignities; and if it be a big match, there will be a sufficient number of onlookers to check any possible inaccuracy of scoring. If you have not faith in a man's scoring, do not play with him; and if you play with a man, do not act in such a way as to suggest that you are suspicious.

But there is a subtler crime than that of miscounting his score, of which a man may be, and of which many often are, guilty in a bunker; and it is a crime which again raises another delicate point of etiquette. He may be touching the sand with his iron. Every golfer knows the rule that you must not touch sand in a bunker, with the club, as you address yourself to the ball—that you must not rest the club-head behind the ball. Almost every golfer does so, however, accidentally, now and again, and some do it habitually. Etiquette has its word to say, not about the touching of the sand, which is a distinct breach of a hard-and-fast rule of the game, but about the tempering justice with mercy in bringing the criminal to account. Let us first see what the custom is, in regard to breach of this rule, and let us then see what the custom ought to be.

With the first class, of those who touch sand accidentally, occasionally, the custom certainly is to continue playing on, lightheartedly, as if they were all unconscious of the rule and of their breach of it. And no one thinks of claiming the stroke as a foul one. Why?—because it is the custom not to claim it, and in the presence of this custom the man who claimed his rights, under the rule, would be regarded as a sharp practitioner. There are, doubtless, also many cases in which the player is himself quite unconscious of having touched the sand; he will indignantly deny having done so, and in the absence of a referee the just claim results in nothing but mutual irritation.

Next, what is the custom with regard to the habitual touchers of the sand? The first two offenses probably go unnoticed. At the third they are possibly cautioned. At the fourth a threat is made to claim the hole. Probably this is about as often as their opponent will have seen their bunker performances, and when the round is over they will tell all their friends what an ungentlemanly fellow their late opponent is, and will probably meet with a great amount of sympathy!

Altogether there is no so-called petty infringement of the rules about which there is so much custom-sanctioned laxity as in the matter of touching sand, and we greatly need that some of our leading golfers should inaugurate a change in that particular. But there are certain other little points wherein a laxity of custom sometimes appears, where a rigid application of the rules of golf would make the game far pleasanter, and far less liable to those little roughnesses of temper which at times crop up in the course of matches.

For instance, it will sometimes happen that, in spite of a player's utmost carefulness in the removal of loose sticks and straws from the neighborhood of his ball, the latter will roll ever so little from its place. This, by clearly expressed rules of the game, counts against him; but there are those who, with full knowledge of the rule, instead of manfully paying the penalty, will appeal to you with a question as to "whether you want them to count that?"

This in itself is a distinct breach of etiquette, for it throws you who are innocent into a position in which a question of etiquette upon your side arises. Of course the proper and honest answer is "Yes," because that is the answer given by the rules of golf, and because, at the moment, you are supposed to be playing golf. But it is just this latter fact that, your opponent does not seem to realize; and if you are too authoritative in pointing it out to him it is not impossible, in consequence of the laxity on these points introduced by custom, that he may, however absurdly, regard himself as rather hardly treated by your assertion of your rights. The very fact of his asking the question indeed is a suggestion that he will so regard it. What are you to say? Is the point at issue, and your respect for your own strength of mind, of sufficient value to compensate for the chance of losing your opponent's good opinion?

These are questions which each will answer according to his temperament; but our great point is that such questions ought never to arise. Nor would they ever arise but for the reprehensible laxity in the application of the rules of the game, which thus gives openings for those very unpleasantnesses which their lax interpretation was presumably intended to avert. Let the rules be applied in their proper strictness; let us play golf according to the rules of golf, and in the strict game we shall find freedom from all such annoyance.

Broadly speaking, there is no breach of true etiquette in enforcing rules; the breaches of etiquette consist, for the most part, in the breaches of the rules.

There are certainly a good many golfers who consider themselves grossly ill-treated if they are asked to hole out a short putt; and, singularly enough, it is just those very golfers who most often justify the request, by missing the short putt, who are most indignant at it. You have a perfect right to ask a golfer to hole out every single putt; and no golfer ought to take offense at your so asking him. There are, of course, putts which it is positively vexatious to ask the veriest duffer to hole. Common sense ought, and does, draw a fair line in the matter. Perhaps one of the most offensive of all breaches of etiquette is committed by him who, after missing one of these little putts, says to his opponent, air-ily, "Oh, I thought you'd have given me that!" It is a remark one is very apt to make in the irritation of the moment, and it is a remark which it well becomes the opponent, in the magnanimity of his triumph, to forgive; but we can only excuse it to ourselves in proportion as we feel a shameful repentance for it afterwards.

It is impossible to frame rules which shall cover every possible contingency, and there should be, between gentlemen, a certain amount of give and take, such as will smooth off the rough edges of injustice or absurdity which in exceptional circumstances appear under the strict letter of the law. In a match played a few years back, a dog seized the ball of one of the players, as it rolled over the putting-green, and bore it off into a carriage which was standing near. According to the then law it was incumbent on the player to play the ball out of the carriage, where the dog had deposited it. This, surely, was one of those exceptional cases wherein the courtesy of the opponent might have suggested a fairer alternative to the, in this case, unjust requirement of the generally fair rule.

Possibly next upon the little list of these delinquents against the unwritten code of golf etiquette comes he who complains outrageously of the good luck which falls to his opponent's share. We all know that there is a great deal of luck in the game; but we also know, in moments of sober reflection, that on the whole the balance of luck, good or bad, for us or against us, hangs very nearly even. Complaints of one's own bad luck are in infinitely bad taste. But this class of offense is nothing compared with aggressive outcries against the good fortune of an opponent. If circumstances *can* aggravate a sin so intrinsically evil, it is even more criminal to complain of the good luck that befalls him with whom you are partnered in a scoring competition than your antagonist in a hand-to-hand match. Generally recognized etiquette goes so far as a kind sympathy and interest in the efforts of your partner for the medal round. A community of trials make you feel in a measure dependent upon each other like fellow knights-errant in a world peopled with monsters in the shape of all the other competitors. Usually a man is generous enough to feel that, if he does not himself win, he would prefer the victory of his partner to that of any other; and when his own fortunes have become desperate, he will lend that partner all the comfort of his sympathy and moral support. This is less the result of the prospect of any little reflected glory than of a genuine fellow-feeling for one passing through the same vale of bunkers as oneself.

The laws of etiquette prescribe for us a certain line of conduct not only to our partner in a foursome, and to our antagonist in a single, but also to our other neighbors on the golf links. One of the first things that the young golfer has to learn is that the prime requisitions for good golf generally are silence and immobility. If he be not careful to preserve these conditions, he will render good golf an impossibility not only within the circle of his own match, but also for the moment with any other of the matches which his own may chance to meet. He who rushes noisily up to a match, demanding with loud geniality "how you stand," irrespective of whether anyone is playing a stroke at the moment, is a nuisance who ought to be abolished from the golf links. At least there is no law of etiquette which should restrain the terms in which such an one should be answered. It seems scarcely necessary to state so universally observed a maxim as that it is your duty to stand perfectly motionless and silent while another is playing. Any breach of this first law of golfing etiquette is, happily, of rare occurrence. Offenses are of that class with which we determine "never to play again." But scarcely less obnoxious than the talker or the walker is he who rushes on wildly after his own ball as soon as he has struck it, partially obstructing our line of aim, and obviously only coming to a halt, at the moment at which we deliver our stroke, out of compulsory respect to the barest exigencies of golfing courtesy.

The proper course of proceeding is this: to drive off first, if it be your honor, and then to stand clear of the teeing ground, behind your adversary's back. Do not stand close enough to him to annoy him, wherever you stand, and do not stand "behind his eye," as it is called—that is, in a line which would be a prolongation, backward, of the line of flight of the ball he is about to drive. Find out where he prefers you to stand, if he be a nervous player; but it is a safe rule to stand, motionless, behind his back. There are men in the golfing world—gentlemen, in some respects—who appear to be not above taking the petty advantage which annoyance to an opponent, caused by neglect of these little points, brings. It is not much use writing on points of etiquette for such as these; but there are also a very large number of golfers who, blessed with prosaic nervous systems themselves, thoughtlessly do not appreciate that others can be affected by the trifles of their surroundings. It is to these that one may say a word which may be gratefully received. They should bear in mind that to be forced to make a complaint upon any one of these trifling conditions is no less trying to a man of finely strung nerves than is the very circumstance of which he complains. Seek, then, to avoid giving him reason for making the complaint.

If it be your opponent's honor, it is far better that you should allow him to drive off from the tee before you think of teeing your own ball. Most teeing places are rather circumscribed, and even if you do not absolutely put down your ball upon its little eminence before your opponent has played, you are very apt to bother him as you crawl about the ground looking for the most likely spot. Let him have his shot in peace, and you may fairly expect him to show you equal courtesy in the happy event of your regaining the honor.

After all, what is courtesy but unselfishness and consideration of others? How grossly then does not he offend against every dictate of courtesy who scalps up the turf with his heavy iron, and leaves the "divot" lying, an unsightly clod of earth, upon the sward! What shall we do to such as he, as playing after him, our ball finds its way into the poor dumb mouth of a wound which he has thus left gaping, to call down upon him the vengeance of gods and men? In vain we print upon our rules that "it is the first duty of every golfer to replace, or see replaced, turf cut out in the act of playing"—in vain we post up the ever-forgotten truism that "golf is not agriculture," with or without the addendum suggested by some cynical landlord—"though both are games of chance." No—in spite of all our efforts, the scalps and divots still lie unsightly on the links, and "nobody seems one penny the worse," though we curse with bell and book and niblick the sacrilegious villain who left the raw, gaping wound on the sacred soil. No golfer is worthy of the name who does not put back his divot. It is no trouble, and is indeed rather amusing, as we watch how, like a piece of a Chinese puzzle, the divot fits back accurately into the chasm from which it was carved. A divot well replaced is, in most conditions of the ground, as a divot that has never been cut.

Under the rules of golf, no player is allowed to drive from the tee until both the sides in the match immediately in front of him have played their respective second strokes. This prohibition contains the obvious implication that it is permissible to drive off the tee-shot the moment after the second shots of the preceding parties are struck. It is an implication which can scarcely be carried to its logical conclusion in practice without danger to life and limb. It is modified by the maxims of etiquette. Under the latest dispensation, this rule has been altered, or, rather, added to, so that it now runs—until those in front shall have played their second shots and got out of range. So that the lives of obese, short-driving old gentlemen are now safe-guarded by law. "Out of range " is strictly a relative measurement. The worm, in the shape of the long driver, terribly kept back, will turn—will turn to and drive into the old and the feeble and the obese, until the latter observing too late the maxim which etiquette and courtesy should have suggested to him without the emphatic hints of the long driver, allows his rapidly traveling pursuer to go before.

But this is the sort of hint which the long driver is only justified in administering under special circumstances—that is to say, where the unwarrantable delay is the fault, solely and entirely, of those parties immediately in front of him whom his artillery will reach. If these parties, on the other hand, are themselves being delayed, it is of course at once a breach both of rules and of etiquette to drive before they are "out of range;" On a crowded green, moreover, it is not of the slightest use passing one couple, to be immediately kept back as badly as ever by the couple again in front.

But these hints should never be administered by the long driver unless the delay has really been of most unconscionable length, often repeated. They should rather be regarded as outbursts of temper, which can be pardoned in proportion as they are repented of. Under any other circumstances, save, perhaps, where a ball has been lost, it is entirely inexcusable to drive into a party along the green, on the putting-green, or before they have played their seconds. Where the parties behind have infringed this great commandment more than once during a round, any means combining due insistence on your rights with adequate courtesy to the offenders seem beyond the suggestions of human ingenuity. Perhaps it may be deemed, however, that players thus offending have forfeited all claim to courteous dealing.

With regard to standing at the hole, the proper etiquette is that the caddie of the player who is nearer to the hole shall go to it, for it is in favor of the striker to play with the chance of hitting the stick; the striker, therefore, should always wait before addressing the ball to give his adversary's caddie a reasonable chance of taking out the flag, but it is a gross breach of etiquette to send on a caddie for this purpose after the player has commenced his "addresses."

Spectators should always remember what is due to the players—silence and attention, if they are to pay the honor of watching the game at all. But it is no less true that a duty of courtesy is owed by the players to those who pay them the compliment of being interested in their performance. Moreover, golf links are commonly public places. The spectator has as good a right there as the most finished golfer, and the latter should not forget that if the former defer to the delicate requirements of his nervous system, it is but an act of courtesy, and should be received with the courteous acknowledgment due to such.

Modesty is a virtue, but the mock modesty, the pride which apes humility, was an occasion of much mirth to Satan; and it is a breach, rather than an observance, of etiquette, and even of honesty, so to underrate your game as to gain an unfair advantage in arranging the conditions of a match. Do not tell a player whom you have defeated that he would be sure to beat you next time. He may think so, but he will not believe that you do, and the remark partakes of the nature of an insult to his understanding.

THE STORY OF LUCK IN GOLF

GARDEN G. SMITH

There can be no question that there is a deal of luck in golf. The extraordinary number of ways in which a badly hit ball can arrive, or the extraordinary number of badly hit balls which do arrive at a given spot, owing to the accidents of the ground, their own inherent eccentricity, and in a manner totally opposed to the intention of the striker, is sufficient proof of the fact. How often the missed iron shot scuffles over or through a bunker and finally rests near the hole. How many a topped putt lands up dead, to the silent joy of its perpetrator and the ill-concealed rage and contempt of his opponent! In addition, the most unfair treatment is often meted out to perfectly played strokes. How frequently a well hit ball despatched on the proper line and with the requisite force to reach the green, is kicked off on alighting either to right or left of the green, how often it drops dead without rolling, or, getting a downward fall, shoots forward over it, and lands in a hazard! This aggravating uncertainty as to what is to be the fate of even the best played strokes, has induced a pessimistic golfing friend to maintain that there is only bad luck at golf, and that good luck, inasmuch as it is only compensatory, and that to the smallest degree, ought not to be considered. Certainly the irritation provoked by certain kinds of bad luck at golf will almost justify this contention, but whether it be called good or bad the game is undoubtedly full of luck, and it is the precise mingling of chance and skill of which it is compound, the kind of pleasing anxiety that accompanies every stroke, that makes up much of the fascination of golf.

Nearly all golfers are superstitious, for golf in its ever changing fortunes is an epitome of life. Here the race is not always to the swift, nor the battle to the strong, and the wicked too often flourishes like a green bay tree. It is the constant presentation of these painful facts that makes the game so difficult. He who thinks the fates are against him will do nothing well in golf, any more than in life. The man who has luck will at once gain courage, and attempt, and succeed at, things which with luck against him he would never have dreamt of essaying.

No doubt the best players are those who, like the average professional, have but little imagination, and if they have any superstition in their natures are not so subtly-minded as to apply it to golf. The writer does not know a single professional who ever regarded himself habitually as unlucky, though he may have complained about his luck on individual occasions. Many amateur players, on the other hand, are always complaining about their bad luck. They believe that they are born under an unlucky star, and are constantly on the outlook for the finger of destiny. This attitude of mind has, of course, a fatal effect on their game, both positively and negatively. For while it robs the golfer who adopts it of all courageous initiative, his game assumes a weak and pusillanimous character, that seems almost to invite the very thunderbolt which he lives in dread of.

To deserve good luck is the sure way, in the long run, to command it. The best player has always the best luck. To be continually whining at the decrees of destiny is to justify their rigorous application to oneself.

It must not be forgotten that the golfer who has got this fatalistic tendency can never be brought to see that any of his misfortunes are the result of his own bad play. It is just his cursed luck. Conversely, the good play of his opponent is only the result of his superior luck. No more disagreeable or depressing partner than the fatalist can be found. His only comments on the game are remarks drawing attention to the marvellous luck that you enjoy, in contrast to the bad luck that invariably pursues him. It is no use getting irritated with such a player. A good plan is to agree and sympathize with him cordially in every particular. This will have an admirable effect in preserving your own game and temper, and may suggest to your opponent, as the game goes on, and if he has any sense of humor, that he is behaving very absurdly.

This habit of blaming luck at golf for all his mistakes, breeds in the golfer all other kinds of absurdities. The player who exclaimed, "Cupped again!" when he topped his tee shot, is a good instance of the disastrous effects of this habit of mind. If he cannot by any possibility set down his bad play to his luck, he will invent all manner of other excuses to account for it. There is a good story told of a St. Andrews player who, having missed a putt, in dead silence, within a foot of the hole, immediately remarked: "Ah, somebody must have moved."

But these distressing symptoms are only, after all, one effect which the existence of luck in golf produces on its votaries. The fatalist elects to suffer the stings and arrows of outrageous fortune, but there is another order of mind less passive and humble which takes arms against the siege of troubles and seeks, by opposing, to end them. There are men whose proud and impatient spirits cannot brook the predominance of matter over mind, which the game of golf so often exemplifies. In "fractured club and cloven ball," in "foozled drives and putts not in," they see not, like their meek brethren, the finger of fate. These Ajaxes defy the lightning, and with their eyes in a fine frenzy rolling, give tongue to the anger which consumes them. When one has the misfortune to play against "the man with a temper," much care has to be exercised to avoid risk of offence, for, like the fatalist, he is always searching for occasions, and goes about like a roaring lion seeking whom he may devour. If, however, his temper has been aroused, the very greatest tact and knowledge of human nature are necessary if one is to attempt to soothe his savage breast. "Touch not the cat without the glove." But the devastating and demoralizing effect of the golfing temper on even the finest natures is so terrible, that it is extremely dangerous to say anything, however apparently sympathetic, and the patient is much better left severely alone till the paroxysm has passed. The breaking of the club wherewith the fatal stroke has been delivered is a common symptom in these cases, and usually this sacrifice is less an act of reprisal on the club itself, than a solemn protest and testimony against the outrageous injustice of which the golfer conceives himself the victim, and a necessary step towards the rehabilitation of his mind. The angry golfer also frequently relieves his pent-up feelings, by hurling his club far from him, after the ball. This is an extremely dangerous habit, as in his anger the golfer is frequently careless of the direction in which it flies, and his partner will do well to keep an eye on his movements.

Like the "fatalist," "the man with a temper," had better be avoided whenever possible. No pleasurable game is to be had in such company, and their peculiar habits are extremely infectious.

The well-balanced mind will not be unhinged by the untoward chances of golf. The wise golfer recognizes that but for these alterations of luck, the game would cease to amuse or charm, and if he has more than his share of bad luck, or bad play today, he says nothing about it, being sure that tomorrow things will go better for him. To go on inventing reasons for one's bad play is fatal to improvement, and can only annoy and irritate your partner. "Deeds, not words," is the true golfer's motto. "In my opeenion," said a wise old caddie, "A man sud niver mak excuses for hissel at gowf. It's like being disrespectfu' to Providence. Gowfers sud jist tak things as they come and be contentit. In my opeenion some fowks like to shaw off a bit, by bletherin' aboot their bad play."

"Be not thy tongue thine own shame's orator,
Look sweet, speak fair."

Jim Epler

THE STORY BEHIND TIGER WOODS' NICKNAME

MATTHEW SILVERMAN

This was a far more innocent question before the Tiger Woods extra marital revelations, but let's just stick to the origin of the name of the world's most famous golfer and the fact that if your name was Eldrick Tont Woods, you would embrace a nickname, too.

Earl Woods gave his son the nickname Tiger at a young age, just as he introduced the boy to golf not long after he could walk. Earl Woods retired as a Lieutenant Colonel, serving in the U.S. Army Special Forces during the Vietnam War. He served as advisor to South Vietnamese Colonel Vuong Dang Phong, whom Earl nicknamed Tiger. Earl credited the original Tiger—or Tiger One—with saving his life from both sniper and viper in the Vietnamese jungle. The two men lost touch after 1971, but Earl vowed if he ever had a son he would call him Tiger.

Though Earl tried to find out what happened to the original Tiger, it was not until Tiger Woods became a golf superstar and international celebrity that the mystery was unraveled. *Golf Digest* reporter Tom Callahan went to Vietnam in 1996 to find out what happened to Tiger One. Callahan used the ruse of covering the 1996 opening of Nick Faldo's golf course in Ho Chi Mihn City, formerly Saigon, to launch his search. Callahan got nowhere, and was reprimanded by the Vietnamese ministry for not going through proper channels. While playing at Faldo's course, however, a businessman he met suggested placing an advertisement in Vietnamese-American newspapers asking for information. Callahan soon learned what happened to the original Tiger.

Tiger One surrendered to the Communists on June 15, 1975—six months before Tiger Woods was born. The colonel died in a re-education camp in 1976, though his family did not learn what happened to him for a full decade. Callahan also learned that Phong's widow, who had nine children, was living in Tacoma, Washington. She was completely unaware of who Tiger Woods was. A meeting was arranged in California between the families of the two Tigers: the colonel's widow and two of her children, plus Earl, Tiger, and Tiger's mother, Kultilda, whom Earl had met while in the service in Thailand.

Another Tiger Woods nickname, Urkel—after the quintessential nerdy kid on the 1990s show *Family Matters*—fell by the wayside by the time he left Stanford University to turn pro. But another, happier nickname stuck with him. Earl Woods often called his son Sam as a boy—"because you look like a Sam." A year after Earl Woods died of cancer in 2006, a daughter, Sam Alexis Woods, was born.

onbekend

BOBBY JONES AND THE STORY BEHIND HIS GOLF COURSE

DAVID BARRETT

Although they had social status and lived comfortably, neither Jones nor his father were rich, and it cost money to compete as an amateur, especially when overseas trips were involved. Jones's grandfather, the original Robert Tyre Jones (Bobby's father was christened Robert Purdemus Jones), was a wealthy textile-mill owner, but Bobby didn't want to lean on him too heavily for support.

So Bobby's weariness of competition dovetailed with his new-found ability to make big money from the game. He didn't have to play professionally to reap the rewards. All he had to do was stop competing as an amateur, which he wanted to do anyway. With two children and a third (and last) on the way at his time of retirement, money was an important consideration. Jones's biographer Stephen R. Lowe writes that the best estimate is that Jones made at least $250,000 from the movie deal (that's about $3.9 million in 2012 dollars).

That's not all. Jones also signed with A.G. Spalding & Brothers to design a "Robt. T. Jones Jr." line of woods and irons, and a copy of his "Calamity Jane" putter. Jones was heavily involved in the design—he wasn't the type to merely put his name on things—and the irons, in particular, were hugely successful. Not only did they have steel shafts (which Jones had never employed during his competitive career but were becoming *de rigueur),* they were among the first perfectly matched sets, and among the first to be numbered one through nine instead of labeled with the old names (mashie, niblick, etc.).

Jones's other main post-retirement venture wasn't a money maker. In fact, it was a money drainer. But it was something dear to his heart. In the late 1920s, he began to dream of forming his own golf club and being involved in designing an "ideal" course that would be the greatest in the South.

He had shared that vision with his friend Clifford Roberts. No sooner had Jones retired than the eager Roberts approached him with a proposal to make that dream a reality.

Jones and Roberts met in about 1925 through a mutual acquaintance, Walton H. Marshall, manager of the Vanderbilt hotels, including the flagship Vanderbilt Hotel in New York and the Bon Air-Vanderbilt in Augusta.

Roberts had set out for New York City in 1918 at the age of 24, leaving his life in the Midwest behind and determined to make his fortune. World War I intervened, and Roberts did his training at Camp Hancock in Augusta—his first connection with the place—before serving in France, mostly after the armistice. Back in New York in 1919, Roberts slowly made his way in the world of investment banking and the stock market. The details of his work in this time aren't clear, but he did well enough to move in high circles even though not particularly wealthy himself.

Roberts joined Knollwood Country Club north of New York City, where he met Marshall. In addition to golf, which Roberts had learned to play during a sojourn in California in his formative years, he and Marshall bonded over bridge and were fellow members of a bridge club in the city.

Jones knew Marshall because he and his father had stayed at the Bon Air-Vanderbilt when visiting Augusta. On a visit to New York during the 1920s, possibly when Jones played an exhibition match at Knollwood, Marshall introduced Bobby to Cliff.

Roberts later wrote about being in a group commiserating with Jones over his loss to George Von Elm in the 1926 U.S. Amateur at Baltusrol in New Jersey. Like nearly everyone, Roberts was a great admirer of Jones. But Roberts had a particular fascination with great men, and a particular ability to get close to them and make himself useful (as later exhibited with President Dwight D. Eisenhower). At some point, Jones told Roberts of his desire to form a club, and when Bobby retired, Cliff sprang into action.

Augusta in those days was a winter resort, favored by those from the Northeast who didn't want to take the longer train ride to Florida. Roberts had made some winter trips to Augusta in the 1920s, and he determined that it would be an ideal site for Jones's club.

Importantly, it had an average high temperature in the winter about five degrees warmer than Atlanta because of its lower elevation. And Augusta's status as a winter resort provided a base of wealthy North-easterners who could be the foundation of a national membership, which is what Jones envisioned.

When Roberts took the idea to Jones in the fall of 1930, Bobby heartily concurred with placing his club in Augusta, as he later expounded on in his book *Golf Is My Game.*

"Living in Atlanta only a short distance away, I had come to Augusta often over a period of years for friendly golf and an occasional charity match [and also the 1930 Southeastern Open]," Jones wrote. "I had always been impressed by the fact that, especially during the winter season, golf courses around Augusta were considerably better conditioned than courses near Atlanta, and since at that time we were doomed to coarse Bermuda grass for putting greens in the summer, it was in winter golf that our best hope lay."

Jones's conception of the ideal golf course he wanted to build included fast, firm greens, which he felt could better be achieved in Augusta.

Also, "Cliff and I had a number of friends among the permanent and winter residents [of Augusta] who could be counted on to form a nucleus around which to build our club. I felt that the financing of such a project would be infinitely more likely to succeed in Augusta than Atlanta."

Roberts also cited a desire for privacy that Jones could achieve better outside his hometown, where it was said that even his casual rounds drew spectators. Jones didn't mention this in his list of reasons for choosing Augusta, and it doesn't really ring true. Every single one of Jones's visits to Augusta was considered a special event and announced in advance in the *Augusta Chronicle.* By comparison, casual rounds in Atlanta would have been easier to keep unpublicized.

But Jones did have a vision of Augusta National as a very private, very exclusive club.

"Our aim was to develop a golf course and a retreat of such nature, and of such excellence," he wrote, "that men of some means and devoted to the game of golf might find the club worthwhile as an extra luxury where they might visit and play with kindred spirits from other parts of the nation."

The clincher was the piece of property that Roberts found. Or, actually, that Roberts's Augusta friend, Thomas Barrett, suggested. Barrett, the vice president of the Bon Air-Vanderbilt, knew just the place—Fruitland, a former plant nursery that had been considered a few years earlier as the site of a new resort hotel and golf course. In November 1930, Barrett, Roberts, and Jones gathered to have a look at the property.

"When I walked out on the grass terrace under the big trees behind the house and looked down over the property, the experience was unforgettable," Jones wrote in 1959 in *Golf Is My Game*. "It seemed that this land had been lying here for years just waiting for someone to lay a golf course upon it. Indeed, it even looked as though it were already a golf course, and I am sure that one standing today where I stood on this first visit . . . sees the property almost exactly as I saw it then."

Jones quickly agreed that this was the place. He told Roberts to arrange the financial backing to purchase the property. In February 1931, Jones headed to California to shoot his film shorts while Roberts set about securing the land that would become Augusta National Golf Club.

Zedcor Wholly Owned

THE STORY OF HOW I TRADED IN MY SHAFT

HAROLD HORSFALL HILTON

Occasionally a player who is in possession of one of these weird, impossible-looking clubs is convinced by some well-meaning friend that this old shaft of his is "done for" and that it would be wise for him to have a new shaft put in the club. It invariably happens that it was an ill day for the possessor of the club when he listened to this well-meaning advice as it is seldom, very seldom indeed, that one can get a new shaft put into an iron club that will prove as reliable or serviceable as the old and trusted friend.

I once had a vivid experience of the truth of this statement. I had an iron club with which I played all manner of shots, a species of "maid of all work" which seldom let me down. A day came when I thought that the shaft was becoming a little past its best, and in the belief that the merit of the club lay in the head I had no hesitation in having the original shaft taken out and a new one put in. The result was not at all happy, and in consequence I decided to have the old shaft resurrected, but unfortunately it could not be found; it had disappeared from the club-maker's shop, as so many apparently worthless shafts do. Well, I tried another new shaft in that head and still another until no less than eight new shafts had been fastened into that head, but not in one single instance did the combination prove as satisfactory as the original one which I had so rudely severed.

Eventually I gave that iron head away in disgust, and the man I gave it to promptly allied it to an old shaft he had lying by, and he told me some three years afterward that never in his life had he had an iron club to equal it. It was just the question of glorious chance; I had thrown a prize away and then drawn eight blanks; he had found another prize at the first attempt. But this has been my experience all through my career, and once a player is in possession of an iron club which suits him and has done him real good service he should not tamper with it, however crooked or bent the shaft may have become, and moreover should not give it away, as he may live to repent the day. A good iron club is of more value than half a dozen good wooden clubs, as the latter are not at all difficult to replace; an iron club always is.

PROBLEMS OF HANDICAPPING: THE STORY

BERNARD DARWIN

Some years ago now, before the war, I saw a friend of mine starting out to play a rather curious match. He was to play one-handed against the better ball of two opponents and to concede the odds of a stroke a hole. Not unnaturally, the game took some time. I had left the club house before it was over. Soon afterwards the hero of it left for India, and I have not seen him since. I am told that he is coming home this year, and the first question I am going to ask him when we meet is whether he won that match. At any rate, his two adversaries could not complain of his lack of generosity, for I have never before or since heard of handicapping on quite so prodigal a scale.

As a general rule it is otherwise. In the immense majority of games, judging by results, the giver of odds is not liberal enough. We have only to look at the records of match-play tournaments under handicap, especially at those of the Calcutta Cup and the Jubilee Vase at St. Andrews, to see how often the players who are handicapped at scratch or better, come through triumphant. In these days of strikes and revolutions it is remarkable that the down-trodden thousands with handicaps in double figures, have not asked for more and got it. They are either very easily dragooned or else a false pride prevents them from acknowledging that they are generally beaten. Perhaps they think that they ought to win if only they played what they are pleased to call their game. But in fact they don't play it, and they don't win.

It is probable that until the receiver of points receives palpably and absurdly too much, he will always have something the worst of it, because he will be to some extent crushed and overawed when he comes up against a golfer of a much higher class than himself. To be left far behind in point of length has a disturbing effect on all but the very level-headed. The stroke to be received seems to dwindle away to nothing. Yet of what enormous value is one stroke. I have played delightful matches against a distinguished naval officer who is neither very young nor very long but of an admirable steadiness. On the course where we play there is a large number of what are called two-shot holes—that is to say, holes such as I pretend to myself that I can' do in four. My opponent with his first drive just clears the bunker from the tee: with his second he is comfortably short of the bunker guarding the green: with his third he is on the green and he is a good putter. If I have to give him a stroke—and I give him too many—the outlook at these holes is a cheerless one for, whatever I pretend, I am by no means good enough to do them all in fours. It is only at the really long holes, or at the short ones when there are some nice deep bunkers, that I begin to pluck up hope against that terrible sailor. If all who receive strokes cut their coat according to their cloth, so judiciously and methodically, what a lot more matches they would win.

If the receiver of odds often grows frightened and regards his allowance as a mere drop in the ocean, there is also another form of fright that afflicts him at times. His strokes appear so numerous that he begins to reflect how foolish he will look if he cannot win with them. With a player in this mood, it is very nearly true that the more strokes you give him the more easily you will beat him. A little while ago there was a discussion on the handicapping question between two players, neither of them very good, of whom A. should officially have given B. about a third or a half. A. was contending that people did not give enough strokes: B. hotly denied it. "Very well," said A., "if you will play on the course I choose I will give you two strokes a hole." The match was made for a considerable stake. A., knowing that his one hope lay in the complete paralysis of B., took him to a course of steep hills and thick heather. Paralysis duly set in: B. topped his drives into the heather and could not get out again. He lost his match and his money, and has resolutely declined ever to play golf again.

I am sometimes inclined to wonder whether the receiver of points did not fare better when there was no pretence that handicapping was an exact science. Golfers either played level or, if odds must clearly be given, then they were given on broad general lines—four strokes as a minimum, and more usually a third or a half. The receiver would not accept charity in small doles or odd amounts, the giver thought shame to be too niggardly and huckstering. Today everything is systematic, and the better player gives three-quarters of the difference between the two handicaps and no more. If every one were rightly handicapped and the system were perfect, it would be all very well. As it is the giver of odds gets the best of it, unless he be one of those whose small vanities are treated sympathetically by committees and of whom it has been said that it costs them a hundred a year to remain scratch players.

It is often said that three-quarters of the difference is not a sufficient allowance. Sometimes it is and sometimes it is not, and there will always be an insuperable difficulty in having a hard and fast rule for all sorts of courses. At Westward Ho! for example, to take one of the hardest of all courses, it is generally not enough, and some years ago when a tournament was played there with the full difference in strokes given, the givers had none the worst of it. At Ranelagh, to take the opposite extreme, it would probably be too much. On a great many inland courses which are not very long or very difficult, it ought to be quite sufficient. Even so much depends on the season and the state of the course. Heavy ground will favour the stronger player. When winter comes, for instance, and the ball sits very close to the ground and declines to run, I am not nearly so frightened of that naval friend of mine. He may then be sometimes seen sadly practising, under the erroneous impression that he is out of form. When the ground is hard and dry in summer and two-shot holes degenerate into what the late Mr. "Teddy" Buckland called "a kick and a spit," the giving of strokes is hard work. The better player's hopes rest no longer on his length but rather on his power, if he has it, of making the ball stop on the keen, hard green. I do not know that there is any reliable remedy for this state of things as regards players who casually make up a match and do not know each other's games, but those who play habitually together need not be hidebound by rules and the rough and ready labels that are called handicaps. They can make their own matches best by the light of their own experience. If I know, by the half-crown test, that X. can give me a third, I am not going to be so foolish as to play him at four strokes because some old gentlemen sitting in a committee room have labelled him "scratch" and me "five." Unless one party be very grasping or the other very conceited, two friends can make their own matches far better than any one else can do it for them.

Besides the orthodox method of handicapping by strokes there are various others, the giving of bisques and holes up, and in three-ball matches there is the better and also the worse ball match. There are also all manner of what may be called "freak" handicaps. Of the matches made under freak handicaps it may be said that they are good fun to talk about and poor fun to play. More generally they are talked about and not played. I remember a lawn-tennis match that was projected between the late Mr. "Laurie" Doherty and a certain plump and dignified friend of his and mine. The articles of agreement provided that Mr. Doherty could only win a point by causing the ball to strike his opponent's person. The match was much chuckled over in advance and then wisely abandoned. It had served its purpose, and would have proved a disappointment. The golf match in which Alfred Toogood played blindfolded against a scratch player at Sunningdale created great interest beforehand and was the very dullest I ever watched in my life. The classic match in which one party was allowed three sudden "Boos" in his opponent's ear and won without using any of them, was probably, if ever played at all, ineffably gloomy and tiresome after the first hole.

There is a form of match sometimes played in which the two players start level. As soon as the stronger player becomes one up he gives a stroke at the next hole, and continues to give a stroke a hole as long as he is up. This may sound exciting. It does provide a close match but also a dull one, for the better man has no great incentive to bestir himself, since by doing so he only hangs a load of debt in the shape of strokes round his neck. The match usually comes to the last hole and there is some small scope for manœuvring, but it too much resembles an unpaced bicycle race in which the riders crawl round lap after lap, waiting for one frenzied burst in the last.

There is something a little freakish about bisques. They are perhaps "no gowf at a', just monkey tricks," but they often produce excellent matches and give scope for generalship. The receiver of bisques must study his adversary's temper and his own. To crowd on all sail and take bisques freely at the beginning of a match may be very good tactics against a player who is easily cowed, but it is of little avail against a dour man who plays better when he is down. We shall then very likely find ourselves stranded high and dry in the middle of the match with no bisques left, a horrid feeling of loneliness, and a strong probability that we shall have that hardest of tasks in all golf, namely, to play up against a decreasing lead.

Against the average opponent it is best if possible to hold a bisque or two, like so many swords of Damocles, over his head. Not only does this give him an unpleasant consciousness of outstanding liabilities but, if he is very imaginative, it keeps him guessing at every hole. Of course it is possible to cling too firmly to a bisque, and to be left with it unused at the end of the round can be as irritating as to be left with a too carefully treasured ace at bridge. I remember a match I once played at Aberdovey the thought of which even now sets me chortling joyfully. My opponent was two up with four holes to play and he had two bisques in hand. He could almost have had me beaten by that time: certainly he could have been dormy, but be enjoyed the refinement of cruelty of keeping me on tenterhooks, or perhaps he had vain visions of winning with a bisque or two unused. Now the fifteenth, sixteenth, and seventeenth at Aberdovey are holes of no great length. They have two features—trouble which may be calamitous, and greens in dells where a lucky approach shot may end very near the hole. The enemy found the trouble; he took six each to those three holes: I had the lucky approach shots and got three threes, and so he had to stand by impotent, his two bisques being no good to him till I became dormy one. He duly halved the match with them at the last hole, but could aught atone? My friend Christopher, if you chance to read this chapter, I am sure you will not have forgotten that match. I trust that something of bitterness, though not enough to endanger our friendship, may still rise at the remembrance.

Holes make rather an unsatisfactory handicap because they tend to a runaway match one way or the ocher. The man who gets first off the mark is too apt to win easily. If the receiver of holes adds to his lead in the first two or three, his pursuer grows fainthearted. If, on the other hand, he loses his lead at the beginning, he feels that he is caught in a trap from which there is no escape. If we were all perfectly level-headed and undaunted these things would not happen, but we are not and they do happen. Moreover, if the difference between the two players is considerable, it is rather a depressing game for the weaker. He may or may not win with his six holes of a start, but he feels that each hole is a match that he has to play on level terms and his hopes centre too exclusively round the other man's mistakes. True, we nearly always win by the enemy's mistakes. "He didn't beat me—I beat myself, sir, I beat myself," I remember hearing Taylor say once with formidable emphasis and fierce shaking of his head. All the same when we win, it is pleasanter to think that we have something to do with it.

Our handicaps are given us by handicapping committees, and the members of those committees are among the many virtuous and hard-working creatures in the world who get more kicks than halfpence for their pains. They have two classes of discontented people to deal with—those who think they have not enough strokes and those who think they have too many. On the whole our vanity is greater than our greed, and I am disposed to think that the second class is the larger of the two. At any rate it is the more difficult to deal with, for it contains a certain number of persons with whom some natural sympathy is felt. They are getting older and shorter and not so good as they were, and in conversation or even in match making they are not above acknowledging the fact, but they do not like to be publicly branded on the handicapping list. Those are often particularly susceptible who have after much pains and labour arrived at the scratch mark. Scratch is very far from meaning what it does in America or in the Ladies' Golf Union, but still it implies a certain honourable status. To be kicked upstairs from it is an unpleasant shock, and golfers who have once been scratch seem, like those "in reduced circumstances," to wear a certain air of faded gentility and "murmur a little sadly" of their past splendours. To have once been "one" is not the same thing at all.

Towards this very human infirmity committees as a rule exhibit considerable tenderness, for they argue very naturally, "If old So-and-so likes to lose his half-crowns, it's his own look-out. Why should we hurt his feelings?" Really there seems no reason why they should, unless they are impelled to it by a sense of duty, and an excessive sense of duty is one of the least attractive of human characteristics.

I should rather have said that there *was* no. reason why they should. Now that the question of limiting the entries to the Championship by handicaps has become an urgent one, there is a good reason for showing neither fear nor favour. At the present time the Championship committee is proposing to tackle the handicapping problem by trying to set up some kind of standard. It is a hard task, but if the thing can be well done it is worth doing.

It is, I think, admitted that the foundation must be the "par" score of the course for which the handicap is framed. It is not a perfect standard, because the par of St. Andrews and the par of a course where most of the holes can be reached with a drive and a pitch may be approximately the same; yet it takes a champion to accomplish the one and a very ordinary mortal on his "day out" to do the other. Still, in estimating the par it may be possible to make some allowance for difficulties besides considering merely the length of the holes, and the par score, if estimated by those who know their business, is as near a constant standard as we can get. On this par score it is proposed to found a scratch score which a scratch player, playing well, should be able to accomplish.

The real difficulty seems to me the question whether there must be a national handicap as well as the individual club handicap. At first sight it would seem a very cumbrous business and to some extent it is so, but without both handicaps there appears no way of dealing with the man who, playing nearly all his golf on one course, naturally plays his best game there and perhaps persists in winning the monthly medal. These small triumphs hardly affect his general position as a golfer. When he comes to play in good company on other courses he takes his normal and proper place. But on the dunghill of which he is the cock he is a formidable person, and his handicap must be reduced if his competitors are to have a fair chance, whether in match or medal play. It may be said that his handicap should not be reduced unless his performances justify it when judged by the scratch score; but if he continues to annex mustard-pots and half-crowns something has got to be done or there will be a revolution. The proper course, I suppose, would be to put up the handicaps of everybody else, but this is a laborious and unpopular course which would not work well in practice. Therefore I am reluctantly driven to the conclusion that, if anything be done at all, there ought to be two handicaps, a national and a club handicap, and without them I am afraid a general scheme would fail.

The Ladies' Golf Union is often and rightly held up to men as a model of business-like organisation, but even the ladies cannot altogether get on without two handicaps, and the L.G.U. handicap and the club handicap of one and the same player seem sometimes to differ very considerably. I doubt if men will ever come to having their handicaps quite so well regulated as those of the L.G.U., for men are either more lazy or less docile and will not constantly go to the trouble of returning a certain number of cards. At least I do not think they will, nor personally do I want them to, for after all handicaps were made for man and not man for his handicap.

THE STORY OF HOW I FOUND "THE SECRET"

J. DOUGLAS EDGAR

Looking back over a period of some years I feel I must have been like a man lost in a thick fog, walking round and round in a circle; or like a man looking for a secret door into an enchanted garden, many times getting near it, but never quite succeeding in finding it. In fact at one time I got so depressed and disgusted with my game that I very nearly abandoned it for farming. That I stuck to it was chiefly due to a sort of inward feeling that there must be in this game some secret or key which, once found, would put me on the right road for the desired destination. I was never lucky enough to be shown it, and it was only after continuous search that I eventually chanced upon it.

Having once found the secret I had no doubt that I was on the right road. Sometimes people have said to me, "Oh! it is all very fine for you, Edgar, you are a natural golfer." Good Heavens! Never was there a more *un*-natural golfer; certainly not you, reader, even if your handicap be 18. Some time or another I must have done everything wrong that it is possible to do. I have worked on countless different ideas, but like the explorer looking for gold have had, as it were, to sink numerous shafts before eventually "striking lucky." In fact my golfing career has been most laborious, and I can safely and truly say that if I could have seen ahead, I probably would not be a golf professional at the present time.

When I first got *the movement* I at once felt it to be what I had long been looking for, and after I had thoroughly tested it in my own game and more especially with pupils who had up to then "beaten me" I knew it was "the goods"; so I set to work to devise some practical contrivance by means of which *the movement* could be most easily and most surely acquired by others.

Stockbyte/Thinkstock

STORIES OF THE HOLE IN ONE

JEROME DUNSTAN TRAVERS

One of the ambitions of every golfer is to make a hole in one shot. The feat, which is a combination of skill and luck, is not uncommon, yet it always causes a mild sensation whenever it is performed. The ball, driven from the tee, lands near or on the edge of the green, rolls toward the hole as if drawn by a magnet and drops in. A. C. Ladd of the Henley-on-Thames Golf Club is credited with having holed out in one shot on a 330-yard hole. One explanation of this phenomenal shot is that the ball was driven down hill and rolled a great distance after it struck the turf. It is extremely probable that Mr. Ladd could try to duplicate the shot on that particular hole for the remainder of his lifetime without succeeding.

I have met hundreds of golfers who never saw a hole made in a single shot, but I have had the good luck to place three of such holes to my credit. The first one was at the old Oyster Bay Golf Club. I drove across a pond a distance of 150 yards to the third green. The shot was only a mashie pitch for an adult player, but I was only fourteen years of age and used a mid-iron. Imagine my delight when, upon reaching the green, I found the ball in the hole!

Four years later I was playing in a four ball match at the Deal Golf Club and used a driving iron on the sixth tee. The ball was at least three feet *off* the line of the flag, but when it struck the green 175 yards distant, it kicked in toward the cup. We saw it roll on the putting green but did not suspect where it was until one of the caddies found it in the hole.

Shortly before I won the championship at Wheaton in 1912, Marshall Whitlatch and I were playing Oswald Kirkby, New Jersey State champion, and Robert C. Watson, who is now president of the United States Golf Association. The match was over the excellent nine hole course of the Mahopac Golf Club. The first hole is about 120 yards from the tee and the green is out of sight. The gallery had gone ahead and members of it called back stating where Kirkby's, Watson's and Whitlatch's balls landed. Then I hit mine.

"It's on the green!" cried the gallery.

Silence for a few seconds.

"It's dead to the hole!"

Another second's silence.

"It's in!!!"

"Travers," said Watson, "you're a robber!"

One day I was practicing putting on the green devoted to that purpose at the Montclair Golf Club. Near by was the regular eighteenth green. "Tom" Anderson, the club professional, took half a dozen balls, went back about two hundred yards to a point from which he could not see the green and practiced brassie shots. Soon he came into the club house and announced with natural pride that out of six brassie shots he had holed one in one shot, two in two shots and three in three shots. After "Tom" had fittingly bought liquid refreshment for the crowd, it was gently broken to him that a mischievous waiter had sneaked upon the putting green, placed one ball in the hole and assembled the remaining five nearby. Then "Tom" said—but no, let me draw the curtain on the scene!

However, it is only fair to "Tom" to state that during his long golfing career he has holed many a drive in a single shot.

Oftentimes a player makes a hole in the second shot under circumstances that give the feat as sensational a character as holing out in one. For example, at the Metropolitan Open Championship on the Englewood links in 1912 Gil Nichols, a well-known professional, holed a second shot with a cleek at a distance of between 180 and 200 yards.

The most remarkable putt I ever saw was one made by Walter J. Travis at Garden City in 1908 during the second round of the national amateur championship. He was playing against H. H. Wilder of the Vesper Country Club in a desperately contested match that went to the forty-first green before Travis won. Wilder had the veteran dormie, 4 up and 4 to play, but Travis won the thirty-third Travis Won and thirty-fourth holes. Travis was playing for life because a single halved hole meant defeat. On the thirty-fifth (seventeenth hole) Travis's ball lay between two mounds on the putting green, each mound being about a foot high, and he had to make a twenty-five foot putt to win the hole. Either because he was stymied, or for some other reason, Travis could not play straight for the hole which was on the same level as his ball. He studied the shot a minute, then deliberately played up the side of one mound toward the hole twenty-five feet distant. The ball climbed the mound, ran along its rounded top for at least fifteen feet, then slantingly ran back to the level green again and rolled into the hole.

On another occasion, when Travis was stymied at this hole, I saw him play directly away from the hole up the side of one of the mounds. The ball ran part way up the slope, then rolled down again and went into the cup.

Now and then holing even the third shot is quite as remarkable as holing the first. Not long ago an Upper Montclair golfer was playing in England with a British professional and his son. When they reached a certain hole, distance about 400 yards, the professional remarked with natural pride:

"I got this hole in 3 once—only time it's ever been done, sir."

"Huh!" cried the American in jest, "I could do it in 3 myself if you would let me play without a coat."

In England it is bad form to play divested of this garment; in America there is no taboo of the sort, and most American golfers cannot play well when wearing a coat.

"I'll lay you thirty shillings to one you can't do it in 3," said the professional.

"And I'll do the same," said his son.

"The bet's on," replied the American, Stripping off his coat. A long drive was supplemented by a strong brassie shot, and the American found his ball in front of a very high bunker, beyond which the green was hidden. Although the hole itself was invisible, he could see the flag marking it and he had one shot left. Taking his mashie he pitched the ball over the bunker, and when they reached the green and found his ball in the hole, the sixty shilling blow almost killed both father and son!

In golf as in every other game of skill there are players who are a bit inclined to draw upon their imaginations in the matter remarkable shots, but now and then even strictly veracious players are fooled by some mischievous person and believe all their lives that they have performed some extraordinary feat. Several years ago a passerby was standing near a certain hole on the links at Essex Falls, N. J., when he noticed two balls, one after another, land on the putting green in front of him. They had come from the tee which could not be seen from the putting green because of intervening trees and bushes. The moment the two balls struck the putting green an equal number of boys dashed out of the bushes, picked up the balls, placed them in the hole and immediately vanished. His curiosity aroused, the passerby waited for further developments. In a few moments a very fat and dignified looking old gentleman and an equally plump and dignified looking old lady, attired in golf costume, sauntered up to the green and made a long, vain search for the balls.

Finally the fat man casually inspected the hole, then frantically beckoned the fat lady to approach. She did so hurriedly and the pair, side by side, peered into the cup.

"Great Scott! We both holed out in *one!*" shouted the fat man.

"Great heavens! so we *did!*" screeched the fat lady, and plucking the two balls from the cup they started on the run to tell their friends the remarkable tale. No doubt they are telling it yet!

THE STORY OF THE "COAT OF TORTURE"

CHARLES EVANS

It was a happy and tremendously exciting day when I played my first round in the British Amateur at Prestwick. I lasted to the fifth round, but I did not play all of them. For the first round I drew a bye, although I was very anxious to begin play, and was a little nervous and excited over the delay.

In my next round my opponent, A. E. Latter of the Royal Blackheath Club, was compelled by illness to forfeit the match.

In the third round I defeated Captain F. H. Stephens of the West Dorset Club, 5 and 3, and in the fourth round I defeated Sidney H. Fry, of the Royal North Devon Club, by 4 and 3. Of course I was pleased with the results and felt that I was playing well.

I might as well confess that I did not expect to lose in my match with Bruce Pearce. I felt that here was a man I would be meeting on more nearly equal terms, for his knowledge of the course could be little if any better than mine, and my game in the Troon tournament had been better than his.

The chief feature of my match with Bruce Pearce, according to reports, was the shedding of my coat on the nineteenth hole. At least that seemed to be the point of the game that attracted the greatest attention, and thereby hangs a tale and the little question of the power of suggestion. Ordinarily a Scottish May is cold and calls for heavy tweeds, which are generally worn. I had been practicing at Atlanta, Georgia, and my clothes were lightweight. Even the new overcoat that I had bought at Liverpool I had lost on the train on the way to Prestwick.

It happened that Silas H. Strawn of Chicago, president of the United States Golf Association and a good friend of mine, was touring the British Isles with William V. Kelley, a member of the Chicago Golf Club, and, of course, they were coming on to the championship at Prestwick. On the way Mr. Strawn made some purchases in Glasgow, and the thought came to him that I would probably need a tweed golfing suit such as was worn for that climate. So he brought one on. I was delighted with it and felt that for once I was properly clothed for the championship. I was experiencing a feeling of satisfaction when the weather began to get warm and I, unaccustomed to tweeds, began to suffer, but I was not willing to change back to my old clothes.

The culmination of my discomfort was reached in my match with Bruce Pearce. The sun beat down mercilessly, and I grew hotter and hotter in my unaccustomed garments. Time and again I felt that I would have to remove my coat, but I had no belt for my knickerbockers. Then the thought began to haunt me that I would ask some one to lend me a belt so that I could remove my coat, but the knickers were not cut to be worn with a belt, but came up on my back in a most extraordinary fashion.

I was 3 up and 5 to go, and with every step I became more irritated by the heat. I began to slip behind. We were even on the eighteenth and had to play an extra hole. Then when I was in a bunker and he on the green, with the match safely his, I did what I had wanted to do throughout the whole match. Before making my shot I took off that coat of torture. It could do me no good then, but instinctively when all was lost I followed a desire that had obsessed me from my first drive to the last niblick shot. It was a great relief, but unproductive at that stage of any good to my game.

THE STORY OF THE GOLF COURSE MYSTERY

CHESTER K. STEELE

There was nothing in that clear, calm day, with its blue sky and its flooding sunshine, to suggest in the slightest degree the awful tragedy so close at hand—that tragedy which so puzzled the authorities and which came so close to wrecking the happiness of several innocent people.

The waters of the inlet sparkled like silver, and over those waters poised the osprey, his rapidly moving wings and fan-spread tail suspending him almost stationary in one spot, while, with eager and far-seeing eyes, he peered into the depths below. The bird was a dark blotch against the perfect blue sky for several seconds, and then, suddenly folding his pinions and closing his tail, he darted downward like a bomb dropped from an aeroplane.

There was a splash in the water, a shower of sparkling drops as the osprey arose, a fish vainly struggling in its talons, and from a dusty gray roadster, which had halted along the highway while the occupant watched the hawk, there came an exclamation of satisfaction.

"Did you see that, Harry?" called the occupant of the gray car to a slightly built, bronzed companion in a machine of vivid yellow, christened by some who had ridden in it the "Spanish Omelet." "Did you see that kill? As clean as a hound's tooth, and not a lost motion of a feather. Some sport—that fish-hawk! Gad!"

"Yes, it was a neat bit of work, Gerry. But rather out of keeping with the day."

"Out of keeping? What do you mean?"

"Well, out of tune, if you like that better. It's altogether too perfect a day for a killing of any sort, seems to me."

"Oh, you're getting sentimental all at once, aren't you, Harry?" asked Captain Gerry Poland, with just the trace of a covert sneer in his voice. "I suppose you wouldn't have even a fish-hawk get a much needed meal on a bright, sunshiny day, when, if ever, he must have a whale of an appetite. You'd have him wait until it was dark and gloomy and rainy, with a north-east wind blowing, and all that sort of thing. Now for me, a kill is a kill, no matter what the weather."

"The better the day the worse the deed, I suppose," and Harry Bartlett smiled as he leaned forward preparatory to throwing the switch of his machine's self-starter, for both automobiles had come to a stop to watch the osprey.

"Oh, well, I don't know that the day has anything to do with it," said the captain—a courtesy title, bestowed because he was president of the Maraposa Yacht Club. "I was just interested in the clean way the beggar dived after that fish. Flounder, wasn't it?"

"Yes, though usually the birds are glad enough to get a moss-bunker. Well, the fish will soon be a dead one, I suppose."

"Yes, food for the little ospreys, I imagine. Well, it's a good death to die—serving some useful purpose, even if it's only to be eaten. Gad! I didn't expect to get on such a gruesome subject when we started out. By the way, speaking of killings, I expect to make a neat one today on this cup-winners' match."

"How? I didn't know there was much betting."

"Oh, but there is; and I've picked up some tidy odds against our friend Carwell. I'm taking his end, and I think he's going to win."

"Better be careful, Gerry. Golf is an uncertain game, especially when there's a match on among the old boys like Horace Carwell and the crowd of past-performers and cup-winners he trails along with. He's just as likely to pull or slice as the veriest novice, and once he starts to slide he's a goner. No reserve comeback, you know."

"Oh, I've not so sure about that. He'll be all right if he'll let the champagne alone before he starts to play. I'm banking on him. At the same time I haven't bet all my money. I've a ten spot left that says I can beat you to the clubhouse, even if one of my cylinders has been missing the last two miles. How about it?"

"You're on!" said Harry Bartlett shortly.

There was a throb from each machine as the electric motors started the engines, and then they shot down the wide road in clouds of dust—the sinister gray car and the more showy yellow—while above them, driving its talons deeper into the sides of the fish it had caught, the osprey circled off toward its nest of rough sticks in a dead pine tree on the edge of the forest.

And on the white of the flounder appeared bright red spots of blood, some of which dripped to the ground as the cruel talons closed until they met inside.

It was only a little tragedy, such as went on every day in the inlet and adjacent ocean, and yet, somehow, Harry Bartlett, as he drove on with ever-increasing speed in an endeavor to gain a length on his opponent, could not help thinking of it in contrast to the perfect blue of the sky, in which there was not a cloud. Was it prophetic?

Ruddy-faced men, bronze-faced men, pale-faced men; young women, girls, matrons, and "flappers"; caddies burdened with bags of golf clubs and pockets bulging with cunningly found balls; skillful waiters hurrying here and there with trays on which glasses of various shapes, sizes, and of diversified contents tinkled musically—such was the scene at the Maraposa Club on this June morning when Captain Gerry Poland and Harry Bartlett were racing their cars toward it.

It was the chief day of the year for the Maraposa Golf Club, for on it were to be played several matches, not the least in importance being that of the cup-winners, open only to such members as had won prizes in hotly contested contests on the home links.

In spite of the fact that on this day there were to be played several matches, in which visiting and local champions were to try their skill against one another, to the delight of a large gallery, interest centered in the cup-winners' battle. For it was rumored, and not without semblance of truth, that large sums of money would change hands on the result.

Not that it was gambling—oh, my no! In fact any laying of wagers was strictly prohibited by the club's constitution. But there are ways and means of getting cattle through a fence without taking down the bars, and there was talk that Horace Carwell had made a pretty stiff bet with Major Turpin Wardell as to the outcome of the match, the major and Mr. Carwell being rivals of long standing in the matter of drives and putts.

"Beastly fine day, eh, what?" exclaimed Bruce Garrigan, as he set down on a tray a waiter held out to him a glass he had just emptied with every indication of delight in its contents. "If it had been made to order couldn't be improved on," and he flicked from the lapel of Tom Sharwell's Coat some ashes which had blown there from the cigarette which Gayrigan had lighted.

"You're right for once, Bruce, old man," was the laughing response. "Never mind the ashes now, you'll make a spot if you rub any harder."

"Right for once? I'm always right!" cried Garrigan. "And it may interest you to know that the total precipitation, including rain and melted snow in Yuma, Arizona, for the calendar year 1917, was three and one tenth inches, being the smallest in the United States."

"It doesn't interest me a bit, Bruce!" laughed Sharwell. "And to prevent you getting any more of those statistics out of your system, come on over and we'll do a little precipitating on our own account. I can stand another Bronx cocktail."

"I'm with you! But, speaking of statistics, did you know that from the national forests of the United States in the last year there was cut 840,- 612,030 board feet of lumber? What the thirty feet were for I don't know, but—"

"And I don't care to know," interrupted Tom. "If you spring any more of those beastly dry figures—Say, there comes something that does interest me, though!" he broke in with. "Look at those cars take that turn!"

"Some speed," murmured Garrigan. "It's Bartlett and Poland," he went on, as a shift of wind blew the dust to one side and revealed the gray roadster and the Spanish Omelet. "The rivals are at it again."

Bruce Garrigan, who had a name among the golf club members as a human encyclopaedia, and who, at times, would inform his companions on almost any subject that chanced to come uppermost, tossed away his cigarette and, with Tom Sharwell, watched the oncoming automobile racers.

"They're rivals in more ways than one," remarked Sharwell. "And it looks, now, as though the captain rather had the edge on Harry, in spite of the fast color of Harry's car."

"That's right," admitted Garrigan. "Is it true what I've heard about both of them—that each hopes to place the diamond hoop of proprietorship on the fair Viola?"

"I guess if you've heard that they're both trying for her, it* s true enough," answered Sharwell. "And it also happens, if that old lady, Mrs. G. O. S. Sipp, is to be believed, that there, also, the captain has the advantage."

"How's that? I thought Harry had made a tidy sum on that ship-building project he put through."

"He did, but it seems that he and his family have a penchant for doing that sort of thing, and, some years ago, in one of the big mergers in which his family took a prominent part, they, or some one connected with them, pinched the Honorable Horace Carwell so that he squealed for mercy like a lamb led to the Wall street slaughter house."

"So that's the game, is it?"

"Yes. And ever since then, though Viola Carwell has been just as nice to Harry as she has to Gerry—as far as any one can tell— there has been talk that Harry is *persona non grata* as far as her father goes. He never forgives any business beat, I understand."

"Was it anything serious?" asked Garrigan, as they watched the racing automobiles swing around the turn of the road that led to the clubhouse.

"I don't know the particulars. It was before my time—I mean before I paid much attention to business."

"Rot! You don't now. You only think you do. But I'm interested. I expect to have some business dealing with Carwell myself, and if I could get a line———"

"Sorry, but I can't help you out, old man. Better see Harry. He knows the whole story, and he insists that it was all straight on his relatives' part. But it's like shaking a mince pie at a Thanksgiving turkey to mention the matter to Carwell. He hasn't gone so far as to forbid Harry the house, but there's a bit of coldness just the same."

"I see. And that's why the captain has the inside edge on the love game. Well, Miss Carwell has a mind of her own, I fancy."

"Indeed she has! She's more like her mother used to be. I remember Mrs. Carwell when I was a boy. She was a dear, somewhat conventional lady. How she ever came to take up with the sporty Horace, or he with her, was a seven-days' wonder. But they lived happily, I believe."

"Then Mrs. Carwell is dead?"

"Oh, yes—some years. Mr. Carwell's sister, Miss Mary, keeps The Haven up to date for him. You've been there?"

"Once, at a reception. I'm not on the regular calling list, though Miss Viola is pretty enough to—"

"Look out!" suddenly cried Sharwell, as though appealing to the two automobilists, far off as they were. For the yellow car made a sudden swerve and seemed about to turn turtle.

But Bartlett skillfully brought the Spanish Omelet back on the road again, and swung up alongside his rival for the home stretch—the broad highway that ran in front of the clubhouse.

The players who were soon to start out on the links; the guests, the gallery, and the servants gathered to see the finish of the impromptu race, murmurs arising as it was seen how close it was likely to be.

And close it was, for when the two machines, with doleful whinings of brakes, came to a stop in front of the house, the front wheels were in such perfect alignment that there was scarcely an inch of difference.

"A dead heat!" exclaimed Bartlett, as he leaped out and motioned for one of the servants to take the car around to the garage.

"Yes, you win!" agreed Captain Poland, as he pushed his goggles back on his cap. He held out a bill.

"What's it for?" asked Bartlett, drawing back.

"Why, I put up a ten spot that I'd beat you. I didn't, and you win."

"Buy drinks with your money!" laughed Bartlett. "The race was to be for a finish, not a dead heat We'll try it again, sometime."

"All right—any time you like!" said the captain crisply, as he sat down at a table after greeting some friends. "But you won't refuse to split a quart with me?"

"No. My throat is as dusty as a vacuum cleaner. Have any of the matches started yet, Bruce?" he asked, turning to the Human Encyclopædia.

"Only some of the novices. And, speaking of novices, do you know that in Scotland there are fourteen thousand, seven hundred—"

"Cut it, Bruce! Cut it!" begged the captain. "Sit in—you and Tom—and we'll make it two bottles. Anything to choke off your flow of useless statistics!" and he laughed good-naturedly.

"When does the cup-winners' match start?" asked Bartlett, as the four young men sat about the table under the veranda. "That's the one I'm interested in."

"In about an hour," announced Sharwell, as he consulted a card. "Hardly any of the veterans are here yet."

"Has Mr. Carwell arrived?" asked Captain Poland, as he raised his glass and seemed to be studying the bubbles that spiraled upward from the hollow stem.

"You'll know when he gets here," answered Bruce Garrigan.

"How so?" asked the captain. "Does he have an official announcer?"

"No, but you'll hear his car before you see it."

"New horn?"

"No, new car—new color—new everything!" said Garrigan. "He's just bought a new ten thousand dollar French car, and it's painted red, white and blue, and   "

"Red, white, and blue?" chorused the other three men.

"Yes. Very patriotic. His friends don't know whether he's honoring Uncle Sam or the French Republic However, it's all the same. His car is a wonder."

"I must have a brush with him!" murmured Captain Poland.

"Don't. You'll lose out," advised Garrigan. "It can do eighty on fourth speed, and Carwell is sporty enough to slip it into that gear if he needed to."

"Um! Guess I'll wait until I get my new machine, then," decided the captain.

There was more talk, but Bartlett gradually dropped out of the conversation and went to walk about the club grounds.

Maraposa was a social, as well as a golfing, club, and the scene of many dances and other affairs. It lay a few miles back from the shore near Lakeside, in New Jersey. The clubhouse was large and elaborate, and the grounds around it were spacious and well laid out.

Not far away was Loch Harbor, where the yachts of the club of which Captain Gerry Poland was president anchored, and a mile or so in the opposite direction was Lake Tacoma, on the shore of which was Lakeside. A rather exclusive colony summered there, the hotel numbering many wealthy persons among its patrons.

Harry Bartlett, rather wishing he had gone in for golf more devotedly, was wandering about, casually greeting friends and acquaintances, when he heard his name called from the cool and shady depths of a summer-house on the edge of the golf links.

"Oh, Minnie! How are you?" he cordially greeted a rather tall and dark girl who extended her slim hand to him. "I didn't expect to see you today."

"Oh, I take in all the big matches, though I don't play much myself," answered Minnie Webb. "I'm surprised to find you without a caddy, though, Harry."

"Too lazy, I'm afraid. I'm going to join the gallery today. Meanwhile, if you don't mind, I'll sit in here and help you keep cool."

"It isn't very hard to do that today," and she moved over to make room for him. "Isn't it just perfect weather!"

At one time Minnie Webb and Harry Bartlett had been very close friends—engaged some rumors had it But now they were jolly good companions, that was all.

"Seen the Carwells' new machine?" asked Bartlett.

"No, but I've heard about it I presume they'll drive up in it today."

"Does Viola run it?"

"I haven't heard. It's a powerful machine, someone said—more of a racer than a touring car, Mr. Blossom was remarking."

"Well, he ought to know. I understand he's soon to be taken into partnership with Mr. Carwell."

"I don't know," murmured Minnie, and she seemed suddenly very much interested in the vein structure of a leaf she pulled from a vine that covered the summerhouse.

Bartlett smiled. Gossip had it that Minnie Webb and Le Grand Blossom, Mr. Carwell's private secretary, were engaged. But there had been no formal announcement, though the two had been seen together more frequently of late than mere friendship would warrant.

There was a stir in front of the clubhouse, followed by a murmur of voices, and Minnie, peering through a space in the vines, announced:

"There's the big car now. Oh, I don't like that color at all! I'm as patriotic as any one, but to daub a perfectly good car up like that—well, it's —"

"Sporty, I suppose Carwell thinks," finished Bartlett. He had risen as though to leave the summerhouse, but as he saw Captain Poland step up and offer his hand to Viola Carwell, he drew back and again sat down beside Minnie.

A group gathered about the big French car, obviously to the delight of Mr. Carwell, who was proud of the furor created by his latest purchase.

Though he kept up his talk with Minnie in the summer-house, Harry Bartlett's attention was very plainly not on his present companion nor the conversation. At any other time Minnie Webb would have noticed it and taxed him with it, but now, she, too, had her attention centered elsewhere. She watched eagerly the group about the big machine, and her eyes followed the figure of a man who descended from the rear seat and made his way out along a path that led to a quiet spot.

"I think I'll go in now," murmured Minnie Webb. "I have to see—"

Bartlett was not listening. In fact he was glad of the diversion, for he saw Viola Carwell turn with what he thought was impatience aside from Captain Poland, and that was the very chance the other young man had been waiting for.

He followed Minnie Webb from the little pavilion, paying no attention to where she drifted. But he made his way through the press of persons to where Viola stood, and he saw her eyes light up as he approached. His, too, seemed brighter.

"I was wondering if you would come to see dad win," she murmured to him, as he took her hand, and Captain Poland, with a little bow, stepped back.

"You knew I'd come, didn't you?" Bartlett asked in a low voice.

"I hoped so," she murmured. "Now, Harry," she went on in a low voice, as they moved aside, "this will be a good time for you to smooth things over with father. If he wins, as he feels sure he will, you must congratulate him very heartily—exceptionally so. Make a fuss over him, so to speak. He'll be club champion, and it will seem natural for you to bubble over about it."

"But why should I, Viola? I haven't done anything to merit his displeasure."

"I know. But you remember what a touch-fire he is. He's always held that business matter against you, though I'm sure you had nothing to do with it. Now, if he wins, and I hope he will, you can take advantage of it to get on better terms with him, and—"

"Well, I'm willing to be friends, you know that, Viola. But I can't pretend—I never could!"

"You're stubborn, Harry!" and Viola pouted.

"Well, perhaps I am. When I know I'm right."

"Couldn't you forget it just once?"

"I don't see how!"

"Oh, you provoke me! But if you won't you won't, I suppose. Only it would be such a good
chance—"

"Well, I'll see him after the match, Viola. I'll do my best to be decent."

"You must go a little farther than that, Harry. Dad will be all worked up if he wins, and he'll want a fuss made over him. It will be the very chance for you."

"All right—I'll do my best," murmured Bartlett. And then a servant came up to summon him to the telephone.

Viola was not left long alone, for Captain Poland was watching her from the tail of his eye, and he was at her side before Harry Bartlett was out of sight.

"Perhaps you'd like to come for a little spin with me, Miss Carwell," said the captain. "I just heard that they've postponed the cup-winners' match an hour; and unless you want to sit around here—"

"Come on!" cried Viola, impulsively. "It's too perfect a day to sit around, and I'm only interested in my father's match."

There was another reason why Viola Carwell was glad of the chance to go riding with Captain Poland just then. She really was a little provoked with Bartlett's stubbornness, or what she called that, and she thought it might "wake him up," as she termed it, to see her with the only man who might be classed as his rival.

As for herself, Viola was not sure whether or not she would admit Captain Poland to that class. There was time enough yet.

And so, as Bartlett went in to the telephone, to answer a call that had come most inopportunely for him, Viola Carwell and Captain Poland swept off along the pleasantly shaded country road.

Left to herself, for which just then she was thankful, Minnie Webb drifted around until she met LeGrand Blossom.

"What's the matter, Lee?" she asked him in a low voice, and he smiled with his eyes at her, though his face showed no great amount of jollity. "You're as solemn as though every railroad stock listed had dropped ten points just after you bought it."

"No, it isn't quite as bad as that," he said, as he fell into step beside her, and they strolled off on one of the less-frequented walks.

"I thought everything was going so well with you. Has there been any hitch in the partnership arrangement?" asked Minnie.

"No, not exactly."

"Have you lost money?"

"No, I can't say that I have."

"Then for goodness' sake what is it? Do I have to pump you like a newspaper reporter?" and Minnie Webb laughed, showing a perfect set of teeth that contrasted well against the dark red and tan of her cheeks.

"Oh, I don't know that it's anything much," replied LeGrand Blossom.

"It's *something!*" insisted Minnie.

"Well, yes, it is. And as it'll come out, sooner or later, I might as well tell you now," he said, with rather an air of desperation, and as though driven to it "Have you heard any rumors that Mr. Carwell is in financial difficulties?"

"Why, no! The idea! I always thought he had plenty of money. Not a multi-millionaire, of course, but better off financially than any one else in Lakeside."

"He was once; but he won't be soon, if he keeps up the pace he's set of late," went on LeGrand Blossom, and his voice was gloomy.

"What do you mean?"

"Well, things don't look so well as they did. He was very foolish to buy that ten-thousand-dollar yacht so soon after spending even more than that on this red, white and blue monstrosity of his!"

"You don't mean to tell me he's bought a yacht, too?"

"Yes, the *Osprey* that Colonel Blakeson used to sport up and down the coast in. Paid a cool ten thousand for it, though if he had left it to me I could have got it for eight, I'm sure."

"Well, twenty thousand dollars oughtn't to worry Mr. Carwell, I should think," returned Minnie.

"It wouldn't have, a year ago," answered LeGrand. "But he's been on the wrong side of the market for some time. Then, too, something new has cropped up about that old Bartlett deal."

"You mean the one over which Harry's uncle and Mr. Carwell had such a fuss?"

"Yes. Mr. Carwell's never got over that And there are rumors that he lost quite a sum in a business transaction with Captain Poland."

"Oh, dear!" sighed the girl. "Isn't business horrid! I'm glad I'm not a man. But what is this about Captain Poland?"

"I don't know—haven't heard it all yet, as Mr. Carwell doesn't tell me everything, even if he has planned to take me into partnership with him. But now I'm not so keen on it."

"Keen on what, Lee?" and Minnie Webb leaned just the least bit nearer to his side.

"On going into partnership with a man who spends money so lavishly when he needs all the ready cash he can lay his hands on. But don't mention this to any one, Minnie. If it got out it might precipitate matters, and then the whole business would tumble down like a house of cards. As it is, I may be able to pull him out But I've put the soft pedal on the partnership talk."

"Has Mr. Carwell mentioned it of late?"

"No. All he seems to be interested in is this golf game that may make him club champion. But keep secret what I have told you."

Minnie Webb nodded assent, and they turned back toward the clubhouse, for they had reached a too secluded part of the grounds.

Meanwhile, Viola Carwell was not enjoying her ride with Captain Poland as much as she had expected she would. As a matter of fact it had been undertaken largely to cause Bartlett a little uneasiness; and as the car spun on she paid less and less attention to the captain.

Seeing this, the latter changed his mind concerning something he had fully expected to speak to Viola about that day, if he got the chance.

Captain Poland was genuinely in love with Viola, and he had reason to feel that she cared for him, though whether enough to warrant a declaration of love on his part was hard to understand.

"But I won't take a chance now," mused the captain, rather moodily; and the talk descended to mere monosyllables on the part of both of them. "I must see Carwell and have it out with him about that insurance deal. Maybe he holds that against me, though the last time I talked with him he gave me to understand that I'd stand a better show than Harry. I must see him after the game. If he wins he'll be in a mellow humor, particularly after a bottle or so. That's what I'll do."

The captain spun his car up in front of the clubhouse and helped Viola out.

"I think we are in plenty of time for your father's match," he remarked.

"Yes," she assented. "I don't see any of the veterans on the field yet," and she looked across the perfect course. "I'll go to look for dad and wish him luck. He always wants me to do that before he starts his medal play. See you again, Captain"; and with a friendly nod she left the somewhat chagrined yachtsman.

When Captain Poland had parked his car he took a short cut along a path that led through a little clump of bushes. Midway he heard voices. In an instant he recognized them as those of Horace Carwell and Harry Bartlett. He heard Bartlett say:

"But don't you see how much better it would be to drop it all—to have nothing more to do with her?"

"Look here, young man, you mind your own business!" snapped Mr. Carwell. "I know what I'm doing!"

"I haven't any doubt of it, Mr. Carwell; but I ventured to suggest" went on Bartlett.

"Keep your suggestions to yourself, if you please. I've had about all I want from you and your family. And if I hear any more of your impudent talk—"

Then Captain Poland moved away, for he did not want to hear any more.

In the meantime Viola hurried back to the clubhouse, and forced herself to be gay. But, somehow, a cloud seemed to have come over her day.

The throng had increased, and she caught sight, among the press, of Jean Forette, their chauffeur.

"Have you seen my father since he arrived, Jean?" asked Viola.

"Oh, he is somewhere about, I suppose," was the answer, and it was given in such p, surly tone and with such a churlish manner that Viola flushed with anger and bit her lips to keep back a sharp retort.

At that moment Minnie Webb strolled past. She had heard the question and the answer.

"I just saw your father going out with the other contestants, Viola," said Minnie Webb, for they were friends of some years' standing. "I think they are going to start to play. I wonder why they say the French are such a polite race?" she went on, speaking lightly to cover Viola's confusion caused by the chauffeur's manner. "He was positively insulting."

"He was," agreed Viola. "But I shouldn't mind him, I suppose. He does not like the new machine, and father has told him to find another place by the end of the month. I suppose that has piqued him."

While there were many matches to be played at the Maraposa Club that day, interest, as far as the older members and their friends were concerned, was centered in that for cup-winners. These constituted the best players—the veterans of the game—and the contest was sure to be interesting and close.

Horace Carwell was a "sport," in every meaning of the term. Though a man well along in his forties, he was as lithe and active as one ten years younger. He motored, fished, played golf, hunted, and of late had added yachting to his amusements. He was wealthy, as his father Had been before him, and owned a fine home in New York, but he spent a large part of every year at Lakeside, where he might enjoy the two sports he loved best— golfing and yachting.

Viola was an only child, her mother having died when she was about sixteen, and since then Mr. Carwell's maiden sister had kept watch and ward over the handsome home, The Haven. Viola, though loving her father with the natural affection of a daughter and some of the love she had lavished on her mother, was not altogether in sympathy with the sporting proclivities of Mr. Carwell.

True, she accompanied him tp his golf games and sailed with him or rode in his big car almost as often as he asked her. And she thoroughly enjoyed these things. But what she did not enjoy was the rather too jovial comradeship that followed on the part of the men and women her father associated with. He was a good liver and a good spender, and he liked to have about him such persons—men "sleek and fat," who if they did not "sleep o' nights," at least had the happy faculty of turning night into day for their own amusement.

So, in a measure, Viola and her father were out of sympathy, as had been husband and wife before her; though there had never been a whisper of real incompatibility; nor was there now, between father and daughter.

"Fore!"

It was the warning cry from the first tee to clear the course for the start of the cup-winners' match. In anticipation of some remarkable playing, an unusually large gallery would follow the contestants around. The best caddies had been selected, clubs had been looked to with care and tested, new balls were got out, and there was much subdued excitement, as befitted the occasion.

Mr. Carwell, his always flushed face perhaps a trifle more like a mild sunset than ever, strolled to the first tee. He swung his driver with freedom and ease to make sure it was the one that best suited him, and then turned to Major Wardell, his chief rival.

"Do you want to take any more?" he asked meaningly.

"No, thank you," was the laughing response. "I've got all I can carry. Not that I'm going to let you beat me, but I'm always a stroke or two off in my play when the sun's too bright, as it is now. However, I'm not crawling."

"You'd better not!" declared his rival. "As for me, the brighter the sun the better I like it. Well, are we all ready?"

The officials held a last consultation and announced that play might start. Mr. Carwell was to lead.

The first hole was not the longest in the course, but to place one's ball on fair ground meant driving very surely, and for a longer distance than most players liked to think about. Also a short distance from the tee was a deep ravine, and unless one cleared that it was a handicap hard to overcome.

Mr. Carwell made his little tee of sand with care, and placed the ball on the apex. Then he took his place and glanced back for a moment to where Viola stood between Captain Poland and Harry Bartlett. Something like a little frown gathered on the face of Horace Carwell as he noted the presence of Bartlett, but it passed almost at once.

"Well, here goes, ladies and gentlemen!" exclaimed Mr. Carwell in rather loud tones and with a free and easy manner he did not often assume. "Here's where I bring home the bacon and make my friend, the major, eat humble pie."

Viola flushed. It was not like her father to thus boast. On the contrary he was usually what the Scotch call a "canny" player. He never predicted that he was going to win, except, perhaps, to his close friends. But he was now boasting like the veriest schoolboy.

"Here I go!" he exclaimed again, and then he swung at the ball with his well-known skill.

It was a marvelous drive, and the murmurs of approbation that greeted it seemed to please Mr. Carwell.

"Let's see anybody beat that!" he cried as he stepped off the tee to give place to Major Wardell.

Mr. Carwell's white ball had sailed well up on the putting green of the first hole, a shot seldom made at Maraposa.

"A few more strokes like that and he'll win the match," murmured Bartlett.

"And when he does, don't forget what I told you," whispered Viola to him.

He found her hand, hidden at her side in the folds of her dress, and pressed it. She smiled up at him, and then they watched the major swing at his ball.

"It's going to be a corking match," murmured more than one member of the gallery, as they followed the players down the field.

"If any one asked me, I should say that Carwell had taken just a little too much champagne to make his strokes true toward the last hole," said Tom Sharwell to Bruce Garrigan.

"Perhaps," was the admission. "But I'd like to see him win. And, for the sake of saying something, let me inform you that in Africa last year there were used in nose rings alone for the natives seventeen thousand four hundred and twenty-one pounds of copper wire. While for anklets—"

"I'll buy you a drink if you chop it off short!" offered Sharwell.

"Taken!" exclaimed Garrigan, with a grin.

The cup play went on, the four contestants being well matched, and the shots duly applauded from hole to hole.

The turn was made and the homeward course began, with the excitement increasing as it was seen that there would be the closest possible finish, between the major and Mr. Carwell at least.

"What's the row over there?" asked Bartlett suddenly, as he walked along with Viola and Captain Poland.

"Where?" inquired the captain.

"Among those autos. Looks as if one was on fire."

"It does," agreed Viola. "But I can see our patriotic palfrey, so I guess it's all right. There are enough people over there, anyhow. But it is something!"

There was a dense cloud of smoke hovering over the place where some of the many automobiles were parked at one comer of the course. Still it might be some one starting his machine, with too much oil being burned in the cylinders.

"Now for the last hole!" exulted Mr. Carwell, as they approached the eighteenth. "I've got you two strokes now, Major, and I'll have you four by the end of the match."

"I'm not so sure of that," was the laughing and good-natured reply.

There was silence in the gallery while the players made ready for the last hole.

There was a sharp impact as Mr. Carwell's driver struck the little white ball and sent it sailing in a graceful curve well toward the last hole.

"A marvelous shot!" exclaimed Captain Poland. "On the green again! Another like that and he'll win the game!"

"And I can do it, too!" boasted Carwell, who overheard what was said.

The others drove off in turn, and the play reached the final stage of putting. Viola turned as though to go over and see what the trouble was among the automobiles. She looked back as she saw her father stoop to send the ball into the little depressed cup. She felt sure that he would win, for she had kept a record of his strokes and those of his opponents. The game was all but over.

"I wonder if there can be anything the matter with our car?" mused Viola, as she saw the smoke growing denser. "Dad's won, so I'm going over to see. Perhaps that chauffeur—"

She did not finish the sentence. She turned to look back at her father once more, and saw him make the putt that won the game at the last hole. Then, to her horror she saw him reel, throw up his hands, and fall heavily in a heap, while startled cries reached her ears.

"Oh! Oh! What has happened?" she exclaimed, and deadly fear clutched at her heart—and not without good cause.

STORIES OF HARRY VARDON'S TRIP TO AMERICA

HARRY VARDON

I was intent on making a bold bid for this American Open Championship. Victory in it seemed to be the one thing essential to make my trip the greatest possible success. My friend Taylor, who had just beaten me for the Open Championship at St. Andrews, had himself come over to the States, and was also a candidate for the premier honours of American golf. As it turned out, we had practically the whole contest at Wheaton to ourselves, and a rare good duel it was, at the end of which I was at the top of the list, but only two strokes in front of my English opponent, while he was eight in front of the next man. The system of deciding the championship was the same as on this side, that is to say, four medal rounds were played, two on one day and two on the next. At the end of the first day's play I was just one stroke better than Taylor, my score for the two rounds bring 157 to his 158, and on the second day I did 156 to his 157, so that on the whole event I was 313 to his 315. Taylor waited on the edge of the green while I holed out my last putt, and was the first to grasp my hand in sincere congratulation. Beautiful weather, the biggest golfing crowd ever seen in America up to that time, and a good links, made the tournament a great success. The partner who went round with me during this championship competition was Will Smith, the holder, who finished fifth.

I had some curious experiences in the course of my journeyings about the country, and I am not sure that they were all good for my game. During the early months I was down in Florida away from the cold and the snow. I met some good golfers there. It was necessary to play an entirely different game from that to which we are accustomed in this country. There was no grass on the putting "greens." They were simply made of loose sand, sprinkled on the baked ground and watered and rolled. When there was a shortage of water and there was wind about, the fine part of the sand was blown away, and the surface of the "greens " then consisted of nothing but little pebbles. It was not easy to putt over this kind of thing, but I must not convey the impression that these sand "greens" were wholly bad. When properly attended to they are really nice to putt upon after you have become accustomed to them. It was impossible to pitch on to them, and one had to cultivate the habit of running up from a very long distance. Thus I got into the way of playing a kind of stab shot. The tees consisted not of grass but of hard soil, and one had to tee up much higher than usual in order to avoid damaging the sole of the driver. This provoked the habit of cocking the ball up, and as a corrective all the teeing grounds in Florida sloped upwards in front. Locusts were responsible for eating all the grass away from some courses, and I had a unique experience when I played Findlay at Portland. When we were on the putting greens, men had constantly to be beating sticks to keep the locusts off the lines of our putts. If it struck a locust the ball would come to a sudden stop. Acres and acres of land about there were without a single blade of grass. The locusts had eaten it all away. After we left Florida we reached some good courses, and resumed the old kind of play. It has often been suggested that the peculiar conditions of play in America, to which I was subjected for a long period, resulted in a permanent injury to my game as played at home, and in the light of reflection and experience I am persuaded to think that this is so. I have played well since then, have felt equal to doing anything that I ever did before, and have indeed won the Championship, but I think I left a very small fraction of my game in the United States.

In the way of other novel experiences I might mention that on one occasion I played as "Mr. Jones." I wanted a quiet day, and did not wish a too attentive public to know where I was. Three friends joined me in a foursome, but when we went into the club-house after our game, another anxious golfer went up to my partner when I was standing by, and inquired of him whether he had heard that Vardon was playing on the links. My friend declared that he knew nothing of such a rumour, and I could hardly refrain from laughter as the anxious one went to pursue his inquiries in other quarters. Another time two other professionals and myself visited a course where we were unknown, and, hiding our identity, pretended that we were novices at the game, and begged of our caddies to advise us as to the best manner of playing each shot, which they did accordingly. We deliberately duffed most of our strokes at several holes, but this course of procedure tired us immensely, and so at last we abandoned it and began to play our natural game. Imagine the consternation and the indignation of those caddies! Each one of them threw down his bag of clubs, and, declining to carry them for another hole, walked sulkily off the course. On one occasion we camped out for the night on the links on which we were playing, and a very pleasant variation from the ordinary routine we found it.

The American newspapers, to which I have frequently referred, do their golf reporting very well. Their journalism may be "sensational" or whatever you like to call it, but the golfing section of it was usually interesting, ingenious, and very intelligent and reliable. On the occasion of one match in which I played, a paper gave up nearly the whole of one of its pages to a large panoramic view of the links. The flight of my ball and that of my opponent, and the places where they stopped after every stroke, from the first to the last, were accurately marked. Thus the whole game was illustrated in a single picture in a very effective manner. As was inevitable, I was sometimes victimised by interviewers who wrote "interviews" with me which I had never accorded, containing most amazing particulars about my methods and habits. Occasionally a reporter was turned on to describe a game when he knew nothing about golf, and then the results were sometimes amusing. One of these writers had it that I "carried away the green with my drive." Another said I "dropped dead at the hole." When playing at Washington against two opponents, I happened to beat bogey at the first hole. One of the reporters was told of this achievement, but did not quite understand it. Going to the next hole, we were walking through a bunker when he came up to me and politely inquired if that—the bunker—was the kind of bogey that I had beaten. I was told a very good story of American golf reporting. A match was arranged between two well-known amateurs, one of whom happened to be a very rich banker. One reporter, who admitted that he "knew nothing about the darned game," arrived rather late on the course, and borrowed the "copy" of an experienced golfing journalist for information of what had already happened. When this "copy" was duly returned with thanks, the late-comer remarked to his obliging friend, "Say, you made a bad mistake in one part." "What was it?" the other asked. "Waal, you say that So-and-so 'lipped the hole for a half.'" "Yes, that is right" "Oh, go away; you don't mean to tell me that a rich man like that would be playing for a paltry fifty cents. I've altered it to 'lipped the hole for a hundred dollars.'" And I remember that once when I was playing the best ball of two amateurs, one of the reporters had been instructed by his chief to keep the best ball score. I happened to lose the match on the last green, but on looking through the paper the next morning I was surprised to see it stated that I was beaten by not one but many holes, making this defeat in fact the biggest inflicted on me during my tour. The paper said that it was. I could not make anything out of it for some time, until at last I discovered that the reporter had reckoned my score also in the best ball figures! Obviously I could not beat myself. The best I could do was to get a half, and that was how it came about that I never won a single hole in the "Harry Vardon *v.* Harry Vardon and two others" match.

Comstock/Thinkstock

THE STORY OF LITTLE POISON IVY

CHARLES E. VAN LOAN

The leopard cannot change his spots—possibly he wouldn't if he could; and, this being the case, the next best thing is to overlook as many of his freckles as possible.

Yesterday I sat on the porch at the Country Club and listened while the Dingbats said kind and complimentary things about young Ambrose Phipps, alias Little Poison Ivy, alias The Pest, alias Rough and Reddy. One short week ago the Dingbats would have voted him a nuisance and a menace to society in general. Yesterday they praised him to the skies. It just goes to show that good can be found in anybody—if that is what you are looking for.

Understand me: there has been no change in Ambrose. He is still as fresh as a mountain breeze. Unquestionably he will continue to treat his elders with a shocking lack of respect and an entire absence of consideration. He was bom with a deep depression where his bump of reverence should have been located, and neither realises nor regrets his deficiency.

He will never change. It is the Dingbats who have changed. The whole club has changed, so far as Ambrose is concerned.

We are all trying to overlook the dark spots in his character and see good in him, whether it is there or not.

Now as to the Dingbats: if you do not know them you have missed something rich and rare in the golfing line. There are four of them, all retired capitalists on the shady side of sixty. They freely admit that they are the worst golfers in the world, and in a pinch they could prove it. They play together six days a week—a riotous, garrulous, hilarious foursome, ripping the course wide open from the first tee to the home green; and they get more real fun out of golf than any men I know. They never worry about being off their game, because they have never been on it; they know they can be no worse than they are and they have no hope of ever being better; they expect to play badly, and it is seldom that they are disappointed. Whenever a Dingbat forgets to count his shots in the bunkers, and comes home in the nineties, a public celebration takes place on the clubhouse porch.

Yesterday it was Doc Pinkinson who brought in the ninety-eight—and signed all the tags; and between libations they talked about Ambrose Phipps, who was practising brassy shots off the grass beside the eighteenth green.

Little Poison Ivy was unusually cocky, even for him, and every move was a picture. At the end of his follow-through he would freeze, nicely balanced on the tip of his right toe, elbows artistically elevated, clubhead up round his neck; and not a muscle would he move until the ball stopped rolling. He might have been posing for a statue of the Perfect Golfer. When he walked it was with a conscious little swagger and a flirting of the short tails of his belted sport coat. He was hitting them clean, he was hitting them far, he had an audience—and well he knew it. Ambrose was in his glory yesterday afternoon!

"By golly!" exclaimed Doc Pinkinson. "Ain't that a pretty sight? Ain't it a treat to see that kid lambaste the ball?"

"Certainly is," agreed Old Treanor with a sigh. "Perfect form—that's what he's got. And confidence in himself," put in Old Myles. "That's the big secret. You can see it in every move he makes. Confidence is a wonderful thing!"

"And youth," said Daddy Bradshaw. "That's the most wonderful thing of all. It's his youth that makes him so—so flip. Got a lot to say, for a kid; but—somehow I always liked him for it."

"Me too!" chimed in Doc Pinkinson. "Dog gone his skin! He used to make me awful mad, that boy.... Oh, well, I reckon I'm kind of cranky, anyway.... Yes; I always liked Ambrose."

Now that was all rot, and I knew it. What's more, the Dingbats knew it too. They hadn't always liked Ambrose. A week ago they would have marked his swaggering gait, the tilt of his chin, the conscious manner in which he posed after every shot; and they would have said Ambrose was showing off for the benefit of the female tea party at the other end of the porch—and they wouldn't have made any mistake, at that.

No; they hadn't always liked young Mr. Phipps. Nobody had liked him. To be perfectly frank about it, we had disliked him openly and cordially, and had been at no pains to keep him from finding it out. We had snubbed him, insulted him and ignored him on every possible occasion. Worst of all, we had made a singleton of him. We had forced him to play alone, because there wasn't a man in all the club who wanted him as a partner or as an opponent. There is no meaner treatment than this; nor is there anything more pathetically lonely than a singleton on a crowded golf course. It is nothing more or less than a grown-up trip to Coventry. I thought of all these things as I listened to the prattling of the Dingbats.

"Guess he won't have any trouble getting games now, hey?" chuckled Old Treanor.

"Huh!" grunted Doc Pinkinson. "He's dated up a week ahead—with Moreman and that bunch! *A week ahead!*"

"And he'll make 'em step!" chirped Daddy Bradshaw. "Here's to him, boys—a redhead and a fighter! Drink her down!"

"A redhead and a fighter!" chorused the Dingbats, lifting their glasses.

Yes; they drank to Ambrose Phipps, and one short week ago they wouldn't have tolerated him on the same side of the course with them. Our pet leopard still has his spots, but we are now viewing him in the friendly shade cast by a battered old silver cup: namely and to wit, the Edward B. Wimpus Team Trophy, permanently at home on the mantelpiece in the lounging room.

II

Going back to the beginning, we never had a chance to blame Ambrose on the Membership Committee; he slipped in on us via the junior- member clause. Old Man Phipps does not play golf; but he is a charter member of the club and, according to the by-laws, the sons of members between the ages of sixteen and twenty-one enjoy all the privileges of the institution.

Ambrose was nineteen when he returned rather hurriedly from college. He did this at the earnest and unanimous request of the Faculty and, it was whispered, the police department of the university town. He hadn't done much of anything, but he had tried very hard to drive a touring car and seven chorus girls through a plate-glass window into a restaurant. The press agent of the show saw his chance to get some publicity for the broilers, and after an interview with the Faculty Ambrose caught the first train for home.

Having nothing to do and plenty of time in which to do it, Ambrose decided to become a golfer. Old Dunn'l MacQuarrie, our professional, sold him a large leather bag full of tools and gave him two lessons. Thus equipped and fortified, young Mr. Phipps essayed to brighten our drab lives by allowing us to play golf with him. Now this sort of thing may be done in some clubs, but not in ours. We do not permit our sacred institutions to be "rushed" by the golfing novice. We are not snobbish, but we plead guilty to being the least bit set in our ways. They are good ways, and they suit us. The club is an old one, as golf clubs go in this country, and most of the playing members are men past forty years of age. Nearly all of the foursomes are permanent affairs, the same men playing together week after week, season in and season out. The other matches are made in advance, by telephone or word of mouth, and the member who turns up minus a game on Saturday afternoon is out of luck.

We do not leap at the stranger with open arms. We do not leap at him at all. We stand off and look him over. We put him on probation; and if he shapes up well, and walks lightly, and talks softly, and does not try to dynamite his way into matches where he is not wanted, some day he will be invited to fill up a foursome. Invited—make a note of that. Now see what Ambrose did.

With his customary lack of tact, he selected the very worst day in the week to thrust himself upon our notice. It was a Saturday, and the lounging room was crowded with members, most of whom were shaking dice for the luncheons. With a single exception, all the foursomes were made up for the afternoon.

A short, sturdily built youngster came through the doorway from the locker room and paused close to the table where I was sitting. His hair was red—the sort of red that will not be ignored—and he wore it combed straight back over the top of his head. His slightly irregular features were covered with large brown freckles, and on his upper lip was a volunteer crop of lightish fuzz, which might, in time, become a moustache. His green sport coat was new, his flannel trousers were new, his shoes were new—from neck to sole he fairly shrieked with newness. Considering that he was a stranger in a strange club, a certain amount of reticence would not have hurt the young man's entrance; but he burst through the swinging door with a skip and a swagger, and there was a broad grin on his homely countenance. It was quite evident that he expected to find himself among friends.

"Who wants a game?" he cried. "Don't all speak at once, men!"

A few of the members nearest the door glanced up, eyed the youth curiously, and returned to their dice boxes. The others had not heard him at all. Harson and Billford looked at me.

"Who's the fresh kid?" asked Billford.

"That," said I, "is Ambrose Phipps, only son of Old Man Phipps."

"Humph!" grunted Harson. "The living, breathing proof that marriage is a failure. What's he want?"

Ambrose himself answered the question. He had advanced to our table.

"You gentlemen got a game?" he asked, laying his hand on Billford's shoulder.

Now if there is anything that Billford loathes and detests, it is familiarity on short acquaintance. He hadn't even met this fresh youth; so he shrugged his shoulder in a very pointed manner and glared at Ambrose. The boy did not remove his hand.

" 'S all right, old top," said he reassuringly. "It's clean—just washed it. Clean as your shirt." He bent down and looked at Billford's collar. "No," said he; "cleaner. . . . Well, how about it? Got your game fixed up?"

"We are waiting for a fourth man." I answered because Billford didn't seem able to say anything; he looked on the point of exploding.

"Oh, a fourth man, eh? Well, if he doesn't turn up you know me." And Ambrose passed on to the next table.

"Insufferable young rotter!" snarled Billford.

"Quite so," said Harson; "but he'll never miss anything by being too bashful to ask for it. Look! He's asking everybody!"

Ambrose made the entire circuit of the room. We could not hear what he said, but we felt the chill he left in his wake. Men glanced up when he addressed them, stared for an instant, and went back to their dice. Some of them were polite in their refusals, some were curt, some were merely disgusted. When he reached the table where Bishop, Gilmore, Moreman and Elder were sitting, they laughed at him. They are our star golfers and members of the team. The Dingbats were too much astonished to show resentment; but when Ambrose left them he patted Doc Pinkinson on the head, and the old gentleman sputtered for the best part of an hour.

It was a discouraging tour, and any one else would have hunted a quiet corner and crawled into it; but not Ambrose. He returned to our end of the room, and the pleased and expectant light in his eyes had given way to a steely glare. He beckoned to one of the servants.

"Hey, George! Who's the boss here? Who's the Big Finger?"

"Misteh Harson, he's one of 'em, suh. He's a membeh of the Greens Committee."

"Show him to me!"

"Right there, suh, settin' by the window."

Ambrose strode across to us and addressed himself to Harson.

"My name is Phipps," said he. "I'm a junior member here, registered and all that, and I want to get a game this afternoon. So far, I haven't had any luck."

Harson is really a mild and kindly soul. He hates to hurt any one's feelings.

"Perhaps all the games are made up," he suggested. "Saturday is a bad day, unless your match is arranged beforehand."

"Zat so? Humph! Nice clubby spirit you have here. You make a fellow feel so much at home!"

"So we notice," grunted Billford.

Ambrose looked at him and smiled. It wasn't exactly a pleasant smile. Then he turned back to Harson.

"How about that fourth man of yours?" he demanded. "Has he shown up yet?"

Billford caught my eye.

"Some one must have left the outside door open," said he. "Seems to me I feel a strong draught."

"Put on another shirt!" Ambrose shot the retort without an instant's hesitation. "Now say, if your fourth man isn't here, what's the matter with me?"

Possibly there is nothing the matter with you," said Harson pleasantly; "but if you are a beginner——"

"Aw, you don't need to be afraid of my game!" grinned Ambrose. "I'll be easy picking."

"That isn't the point," explained Harson. "Our game would be too fast for you."

"Well, what of it? How am I ever going to learn if I never play with anybody better than I am? Don't you take any interest in young blood, or is this a close corporation, run for the benefit of a lot of old fossils, playing hooky from the boneyard?"

"Oh, run away, little boy, and sell your papers!" Billford couldn't stand it any longer.

"I will if you lend me that shirt for a make up!" snapped Ambrose. "Now don't get mad, Cutie. Remember, you picked on me first. A man with a neck as thick as yours ought not to let his angry passions rise. First thing you know, you'll bust something in that bonemeal mill of yours, and then you won't know anything." Ambrose put his hands on his hips and surveyed the entire gathering. "A nice, cheerful, clubby bunch!" he exclaimed. "Gee! What a picnic a hermit crab could have in this place, meeting so many congenial souls!"

"If you don't like it," said Billford, "you don't have to stay here a minute."

"That's mighty sweet of you," said Ambrose; "but, you see, I've made up my mind to learn this fool game if it takes all summer. I'd hate to quit now, even to oblige people who have been so courteous to me. . . . Well, good-by, you frozen stiffs! Maybe I can hire that sour old Scotchman to go round with me. He's not what you might call a cheerful companion, but, at that, he's got something on you. He's *human,* anyway!"

Ambrose went outside and banged the door behind him. Billford made a few brief observations; but his remarks, though vivid and striking, were not quite original. Harson shook his head, and in the silence following Ambrose's exit we heard Doc Pinkinson's voice:

"If that pup was mine I'd drown him; dog gone me if I wouldn't!"

Young Mr. Phipps, you will observe, got in wrong at the very start.

III

Bad news travels fast when a few press agents get behind it, and not all the personal publicity is handed out by a man's loving friends. Those who had met Ambrose warned those who had not, and whenever his fiery red head appeared in the lounging room there was a startling drop in the temperature.

For a few weeks he persisted in trying to secure matches with members of the club, but nobody would have anything to do with him—not even old Purdue McCormick, who toddles about the course with a niblick in one hand and a midiron in the other, *sans* bag, *sans* caddie, *sans* protection of the game laws. When such a renegade as Purdne refused to go turf-tearing with him Ambrose gave up in disgust and de voted himself to the serious business of learning the royal and ancient game. He infested the course from dawn till dark, a solitary figure against the sky line;

our golfing Ishmael, a wild ass loose upon the links, his hand against every man and every man's hand against him.

He wore a chip on his shoulder for all of us; and it was during this period that Anderson, our club champion and Number One on the team, christened Ambrose "Little Poison Ivy," because of the irritating effect of personal contact with him.

Ambrose couldn't have had a great deal of fun out of the situation; but MacQuarrie made money out of it. The redhead hired the professional to play with him and criticise his shots. The dour old Scotch mercenary did not like Ambrose any better than we did, but toward the end of the first month he admitted to me that the boy had the makings of a star golfer, though not, he was careful to explain, "the pr-roper temperament for the game."

"But it's just amazin', the way he picks up the shots," said Dunn'l. "Ay, he'll have every thing but the temperament."

As the summer drew to a close the annual team matches began, and we forgot Ambrose and all else in our anxiety over the fate of the Edward B. Wimpus Trophy.

Every golf club, you must know, has its pet trophy. Ours is the worn old silver cup that represents the team championship of the Association. A pawnbroker wouldn't look at it twice; but to us, who are familiar with its history and the trips it has made to different clubhouses, the Edward B. Wimpus Trophy is priceless, and more to be desired than diamonds or pearls.

When the late Mr. Wimpus donated the cup he stipulated that it should be held in trust by the club winning the annual team championship, and that it should become the property of the club winning it three times in succession. For twenty years we had been fighting for permanent possession of the trophy, and engraved on its shining surface was the record of our bitter disappointment—not to mention the disappointment of the Bellevue Golf Club. Twice we had been in a position to add the third and final victory, and twice the Bellevue quintet had dashed our hopes. Twice we had retaliated by preventing them from retiring the Wimpus Trophy from competition; and now, with two winning years behind us and a third opportunity in sight, we talked and thought of nothing else.

According to the rules governing team play in our Association, each club is represented by five men, contesting from scratch and without handicaps of any sort. In the past, two teams have outclassed the field, and once more history repeated itself, for the Bellevue bunch fought us neck and neck through the entire period of competition. With one match remaining to be played, they were tied with us for first place, and that match brought the Bellevue team to our course last Friday afternoon.

I was on hand when the visitors filed into the locker room at noon—MacNeath, Smathers, Crane, Lounsberry and Jordan—five seasoned and dependable golfers, veterans of many a hard match; fighters who never know when they are beaten. They looked extremely fit, and not in the least worried at the prospect of meeting our men on their own course.

They brought their own gallery, too, Bellevue members who talked even money and flashed yellow-backed bills. The Dingbats formed a syndicate and covered all bets; but this was due to club pride rather than any feeling of confidence. We knew our boys were in for a tough battle, in which neither side would have a marked advantage.

Four of our team players were on hand to welcome the enemy—Moreman, Bishop, Elder and Gilmore—and they offered their opponents such hospitality as is customary on like occasions.

"Thanks," said MacNeath with a grin; "but just now we're drinking water. After the match you can fill the cup with anything you like, and we'll allow you one drink out of it before we take it home with us. Once we get it over there it'll never come back. It's not in the cards for you to win three times running. . . . Where's Anderson?"

"He hasn't shown up yet," said Bishop.

"He's on the way out in his car," added Moreman. "I rang up his house five minutes ago. He'd just left."

"Oh, very well," said MacNeath, who is Number One man for Bellevue, as well as captain of the team. "Suppose we have lunch now, Bishop; and while we're eating you can give me the list of your players and I'll match them up."

In team play it is customary for the home captain to submit the names of his players, ranked from one to five, in the order of their ability. The visiting captain then has the privilege of making the individual matches; and this is supposed to offset whatever advantage the home team has by reason of playing on its own course.

Bishop, our captain, handed over a list reading as follows: 1—Anderson; 2—Moreman; 3—Bishop; 4—Elder; 5—Gilmore. MacNeath bracketed his own name with Anderson's, and paired Crane with Moreman, Lounsberry with Bishop, Smathers with Elder, and Jordan with Gilmore.

After luncheon the men changed to their golfing togs; but still there was no sign of Anderson. Another telephone call confirmed the first message; his wife reported that he had left his home nearly an hour before, bound for the club.

"Queer!" said MacNeath. "Engine trouble or a puncture—possibly both. It's not like the Swede to be late. Might as well get started, eh? Anderson and I will go last, anyhow."

A big gallery watched the first pair drive off, Gilmore getting a better ball than Jordan, and cheering those who believe in omens. Then at five-minute intervals, came Lounsberry and Bishop, Smathers and Elder, and Crane and Moreman. Each match attracted a small individual gallery, but most of the spectators waited to follow the Number One men. MacNeath, refusing to allow himself to be made nervous by the delay, went into the clubhouse; and many and wild were the speculations as to the cause of Anderson's tardiness. The wildest one of them fell short of the bitter truth, which came to us at the end of a telephone wire located in the professional's shop. It had been relayed on from the switchboard in the club office:

"Anderson blew a front tire at the city limits. Car turned over with him and broke his leg."

A bombshell exploding under our noses could not have created more consternation. There we were, with four of the matches under way, our best man crippled, and up against the proposition of providing an opponent for MacNeath, admittedly the most dangerous player on the Bellevue team. Harson, as a member of the Greens Committee and an officer of the club, assumed charge of the situation as soon as he heard the news.

"No good sending word to poor old Bishop," said he. "He's the team captain, of course; but he can't do anything about it. Besides, he's already playing his match, and this would upset him terribly. Is there any one here who can give MacNeath a run for his money?"

"Not unless you want to try it," said I.

"He'd eat me alive!" groaned Harson. "We might as well forfeit one match, and put it up to the boys to win three out of four. Oh, if we only had one more good man!"

"Ye have," said MacQuarrie, who had been listening. "Ye've overlooked young Mister Phipps."

"That kid?" demanded Harson. "Nonsense!"

"Ay," said Dunn'l; "that kid! Call it nonsense if ye like, sir, but he was under eighty twice yesterday. This mor-min' he shot a seventy-seven, with two missed putts the length o' your ar-rm. He's on top of his game now, an' goin' strong. If he'll shoot back to his mor- min' round he'll give Mister MacNeath a battle; but the lad has never been in a competition, so ye'll have to chance his ner-rves."

"Ambrose!" I exclaimed. "I never should have thought of him!"

"Of course ye wouldn't," said MacQuarrie. "Ye've never played with him—never even seen him play."

"But he's such a little rotter!" mumbled Harson.

"Ay," said Dunn'l; "an', grantin' ye that, he's still the best ye have. He's in the club house now, dressed an' ready to start, once the crowd is out of the way."

"And he really did a seventy-seven this morning?" asked Harson.

"With two missed putts—wee ones."

I looked at Harson and Harson looked at me.

"You go in and put it up to him," said he at last. "I can't talk to him without losing my temper."

I found our little red hope banging the balls about on the billiard table, carefree as a scarlet tanager.

"Young man," said I, "your country calls you."

"I'm under age," said Ambrose, calmly squinting along his cue. "Don't bother me. This is a tough shot."

"Well, then," said I, "your club calls you."

"My club, eh?" remarked the redhead with nasty emphasis. "Any time this club calls me I'm stone-deaf."

"Listen to me a minute, Phipps. This is the day of the big team match and we're up against it hard. Anderson turned his car over on the way out and broke his leg. We want you to take his place."

"Anderson," repeated Ambrose. "Ain't that the squarehead who calls me Little Poison Ivy? Only his leg, eh? Tough luck!"

"You bet it is!" I exclaimed, ignoring his meaning. "Tough luck for all of us, because if we can't dig up a man to take Anderson's place we'll have to forfeit that particular match to MacNeath. We'd set our hearts on winning this time, because it would give us the permanent possession of the team trophy that we've been shooting at for twenty years——"

"Let your voice fall right there!" commanded Ambrose. "Trophies are nothing in my young life. This club is nothing in my life. Everybody here has treated me worse than a yellow dog. Go ahead and take your medicine; and I hope they lick you and make you like it!"

I saw it was time to try another tack. Ambrose had used one word that had put an idea into my head.

"All right," said I. "Have it your own way. Perhaps it was a mistake to mention MacNeath's name."

"What do you mean—a mistake?" He fired up instantly.

"Well," said I, "you must know Mac by reputation. He's one of the best golfers in the state and a tough proposition to beat. He's their Number One man—their star player. He shoots pretty close to par all the time."

"What's that got to do with it?" asked Ambrose.

"Why, nothing; only——"

"Only what?"

"Well, they all said yon wouldn't want to go up against such a strong player."

"Who said that?"

"Oh, everybody. Yes; it was a mistake to mention his name. I'm frank enough to say that I wouldn't tackle him without a handicap. MacNeath is hard game."

"Look here!" snapped the redhead. "You're off on the wrong foot entirely. You're barking up the wrong tree. It's not because I'm afraid of this MacNeath, or anybody else. I licked that sour old Scotchman this morning, and I guess you'll agree he's not soft picking. It's just that I don't feel that this club ought to ask a favour of me."

"A favour! Why, man alive, it's a compliment to stick you in at Number One—the biggest compliment we can pay you!"

"Well," said Ambrose slowly, "if you look at it in that light——"

"I most certainly do. . . . But if you'd rather not meet MacNeath——"

Ambrose dropped his cue with a crash. "You don't really think I'm *yellow*, do you?" he cried.

"If you are," said I, "you're the first redhead that ever got his colour scheme mixed."

The little rascal grinned like a gargoyle. "Listen!" said he confidentially. "You've used me pretty well—to my face, anyhow—and I'll tell you this much: I don't care the snap of my fingers for your ratty old cup. I care even less for the members of this club—present company excepted, you understand; but I can't stand it to have anybody think I'm not *game*. Ever since I was a runt of a kid I've had to fight, and they can say anything about me except that I'm a quitter. . . . Why, I've stuck round here for nearly five months just because I wouldn't let a lot of old fossils drive me out and make me quit—five months without a friend in the place, and only MacQuarrie to talk to.

"If I'd been yellow it would have shown that first Saturday when everybody turned me down so cold. I wanted to walk out and never come back. I wanted to; but I stuck. Honest, if I'm anything at all I'm game—game enough to stand the gaff and take the worst of it; and I'll prove it to you by playing this bird, no matter how good he is. I'll fight him every jump of the way, and if he licks me he'll have to step out some to do it. What's a licking, anyway? I've had a thousand of 'em! Plenty of people can lick me; but you bet your life nobody ever scared me!"

"Good kid!" said I, and held out my hand.

After an instant's hesitation Ambrose seized it. "Now lead me to this MacNeath person," said he. "I suppose we ought to be introduced, eh? Or has he been told that I'm the Country Club leper?"

It was a sorely disappointed gallery that welcomed the substitute—disappointed and amazed; but the few Bellevue members were openly jubilant. They had reason to be, for word had been brought back to them that Lounsberry and Crane were running away with their matches. Between them and the cup they saw only a golfing novice, a junior member without a war record. They immediately began offering odds of two to one on the MacNeath-Phipps match; but there were no takers. The Dingbats held a lodge of sorrow in the shade of the caddie house and mournfully estimated their losses, while our feminine contingent showed signs of retreating to the porch and spending the afternoon at bridge.

MacNeath was first on the tee—a tall, fiat-muscled, athletic man of forty; and, as the veteran was preparing to drive, Ambrose and MacQuarrie held a whispered conversation.

"I'd like to grab some of that two to one," said the boy.

"Don't be foolish," counselled the canny Scot. "Ye'll have enough on your mind wi'out makin' bets; an' for pity's sake, remember what I've told ye—slow back, don't press, keep your head down, an' count three before ye look up. Hit them like ye did this mor-min' an' ye've a grand chance to win."

MacNeath sent his usual tee shot straight down the course, a long, well-placed ball; and Ambrose stepped forward in the midst of a silence that was almost painful.

"Mighty pretty," said he with a careless nod at his opponent. "Hope I do as well."

"Ye can," muttered old Dunn'I, "if ye'll keep your fool mouth shut an' your eye on the ball!" As Ambrose stooped to arrange his tee he caught a glimpse of the gallery—a long, triple row of spectators, keenly interested in his next move—expectant, anxious, apprehensive. Something of the mental attitude of the audience communicated itself to the youngster, and he paused for an instant, crouched on one knee. When he rose all the nonchalant ease was gone from his manner, all the cocksureness out of his eyes. He looked again at MacNeath's ball, a white speck far down the fairway. MacQuarrie groaned and shook his head.

"Never mind that one!" he whispered to himself savagely. "Play the one on the tee!" Ambrose fidgeted as he took his stance, shifted his weight from one foot to the other, and his first practise swing was short and jerky. He seemed to realise this, for he tried again before he stepped forward to the ball. It was no use; the result was the same. He had suddenly stiffened in every muscle and joint—gone tense with the nervous strain. He did manage to remember about the back swing—it was slow enough to suit anybody; but at the top of it he faltered, hesitating just long enough to destroy the rhythm that produces a perfect shot. He realised this, too, and tried to make up for it by lunging desperately at the ball; but as the club-face went through he jerked up his head and turned it sharply to the left. The inevitable penalty for this triple error was a wretchedly topped ball, which skipped along the ground until it reached the bunker.

"Well, by the sweet and suffering——"

This was as far as Ambrose got before he remembered that he had a gallery. He scuttled off the tee, very much abashed; and MacNeath followed, covering the ground with long, even strides. There was just the thin edge of a smile on the veteran's lean, bronzed face.

Moved by a common impulse, the spectators turned their backs and began to drift across the lawn to the Number Ten tee. They had seen quite enough. Old Doc Pinkinson voiced the general sentiment:

"No use following a bad match when you can see a good one, folks. Gilmore and Jordan are just driving off at Ten. I knew that redhead was a fizzer—a false alarm."

"Can't understand why they let him play at all!" scolded Daddy Bradshaw. "Might just as well put *me* in there against MacNeath! Fools!"

MacQuarrie obstinately refused to quit his pupil.

"He boggled his swing," growled Dunn'l; "he fair jumped at the ball, an' he looked up before he hit it. He'll do better wi'out a gallery. Come along, sir!"

I followed as far as the first bunker. Though his ball was half buried in the sand, Ambrose attempted to skim it over the wall with a mashie, an idiotic thing to do, and an all but impossible shot. He got exactly what his lunacy deserved—a much worse lie than before, close against the bank—and this exhibition of poor judgment cost him half his audience.

"What, not going already?" asked Ambrose after he had played four and picked up his ball. "Stick round a while. This is going to be *good*."

I said I wanted to see how the other matches were coming on.

"Everybody seems to feel the same way," said the redhead, looking at the retreating gallery. "All because I slopped that drive! I'll have that audience back again—see if I don't! And I'll bet you I won't look up on another shot all day!"

"If ye do," grumbled MacQuarrie, "I'll never play wi' ye again as long as ye live!"

"That's a promise!" cried Ambrose. "One down, eh? Where do we go from here?"

IV

Our team veterans did not lack sympathetic encouragement on the last nine holes, and all four matches tightened up to such an extent that we wavered between hope and fear until Crane's final putt on the seventeenth green dropped us into the depths of despair.

Gilmore, setting the pace with Jordan, gave us early encouragement by maintaining a safe lead throughout and winning his match, 3 to 2. First blood was ours, but the period of rejoicing was a short one; for the deliberate Louns- berry, approaching and putting with heartbreaking accuracy, disposed of Bishop on the seventeenth green.

"One apiece," said Doc Pinkinson. "Now what's Elder doing?"

The Elder-Smathers match came to Number Seventeen all square; but our man ended the suspense by dropping a beautiful mashie pitch dead to the pin from a distance of one hundred yards. Smathers' third shot also reached the green; but his long putt went wide and Elder tapped the ball into the cup, adding a second victory to our credit.

"It's looking better every minute!" chirped the irrepressible Doc Pinkinson. "Now if Moreman can lick his man we're all hunky-dory. If he loses—good-a-by, cup! No use figuring on that red-headed snipe of a kid. MacNeath has sent him to the cleaner's by now, sure!"

The gallery waited at the seventeenth green, watching in anxious silence as Crane and Moreman played their pitch shots over the guarding bunker. Both were well on in threes; but the

Bellevue caddie impudently held his forefinger in the air as a sign that his man was one up. Moreman made a good try, but his fourth shot stopped a few inches from the cup; and Crane, after studying the roll of the green for a full minute, dropped a forty-foot putt for a four—and dropped our spirits with it.

"That settles it!" wheezed Daddy Bradshaw.

"No need to bother about that other match.... Oh, if Anderson was so set on breaking his leg, why didn't he wait till to-morrow?"

"Then he could have busted 'em both," remarked the unfeeling Pinkinson, "and nobody would have said a word. Might's well pay those bets, I reckon. We got as much chance as that snowball they're always talking about. If it didn't melt, somebody would eat it."

He turned and looked back along the course. Two figures appeared on the skyline, proceeding in the direction of the six-teenth tee. The first one was tall, and moved with long, even strides; the second was short, and even at the distance it seemed to strut and swagger.

"Hello!" ejaculated Pinkinson. "Ain't that MacNeath and the kid, going to Sixteen? It is, by golly! D'you reckon they're playing out the bye holes just for fun—or what?"

"It can't be anything else," said Bradshaw. "The boy couldn't have carried him that far." Somebody plucked at my sleeve. It was a small dirty-faced caddie, very much out of breath.

"Mister Phipps says—if you want to see—some reg'lar golf—you'd better catch the finish—of his match. He says—bring all the gang with you."

"The finish of his match!" I cried. "Isn't it over? You don't mean that they're still playing?"

"Still playin' is right!" panted the caddie. "They was all square—when I left 'em."

All square! Like a flash the news ran through the gallery. The various groups, already drifting disconsolately in the direction of the clubhouse, halted and began buzzing with excitement and incredulity. All square? Nonsense! It couldn't be true. A green kid like that holding MacNeath to an even game for fifteen holes? Rot! But, in spite of the doubts so openly expressed, there was a brisk and general movement backward along the course, with the sixteenth putting green as an objective point.

It was a much augmented gallery that lined the side hill above the contestants. All the other team members were there, our men surprised and skeptical, and the Bellevue players nervous and apprehensive. There was also a troop of idle caddies, who had received the word by some mysterious wireless of their own devising.

"MacNeath is down in four," whispered one of the youngsters; "and Reddy has got to sink this one."

Ambrose's ball was four feet from the cup. He walked up to it, took one look at the line, one at the hole, and made the shot without an instant's hesitation—a clean, firm tap that gave the ball no chance to waver, but sent it squarely into the middle of the cup. MacQuarrie himself could not have shown more confidence. Mac-, Neath's caddie replaced the flag in the hole, dropped both hands to his hips, and moved them back and forth in a level, sweeping gesture. His sign language answered the question uppermost in every mind. Still all square! A patter of applause gave thanks for the information and Ambrose looked up at us with a quizzical grin. I caught his eye, and the rascal winked at me.

He was first on the seventeenth tee, and this time there was no sign of nervous tension. After a single powerful practise swing he stepped forward to his ball, pressed the sole of his club lightly behind it, and got off a tremendous tee shot. I noticed that his lips moved; and he did not raise his head until the ball was well down the course.

"He's countin' three before he looks up!" whispered a voice in my ear; and there was MacQuarrie, the butt of a dead cigar between his teeth, and his eyes alive with all the emotions a Scot may feel but can never express in words.

"Then he's really been playing good golf?" I asked.

"Ay. Grand golf! They both have. It's a dingdong match, an' just a question which one will crack fir-rst."

MacNeath's drive held out no hope that he was about to crack under the strain of an even battle. He executed the tee shot with the ma- chinelike precision of the veteran golfer—stance, swing and follow-through standardised by years of experience.

Our seventeenth hole is a long one, par 5, and the approach to the putting green is guarded by an embankment, paralleled on the far side by a wide and treacherous sand trap, put there to encourage clean mashie pitches. The average player cannot reach the bunker on his second, much less carry the sand trap on the other side of it; but the long drivers sometimes string two tre- mendous wooden-club shots together and reach the edge of the green. More frequently they get into trouble and pay the penalty for attempting too much.

The two balls were close together; but Ambrose's shot was the longer one by a matter of feet, and it was up to MacNeath to play first. Would he gamble and go for the green, or would he play short and make sure of a five? The veteran estimated the distance, looked carefully at his lie, and then pulled an iron from his bag. Instantly I knew what was passing in his mind—sensed his golf- ing strategy: MacNeath intended to place his second shot short of the bunker, in the hope that Ambrose would be tempted into risking the long, dangerous wooden-club shot across to the green.

"Aha!" whispered MacQuarrie. "The old fox! He'll not take a chance himself, but he wants the lad to take one. ' "Will ye walk into my parlour?" says the spider to the fly.' Ay; that's just it—will he, now?"

Ambrose gave us no time for suspense. MacNeath's ball had hardly stopped rolling before his decision was made—and a sound one at that! He whipped his mid-iron from the bag.

" 'Fraid I'll have to fool you, old chap," said he airily. "You wanted me to go for the green—eh, what? Well, I hate to disappoint you; but I can't gamble in an even game—not when the kitty is a sand trap. . . . Ride, you little round rascal; ride!"

The last remark was addressed to the ball just before the blade of the mid-iron flicked it from the grass. Again there were two white specks in the distance, lying side by side. If MacNeath was disappointed he did not show it, but tramped on down the course, silent as usual and absorbed in the game. Both took fives on the hole, missing long putts; and the battle was still all square.

Our home hole is a par 4—a blind drive and an iron pitch to the green; and the vital shot is the one from the tee. It must go absolutely straight and high enough to carry the top of the hill, one hundred and forty yards away. To the right is an abrupt downward slope, ending in a deep ravine. To the left, and out of sight from the tee, is a wide sand trap, with the father of all bunkers at its far edge. The only safe ball is the one that sails over the direction post.

Ambrose drove; and a smothered gasp went up from the gallery. The ball had the speed of a bullet, as well as a perfect line; and, at first, I thought it would rise enough to skim the crest of the hill. Instead of that, it seemed to dudk in flight, caught the hard face of the incline, and kicked abruptly to the left. It was that crooked bound which broke all our hearts; for we knew that, barring a miracle, our man was in the sand trap.

"Hard luck!" said MacNeath; and I think he really meant to be sympathetic.

Ambrose looked at him as a bulldog might look at a mastiff.

"Oh, I wouldn't say that!" he answered, rather stiffly. "I like to play my second shot from over there."

"You're welcome!" said MacNeath; and completed our discomfiture by poling out a tremendous shot, which carried well over the direction post and went sailing on up the plateam toward the clubhouse.

No man ever hit a longer ball at a more opportune time. As we toiled up the hill I tried to say something hopeful.

"He may have stopped short of the trap."

"Not a hope!" said MacQuarrie, chewing at his cigar. "He'll be in—up to his neck."

Sure enough, when we reached the summit there was the caddie, a mournful statue on the edge of the sand trap. The crowd halted at a proper distance and Ambrose and MacNeath went forward alone. MacQuarrie and I swung off to the left, for we wanted to see how deep the ball was in and what sort of a lie it had found.

"Six feet in from the edge," muttered Dunn'l, "an' twenty feet away from the wall. Lyin' up on top of the sand too. An iron wi' a little loft to it, a clean shot, a good thir-rd, an' he might get a four yet. It's just possible."

"But not probable," said I. "What on earth is he waiting for?"

Ambrose had taken a seat on the edge of the trap; and as he looked from the ball to the bunker looming in front of it, he rolled a cigarette.

"You don't mind if I study this situation a bit?" said he to MacNeath.

"Take your time," said the veteran. "Because I wouldn't want to use the wrong dub here," continued Ambrose.

The caddie said something to him at this point; but Phipps shook his red head impatiently and continued to puff at his cigarette. He caught a glimpse of me and beckoned.

"How do the home boys stand on this cup thing?" he asked.

"All even—two matches to two."

"That," said Ambrose after a thoughtful pause, "seems to put it up to me."

At last he rose, tossed away the cigarette end and, reaching for his bag, drew out a wooden club. Again the caddie said something; but Ambrose waved him away. There was not a sound from his audience, but a hundred heads wagged dolefully in unison. A wooden club—out of a trap? Suicide! Sheer suicide! Am iron might give him a fighting chance to halve the hole; but my last lingering hope died when I saw that club in the boy's hand. The infernal young lunatic! I believe I said something of the sort to MacQuarrie.

"Sh-h!" he whispered. "Yon's a baffy. I made it for him."

"What's a baffy?"

"Well, it's just a kind of an exaggerated bulldog spoon—ye might almost call it a wooden mashie, wi' a curvin' sole on it. It's great for distance. The lie is good, the wind's behind him, an' if he can only hit it clean—clean!———Oh, ye little red devil, keep your head down—keep your head down an' hit it clean!"

I shall never forget the picture spread out along the edge of that green plateau—the redheaded stocky youngster in the sand trap taking his stance and whipping the clubhead back and forth; MacNeath coolly leaning on his driver and smiling over a match already won; the two caddies in the background, one sneeringly triumphant, the other furiously angry; the rim of spectators, motionless, hopeless.

Everybody was watching Ambrose, and I think Old MacQuarrie was the only onlooker who was not absolutely certain that the choice of a wrong club was throwing away our last slender chance.

When the tension was almost unbearable the redhead turned and grinned at MacNeath.

"I suppose you'd shoot this with an iron," said he; "but the baffy is a great club—if you've got the nerve to use it."

Ambrose settled his feet firmly in the sand, craned his neck for a final look at the flag, two hundred yards away, dropped his chin on his chest, waggled the clubhead over the ball, and then swung with every ounce of strength in his sturdy body. I heard a sharp click, saw a tiny feather of sand spurt into the air, and against the blue sky I caught a glimpse of a soaring white speck, which went higher and higher until I lost it altogether. The next thing I knew, the spectators were cheering, yelling, screaming; and some one was hammering me violently between the shoulder blades. It was the unemotional Dunn'l MacQuarrie, gone completely daft with excitement.

"Oh, man!" he cried. "He picked it up as clean as a whistle, an' he's on the green—on the green!"

"Told you that was a sweet little club!" said Ambrose as he climbed out of the trap. "Takes nerve to use one though. On the green, eh? Well, I guess that'll hold you for a while."

His prediction soon had a solid backing of fact. MacNeath, the iron man, the dependable Number One, the match player without nerves, was not proof against a miracle. Ambrose's phenomenal recovery had shaken the veteran to the soles of his shoes.

MacNeath's second shot was an easy pitch to the green, but he lingered too long over it; the blade of his mashie caught the turf at least three inches behind the ball and shot it off at an angle into the thick, long grass that guards the eighteenth green. He was forced to use a heavy niblick on his third; but the ball rolled thirty feet beyond the pin. He tried hard for the long putt, but missed, and picked up when Ambrose laid his third shot on the lip of the cup.

By the most fortunate fluke ever seen on a golf course our little red Ishmael had won for us the permanent possession of the Edward B. Wimpus Trophy.

MacNeath was game. He picked up his ball with the left hand and offered his right to Ambrose. "Well done!" said he.

"Thanks!" responded Ambrose. "Guess I kind of jarred you with that baffy shot. It's certainly a dandy club in a pinch. Better let MacQuarrie make you one."

MacNeath swallowed hard and nearly managed a smile.

"It wasn't the club," said he. "It was just burglar's luck. You couldn't do it again in a thousand years!"

"Maybe not," replied the victor; "but when you get back to Bellevue you tell all the dear chappies there that I got away with it once—got away with it the one time when it counted!"

At this point the gallery closed in and overwhelmed young Mr. Phipps. Inside of a minute he heard more pleasant things about himself than had come to his ears in a lifetime. He did not dispute a single statement that was made; nor did he discount one by so much as the deprecating lift of an eyebrow. For once in his life he agreed with everybody. In the stag celebration that followed—with the Edward B. Wimpus Cup in the middle of the big round table—he was easily induced to favour us with a few brief remarks. He informed us that tin cups were nothing in his young life, club spirit was nothing, but that gameness was everything—and the cheering was led by the Dingbats!

Now you know why we feel that we owe Ambrose something; and, if I am any judge, that debt will be paid with heavy interest. Dunn'l MacQuarrie is also a winner. He has booked so many orders for baffies that he is now endeavouring to secure the services of a first-class club maker.

As Ambrose often tells us, the baffy is a sweet little club to have in the bag—provided, of course, you have the nerve to use it.

STARTING THE SWING—THE UNIVERSAL METHOD

DAVID SMITH HUNTER

L ast winter I spent some months as an instructor in the larg-est indoor golf school in New York (or America). There were a number (at least a dozen) of other professionals engaged, and I had a splendid opportunity to watch not only their methods of teaching, but also their various styles of play. Some used the open, some the square, stance; some used a flat, some a medium, and others an upright, swing. They had various methods of gripping the club, but whatever their method of doing these various things, they all—without an exception—had the same way of starting the club back from the ball, although the effects were very different, owing to different characteristics and physical make-up.

As already stated, the effects were different but the start of the back swing was always the same—the back movement and the turning of the wrists and forearms always started simultaneously and there was no jerkiness—even though some of them had a very quick swing. Their use of it may have been instinctive or subconscious, but it was there, nevertheless.

The simplicity of this principle and rule in golf is its chief charm. It is applicable to all styles of play, whether upright, flat, or medium, and applies to all the shots in your bag. Analyze everything from the back swing. Never work to improve "effects," always go back to "cause."

Briefly, my theory—which is now no longer a theory, but a fact, proved demonstrable, through years of experience—may be summed up as follows:

With grip and stance properly adjusted, be sure you start your club-head back from ball correctly. Do not jerk, start slowly. Let the backward movement and the turn of the wrists and forearms start at exactly the same moment. Keep control in the left hand. Pronate properly. (And to know when you are doing this, notice the position of the club-head when club is horizontal). And finally, when you "go off your game," no matter in what respect—whether because of slicing, pulling, topping, whatever it may be—do not try to correct the "effect" but *go back to first principles* and thereby remove the "cause."

THE STORY OF PHYSIQUE IN GOLF

HAROLD H. HILTON

I once heard a Scotch professional say: "Yon man's o'er strong to play." He was referring to one of those individuals of Samsonlike development who could put the shot an incredible number of feet and who, by pure muscular power, could lift a comparatively heavy man with one hand and hold him up for some considerable period of time. There was much of truth in this professional's remark, for the Goliath could make nothing of the game of golf. He could not even hit the ball a long way, for the simple reason that he was muscle-bound in every limb in his body, and in consequence could not swing the club with even a relative degree of freedom.

The whole result of his most frantic muscular efforts was to push the ball a distance of about one hundred and fifty yards. I say push advisedly, as his swing was nothing more or less than a species of push, a swing which took the club up with rigid muscles. He did not seem able to relax those abnormal muscles of his, and then tighten them up again on the downward swing, but the mere effort of taking hold of the club seemed to have the effect of bringing his frame into an absolute state of rigidity.

I do not wish to imply by this, however, that actual physical strength is of no avail in the game of golf. If a man who is well blessed with physical power can only apply that power to its best advantage, it must of necessity be a great asset to him, as there are quite a number of strokes to be played in the game which necessitate the use of more than an average degree of strength, and the man who is not blessed with a sufficiency for the occasion must necessarily suffer. But it is better to be blessed with a comparatively limited degree of physical strength and know how to apply it to its fullest advantage than to have the gift of exceptional physical power and not know how to utilize it advantageously. In the one instance the physical power is in excellent control, while in the other it cannot be.

If there is one muscle, or rather set of muscles, in the human frame which are of no use to man in the pursuit of the game of golf, they are those which act in relation to what is usually termed the biceps. No doubt these muscles have their uses in this world. For instance, one could imagine that they are particularly serviceable in the removal of pianofortes or other heavy domestic material, but for the propulsion of a golf ball they are worse than useless, as they are apt to get in the way and hinder the swing of the player.

That they are of little avail to the golfer is evidenced by the fact that among professionals whose physical exercises are very much limited to the playing of golf there is almost an entire absence of development. Some few years ago I had occasion to receive very emphatic testimony on this point. We were discussing the question of golf and physical development consequent to it, and I expressed the opinion that not only were the biceps of no use to the player, but, moreover, there were very few first-class players who could claim any particular development in this part of the arm and that the majority were almost devoid of such development. These opinions were received with a certain degree of incredulity, not to say unbelief. Just at that moment J. H. Taylor, the four-times champion, arrived on the scene, and I suggested that they should utilize his anatomy as a test.

Now, Taylor is an exceptionally sturdy, strongly built man who looks the very embodiment of physical strength, the kind of man one would on first sight be excused in assuming was something akin to a professional wrestler. On the mere question of appearance, a more unlikely subject could not have been chosen by which to prove the truth of my contention, but I was not in the least alarmed, as I knew that Taylor played golf and no other game. The reply to the query as to the development of his biceps was much as I anticipated, as it came in the most emphatic manner; "Soft as butter, sir, just like a child's" and a physical demonstration proved this to be correct in every way. John Henry Taylor was almost completely devoid of muscular development in his biceps, and in this respect was only much the same as the majority of men who have made the game of golf their favorite physical pastime.

But it must not be understood that golf does not develop the physical attributes, as in truth it is a wonderful all-round developer of physique, and in particular of the muscles at the back of the arm, and those which have their resting place in the shoulders; the majority of those who have played much golf in their younger years have splendidly developed shoulder muscles. Again it develops the leg and chest muscles; in fact, as a general, all-round developer of the frame there are very few games as good as golf. It is a peculiar fact that the muscles that it does not materially aid are the biceps and the forearm muscles. Although many good golfers have well-developed forearms, it is, to my way of thinking, possible to have too great a development of forearm for the playing of successful golf.

What I do think the game of golf tends to develop is strength of sinew, particularly those which pass through the wrists, as it is almost impossible for a golfer to be a great player without he has an average degree of strength in the sinews of the wrists. This does not mean necessarily that he must be possessed of those big, strong, square-boned species of wrists which indicate exceptional strength in this part of the anatomy. In fact, the bone development may be slight and the wrist apparently a comparatively weak example, but provided there is strength and suppleness of sinew, the player need not worry about the lack of bone. The sinews will do all that is required and some of the longest drivers I have ever come across have had wrists which in appearance would have seemed more in keeping on the arms of a woman.

THE SECRET OF LENGTH

The secret of being able to hit a golf ball a very long way, is freedom of action and the application of strength. To be a long driver it is not altogether necessary to be abnormally strong muscularly. Strength is useful, but not in any way essential, as is evidenced by the fact that many men of comparatively light physique are very long drivers, a fact which is no doubt due to strength of sinew and the gift of being able to apply the strength they have at command. In connection with the evidence of power when hitting a golf ball, I am convinced on one point and that is that long arms are a great aid to the player, as not only do they enable him to obtain a fine, free sweep of the club without the use of any excessive body action, but, moreover, long arms are invariably set on the body on somewhat free principles, and the player who is blessed with this freedom is enabled to get his arms well away from his body.

The ideal combination for long driving is a pair of long, sinewy arms combined with long, powerful hands and fingers, and the majority of players who drive a long ball without much apparent effort are invariably thus blessed. Of course, there are players who obtain length by other means, men who are compactly built and are comparatively short in the arms, but they usually obtain their length by forcing with the body, that is, by throwing the whole of their physique into the blow. It is a forcing style of driving which is not altogether elegant and, moreover, it is a style of play which is apt to go to pieces under pressure. Again there is always a danger in connection with players who, on account of their physique, have recourse to these methods, and the danger lies in the fact that with increasing years they are naturally prone to put on avoirdupois, and what freedom they originally possessed is apt to leave them, and they inevitably lose their length.

Of all the golfers I have come across I cannot think of any who to my mind would appear as ideally built for the playing of the game as Harry Vardon. He is sufficiently tall without being ungainly, he is strong without being muscle-bound, and he has the strength in the correct places, viz.: the shoulders, wrists, and hands. There may be many men playing golf who are infinitely better physically developed than Harry Vardon, but perhaps none whose physique is better adapted for the game. George Duncan is another player whose physique is also well fitted for the game, but Ray, whom Americans will see performing this fall in their open championships, would appear to be a somewhat clumsily fashioned individual and does not in any way give one the impression of being an athlete. But he has wonderful strength and great freedom of action.

At one time in his career he was probably too free in his actions, but since he has filled out into a big, heavy man, his freedom has come much more under control, and he is in consequence a more reliable long-game player. Comparing his form of the present day with that when he was a man of comparatively light physique, one cannot heip but think that the extra avoirdupois which has gradually appeared during the past few years has had a very sobering effect upon his swing, and many young players who are inclined to be weedy of physique would, no doubt, benefit by the addition of weight to their physique, much as Ray would appear to have benefited.

Reviewing golfers who have learned the rudiments of the game in the States, one cannot help being struck with the fact that the four players who stand out as having made the biggest name for themselves are all men of comparatively light physique. The four I mean are Messrs. Walter Travis, Jerome Travers, Chick Evans, and MacDermott. Not by the wildest stretch of imagination can any of this quartet be called big men. In truth, one would be inclined to class them all as comparatively small men. Jerome Travers is probably the tallest of the four, but he is not by way of being a giant.

SUCCESSFUL SMALL MEN

Of course, it may be only a pure coincidence that the four most successful golfers in America are all of small physique, but it is nevertheless remarkable that they should exhibit more control over their clubs than the men of more commanding stature. There is a saying that a good "big one" will always defeat a good "little one," and one cannot get away from the truth of this opinion, as provided that both are equally gifted from the point of view of scientific application, the greater strength of the bigger man must prevail in the end. But, on the other hand, it will generally be found that the smaller man has the better balanced physique, better balanced in the respect that he can control his actions more successfully. On this assumption the small man should be the more stable and consistent player than the big man, and I am inclined to think that on the average he is, as he has certainly proved himself so in America.

It is in events such as open championship contests that the smaller man is at a disadvantage with his stronger opponents. He may be likely to do as well as any of his opponents, for argument's sake we will say even better than any individual opponent, but on account of the limitations to his power he cannot expect with just average fortune, to accomplish anything as great as that which several of his stronger opponents may accomplish. However well the smaller man may play, there is always the great chance that one or other of his more powerful opponents may do even better, for the reason that they are gifted with greater power, and in an open event one has to defeat all opponents and not any particular individual one.

In England the open championship during recent years has invariably fallen to one of the big men. Players like J. H. Taylor or Tom Ball, who are representatives of the accurate, scientific class of player, have a habit of finishing in second position, suffering defeat because they have the misfortune to run up against just *one* player possessed of greater power, who is on the top of his game on this particular occasion. The difficulty for the Taylors and the Balls is to defeat the whole fleet of these big men, and the fleet is such a numerous one nowadays.

In the old days the sound, accurate golfer had a much better chance of success in the open championship than he has at present, as the ever-growing number of powerful big hitters has had the effect of increasing the pace, so to speak, in that the players now realize that to win the championship something more than steady play is required. One or other of the strong men is almost sure to be on his game, and the men less gifted in physique have to go full steam ahead from the very start of the event and often crack under the strain.

Aside and apart from the question of a good wrist and a good wrist action, which is undoubtedly the most essential possession for a golfer who hopes to be a first-class exponent of the game, perhaps the most useful asset is a powerful pair of hands, and if the fingers are long all the better for the player. To my way of thinking, long, strong fingers are an aid to the golfer in every way, with the possible exception of when he is on the putting greens, where it may be an advantage to have slight, delicate fingers. But in the more powerful phases of the game the long, strong fingers have it in every way, as they are able to control a comparatively heavy club with ease, and long driving, in consequence, becomes more or less a simple manner.

But it is in the really heavy work from indifferent lies that the long, strong fingers hold the great advantage, as they enable the player to grip the club firmly and get that quick, sharp nip into the swing which is so useful when playing from rough, heavy grass. I speak feelingly on this point, as nature gave me short fingers, and I look with envy upon men like Braid, Ray, and Vardon when they take heavy medium irons from lies from which I would have to rest content with a niblick shot for safety. They have the combination of length in the fingers and strength in the hand, which allows them to put sufficient snap behind the shot to enable the club to come through all obstructions.

Personally, I may have the requisite strength in the hand, but I am certainly not possessed of the requisite grip with the fingers, and if I attempt any of these Goliathlike feats when playing from long grass, it invariably ends in my losing possession of the club. It is not due to the lack of strength in my fingers, but to the lack of firmness of grip owing to the shortness of finger.

THE VIRTUE OF SLOPING SHOULDERS

One excellent physical attribute for a golfer to possess is sloping, or what are generally termed bottle-neck, shoulders, as there cannot be the slightest shadow of doubt that the man with these sloping shoulders is always gifted with exceptional freedom in this part of his anatomy. There are two of our noted players, viz.: Mr. John Ball and Alexander Herd, who are blessed with this class of shoulders, and for freedom of swing these two are not excelled by any. The ease with which they can swing a golf club is simply extraordinary.

Rather remarkable to say, both Mr. Ball and Mr. Herd grip the club in the palm of the right hand, with the knuckles pointing to the ground, and I feel assured that neither of them could employ this underhand grip and nevertheless swing with such freedom and truth if it were not for the sloping shoulders that they possess. In swinging a golf club a square-shouldered man is, to my way of thinking, at a disadvantage in comparison with men who are physically modeled on the lines of Mr. Ball and Mr. Herd.

Although in the swinging of a golf club the upper part of a player's anatomy is admittedly a more important factor than the lower part, still in the truth of a golfing swing much depends upon the use the player makes of his legs and feet, and in consequence a player is a good deal dependent upon the physique of his lower limbs. There can be but little doubt that it *is* an advantage to be strong in the legs, as strength in this part of the anatomy enables a player to maintain his balance. But as against this many men who are abnormally strong in the legs are not a little prone to try to utilize them too much, and are not only apt to move about on their feet, but, moreover, are sometimes inclined to place so much pressure on the feet that there is a continual risk of their slipping.

One thing I have noticed is that nearly all players who are exceedingly well developed below are inclined to take a very wide stance. This is only natural, as they are naturally inclined to obtain a more than average degree of impetus from the legs and feet

Another point which is noticeable in connection with the general run of golfers who have played from their youth up is that they are much inclined to turn their toes up, and in a true, free golfing swing players undoubtedly utilize their toes a great deal. Moreover, they turn on the ball of the foot, and this tends to turn the toes skywards.

THE STORY OF THE CHARM
OF GOLF

ALAN ALEXANDER MILNE

When he reads of the notable doings of famous golfers, the eighteen-handicap man has no envy in his heart. For by this time he has discovered the great secret of golf. Before he began to play he wondered wherein lay the fascination of it; now he knows. Golf is so popular simply because it is the best game in the world at which to be bad.

Consider what it is to be bad at cricket. You have bought a new bat, perfect in balance; a new pair of pads, white as driven snow; gloves of the very latest design. Do they let you use them? No. After one ball, in the negotiation of which neither your bat, nor your pads, nor your gloves came into play, they send you back into the pavilion to spend the rest of the afternoon listening to fatuous stories of some old gentleman who knew Fuller Pilch. And when your side takes the field, where are you? Probably at long leg both ends, exposed to the public gaze as the worst fieldsman in London. How devastating are your emotions. Remorse, anger, mortification fill your heart; above all, envy—envy of the lucky immortals who disport themselves on the green level of Lord's.

Consider what it is to be bad at lawn tennis. True, you are allowed to hold on to your new racket all through the game, but how often are you allowed to employ it usefully? How often does your partner cry "Mine!" and bundle you out of the way? Is there pleasure in playing football badly? You may spend the full eighty minutes in your new boots, but your relations with the ball will be distant. They do not give you a ball to yourself at football.

But how different a game is golf. At golf it is the bad player who gets the most strokes. However good his opponent, the bad player has the right to play out each hole to the end; he will get more than his share of the game. He need have no fears that his new driver will not be employed. He will have as many swings with it as the scratch man; more, if he misses the ball altogether upon one or two tees. If he buys a new niblick he is certain to get fun out of it on the very first day.

And, above all, there is this to be said for golfing mediocrity— the bad player can make the strokes of the good player. The poor cricketer has perhaps never made fifty in his life; as soon as he stands at the wickets he knows that he is not going to make fifty today. But the eighteen-handicap man has some time or other played every hole on the course to perfection. He has driven a ball 250 yards; he has made superb approaches; he has run down the long putt. Any of these things may suddenly happen to him again. And therefore it is not his fate to have to sit in the club smoking-room after his second round and listen to the wonderful deeds of others. He can join in too. He can say with perfect truth, "I once carried the ditch at the fourth with my second," or "I remember when I drove into the bunker guarding the eighth green," or even "I did a three at the eleventh this afternoon"— bogey being five. But if the bad cricketer says, "I remember when I took a century in forty minutes off Lockwood and Richardson," he is nothing but a liar.

For these and other reasons golf is the best game in the world for the bad player. And sometimes I am tempted to go further and say that it is a better game for the bad player than for the good player. The joy of driving a ball straight after a week of slicing, the joy of putting a mashie shot dead, the joy of even a moderate stroke with a brassie; best of all, the joy of the perfect cleek shot—these things the good player will never know. Every stroke we bad players make we make in hope. It is never so bad but it might have been worse; it is never so bad but we are confident of doing better next time. And if the next stroke is good, what happiness fills our soul. How eagerly we tell ourselves that in a little while all our strokes will be as good.

What does Vardon know of this? If he does a five hole in four he blames himself that he did not do it in three; if he does it in five he is miserable. He will never experience that happy surprise with which we hail our best strokes. Only his bad strokes surprise him, and then we may suppose that he is not happy. His length and accuracy are mechanical; they are not the result, as so often in our case, of some suddenly applied maxim or some suddenly discovered innovation. The only thing which can vary in his game is his putting, and putting is not golf but croquet.

But of course we, too, are going to be as good as Vardon one day. We are only postponing the day because meanwhile it is so pleasant to be bad. And it is part of the charm of being bad at golf that in a moment, in a single night, we may become good. If the bad cricketer said to a good cricketer, "What am I doing wrong?" the only possible answer would be, "Nothing particular, except that you can't play cricket." But if you or I were to say to our scratch friend, "What am I doing wrong?" he would reply at once, "Moving the head" or "Dropping the right knee" or "Not getting the wrists in soon enough," and by tomorrow we should be different players. Upon such, a little depends, or seems to the eighteen-handicap to depend, excellence in golf.

And so, perfectly happy in our present-badness and perfectly confident of our future goodness, we long-handicap men remain. Perhaps it would be pleasanter to be a little more certain of getting the ball safely off the first tee; perhaps at the fourteenth hole, where there is a right of way and the public encroach, we should like to feel that we have done with topping; perhaps

Well, perhaps we might get our handicap down to fifteen this summer. But no lower; certainly no lower.

THE STORY: SHOULD MARRIED MEN PLAY GOLF?

JEROME KLAPKA JEROME

That we Englishmen attach too much importance to sport goes without saying—or, rather, it has been said so often as to have become a commonplace. One of these days some reforming English novelist will write a book, showing the evil effects of over-indulgence in sport: the neglected business, the ruined home, the slow but sure sapping of the brain—what there may have been of it in the beginning—leading to semi-imbecility and yearly increasing obesity.

A young couple, I once heard of, went for their honeymoon to Scotland. The poor girl did not know he was a golfer (he had wooed and won her during a period of idleness enforced by a sprained shoulder), or maybe she would have avoided Scotland. The idea they started with was that of a tour. The second day the man went out for a stroll by himself. At dinner-time he observed, with a far-away look in his eyes, that it seemed a pretty spot they had struck, and suggested their staying there another day. The next morning after breakfast he borrowed a club from the hotel porter, and remarked that he would take a walk while she finished doing her hair. He said it amused him, swinging a club while he walked. He returned in time for lunch and seemed moody all the afternoon. He said the air suited him, and urged that they should linger yet another day.

She was young and inexperienced, and thought, maybe, it was liver. She had heard much about liver from her father. The next morning he borrowed more clubs, and went out, this time before breakfast, returning to a late and not over sociable dinner. That was the end of their honeymoon so far as she was concerned. He meant well, but the thing had gone too far. The vice had entered into his blood, and the smell of the links drove out all other considerations.

We are most of us familiar, I take it, with the story of the golfing parson, who could not keep from swearing when the balls went wrong.

"Golf and the ministry don't seem to go together," his friend told him. "Take my advice before it's too late, and give it up, Tammas."

A few months later Tammas met his friend again.

"You were right, Jamie," cried the parson cheerily, "they didna run well in harness; golf and the meenistry, I hae followed your advice: I hae gi'en it oop."

"Then what are ye doing with that sack of clubs?" inquired Jamie.

"What am I doing with them?" repeated the puzzled Tammas. "Why I am going to play golf with them." A light broke upon him. "Great Heavens, man!" he continued, "ye didna' think 'twas the golf I'd gi'en oop?"

The Englishman does not understand play. He makes a life-long labour of his sport, and to it sacrifices mind and body. The health resorts of Europe—to paraphrase a famous saying that nobody appears to have said—draw half their profits from the playing fields of Eton and elsewhere. In Swiss and German kurhausen enormously fat men bear down upon you and explain to you that once they were the champion sprinters or the high-jump representatives of their university—men who now hold on to the bannisters and groan as they haul themselves upstairs. Consumptive men, between paroxysms of coughing, tell you of the goals they scored when they were half-backs or forwards of extraordinary ability. Ex-light-weight amateur pugilists, with the figure now of an American roll-top desk, butt you into a comer of the billiard-room, and, surprised they cannot get as near you as they would desire, whisper to you the secret of avoiding the undercut by the swiftness of the backward leap. Broken-down tennis players, one-legged skaters, dropsical gentlemen-riders, are to be met with hobbling on crutches along every highway of the Engadine.

They are pitiable objects. Never having learnt to read anything but the sporting papers, books are of no use to them. They never wasted much of their youth on thought, and, apparently, have lost the knack of it. They don't care for art, and Nature only suggests to them the things they can no longer do. The snow-clad mountain reminds them that once they were daring tobogannists; the undulating common makes them sad because they can no longer handle a golf-club; by the riverside they sit down and tell you of the salmon they caught before they caught rheumatic fever; birds only make them long for guns; music raises visions of the local cricket-match of long ago, enlivened by the local band; a picturesque estaminet, with little tables spread out under the vines, recalls bitter memories of ping-pong. One is sorry for them, but their conversation is not exhilarating. The man who has other interests in life beyond sport is apt to find their reminiscences monotonous; while to one another they do not care to talk. One gathers that they do not altogether believe one another.

The foreigner is taking kindly to our sports; one hopes he will be forewarned by our example and not overdo the thing. At present, one is bound to admit, he shows no sign of taking sport too seriously. Football is gaining favour more and more throughout Europe. But yet the Frenchman has not got it out of his head that the *coup* to practise is kicking the ball high into the air and catching it upon his head. He would rather catch the ball upon his head than score a goal. If he can manoeuvre the ball away into a corner, kick it up into the air twice running, and each time catch it on his head, he does not seem to care what happens after that. Anybody can have the ball; he has had his game and is happy.

They talk of introducing cricket into Belgium; I shall certainly try to be present at the opening game. I am afraid that, until he learns from experience, the Belgian fielder will stop cricket balls with his head. That the head is the proper thing with which to play ball appears to be in his blood. My head is round, he argues, and hard, just like the ball itself; what part of the human frame more fit and proper with which to meet and stop a ball.

Golf has not yet caught on, but tennis is firmly established from St. Petersburg to Bordeaux. The German, with the thoroughness characteristic of him, is working hard. University professors, stout majors, rising early in the morning, hire boys and practise back-handers and half-volleys. But to the Frenchman, as yet, it is a game. He plays it in a happy, merry fashion, that is shocking to English eyes.

Your partner's service rather astonishes you. An occasional yard or so beyond the line happens to anyone, but this man's object appears to be to break windows. You feel you really must remonstrate, when the joyous laughter and tumultuous applause of the spectators explain the puzzle to you. He has not been trying to serve; he has been trying to hit a man in the next court who is stooping down to tie up his shoe-lace. With his last ball he has succeeded. He has hit the man in the small of the back, and has bowled him over. The unanimous opinion of the surrounding critics is that the ball could not possibly have been better placed. A Doherty has never won greater applause from the crowd. Even the man who has been hit appears pleased; it shows what a Frenchman can do when he does take up a game.

But French honour demands revenge. He forgets his shoe, he forgets his game. He gathers together all the balls that he can find; his balls, your balls, anybody's balls that happen to be handy. And then commences the return match. At this point it is best to crouch down under shelter of the net. Most of the players round about adopt this plan; the more timid make for the club-house, and, finding themselves there, order coffee and light up cigarettes. After a while both players appear to be satisfied. The other players then gather round to claim their balls. This makes a good game by itself. The object is to get as many balls as you can, your own and other people's—for preference other people's—and run off with them round the courts, followed by whooping claimants.

In the course of half-an-hour or so, when everybody is dead beat, the game—the original game—is resumed. You demand the score; your partner promptly says it is "forty-fifteen." Both your opponents rush up to the net, and apparently there is going to be a duel. It is only a friendly altercation; they very much doubt its being "forty-fifteen." "Fifteen-forty" they could believe; they suggest it as a compromise. The discussion is concluded by calling it deuce. As it is rare for a game to proceed without some such incident occurring in the middle of it, the score generally is deuce. This avoids heart-burning; nobody wins a set and nobody loses. The one game generally suffices for the afternoon.

To the earnest player, it is also confusing to miss your partner occasionally—to turn round and find that he is talking to a man. Nobody but yourself takes the slightest objection to his absence. The other side appear to regard it as a good opportunity to score. Five minutes later he resumes the game. His friend comes with him, also the dog of his friend. The dog is welcomed with enthusiasm; all balls are returned to the dog. Until the dog is tired you do not get a look in. But all this will no doubt soon be changed. There are some excellent French and Belgian players; from them their compatriots will gradually learn higher ideals. The Frenchman is young in the game. As the right conception of the game grows upon him, he will also learn to keep the balls lower.

I suppose it is the continental sky. It is so blue, so beautiful; it naturally attracts one. Anyhow, the fact remains that most tennis players on the Continent, whether English or foreign, have a tendency to aim the ball direct at Heaven. At an English club in Switzerland there existed in my days a young Englishman who was really a wonderful player. To get the ball past him was almost an impossibility. It was his return that was weak. He only had one stroke; the ball went a hundred feet or so into the air and descended in his opponent's court. The other man would stand watching it, a little speck in the Heavens, growing gradually bigger and bigger as it neared the earth. New comers would chatter to him, thinking he had detected a balloon or an eagle. He would wave them aside, explain to them that he would talk to them later, after the arrival of the ball. It would fall with a thud at his feet, rise another twenty yards or so and again descend. When it was at the proper height he would hit it back over the net, and the next moment it would be mounting the sky again. At tournaments I have seen that young man, with tears in his eyes, pleading to be given an umpire. Every umpire had fled. They hid behind trees, borrowed silk hats and umbrellas and pretended they were visitors—any device, however mean, to avoid the task of umpiring for that young man. Provided his opponent did not go to sleep or get cramp, one game might last all day. Anyone could return his balls; but, as I have said, to get a ball past him was almost an impossibility. He invariably won; the other man, after an hour or so, would get mad and try to lose. It was his only chance of dinner.

It is a pretty sight, generally speaking, a tennis ground abroad. The women pay more attention to their costumes than do our lady players. The men are usually in spotless white. The ground is often charmingly situated, the club-house picturesque; there is always laughter and merriment. The play may not be so good to watch, but the picture is delightful. I accompanied a man a little while ago to his club on the outskirts of Brussels. The ground was bordered by a wood on one side, and surrounded on the other three by *petites fermes*—allotments, as we should call them in England, worked by the peasants themselves.

It was a glorious spring afternoon. The courts were crowded. The red earth and the green grass formed a background against which the women, in their new Parisian toilets, under their bright parasols, stood out like wondrous bouquets of moving flowers. The whole atmosphere was a delightful mingling of idle gaiety, flirtation, and graceful sensuousness. A modern Watteau would have seized upon the scene with avidity.

Just beyond—separated by the almost invisible wire fencing—a group of peasants were working in the field. An old woman and a young girl, with ropes about their shoulders, were drawing a harrow, guided by a withered old scarecrow of a man. They paused for a moment at the wire fencing, and looked through. It was an odd contrast; the two worlds divided by that wire fencing—so slight, almost invisible. The girl swept the sweat from her face with her hand; the woman pushed back her grey locks underneath the handkerchief knotted about her head; the old man straightened himself with some difficulty. So they stood, for perhaps a minute, gazing with quiet, passionless faces through that slight fencing, that a push from their work-hardened hands might have levelled.

Was there any thought, I wonder, passing through their brains? The young girl—she was a handsome creature in spite of her disfiguring garments. The woman—it was a wonderfully fine face: clear, calm eyes, deep-set under a square broad brow. The withered old scarecrow—ever sowing the seed in the spring of the fruit that others shall eat.

The old man bent again over the guiding ropes: gave the word. The team moved forward up the hill. It is Anatole France, I think, who says: Society is based upon the patience of the poor.

THE STORY OF THE TRAGEDIES OF THE SHORT PUTT

HARRY LEACH

The case of an earth so well explored by golfing travellers having been considered as the third of the wonders of the sphere, and the peculiarity of St. Andrews as the fourth, there is a clear suggestion as to which is the next or fifth wonder of the series. Inevitably one recalls the tearful situation of the mighty hunter in a story which is passed in company as fact. He declared he had encountered all the manifold perils of the jungle, had tracked the huge elephant to its retreat, and had stood eye to eye with the man-eating tiger. It is believed that he had done all these things. Then he added, "And never once have I trembled until I came to a short putt." For me one of the most remarkable things I have seen in golf was at an Open Championship meeting at St. Andrews when, watching and musing by the side of the eighteenth green, I saw four of the greatest players of this or any other time come up to it in the competition one by one and have putts of less than eighteen inches at that hole. Three of the four missed! In the old days, at all events, when the greens were not quite as they are now, but became very glassy and slippery with much wind and constant play upon them, I believe there were more short putts missed on the old course at St. Andrews than on any other two courses in the world, and the task of holing the little stupids on that home green was a most tormenting ordeal.

So, with the broken-hearted explorer, and the tragedy of St. Andrews, there is pointed to us for the next wonder of the game the missing of the short putt. And I do believe, and so must others, that the missing of such a short putt as it seems humanly impossible for any man, having the control of his limbs and being *compos mentis*, to miss is one of the most remarkable features of any game, and one that would be completely and absolutely inexplicable did it not in itself offer a most splendid illustration of the full effect of strain of mind on physical action, of the pressure of great responsibility on an over-anxious man. It embraces nearly the whole psychology of golf. The short putt largely explains the game, and it is testimony to the soundness of this view, and the rightful selection of this as a permanent wonder, that the general public would never believe the truth as we know it, that it is possible for the greatest players with what is to them, for the time being, almost as much as their lives depending on it, to miss putts so little that no walking baby properly fed would miss. The general public, with its vast stores of common sense, would not believe the fact; it would ridicule it and treat the whole suggestion with contempt, and it might in a sense be right; but then the general public has not been fighting its way round a golf course against another and very truculent general public, driving, playing seconds and thirds, getting bunkered and recovering, and encountering all manner of difficulties and dangers, and then had its fate for the day depending on a short putt at the eighteenth green! By psychology of the game, as just mentioned, we mean, of course, the way in which the mind and the emotions act and react upon the physical system and its capacity, how doubts and fears are engendered, and things from not seeming what they are become really different, so far as the attitude of the player to them is concerned. Thus, as has been well said, a putt of ten inches on the first green is, as one might feel, a putt of thirty inches—though still in fact of the same length—when that green is not the first but the thirty-seventh, and that on which a long-drawn-out match is being finished.

One summer's day, on a course in France, a little party of us were discussing the slow and sure methods of certain Americans then in Europe—if, really, they were quite so sure as they were slow. Indeed they hustled not. The point was put forward by one of us that there is a moment in waiting when inspiration and confidence come together, or at least come then as well as ever they can or will, and that if the hesitation is prolonged beyond that moment, the result is inevitably loss of faith, increasing doubt and timidity, and a distorted view of the situation arising from fear of fate. Half the difficulties of golf are due to the fact that the player has an abundance of time to think about what he is engaged to do and how it should be done. In that time hopes and fears and many emotions race through his mind, and tasks which were originally simple become every moment harder. In no other game has the player such ample leisure in which to think, to be careful, to be exact, and to decide upon the proper action, and thus responsibility is heaped upon him for what he does as it is in no other sport or recreation. He is oppressed with a mighty burden.

That which he does he is entirely responsible for, and it can never be undone. It follows that this game has an extensive and peculiar psychology such as is possessed by no other. I shall proceed to tell a little story, dramatic in its circumstances, abounding in significance. It embraces the meanings and mysteries of golf.

* * * * *

The strange case of Sir Archibald Strand is one that caused much excited attention among the members of the golf community in general some months ago, and it is still discussed in the club-houses. Sir Archibald Strand, Bart., is a fair example of the thorough, enthusiastic, middle-aged player, who treats golf as something rather more than a game, which is as it should be. He is one of tolerably equable temperament, a good sportsman, and a man of strong character and physique, who did a long term of military service in India. Nowadays he spends an appreciable portion of his time in golfing, and a fair part of the remainder in contemplating the enduring mysteries and problems of the links. The game worries him exceedingly, occasionally it leads him to unhappiness, but, on the whole, he feels he likes it. He is a member of several London clubs, including Sunningdale, Walton Heath, Mid-Surrey, Coombe Hill, and Woking, and of his seaside clubs those he most frequents are the Royal St. George's at Sandwich, and Rye. His handicap is 5, and generally he is what we consider and call a good reliable 5.

He and his opponent, to whom, as a matter of discretion and confidence, we must refer as Mr. A., had just ended their match at Mid-Surrey one pleasant day, and Sir Archibald was trying his last putt over again as golfers often do. It was a putt of two feet. He had missed it before; but now, of course, he rolled the ball in every time. A question arose about circumstances altering cases, as they so commonly do in golf, and of responsibility weighing heavily on the mind that hesitates; and Sir Archibald declared that nobody in good health could be such a fool as to miss a two-feet putt like that, if he really examined the line thoroughly, and took the proper pains. Just then the open champion of the period was passing by the green, and they called him up and asked his views upon the missing of two-feet putts. Taylor denied that a man was a fool for missing them. He mentioned the psychology of the business, and very forcibly argued that a two-feet putt was a very difficult thing, that the more important it was the more difficult it became, and that the longer one thought about it the more impossible did it seem to hole it. "Ah! " said he, with the solemn countenance he assumes when discussing the terrors of this game, and the deep emphasis he makes when he admits the difficulties it creates for him, "Ah!" he murmured, "if I had never missed any putts of one foot, let alone the putts of two! I tell you, sir, the two-feet putt, when it has to be done—mind you when it has got to be done—is one of the most difficult things in the world to do, and never mind the fact that your babies can do it all the time! Take that from me, sir!" This was a touch of the real Taylor, the true philosopher, one who knows the game.

Mr. A., who is sometimes aggressive in manner, brought the matter in discussion to a pretty point at once. "Look here, Strand," said he, "I will tell you what I will do. I will place this ball here, so, exactly two feet from the hole, and I will give you a fortnight, but not less than a fortnight, to hole that putt. You are not to practise it here at this hole on this green in the meantime; but you may place the ball in position if you like, and look at it. And a fortnight today, at ten o'clock in the morning, you must make the putt, and I will bet you fourteen guineas, being a guinea a day for waiting, that you do not hole it. We will have the position of the hole properly marked, so that a fortnight hence it shall be in the same place."

The champion said he would tell Lees, the green-keeper, and that should be done. Strand, with a laugh, accepted the wager, and the matter was settled.

The events that followed were curious. In the club-house there was then little disposition to attend to the accounts of the proceedings that were furnished by both parties. The men who had finished rounds were too much occupied with their own troubles or joys.

At his club in town that evening, Sir Archibald, over dinner, related the circumstances of the wager to a few friends, with an appearance of considerable satisfaction with himself, and seemed a little surprised that the other members of the party did not at once approve of his proceeding as sound and business-like.

"Of course, you know, Strand, my good man," said Mr. Ezekiel Martin, a successful stockbroker, "these putts are missed sometimes, and I don't suppose it makes it any easier for you by waiting a fortnight. It's like carrying over in the House till one is a very tired bull."

"Nonsense!" exclaimed Sir Archibald, "I could go out now and hole that putt nineteen times out of twenty in the dark!"

"I believe you could," answered Martin, "but doing it in the dark, when you cannot see the hole and realise all the imaginary difficulties, is very different from doing it in broad daylight; and putting now, on the spur of the moment, as it were, is very different from putting when you have a whole fortnight to think about what you are going to do."

"I don't see it," replied Sir Archibald, yet he began to feel a little uneasy. On returning home that night, instead of going to bed at once he went into his study, laid a tumbler on its side on the carpet, and putted from a measured two feet for about half an hour. He holed most or them, and tumbled into bed feeling that Martin had been "pulling his leg," as people say. In the morning he engaged a gardener to smooth down a piece of his lawn, planting in a little putting-green turf, and he had a hole made in it, and a circle with two feet radius drawn round the hole, so that he could putt from every point. When this work was done, he spent an hour in practising there, and succeeded well. He only missed about one in ten. He tried seven different putters, with approximately equal results. In the afternoon he went down to

Mid-Surrey, played a match, and lost it by missing a short putt at the home hole. After tea, he went out on to the eighteenth green, found the spot where the hole was the day before, examined it carefully, and saw that there were slight differences in the texture of the grass round about, and that there was a little depression to the left side. He had not noticed this before. However, said he to himself, it would be easy to make allowances for these things, but he began now to doubt whether thirteen days ahead he would use his wry-necked putting cleek or bolt the putt with an aluminium putter. Where there are troubles of that kind it is often better to make short work of the putt by the bolting way, and have an end of it. At home that evening he did more putting practice on the carpet, and did not hole them quite so well. Lady Strand, who understands her husband thoroughly, and is the sweetest, gentlest sympathiser, coaxed him to telling her the trouble, for she saw that one existed. With perfect wisdom she suggested that he should wipe the fourteen guineas from the current account as already lost, and face the task as one who had all to gain and nothing to lose. Of course, her husband said, it was not the money, but the frightful jackass he would look if he missed the putt.

He went to his club in town the next day instead of going to golf, and took with him a book containing a chapter on putting, by Willie Park. He stretched himself out on a Chesterfield in a corner of the library, and gazed at two spots on the carpet which he had measured as being two feet from each other. Eventually, he decided that that was not good for him, since equal distances in furnished rooms, as is well known, look longer than they look outside. He lunched with a few friends, and brought up the subject again.

"Give him the money and have done with it, Strand. You are sure to lose!" said the brutish Martin.

"I wish I had not to wait for a fortnight," murmured Strand.

"Ah! He knew! The other man knew!" rejoined Martin. "He knows the game of golf! What I cannot understand is why he did not give you a year and make it 365 guineas. You would have sold out in six weeks at £200!"

Sir Archibald wrote a letter to Mr. A. that evening, intimating that he would probably have to leave town the week after the next. He hinted that it might be convenient if they got their wager out of the way beforehand, and if he putted a week from then. Mr. A. replied that he was sorry it would not be convenient for him to attend then, and that the signed terms of the contract had better be abided by.

Sir Archibald bought two new putters on the following day, and in the afternoon he had Taylor out for an hour, and they went practising on the putting lawn just outside the garden gate. Sir Archibald was putting very well then; but he insisted that it would be a good thing to change the ball he was using, which was rather lively. After he had done with Taylor, he went to look at the place on the eighteenth green where he would have to putt, and it seemed that the coarse grass had fattened up considerably with the rain that had fallen, and that the sand below it was distinctly gritty. It began to seem that he would have to run the ball in at the right side of the hole. He asked Lees some questions about the grasses on that green, and was sorry he could not take a little Mid-Surrey turf home with him. He was feeling a little tired when he reached his home that night, and as it was Thursday he suggested to Lady Strand that they should go to Folkestone for the week-end, and not bother at all about golf, which they did accordingly. He found it delightful to linger on the leas and not be worried with the game.

This kind of thing continued and became worse and worse again during the days that followed. There was practice, thought, and purchase continually, and unfortunately the proportion of missed putts at two feet, both on the carpet, on the practice lawn, and on the greens at Mid-Surrey, Coombe Hill, and Woking, began to increase. At putts of three feet, four, and five, Sir Archibald was marvellous, and, of course, he never missed the very little ones;

but the two-feet putts bothered him all the time. He attributed it to his liver; and he was certainly looking worn. Matters were not improved by such inconsiderate remarks as were made by Martin, Evans, and others, whenever he had a two-feet putt to do, such as "Now, Strand, that's just your distance!" It was only a joke; but in the circumstances it was not perhaps in good taste.

On the evening of the twelfth day Strand, after deliberation, wrote a letter to A. in which he said he feared he would not be able to go down to the course at the appointed time, and intimated that, according to the terms of the wager, he would hand over the fourteen guineas to him when next they met. Before posting this letter he went and did a little practice in the dusk on the lawn outside the house. He seemed to get them down with some confidence on this occasion, and Lady S., watching him, called out cheerily, "Silly boy! as if you could really miss! Now what shall I buy with the fourteen guineas?"

So Strand tore up the letter and went to bed for rest.

On the night before the appointed day he slept badly. He was putting in his mind until three o'clock in the morning. Then he rose, went in his pyjamas into the study, made a line on the top of his aluminium putter indicating the striking point, and went back to bed, but did not sleep. For some time he tried an imaginary humming of the "Jewel Song" from *Faust*, and repeated a few lines from Scott's "Lady of the Lake"—old dodges of his for assisting distraction and sleep—but they did not serve, nor did a fixed vision of millions of balls falling in an endless stream from the mouth of a pump and disappearing instantly through a golf hole in the ground.

At five-thirty he rose again and took his bath. He hesitated as to what golfing suit he should wear. Finally, for the sake of complete ease, and that there should be nothing to attract his eye from the ball, he put on some dark-blue flannels.

He looked at his breakfast, pecked at a sole, and at nine-fifteen, feeling distinctly unwell, he took a taxi for the course. He had one great consolation upholding him. At five minutes past ten it would all be over. He felt that he knew how glad a condemned criminal must be that at five minutes past eight on a certain morning—or a minute or two earlier with a little luck—a black flag would be hoisted on the prison pole.

At seven minutes to ten he drank a large brandy and soda and went out to the eighteenth green. Mr. A. and a few others were there to see the business properly carried out. Taylor placed the ball exactly two feet from the hole, which was cut in the proper place. He had his watch in his hand.

Sir Archibald bent down and examined the putt with great care. He essayed to pick up what seemed to be a "loose impediment" on his line, but saw that it was not loose. The putt seemed very difficult now, and he wished he had brought his plain putting cleek out with him, but it was too late.

At ten o'clock exactly, Taylor said, "Now, Sir Archibald, will you kindly putt?"

Sir Archibald Strand looked like a man who had been hunted down. He made one swift glance around him, but saw no escape, so he pulled himself together, smiled a little sadly, and said to himself, "Don't be a fool, Archie!" Then he faced the putter to the ball; the club was trembling slightly. He swung it back much too far, checked it in the return swing, and came on to the ball in a nervous, stupid sort of way, doing little more than touch it. The ball took a line to the right of the hole, and did not run more than fourteen inches.

You may have thought that Sir Archibald used unfortunate words and was dismayed. He did not. A look of established happiness and placid contentment spread upon his countenance, as a streak of sunlight might flash across a plain. "Ha!" he sighed in relief. He took from his pocket a cheque for fourteen guineas already made out, and handed it to Mr. A., and then joyfully exclaimed: "Thank heaven, it is finished! Now, my friends, we will honour this unusual occasion in a suitable manner at your convenience, and this afternoon I leave for Sandwich for a week of golf. And no letters are being forwarded."

* * * * *

Let us now enter consideration of this matter in a proper frame of mind, seriously and not looking contemptuously upon the problem of holing even the very shortest of putts as no problem at all after the affected manner of the inexperienced and uninformed general public. Let us approach it cautiously and in an analytical spirit. We should take the evidence of expert witnesses upon happenings in their careers, in our endeavour to discover the real truth. We have already remarked upon the case of the hunter who shot tigers and cringed at putts, and of the great champions who all missed them on the eighteenth green at St. Andrews, when they were playing for nothing less than the championship. We have also contemplated the circumstances of the distressed baronet who was given a fortnight in which to hole a two-feet putt, suffered intolerable agonies during the period, and was only restored to happiness when he had failed at the stroke. Now let us pay regard to the experience of a little child only six years old, who was completely successful at many putts in succession, at distances of from one to six feet, all the most perilous situations. This remark able demonstration was witnessed by the proud parents, by a great professional, and by myself.

The child is a boy, and not, as has been stated, a winsome little girl. There is, if I may say it without offence, nothing remarkable about his parents. They are excellent kindly-mannered people, of tolerable middle-class education, simple in their manner of life, and of no pronounced tastes in any direction. The father is in a large timber business in the Midlands, and has probably an income of about six hundred pounds a year. His handicap is 14. He is not a very keen golfer, and seems to spend a fair amount of his time in his garden. A total abstainer, he smokes little, and has no strong tastes in art and literature; but he once told me that in addition to much Scott and a sufficiency of Dickens he had read one of my books on golf. That is the father. As to the mother, she is just one who might be called in the north a nice little body. She is a thoroughly good housewife, domesticated, affectionate, and if she does not play golf she sympathises with it. These are people who are tolerably satisfied with their state. They live in a pleasant house, employ two maidservants, and have no motor-car. Here, surely, is nothing to suggest the creation of genius. Yet they are the parents of this remarkable child who did, with no hesitation, with confidence, certainty, and frequency, what the mighty hunter, the champions, the bold but misguided baronet, and you and I have failed to accomplish.

There is a man of wit and wisdom, Andrew Kirkaldy, who, when you inquire of him what is the most difficult thing in golf, responds with no hesitation that it is to hole "a wee bit divvle of a putt that long!" and so saying he will hold his hands four feet apart. Occasionally he may vary the phraseology, not to its advantage, but the meaning and effèct remain the same. Andrew is solid on four feet. But authorities differ a little in this matter of measurement. Some will reduce the distance to thirty inches; others have it that the yard putt is the most trying; I have heard eighteen inches put forward. But it all amounts to much the same thing, that what looks ridiculously easy is very, very difficult. Now this tender little child, who knew nothing of the fears and dangers of this awful game, placed the ball at a distance of two feet from the hole on a curly and slippery green, and with a sublime aplomb hit it straight to the middle of the hole—the first putt of his life and a good one. Then he putted from a yard and holed it again, then from Kirkaldy's distance and played the stroke just as surely and successfully, and then repeated them many times, never faltering, never failing. We who watched were a trifle sad, and perhaps ashamed. We knew that with all our thought and skill and golfing learning, all our strength and manhood, we could not do the same when at our games, and that, the more we needed to do it by the importance of the golf that was being played, the more difficult it was. Our selfish consolation was that in time the little child would grow up and then he would not be able to hole those putts, for then he would know that it was a difficult thing to do, and would be embarrassed and defeated accordingly. For it is the golfer's consciousness of imaginary difficulties that makes him such a strange coward when this putting business is being done. He knows that really the putting is easy, but he knows also that he must not miss, that an inch lost here is as much of a loss as two hundred yards in the driving—and he fears his fate. It is consciousness of the stupidity of missing, nerves, fears, imagination, that make this missing of short putts by the cleverest players, champions as much as any others, the most remarkable thing that happens constantly in any game. There is nothing like it. If it were not so easy, if there were good excuse for failure, those putts would not be missed so frequently. In putting, said Sir Walter Simpson, there is much to think about and much more not to be thought of. "When a putter," he reflected, "is waiting his turn to hole out a putt of one or two feet in length, on which the match hangs at the last hole, it is of vital importance that he think of nothing. At this supreme moment he ought studiously to fill his mind with vacancy. He must not even allow himself the consolations of religion. He must not prepare himself to accept the gloomy face of his partner and the derisive delight of his adversaries with Christian resignation should he miss. He must not think that it is a putt he would not dream of missing at the beginning of the match, or, worse still, that he missed one like it in the middle. He ought to wait, calm and stupid, till it is his turn to play, wave back the inevitable boy who is sure to be standing behind his arm, and putt as I have told him how—neither with undue haste nor with exaggerated care. When the ball is down, and the putter handed to the caddy, it is not well to say, 'I couldn't have missed it.' Silence is best. The pallid cheek and trembling lip belie such braggadocio."

* * * * *

The truth is that the man who golfs will unceasingly think of the things he should not think of, and that is what makes this easy putting so difficult, and it explains why the innocent child, unthinking, finds the business as simple and pleasant as swinging under the boughs of a tree on a sunny day in June. While there is one quite easy way of doing nearly every putt, there are perhaps a dozen more or less difficult ways of missing it, and it is these that are uppermost in the golfer's mind when the time of his trial comes, and so once more is vice triumphant while angels are depressed. There is the hole, a pit that is deep and wide, four and a quarter inches in diameter, and there is the little ball, only an inch and a half through the middle, and the intervening space between the two is smooth and even. It would seem to be the easiest thing in theory and practice to knock the ball into the large hole; but how very small does the hole then appear to be and how much too big for it is the ball! But the golfer knows that he should hole that putt, and that if he fails he will never, never have the chance again. Should he putt and miss the act is irrevocable; the stroke and the hole, or the half of it, are lost, and nothing that can happen afterwards can remove that loss. Should he at the beginning of the play to a hole make a faulty drive, or should his approach play be very inaccurate, he knows that he may atone for these mistakes by special cleverness displayed in subsequent strokes, and with the buoyant hope that constantly characterises him he thinks he will. But the hope seems often to desert him at the end; confidence lapses. The short putt is the very last stroke in the play to that hole, and if it is missed there is no further opportunity for recovery. In this way it does seem sometimes that there is a little of the awful, the eternal, the infinite about that putt. The player is stricken with fear and awe. He knows it is an easy thing to do in the one proper way of doing it, but raging through his mind are hideous pictures of a dozen ways of missing. Once upon a time I put the question to a number of the greatest players of the age as to what were their thoughts, if any, when they came to making one of these little putts on which championships or other great affairs almost entirely depended, and almost invariably their answer was that at the last supreme moment a thought came into their minds and was expressed to themselves in these words: "What a fool I shall look if I miss this putt!" Those words exactly did Willie Park, the younger, say quietly to himself just as he was about to make the last short putt of a round at Musselburgh, which would or would not give him a tie for the championship with Andrew Kirkaldy. He did not say that if he missed the putt he would lose the championship. He said he would look a fool.

The other day in a quiet corner of London, away from the game but, as it happened, not from the thought of it, I had Harry Vardon with me engaged in some serious talk in a broad and general way upon golfing men and things. Ten years ago, when we were doing some kind of collaboration in the production of a new book, he said to me very impressively and as one who wonders exceedingly, "It is a funny game; let us impress that upon them all, it is a very funny game," and now, having played perhaps five thousand more rounds and won another Open Championship, he went forward to the admission, "It is an awful game." He meant it, and one reason why we like our Harry Vardon is because he too has always been awe-stricken by this so-called game, and because there is no other man in golf who sympathises better with the trials and tortures of the moderate player. On this morning of spring he was telling me of another new and great discovery he had made in putting methods, and in giving to me an account of his pains, his sufferings in missing all the short putts he had failed at in recent times—how dearly have they cost him!—he said it was the two-feet putt that frightened him most of all, and declared solemnly and seriously that he would rather have a three-yarder than such a putt, and that he would hole the former oftener than the latter. He said the two-feet putts frighten him, that as soon as he settles himself down to the business of putting in such a case the hole seems to become less and less. "I am overcome," says he, "with the idea that in a moment it will be gone altogether. Then I am in a state of panic, and I snatch at my putter and hit the ball quickly so that with a little luck it may reach the hole before it goes away altogether and there is nothing to putt at. When I have missed I see that the hole is there, and as big as ever or bigger!" Vardon once tried putting left-handed, a doctor having advised him to do so, and he found that the idea worked splendidly, but he did not like the look of it. He believes after all his sorrows that one of the greatest and best secrets of good putting is to keep more absolutely still than do most golfers, who seem to think it matters less in putting when it matters so much more.

* * * * *

Now the golfer in his wisdom, ingenuity, and resource has tried every way he can think of to solve this problem of nerves and doubts by mechanical and other means. Those who would be successful in competitions have retired to bed at nine o'clock in the evening for a month, and some of them have sipped from bottles of tonics hoping that physic would serve to give them strong nerve, steady hands and courage, but such methods have not availed. For no part of this or any other game have so many different kinds of instruments been invented, though the little child could do the putts with the head of a walking-stick or a common poker. Scarcely a week goes by in the season but some new kind of putter is introduced to the expectant multitude of harassed players, and now and then a thrill runs through the world as they receive a clear assurance that at last some special device has been discovered which will make their putting ever afterwards easy and certain. There is a thrill as if a secret of long life had been found. But the chill of disappointment follows quickly. Golfers have now tried all things known, and more short putts are missed than ever. Hundreds of different kinds of putters have been invented. They have been made with very thin blades, and with thick slabs of metal or other substance instead of mere blades. They have been made like spades, like knives, like hammers, and like croquet mallets. They have even been made like putters. They have been made of wood, iron, aluminium, brass, gun-metal, silver, bone, and glass. Here in my room I have the sad gift of the creator of a forlorn and foolish hope. It is a so-called putter made in the shape of a roller on ball bearings which is meant to be wheeled along the green up to the ball. Like some others it was illegal according to the rules. To such extravagances of fancy the desperate golfers have been led in their desire to succeed in this putting that the authorities have had to step in for the defence of the dignity of the game to declare a limit to the scope of invention in this matter. And yet I once knew a man who for a long period did some of the best putting that you would ever fear to play against with a little block of wood that had once served to keep the door of his study ajar, to which had been attached a stick that was made from a broom handle. This improvised putter was a freak of his fancy at a time when he thought there might be some virtue in a return to prime simplicity. Then Mr. James Robb, who has won the Amateur Championship once and been in the final on two other occasions, has putted all his life with a cleek that his sister won in a penny raffle when he was a boy and gave to him. Likewise Mr. John Laidlay has also putted uninterruptedly since he was a boy with a cleek that is now so thin with much cleaning that his friends tell him he may soon be able to shave himself with it. But these are the grand exceptions after all. Such fine settlement and constancy are unknown to the average player. It was but the other day that I learned that a friend of mine, one most distinguished in the game and of the very highest skill, had used fifteen different putters on the day of an important competition—three in the morning's play, nine others in noonday practice, and three quite fresh ones in the afternoon game. The same good man carried a choice assortment of his own putters to a recent amateur championship meeting, but at the beginning of the tournament made love to one of mine, borrowed it, and used it until he was beaten— not a long way from the end of the competition. Sometimes it seems that what is rudest in design, almost savage, is now best liked when in our frenzy we have ransacked art, science, and all imagination in search of the putter with which we can putt as we would. There is the spirit of reaction; we would return to the primitive. Putters that look as if they might be for dolls, some of those stumpy little things made of iron on a miniature aluminium putter model, which some of the great champions have been using, have hardly become popular. The crude and the bizarre, suggestive of inspiration, please well. I shall not forget Jean Gassiat, good golfer of France, coming up to me one championship day at Hoylake, holding forward in his right hand, and with its head in the air, what was evidently meant for a golf club, but which was as much unlike one as anything we had ever seen. On the face of the player was spread the grin of pleasure; wordlessly he suggested that at last he had found it, the strangest, the most wonderful. In principle this new club, as it has to be called for courtesy, is akin to the affair of the door-stopper and the broomstick. It consists of a plain flat rectangular piece of wood about four inches long, two inches wide, and three-quarters of an inch deep, and its two-inch nose is cut quite square, while for a couple of inches at the end of the shaft the grip is thickened to twice its usual size. It is weighted and balanced by large and small lead bullets in the sole. It is possible to frame a good argument in favour of a putter made of anything; nothing is without some advantage. It could be said for a gingerbeer bottle that it would insist on the ball being most truly hit from the middle of the vessel as the ball ought to be hit, and, given notice, one could prepare a statement of claim on behalf of an old boot seeking to be raised to the putterage. So there are good things to be said for this putter from France, and one of the best is that after smiling upon it Jean Gassiat began to wonder, then thought, experimented, and fell in love with this putter completely. Some weeks later I saw him doing those marvels on the green as are only done when man and putter have become thoroughly joined together, and Gassiat has always to be taken seriously in these matters, for, like Massy, he is a Basque, and, like the old champion, he is one of the most beautiful putters, with an instinct for holing. This most remarkable invention, without desiring its extinction in the least, one would say, surely departs a whole world of fancy farther from the traditional idea of what a golf club should be than the poor Schenectady of the Americans which St. Andrews proscribed. It was not the idea of Gassiat, nor of any other than the Marquis de Chasseloup-Laubat, a French sportsman of thoroughness and a very keen golfer. Seeing what Gassiat was doing James Sherlock obtained one of these barbaric tools, and at this the public came in.

* * * * *

Every thinkable variety of putting method has been adopted. Bodies, hands, feet have been placed in all positions, and the stroke has been made in every conceivable way. Are there any two players who do it just the same, or have the same advice to give? For a violent contrast take two of the most able amateurs of the time, both of them long since distinguished in the foremost competitions, Mr. John Low and Mr. H. S. Colt. The former favours the wooden putter, and he has one of that kind to which he is keenly attached, but he putts with all sorts of things as the spirit moves him on consideration of special circumstances. He was one of the early members of the thoughtful school of golf which has made such a strong advance in recent times. Nearly always, however, you will find him standing nearly upright when doing his putting, grasping a club with a tolerably long shaft somewhere quite near to the top of the handle. This erect attitude is that which our forefathers of the traditions mostly favoured. Those splendid gentlemen, as we have agreed, were fine golfers who conducted their game nobly, but it has always seemed to me that they were an unimaginative lot. It never appears to have occurred to them that because the club has a handle at the top was no reason why they should grasp it up there instead of nearly at the opposite end, as do a large body of the most enterprising and inquiring amateurs these days. Of this advanced party the eminent architect is a shining example, for he holds his putting cleek so far down, so near to the ironwork, that the shaft seems useless, and in addition to this he defies all teaching in putting by planting the heel of the club down on the green and holding the hands so low that the toe of the putter is cocked up, and with this toe he hits the ball, and, as it looks, he tops it. But that putting of his is too much for most of the men who have to play against it. When those who do not understand see men putting in this way, or something like it, they say to themselves, and perhaps to others, that they cannot see why the men do not have the unused part of the shaft cut off so that it may not be in the way. But there they show their deficiencies of knowledge, though one is not sure that all the men who putt with a low grip quite know why they do so. They only know that the method suits them, but the truth is often that in these cases the balancing piece of the shaft above the hands acts as a steadier for the piece below. A few students have carried this idea a point further by having a piece of lead attached to the top of the handle to increase the weight and the balancing influence of that part. Mr. Hammond Chambers is one of them. The amateurs are the most original and peculiar in their putting methods. For the most part the professionals, although adopting widely different stances, hold themselves fairly well up when doing their work on the green, and putt with an easy following-through stroke as is recommended by the old masters. Strange that we should realise that quite the most impressive, stylish, and beautiful putter of the erect school is M'Dermott, the brilliant young American champion, who stands straight up with his legs and heels touching, grips his putter at the very end, and moving nothing but his club and hands, makes the most delightfully smooth swing. The low-grip method is not at all conducive to the gentle swinging, following-through putt, but encourages a sharp little tap.

All the old original philosophy and instruction in putting can be summarised in a very few words, but hundreds of thousands would be needed for discussion of the variations, most of which have been used successfully at some time. The majority of advisers make a point of it that the ball must be hit truly, but they would not all be agreed on what that "truly" was except that it was hitting it as they meant to do. What most of them have in mind is that there is on the face of the putter a proper hitting point, from which the ball will run more accurately and with less disposition to slide off the right line than when hit with any other part, that being the point of balance or the sweet spot which every iron club possesses, and this point should be brought to the ball by an even swing from the back, and the swing should be continued after impact by the steady smooth advance of the head of the club along the line that it was making at the moment of striking. Absolute steadiness of the body is quite essential, and lack of it—just the most trifling and almost undiscernible lack—is responsible for more putting failures than almost any other cause. Most of those who tell us what to do in golf advise that we should keep the arms and forearms quite still also, and putt entirely from the wrist. And yet even these canons, as they are considered, are defied by large bodies of players. There are thousands of golfers who putt from the toes of their clubs, and believe in the method. They say they can feel the ball better and direct it more surely.

I quote again one of the first preceptors, Sir Walter Simpson, because I think in most matters of feeling and practice he stands so well for the old solid school of golf that has nearly died away. He insists on the wooden putter, to begin with, and maintains that no good thing upon the green can come out of iron, but therein he was mistaken and time has cried him down. And then he writes: "I have just said there are, at most, two or three attitudes in which good putting is possible. We are nowadays inclined to be more dogmatic, and to assert that there is but one. The player must stand open, half facing the hole, the weight on the right leg, the right arm close to the side, the ball nearly opposite the right foot. To putt standing square, the arms reached out, is as difficult as to write without laying a finger on the desk." Had he lived on to these more modern days he would not have been nearly so dogmatic as that. Some of the very best putters do not play with the open stance, but putt entirely from the left leg, that leg thrown forward and in front and bearing all the weight, the right being merely hanging on behind. Then they have the ball right opposite the left toe, and they putt with a sense or strain which they believe in such circumstances is conducive to delicacy. Tens of thousands of others could not putt in this way, but those who can are very successful, and this is just another indication of the danger of dogma in golf. As to the right arm at the side, it may be said that there is now a fast increasing practice on the part of those who bend down somewhat to their putting to rest the right elbow or forearm on the right knee. J. H. Taylor experimented with this idea on the very eve of the 1913 championship at Hoylake, his putting for some time having been bad. He adopted it, won the championship, and gave the new way of putting all the credit.

Now see how high and deeply thinking authorities can differ about the ways and means of doing this thing that the little child does so thoroughly and well. "A great secret of steady putting is to make a point of always 'sclaffing' along the ground," said the baronet. "The best putters do this, although it is not evident to an onlooker, the noise of the scrape being inaudible. To be sure of the exact spot on the putter face which is invariably to come in contact with the ball, is, of course, essential to the acquirement of accuracy. If you play to hit clean, your putter must pass above the ground at varying heights, as it is impossible to note how much air there is between it and the turf. In the other way you feel your road. But the greatest gain from treating putting as a sclaffing process is the less delicate manipulation required when short putts are in question. At a foot and a half from the hole the clean putter often fails, from incapacity to graduate inches of weakness, whilst the sclaffer succeeds because he is dealing with coarser weight sensitiveness."

Now time and experience have showed us all that we cannot be dogmatic about anything in golf except that the ball must be struck somehow, and least of all may we venture to dogmatise in the matter of putting, and we will only say now that the late Sir Walter has a heavy majority against him on this suggestion that in doing the short putts it is well to let the putter scrape along the grass when going forward to the ball. It seems a small matter (that little man child never thought of it, but I noticed he did not sclaff), yet a whole world of good and ill upon the links is bound up with it. We shall set this happy golfer as he was, and friend of Robert Louis Stevenson, against one of the great champions and one of the finest putters who have ever handled clubs, and that is Willie Park, the younger, who says, "One of the secrets of putting is to hit the ball, and the ball only—a sclaffy style of putting is fatal; and, with the object of making absolutely certain of avoiding it, rather aim to strike the globe just the least thing above the ground. The ball should be smartly tapped with the putter, the stroke being played entirely from the wrists; and it should be neither struck a slow, heavy blow, nor shoved, nor should it be jerked."

Most golfers will be with Willie in this matter, and those who have not tried already that way of putting, the sole of the club being kept clear from the turf when the stroke is being made, might do so to their very likely advantage. It is a point that a player of limited experience might never think about, and I know many who have been converted from bad putters to good ones by it. Some of the leading players of the Hoylake school have long been addicted to a slight elaboration or variation of this method. As they bring the club on to the ball they lift it slightly so that at the moment of impact a peculiar running spin is given to the ball, one that is not quite the same thing as is imparted by merely topping it. The way appears to help the hole to gather the ball when it arrives, but it is a method that needs natural aptitude and much practice to make it quite safe in application. And then again, right away to the contrary, I have witnessed in recent weeks a way of putting by one or two of the best players in the country, which is new, and which they declare to be most effective when dealing with the small heavy balls that are now in vogue and which are so difficult to manage, especially on very keen greens. We have all heard of the push shot, generally done with cleeks and the more powerful irons—and many of us have tried to play it as Harry Vardon does, and the things that I have seen done and described as push shots by ordinary amateurs have been very dreadful. But, no matter; the idea of the push shot is to hit the ball a kind of downward glancing blow, the club coming to ground after impact, the result being that the ball starts off quickly and pulls up suddenly. The players to whom I have referred have applied this stroke to their putting, coming on to the ball above the centre and gently pushing the club through it, and in the circumstances I have indicated there can be no doubt they have succeeded. Balls being so tricky now, these matters are worth considering.

You would perceive how boldly dogmatic was the writer of the early classic on the question of stance. On that point there is just one more word to say. The tendency seems to be increasing in these days towards holding the feet closely together. It is a stance to which Harry Vardon, after all his putting troubles, has nearly settled down, and many of the best men on the green, Tom Ball for one, are given to it. But there is no law, no recommendation even, only the most timid suggestion to be made to any man in this matter. That way which suits him and gives him confidence is the best, and one may find men putting marvellously well when their stance and attitude seem to be so ungainly and difficult as to cause them pain.

* * * * *

The method of holding the club has, at least, as much to do with good putting as anything else, and in this matter one may almost dare to dogmatise. The majority of players hold their putters with the two hands close together but detached from each other, in much the same way as they hold their other clubs. All of them have heard of what they call the Vardon grip, or the overlapping grip, by which, when the club is held, the left thumb is brought into the palm of the right hand, and the little finger of that right hand is made generally to ride upon the first of the left hand. Many try this grip for their long shots, but few persist with it, as they become convinced either that their hands and fingers are not strong enough for it, or that before they could master the method they would need to suffer too much in loss of the game that they already possess. Therefore they renounce the overlapping grip entirely. But if they would try it in putting they would experience none of the difficulties with which they are troubled when applying it to their wooden club shots, no sort of force having to be given to the stroke, and almost from the first attempt they would enjoy an advantage. It is a matter of the most vital importance in putting that the two hands should not interfere with each other to the very slightest extent. One of them should have the general management of the putting, and the other, if detached from it, should do little save act in a very subordinate capacity as a steadying influence. Everybody is agreed upon that; it is absolute. But when we have the two hands separate, as with the ordinary grip, there is always a danger of the subordinate asserting itself too much, or at all events varying in the amount of work that it does. It cannot be avoided; it is inevitable. This, we may be sure, is the cause of much bad and uncertain putting.

Join the two hands together, as with the overlapping grip, and we have them working as one completely, and the risk of undue interference by the subordinate vanishes. This is the best hint on putting that all our counsellors have to give, and they one and all declare it will do more than anything else to raise a man to the high level of excellence of the innocent child. Sometimes we see men putting one-handed, and one may believe that for medium and short putts this way is more certain than the separate hands. Mr. Hilton once putted that way in the Amateur International match, and I have seen many other good putters do well with it. But it savours of freakishness, and, as a famous professional said to the distinguished player who adopted the method, "God did not give us two hands for one to be kept in a pocket while the putting was being done." The simple truth is that the one-hand way approximates very closely to the two-hand overlapping method. It is nearly the same thing, the same principle—all the work being done from one point. Upon thought, we often come to realise that what appear to be some of the most freakish methods of putting have the same fundamental principle at their base. Thus, take the case of Sherlock, who putts extremely well and consistently. He almost alone, among players of the game, holds his two hands wide apart on the handle of the putter, the left one uppermost, of course. This looks very strange, and at the first consideration it might seem that surely one hand will upset all the good work and reckoning that is done by the other. But the simple fact is that the left is so far away that it cannot interfere, and that is the secret of the quality of this method.

When the left is dose up to the right we cannot prevent it from meddling; we are unconscious of it when it is doing so; but get it far away and we have it in subjection, and all that it does in Sherlock's case is just to steady things up a little while the right hand does the business of the time.

Mr. Walter Travis, the most eminent American, than whose putting in the Amateur Championship he won at Sandwich nothing better has ever been seen since time and the game began, long since adopted a slight variation of this overlapping grip, specially for his putting, which, I think, has something to commend it. Instead of letting the little finger of the right hand rest on the forefinger of the left, he reverses the situation, and puts the forefinger of the left hand on the little one of the right, thus leaving the right hand in full possession of the grip, both thumbs being down the shaft. In the other way it is the left hand that has hold of the club with all its fingers, and it will now be remembered that while the left hand is the chief worker in driving and playing through the green, the right is the one that most frequently does the putting.

Having thus mentioned Mr. Travis, one can hardly refrain from quoting some of his instruction in this matter as he once conveyed it to me. "I believe," said he, "that putting should always be done with one hand—with one hand actively at work, that is. The left should be used only for the purpose of swinging the club backwards preparatory to making the stroke. When it has done that its work is ended and the right hand should then be sole master of the situation, the left being merely kept in attachment to it for steadying purposes. When only one hand is thus employed the gain in accuracy is very great. Two hands at work on a short putt or a long one tend to distraction. When the stroke is being made the grip of the right hand should be firm, but not tight, and after the impact the clubhead should be allowed to pass clean through with an easy following stroke. The follow-through should indeed be as long as it is possible to make it comfortably, and, with this object in view, at the moment of touching the ball the grip of the fingers of the left hand should be considerably relaxed, so that the right hand may go on doing its work without interruption. Never hit or jerk the ball as so many players do. There is nothing that pays so well as the easy follow-through stroke."

Yet we find that there is less than ever of that easy follow-through being done in these days, and putting may be no better for the fact, almost certainly is not. These are days when old maxims are being abandoned and new systems are being proclaimed season by season. Jack White, a splendid putter and a magnificent heretic, lately declared that it is time to get rid of what has been regarded as the most inviolable of maxims, "Never up, never in," asserting that the determination to be past the hole in putting, if not in it, leads with these lively balls we now play with to far too many of them running out of holing distance on the other side. His counsel, therefore, is that the ball should be coaxed gently up to the hole with as much drag applied to it as can be. Then for years past it has been recommended that one of the best ways of managing the putting with these speedy balls is to have much loft on the putter, and so in that way do something to create the drag; but lately a change of opinion began to be made, and I am finding some of the best players using putters that are perfectly straight in the face, believing that by their agency they can putt more delicately and with a surer judgment of strength.

It is a little bewildering. Arnaud Massy, the French player who once won the Open Championship, and who is better at the putts of from six to ten or twelve feet than any man I know, says that he has come to believe that Nature has planted deep down in us a sixth sense, and it is that of putting. In the development of that sense lies the way to success. But after all such meditations as this, I go back to the remembrance of that wonderful little child who could never miss, and then from it all there emerges the only real secret of success in putting. The child has a quality which we elders do not enjoy, and never shall have it for any length of time. He knows not the hardness of the world. Having innocence and faith he looks trustingly upon it, and the old world and its four and a quarter inch hole is a little ashamed, perhaps. The child has Confidence.

THE STORY: IF YOU DON'T MIND MY TELLING YOU

HOLWORTHY HALL

MR. Valentine Mott, scowling ferociously, made a fierce gesture toward his wife, five miles distant, and removed the hand which he had fitted over the transmitter as soon as the men in the nearest locker unit had begun to sing "How Dry I Am!" in close and execrable harmony. Mr. Mott leaned in utter impatience against the wall, and glowered mercilessly at his distant wife, and forthwith interrupted her in a voice freighted with glucose and saccharin.

"Well, I'm awfully sorry," he said. "Yes, I *know* I promised to come back for lunch; I know all that. . . . I certainly did intend to come back, but . . . Well, you know how it is; I met this man, and he's a good customer of ours and he wants me to play another round with him. I was just getting ready to change my clothes when he . . . Oh, I *could,* but I don't like to offend a man; these big buyers are so touchy sometimes you wouldn't hardly . . . Well, of *course;* but it's the little personal attentions that count. It's a real opportunity to get in solid with him. . . . Well, I don't see exactly how I can get out of it now; he's waiting for me at the first tee this minute. . . . I hope you don't think I'm *enjoying* it; it's a cold-blooded business proposition; we're not really going out for the *golf;* he just sort of wants to walk around for the exercise and talk business between shots. . . . Well, I *would* bring him home, but he wants the exercise. . . . Oh, absolutely! Why, I'll take you anywhere you say; I hadn't planned anything for to-morrow. . . . Not to-night, dear; I can't go out anywhere to-night. . . . Yes, to-morrow, and any night next week, too. . . . I certainly *don't!* . . . Well, I didn't even expect to play this afternoon, and to-morrow I'll drive you anywhere you . . . Oh, it might easily mean a thousand dollars to me. . . . Yes, a thousand. . . . Just as soon as we finish. . . . Oh, no, I wouldn't do that! The greens committee doesn't like to have women on the course on Saturdays. I'll start home the minute we finish. . . . All right; I'm just as sorry as you are. Goodbye!"

Mr. Mott hung up the receiver, exhaled in an abandon of relief, and smartly accosted a cadaverous friend, who happened to be passing through the locker room.

"Oh, Smithson! Made up yet for the afternoon?" Smithson paused, and shook his head disconsolately.

"I'm sorry, but I've got to go home, Val. Where's the crowd you had this morning?"

"They had to go home, too," said Mr. Mott, implying unutterable weakness on the part of the henpecked miscreants. *"I'm going to play eighteen more."*

How in thunder do you do it?" asked the cadaverous one in frank envy and injured righteousness. "If I ever managed to get in thirty-six holes just *once*—"

Mr. Mott waved the hand which had recently done duty as a silencer.

"Easiest thing in the world. Mrs. Mott wouldn't any more think of spoiling my Saturdays than—well, she just wouldn't think of it. She knows I'm working like a dog all the week; a man's got to have *some* recreation."

"That's so; but I can't ever seem to get it over. Well, how were you shooting?"

"Pretty fair—for me." Mr. Mott nodded, moved off in the direction of the grill, and halted on the outskirts of a loquacious group which was actively engaged in filing demurrers and replications. "Everybody made up?" he inquired genially. With discouraging unanimity they answered in the affirmative; and in the same breath they asked him how he was traveling.

"Not bad—that is, for me," said Mr. Mott. He hailed a lone wayfarer who was hurrying along the aisle. "Anybody looking for an extra man?"

"Sorry! Say, Val, there's a special competition on for the afternoon; heard about it?"

"*No,*" said Mr. Mott, alert. "What is it?"

"Straight medal-play, handicap. Special prize put up by one of the newcomers. Wasn't on the regular program."

"Is that so? I'll have to see about it. Well, how're you hitting 'em?"

"Vile!" The lone man took up his march in the direction of the attendant's room, and Mr. Mott shook his head in profound sympathy, and went on to the bulletin-board, where he delayed for a moment to inspect the current handicap-list. As he stood there, sniffing contemptuously at his own modest rating, a trio of late arrivals burst through the side door, and bore down upon him, laughing and talking and forecasting the future with that incorrigible golfing optimism which is Phoenix-born everyday out of the black ashes of yesterday's sodden facts. Mr. Mott knew all three, and he hailed them cheerfully.

"Hello! Looking for a fourth man?"

"No; somebody's waiting for us. No competition this afternoon, is there?"

"Of course there is! Special prize for straight medal-play," said Mr. Mott. "Don't you fellows ever read the announcements?"

"Is that so? That's fine! Thought there wasn't anything doing! Well, how were you going this morning?"

"Oh, pretty fair—for me, of course."

The trio hurried away, and Mr. Mott, lingering only to make sure that the tabular results of the competition for the treasurer's cup still remained on the board,—he hadn't been put out until the semifinals, and liked to see his name in the bracket,—strolled into the grill, and cast about him for companionship.

The low-studded room, as Mr. Mott entered, echoed the mad confusion of a political convention crossed with a dairy restaurant. Crockery clattered against wooden surfaces, plated silver clattered against crockery, tumblers clinked to tumblers, and hobnails grated on the red-tiled floor. Men in knickerbockers and men in flannels huddled close to the round tables and bawled statistics at one another; men in street clothes dragged rattling caddy-bags through from the office; men flushed and perspiring stamped in from the eighteenth green, and clamored loudly at the bar. Disheveled waiters dodged aimlessly about in answer to the insistence of a dozen members simultaneously. Half a hundred voices swelled in extenuation, alibi, defense; half a hundred voices rang clear in joyous prophecy. Drifting clouds of light-gray smoke clung like a canopy to the ceiling. The atmosphere was surcharged with excitement, and Mr. Mott's nostrils dilated as he scented it. The air quivered to the ungodly tumult, and Mr. Mott's ear-drums vibrated as he heard it.

"Waiter! Hang that waiter! Here, you! I—"

"I had a putt for a forty-seven coming in; without that nine on the tenth I'd have had a putt for a forty-one—"

"Come on; be a sport; make it a ball Nassau—"

"Why should *I* give you a stroke? Here's *my* suggestion—"

"All right! All right! Count it up yourself! 5, 7, 4, 9, 6, 6, 8—"

"Five aces in one! *I'*ll stand!"

"Hey, Jim! I had a par five—"

"Waiter! Waiter! I didn't order soup!"

"That's ground under repair. It says so on the card—"

"Oh, I couldn't hit a balloon. Worst I *ever* did!"

"Well, if you start us one up on each nine and—"

"Confound it! *I* didn't make the rules! It costs you two strokes!"

"Telephone! Telephone for Mr. Smithson! Mrs. Smithson calling—"

"Well, my handicap's too low. He's been under ninety twice this year, and the best I ever made in my life was a ninety-four, and still I've got to give him three strokes—"

"*Waiter!* Hurry along that club sandwich, will you?"

"If you'd just keep that left shoulder down, Bill, and remember to follow through—"

"I'll *bet* you I break 110—"

"Oh, if I could putt, I'd be all right. I just can't putt."

"Here, give *me* that check! Oh, come now; that's not right—"

"Then I went all to pieces—"

"Well, if I'd been playing my game—"

"Honest, I'd like to play you even, but I haven't touched a club since June—"

"Oh, I was *awful!*—How about you?"

"*Waiter!*"

Mr. Mott smiled happily, and button-holed the chairman of the handicap committee.

"Made up yet?" he inquired.

The chairman was prone to brevity.

"Yes. How'd you come out this morning?"

"Rotten!" said Mr. Mott, promptly. "Tore up my card; I was fierce. Know anybody that's looking for a match?"

"Yes, there's a new member out by the caddy-house. Don't know who he is, but he's alone. I thought somebody ought to give him a welcome. *You* do it, Val."

"Good idea—I will." Mr. Mott edged his way to the outer door, bellowed over his shoulder to one who had bellowed a question at him—the answer was "Pretty fair—for me!"—and emerged to the gravel walk. At this hour the vicinity of the first tee was deserted, but before the professional's tiny house Mr. Mott saw a lanky stranger dallying in an attitude of longing; Mr. Mott drew near and grinned. The stranger looked up, and presently grinned in return.

"Waiting for somebody?" asked Mr. Mott.

"No," said the stranger. "Just taking my chances; I'm a new member."

"Indeed! My name's Mott."

"Chapman's mine."

They shook hands. Mr. Mott glowed with the consciousness of duty well done.

"I'm alone, too. Suppose we try it?"

"I'd be glad to. Your name up for the handicap?"

"Not yet."

"I'll put it up," volunteered Mr. Mott In the top space on the ruled sheet tacked to the scoreboard he scrawled his own patronymic, and added his stroke allowance. "What's yours?"

"They haven't given me one. I've been in the club only a week."

"*Well*" said Mr. Mott, uncertainly, "then you can't very well compete—"

"Oh, I'm not going to. I'm not strong for tournaments, anyway. If you don't mind, I'll just attest your round; I'm not in condition anyway."

"All right." Mr. Mott dusted his hands, and stepped over to the caddy-master. "A couple of boys ready? Who do I draw? This one? My bag there? Now, son, your job is to *watch the ball*. You remember that, will you? Let's have the driver." He strode within the fatal inclosure, and swung the club experimentally at a trespassing cigarette stub. The stub leaped forward a yard, accurately on the line. "What do you play around in?"

"Oh, I'm erratic," said Chapman, watching intently. "You take the honor, please."

"Well, if you say so." He chuckled. "Might as well take it when I can get it. I may never have another chance." He teed an almost new ball, and took his stance; waggled, hesitated, stooped, glanced at his caddy, and glared at him. "Another ball," he said shortly. "Red-line Silver King out of the pocket." The caddy, overwhelmed with guilt, furnished it. It was of the same brand, the same marking, the same weight, and showed the same degree of wear and tear as the original choice; but Mr. Mott, for reasons comprehended only by golfers, regarded it with far greater satisfaction. It was the ball with which he had made the last hole in a par five on the morning round. It was, so to speak, already broken in, trained, biddable. Mr. Mott teed it, and after swinging once or twice in exaggeratedly correct form, lunged downward savagely.

"Good ball!" approved Chapman.

"Too high," said Mr. Mott, with meretricious disgust. It was the longest drive he had made from the first tee in six weeks.

The stranger hit a prodigious hook out of bounds. On his second attempt the hook was less pronounced; he was in the rough. The two players set out fraternally on their journey.

"Been playing much lately?" inquired Mr. Mott.

"Not a great deal. Only once or twice since April."

"You've got a fine follow-through, though."

"Unfortunately, there's more to the game than that," deprecated Chapman. He selected a spoon, and was hole-high to the left of the green.

"Beautiful! Just a trifle off," commented Mr. Mott. With the sole of his club he patted down a worm-cast; with his heel he deleted a tuft of grass from the complications of his lie. He made his effort, and afterwards he held himself rooted to the spot until he had verified, by three swings at vacancy, his unexpressed opinion that, given another opportunity, he would have split the flag, instead of dubbing fifty feet down-hill. "I can't keep my head down," he lamented. "Oh, well—" He turned suddenly to his caddy, and sent a bolt of lightning at him. "*Watch* this one!" he ordered. And the caddy obediently watched it hobble a hundred yards, and disappear among the leaves of a dry trench.

As Mr. Mott, looking aggrievedly at a pair which had come up behind him and were yelling "Fore!" at the top of their lungs, stood on the first green and noted his score, he was impelled to quote history.

"I had a six here this morning," he sighed. "It's a tricky green, isn't it?"

"Very," agreed his partner. "You keep the honor all the way, will you? You're in the tournament, and I'm not."

"Just as you say. On this one you want to aim pretty well to the left of the mound." Mr. Mott drove thirty yards to the right of it. "Doggone it!" he exclaimed, with his hands on his hips, "that club's no earthly good; I can't hit the broad side of a barn with it! It isn't balanced, or something. Further to the left, Mr. Chapman." Here Chapman sent forth a towering drive which at least was out of trouble. "*That's* safe! You're lucky."

"Oh, I'm not kicking," said Chapman placidly. "But I'm afraid you're in the pit."

"I see," said Mr. Mott, getting into his stride, "that that Bobby Jones hasn't been doing as well this season as he did last. Well, that's the way it ought to work out. He's too young to have all that success; it might have spoiled him. Besides, the national's no place for a boy like that. I was hoping he wouldn't go too far at Merion a year ago."

"He made a seventy-four," said Chapman, shrugging his shoulders, "and a seventy-six and a seventy-seven—"

"Oh, that's not so very remarkable. You take these caddies; they watch good players, and get hold of a good swing, and they're not bothered with nerves—"

"Pardon me, but I think you're back there about ten yards, Mr. Mott."

"So I am! Much obliged! Fore!"

Within a quarter of a mile there was no one who might conceivably have been endangered by Mr. Mott's recovery from the sand-pits, but his warning cry was both mechanical and peremptory. He eyed the flag, three hundred yards in advance, and with his eye still on it he played the mashie-niblick in the stroke which made Edward Ray internationally famous. It made Mr. Mott apoplectic. Thenceforward he progressed by slow and circuitous stages to the sloping green, and upon his arrival he was too deeply perturbed to sympathize with Chapman, whose iron shot had found a trap, and whose approach was beyond the hole. To be sure, the sinking of a long putt did much to salve the irritation in Mr. Mott's bosom, and although Chapman also holed a twenty-footer, Mr. Mott secretly felt, and generously withheld the statement, that Chapman had been excessively fortunate in the roll of the green. And he was too much absorbed in his own cosmos to inquire Chapman's score.

The third hole was short; that is, it was short for scratch-players. Mr. Mott had seen Tommy Kerrigan, the club professional, once play it with a heavy mashie; he had seen Sumner Hollander, who, although rated at nine, was Mr. Mott's ideal performer, overplay it with a mid-iron. Therefore Mr. Mott, who, if he could have reached the pin with a full brassey once out of three trials, would have owed sacrifices to the gods and blessings to a beam wind, chose a mid-iron.

"I'm not generally as bad as this," he explained when the ball had found cover in a growth of underbrush. "I'm not getting my wrists into it, that's all. I don't know what's the matter with me today. I don't seem to have any snap. It's costing me a stroke a hole, too."

"Easily," said Chapman. He, too, was off the line, but he was near enough to the green to use a putter while Mr. Mott was still flailing at the underbrush, and he was down in four to Mr. Mott's six.

"Now for a long one," complained Mr. Mott, climbing the eminence to the fourth tee. "Well, I suppose I'll have to take that driver of Kerrigan's again. If I had any sense I'd drive with an iron. Well, never mind. I believe in playing the right club. Watch it, boy!" He hit a screaming liner down the alley for more than two hundred precious yards, and posed diligently and without motion, until the ball had not only come to rest, but had also lain quiescent for several seconds. He regarded the club-head in general perplexity. He tested the spring of the shaft. He breathed deeply, and made way for Chapman; and after Chapman, owing to a half-top, had failed by a full rod to equal that drive of Mr. Mott's, he relentlessly fought down the smile which struggled for its outlet. Indeed, he was rather astonishingly severe and unemotional for a man who had just accomplished a praiseworthy feat, and got back on his game. He endeavored by conversation to disguise his glory.

"You've just joined the club, Mr. Chapman?"

"Only a week ago, Mr. Mott."

"Pretty nice course, don't you think? It's very hard. It's harder by three strokes than any other course in the metropolitan district, and the fairway's a bit ragged, and the greens are pretty nearly hopeless; but you wait five years! I tell you, a man's got to keep out of the rough on this course or he's dished. I like a stiff course; it's the only kind to have. Where did you play formerly?"

"Over in Boston—Woodland."

"Oh! Do you know Francis Ouimet?"

"I should say I do! Do *you?*"

"Well, not personally," said Mr. Mott, with some haste. "But of course . . . If he had more time to play, he'd be a wizard, wouldn't he? Fore!"

"You're in the pit!" shrilled Mr. Mott's caddy.

"Well, don't tell me about it *now!*" roared Mr. Mott, turning livid. He glanced at Chapman. "Excuse me, I thought you'd played. Well, of all the—" He saw Chapman's stinging brassey, which had threatened to sail into a grove of pines to westward, suddenly veer to the east, and drop lazily abaft the green.

"Pretty lucky," said Chapman. "I played for a slice, but—"

"*Lucky!* I wish I had *half* your luck! I'd be down to a three handicap, by gosh! See my ball anywhere, caddy? You said it was in the pit."

The boy indicated it.

"It bounced over, sir."

"Humph!" said Mr. Mott, accepting the gift of the fates without evident thankfulness. "Well, why don't you *watch* it, boy? Tell me it's in the pit, and then . . . Stand still, will you? Stop rattling those clubs!" He hit a high iron and lost it in the sun. "Say, I didn't see that one at all."

"Neither did I," said Chapman. "But it sounded like a clean hit."

Mr. Mott shifted the responsibility to his faithful retainer, who was nonchalantly chewing gum.

"Did you mark it, caddy?"

"No, sir; couldn't see it drop, Sun's in my eyes." Mr. Mott snorted, and tossed his cleek to the ground.

"Good Lord!" he snapped. "What d'you think you're paid for? D'you think I hire you to *lose* balls? Anybody can carry the clubs; your job is to *watch* the *ball!* Why didn't you mark it? That'll make three I've lost today, and you—"

"It's on," stated the caddy, chewing rapidly.

"*On!* Where?"

"On the green. Over by the sprinkler."

Mr. Mott coughed delicately, and looked at Chapman under his lashes. Chapman wasn't on; Chapman wasn't on by a good ten yards, but Mr. Mott was on in three, and the hole was a par five.

"I've got a chance for a birdie," he whispered to himself, "a chance for a four. It's four hundred and eighty yards, and I've got a chance for a four. For a birdie. . . . *Good shot!*" Chapman had clipped up neatly.

Mr. Mott took his putter, and made an awkward jab at the ball. It fled at a disconcerting angle. Mr. Mott flushed, pursued the gutty, and jabbed again. Then he lifted himself erect, and poured out into the world the offscourings of his innermost soul. He reviled himself, the Silver King golf-ball, the Vaile putter, the greenskeeper, the turf, the contour of the land, the Scotch who had invented the game, and the promoters who had organized the club. As an afterthought, he hurled the putter into a convenient hazard, and, seizing the first weapon which came to hand,—a niblick,—struck so fair and true that the ball went down for a six, one over par.

"Too bad!" said Chapman. "I missed an easy one, myself."

"I had a chance for a four," declared Mr. Mott, loudly. "Of all the rotten putting I ever saw in my *life* that was the worst! On the green in three, and three putts! These greens are rotten! Worst in the world; and believe me, I've seen some bad ones! Where's my driver? Hurry up, there!"

While his mood was of grim resolution, and he concentrated rigidly upon the act, he drove off in excellent form and with highly creditable results.

"There!" he ejaculated. "*Now* I'm getting back on my game. That old war-club certainly does poke 'em out when I hit 'em right. But three putts, and only one over par at that! If our greens were as good as they've got at Wykagyl or Sleepy Hollow—"

He observed that his companion had again hooked, and by virtue of his own superiority of direction he was vastly exhilarated. The second shots, too, filled him with passionate joy, for he was safely over the brook, while Chapman had pulled into tall grass. Mr. Mott sidled toward his partner, and made diplomatic overtures of assistance.

"If you don't mind my telling you," he said, "you stand too far back of the ball. You can't help hooking when you do that. You push the face of the club right across the ball. It's like a masse shot in billiards. You're getting good distance, but you hook all the time. Just straighten 'em out and you'll be 'way out every time. Stand farther ahead, and you'll be all right."

"I certainly am hooking 'em," acknowledged the lanky man.

"Well, if you don't mind my telling you—"

"Not a bit!"

"More like this," said Mr. Mott, illustrating. "Go back slower, and let go with your right hand at the top of the swing. Then take hold hard with your left when you start to come down. It's the left hand that does the business. And follow through more. Now, you take that last shot of mine; I hit three inches behind the ball, and the follow through saved it. All of it was bad but the follow through; but what happened? It went as straight as a die. Say, are those people going to stay on that green all *night?* Fore!"

"Oh, they haven't holed out yet."

"Yes, they have; they're counting their scores. Some people don't realize there's such a thing as etiquette in this game. *Fore!*"

He topped into the brook.

"Fore!" said Mr. Mott, waving his niblick.

He hammered the ball into a bank of yielding clay.

"Fore!" rasped Mr. Mott, setting his teeth.

He essayed a pitching stroke, a lofting stroke, an extricating stroke, and two shoveling strokes, and the last of these brought him to solid earth.

"Fore!" shouted Mr. Mott, wild-eyed. He ran an approach to the edge of the green and panted violently. "Four—and I'm on in five," said Mr. Mott, utterly innocent. "Where'd *you* go?"

"Just off—over by the water-pipe."

Mr. Mott exhaled luxuriously, and fanned himself with his hat.

"That isn't bad. One of you boys take the flag. Good work!" Secretly he held that Chapman's run-up was a fearful fluke.

"Sink it now," urged Chapman, encouragingly.

Mr. Mott tried his best to sink it, and missed by a bare inch.

"Throw that back here!" he ordered.

The second endeavor was flawless. Legally, Mr. Mott had taken two putts; morally, he had taken one—the last one. It was this consciousness of innate ability, this realization that if he had aimed a hair's-breadth farther to the left he would have sunk the first attempt that cheered and inspired him. He could have done it if he had really cared about it. And Chapman missed a two-footer!

"If you don't mind my telling you," said Mr. Mott, with admirable restraint, "you can putt a whole lot better if you turn the face of your putter over toward the hole. It puts a drag on the ball. It makes it run close to the ground. I had a six; no, seven. That first one should have gone down. Seven."

"Twelve," said his caddy, apprehensive, but judicial.

Mr. Mott turned upon him vehemently.

"*Twelve!* What in thunder are you talking about? Five on the green—"

"No, sir, ten—"

"Listen! Three in the brook,—" Mr. Mott's mouth opened slowly, and his jaw fell,—"three in the brook," he repeated in horror, "and—"

"And nine out, sir. You yelled 'Fore!' and counted the next stroke five—"

"Give me the mid-iron," said Mr. Mott, abruptly. "Get down there and mark this shot!" He wheeled to gaze at the scene of his recent dredging operations. "Three in the brook, four, five, six, seven—*Hey! Stop swinging those clubs!* Well, I *said* it was seven! Three in the brook—"

"Your honor, Mr. Mott."

"Thank you." He teed for the short sixth across a threatening ravine. "*Caddy!* wake up there!" He turned to his partner with a gesture of Christian resignation. "Don't you wish," he asked, "that just once in a while you'd find a caddy that showed some *interest* in the game?"

The sixth hole was a trifling matter of a hundred and fifty yards; but to render it attractive to experts, there were mental, physical, and psychological hazards cunningly placed by nature, aided and abetted by Donald Ross. As Mr. Mott wavered on the tee, he saw a deep gully, weed-infested and spotted with frowning rocks; he saw pits limiting and guarding the green; he saw trees and excavations and a stone wall. Upon its misshapen mound of sand he saw the Silver King waiting resignedly for its certain punishment. He saw his mid-iron, broad bladed and heavy, a club capable of propelling thirty pennyweight of rubber and silk an eighth of a mile and more if properly coerced. Yet Mr. Mott discounted the inherent qualities of that iron, just as he discounted the elasticity of the golf-ball and the power of his wrists and forearms. He recalled that on the last few occasions of his attack upon this hole he had shafted his ball over the stone wall, and he wondered dumbly how he might prevent a repetition of the error. Instinct warned him to go for the hole, and play with assurance; but for several minutes he hadn't been on good terms with his instinct. He struggled to revive the warnings of those who have written text books, to remember what Taylor or Braid or Travers has prescribed as antidotes for shafting tee-shots. "Stop talking!" he growled at the caddies. "How d' you think I can drive when you're talking!" Out of the obscurity of printed words a phrase flashed to his brain and he was aware that as Haultain says, he was about to pivot on the head of the left thigh-bone, working in the cotyloidal cavity of the *os innominatum.* He placed the mid-iron in position, and told himself that upon his life he wasn't to move his right gastrocnemius or sartorius except torsionally. He rehearsed, in one mad instant, platitudes affecting the right elbow, the eyes, the left knee, the interlocking grip, and the distribution of weight. He lifted the club stiffly, and brought it down again. Too cramped!

He settled himself more comfortably, and peered at the stone wall. The green, half bathed in golden sunshine, half purplish in dense shadow, seemed to reach out yearning arms to draw the Silver King to its broad bosom. A hundred and fifty yards, par three. Mr. Mott caught his breath in a quick intake, and drove sickeningly into the stone wall.

"Oh, tough!" said Chapman.

But the features of Mr. Mott expressed no rage. On the contrary, he was smiling placidly, as a parent smiles at a wayward child. The crisis had come and gone; the most difficult obstacle of the entire round was now a matter of indifference to him; he had known positively that he was destined somehow to entangle himself with that stone wall, and now he had done it. Even so, he didn't begrudge his partner that arching shot which spanned the ravine, and lacked not more than a yard or two of carrying the green; on the contrary, he was glad that Chapman had done so well.

"I *always* dub this hole," he said cheerfully. "I got a two on it last July, but ordinarily I'm satisfied if I get a four. You're well up there; still a tiny bit of a hook, though. But you're doing a lot better since I told you."

"I'm working hard enough to straighten 'em out," deprecated Chapman.

"Well, if you take a nice, easy swing, and don't pull your body round, you'll get good results. I hope you don't mind my telling you."

"Far from it," said Chapman, humbly.

Mr. Mott's caddy pointed to the ball, which was virtually unplayable among the stones. Mr. Mott, now that he had passed the climax of his round, was suddenly dogged and determined. It was all well enough to flub the drive, but this approach of his was serious business. He broke off a reed or two which interfered with his stance; he commandeered both caddies to assist him in the removal of sundry large rocks; he bent the grasses so that he had a fighting chance to smash through with his deep-faced mashie. Down on the green Chapman was watching earnestly. On the sixth tee a fast-moving foursome was emitting comments which blew across the ravine, and caused the muscles of Mr. Mott's jaw to tighten significantly. Duffer, was he! He'd show 'em whether he was a duffer or not! He focused on the flag, and swung the mashie in a wide ellipse.

Mr. Mott, by virtue of that mysterious and extraordinary sense with which some men are sometimes gifted, had known with utter privity of knowledge that he was sure to recover from the rough. There was no doubt about it; it was his destiny. What he hadn't known, or remotely suspected, was that he would cover sixty good yards with that clean swipe, and lose his ball in the wilderness of the adjacent jungle. And even in that moment when he most commiserated with himself for the gross faultiness of the club and the grave defects of the ball, he wasn't nearly so much tortured by the necessity of playing three, still from trouble, as he was by the necessity of allowing that cynical foursome to go through. His gorge rose at the mere conception of being passed; in match-play he would have conceded the hole instanter rather than suffer the ignominy of signaling a foursome to take precedence; but in medal-play he must finish every hole and hole every putt; so that he fretted impatiently for five long minutes, spoke to his caddy in curt monosyllables, and majestically expelled from the course, as a thief and a pirate, a soiled and tattered renegade who leaned over the wall and offered to sell him two second-hand floaters for a quarter. In days gone by Mr. Mott had bought perhaps two dozen balls from that self-same urchin, that boy who wearily spent the long summer evenings in beating thicket and brush for abandoned gutties; but today he looked askance upon the scoundrel, and saw him plainly for what he was, a trafficker in illicit wares, a golf-hound outlawed and thrice condemned. Besides, last Saturday Mr. Mott had purchased four old balls from him only to discover later that two of them were balls which Mr. Mott himself had lost a fortnight ago. They had his initials on them.

The foursome, completing their routine with incredible speed and skill, disappeared in the middle distance. Mr. Mott played three, and Mr. Mott played four, and if he hadn't kept majestic control over his temper, he would have dumped his clubs in the nearest pit, brained his caddy with a patent putter, and started incoherently for Bloomingdale. As it was, he merely confirmed the theory that the terminology of masculine hysteria is limited to four suffixes, and played five without caring whether he found the hole or Long Island Sound. As a matter of fact, he found the hole.

"Bully!" said Chapman. "I made mine, too; thought we'd better save time. I putted while you were hunting."

Mr. Mott, red and perspiring, shook his head sadly.

"I ought to have had a four," he maintained. "I wasted a shot. That's eight strokes I've absolutely thrown away this round. I ought to have had a four-easy. If you don't mind my telling you, you'd better play straight for the big tree. Then your hook'll make it come around into the fair." Whereupon Mr. Mott hit a very high, very short hook, and as he postured in the guise of Ajax,— save that Ajax presumably had no such costume and no such implement to intensify the dramatic value of his gestures,—he fervently apostrophized the wind, which had taken a perfectly straight ball and blown it into a trap. He wasn't influenced in his decision by the sight of a marker-flag drooping lazily on its staff, nor by the circumstance that Chapman's drive, which attained almost equal height, came to earth without a single degree of deviation from the line of shortest distance.

"The wind took it right around!" flamed Mr. Mott, snatching his niblick. "*Fore!*"

It was a good out, and Mr. Mott played a goodly third. His fourth, however, was abortive, although the divot flew gracefully. Mr. Mott withheld his analysis until Chapman had curved an approach within striking distance of the green, and then his finer sensibilities prompted him to disregard himself and to tutor Chapman.

"That was a nice ball," he began sincerely, "but you're still hooking. Why don't you try addressing it with the heel of the club? That makes you come around in after it. You try that, and see what it does. And I've noticed you go back too fast. You can't do that and keep your balance unless you're a good player. Slow back, and crook your left knee more. In at the ball, I mean. Like this!" His delsarte was masterly; and although he foundered the shot, the ball rolled and rolled until it trickled on to the green and stopped dead. "Well, that's the idea, but I didn't get it up enough," said Mr. Mott with decent reserve. Subsequently they each used the putter twice.

The eighth was a respite, and they halved it in four. On the ninth tee, to the frank annoyance of another foursome which had overtaken them, Mr. Mott refused to drive until the quartet ahead had left the green, two hundred and twenty-two yards away, uphill.

"A good wallop'll carry that far sometimes," he explained with dignity. "I've done it myself. Almost did it this morning. They're off now, anyway." Before proceeding to the shot, he condescended to lighten the situation with a ray of humor. "I'd hate to kill anybody," he said, and after an enormous swing topped not more than a mallet's length into the tall grass.

From the restive foursome a gruff voice struck harshly upon Mr. Mott's sensitive ears:

"Well, that was a damn' humane impulse all right!"

With a medal score of sixty-three for the first nine, Mr. Mott bade farewell to all thought of a silver trophy for his library, and devoted himself to a keen study of ballistics as exemplified by his partner's chronic hook. For two holes he fairly exuded advice and encouragement, but at the twelfth tee he was staggered to discover that he had counseled an ingrate. Without question, Chapman was improving steadily; the hook was appreciably less, and Mr. Mott had merely said, with the kindest of motives, that Chapman *was* improving, and that if he'd only remember to stare while he counted three at the spot where the ball had rested before he hit it, he'd do even better. And Chapman, smiling faintly, replied in a gentle tone which contained rebuke:

"Perhaps if you'll play your own game, Mr. Mott, and let me play mine, we'll get along well enough as it is."

Mr. Mott wouldn't have been human if he hadn't taken seven on the next hole, and he wouldn't have been human if he hadn't experienced a thrill of primitive triumph when Chapman not only hooked his drive, but also his full mid-iron. Granted that his approach was moderately efficient, Chapman deserved nothing better than a seven, or possibly a six, with divine aid; but when he putted wretchedly off direction, and the ball, obviously deflected by the agency of a slope which Mr. Mott hadn't seen and couldn't discern curled sharply in toward the cup, and tottered to the lip of it, and dropped, Mr. Mott compressed his lips and said nothing. He realized* that comment was superfluous; when a man had that sort of luck, which simply compensated for two earlier mistakes, there was nothing for a righteously indignant opponent to say. Chapman had even forfeited his earlier right to be joked about it.

But when Chapman achieved a perfect drive on the thirteenth Mr. Mott burst with information.

"That's the queerest thing I ever saw in my life!"

"What is?"

"Why, that ball was straight as a die! And you stood for another hook!"

"No!" said Chapman.

"But—why, certainly you did. I'd have told you, but you'd begun your swing, and I was afraid of spoiling your shot. It's the funniest thing I ever saw! Where am I, caddy?"

"In the pit," said the stolid caddy.

By the time he got out, he perceived that his companion had finished, and was sitting on the bench in the shade. Highly offended at the discourtesy, Mr. Mott whistled as a demonstration of independence, and utilized an unconscionable length of time in a study of topography. To do him justice, he wasn't seeking to retaliate; he was resolved that by his own excellence in the short game he would display his lack of nerves and his imperturbability in a trying moment. The man whose partner has played out rather than to wait politely while sandpits are under exploration is subject to an adjustment of poise; and although Mr. Mott had the satisfaction of leaving no loophole for criticism, and of holing prettily, he was nevertheless too fundamentally introspective to drive well on the dog-leg fourteenth.

Furthermore, although the region immediately surrounding his ball wasn't placarded as ground under repair when Mr. Mott began his onslaught upon the turf, it was indubitably in need of repair when Mr. Mott got through with it. He quarried out a blanket of gravelly soil at each of four desperate offensives, and when he toiled wearily up the hillside to the rolling green he took two putts for a nine, and was aware that Chapman, whether befriended or betrayed by fortune, hook or no hook, had beaten him by a margin of many strokes.

But the sun was setting, the end was near, and Chapman was a new member. Mr. Mott relaxed somewhat, tore his tournament score-card to bits, and scattered them on the grass.

"No use keeping *that* any more," he said. "I can't putt on these plowed fields they call greens. They're a disgrace to the club, that's what they are. Now, this is what I call a beautiful hole. Four hundred and sixty—over beyond the farthest line of trees. Par five; it ought to be par six."

"Why?"

Mr. Mott was mildly astonished.

"Because it's a hard hole."

"But par's arbitrary, Mr. Mott."

"Yes, but the greens committee—"

"The greens committee hasn't anything to do with it. Any hole up to two hundred and fifty is par three, from that to four fifty is par four, from four fifty-one to six hundred is par five. So this is a par five—and it's only ten yards too long to be a par four."

Mr. Mott blinked at the sun.

"What makes you think that?"

"I don't think it; I *know* it. The U. S. G. A. changed the figures in April, but the ruling didn't affect this particular distance at that."

"Well, I may be wrong, but my impression is that the greens committee fixes the par for the different holes. Anyway, here goes!"

"Nice ball!" said Chapman.

Mr. Mott smiled conciliatingly.

"Tommy Kerrigan made that driver for me," he said. "It's a pippin. As soon as I swing I can *feel* I'm going to hit it clean. I *beg* your pardon! Did I take your mind off your shot?"

"Not at all. I'm out there about where you are."

"It was a screamer," said Mr. Mott, unaware of the inference to be drawn from the compliment. "As good a drive as I've seen in a month."

To his immense gratification, he was hole-high on his second shot, and home on his third. He compelled himself to plan for two putts, to insure himself a par five instead of risking all on a bold steal which might prove, by metamorphosis, to be a gift to the devil. In consequence he very nearly holed out, and he was far too enraptured to care what Chapman got. Chapman had manhandled his chip shot, and Mr. Mott hadn't noticed the others. Let Chapman account for himself. Par five! Who cared what Chapman got?

According to the custom duly laid down in such cases, Mr. Mott took many practice swings on the sixteenth tee. Temporarily, he had struck his head upon the stars, and with the pride of a champion he swung with a champion's ease and freedom. Par five! Mr. Mott, with the image of victory statue hovering before his eyes, clipped bits of turf from the scarred tee and ogled the green. Kerrigan had often overdriven it; once when the ground was baked out; it wasn't much more than two hundred and forty yards. And the rough directly before the tee, the trap to the left, and the rough to the right, what were they? Who but novices were to be alarmed by puny obstacles such as these? Surely not the man who has made the long fifteenth in a par five!

"Fore!" he said mechanically.

Mr. Mott drove magnificently, and started hastily over the foot-bridge, then halted at the pleasant laughter of his companion; and shamefacedly stood aside. He never looked to see where Chapman drove; his consciousness was riveted upon a small white object far up on the slope. And since, during his walk, he told himself exactly how he should play his approach, how he should stand, how he should swing, he later stood and swung without destructive uncertainty, and so pitched fairly to the pin. The putt was simple; Mr. Mott achieved it without a tremor.

"Three!" he whispered to himself. "One under par! One under par for two holes! Gosh! If I hadn't been so rotten up to the fifteenth I'd have had a chance!" Aloud, he said: "Par four's too much for this hole. It ought to be three. What was yours?"

"Four," said Chapman. "Your approach was too good; it was a wonder."

"Pure wrist shot. Notice how I took the club back? Sort of scoop the ball up—pick it up clean? That's what I've been working for—pick 'em up clean with lots of back spin. You get that by sort of sliding under the ball. Well, two more to go!"

"Let's make 'em good!" adjured Chapman.

"One under par for two holes," thought Mr. Mott, slashing a low drive to the open. "Say, I guess somebody wouldn't turn up his nose at that, eh? A five and a three! I was—let's see—thirty-eight for five holes, and a five and a three make forty-six. Oh, I beg your pardon!" He was wool-gathering squarely in front of Chapman, who presently put a hooked ball somewhat beyond Mr. Mott's. "My! what a wonderful day for golf!" said Mr. Mott, enthusiastically. "Not a breath of wind, not too hot, just right."

"It suits me. You got a nice drive there."

"Too high," said Mr. Mott. He played a jumping shot which ran briskly over the shallow pit guarding the green, and came to a standstill not twenty feet from the cup. He putted, and was dead. He holed out with neatness and precision, and knew that he had beaten Chapman by a stroke. "Gad, what a green!" said Mr. Mott, pop-eyed. "Like a billiard-table. We've got an English greens-keeper here; he's a wonder. Best greenskeeper in the East. Sleepy Hollow and Pine Valley have nothing on *us*"

"You're finishing strong, Mr. Mott. Go to it!"

"One under par for three holes," shouted Mr. Mott's dual personality to Mr. Mott. "And—how many am I to here?" To Chapman he said, "I'm trying to remember—what did I have on the tenth?"

"Six," said Chapman.

"Why, are you sure?"

"Positive."

"Well, I *thought* I remembered it was six,—I've been counting up,—but—"

"I can name every stroke you've played since you started," said Chapman. "It gets to be second nature after a while. It's only a knack; but sometimes it's very valuable. I know every shot we've *both* played."

Mr. Mott looked doubtful.

"I'd take the short end of a sizable bet on that proposition. What was my fourth shot on the fourth hole?"

"Brassey to the green," said Chapman. "You got a six."

"Well, I'll be—what did I make on the seventh hole? "

"Seven."

"Well, what was my third shot on the tenth?"

"Just a minute—why, it was a topped mashie into the trap. You were on in four and down in six."

Mr. Mott prepared to drive.

"Do you always remember scores like that?"

"Always."

Mr. Mott drove far down the fairway. Exalted and emboldened, he ventured to explain briefly just how he had done it. Then when Chapman had hit a long, low ball which developed a faint hook as it dipped to the hollows, Mr. Mott was constrained to offer condolence.

"If you just get that kink out of your shots you'll play under a hundred," he stated flatly. "Under a hundred with no trouble at all."

His companion chuckled involuntarily.

"Well, I hope I should."

"Nothing in the world but too much wrist action. Look! You don't see *me* hooking many balls, do you? Watch how I get my wrists into this one!" He was unerring on the line, and Chapman nodded understandingly.

"You couldn't ask anything better than that."

"And the best of it is," said Mr. Mott, glowing, "that I always know what's the matter with me. I wasn't always that way; there was a time when I was way up in the air about it, so I know just how you feel. Now go after this one! Easy—and follow through! Oh—too bad!"

Chapman, however, wasn't overly discouraged.

"It's safe, isn't it?"

"Yes, it's almost up on the brook; but if you'd gone into the woods, it would have been a lost ball. *This* way!" Mr. Mott illustrated once more. "Here she goes!" And he made his third consecutive shot which was without reproach.

Chapman, however, hooked a trifle even with his full mashie, which was barely off the green, and Mr. Mott sighed for him. For himself, he ran up alongside. If he could go down in two more, he would have played the last four holes in par! Mr. Mott reached for his putter, and fumbled with it. He bent over the ball, and observed that it was smaller than he had suspected; he told himself that he should have chosen a larger size. Mr. Mott's lips formed the word "Fore!" and he tapped impotently. The ball rolled in, swerved, struck a transient leaf, and Mr. Mott, his mind erased of any conception of a partner, or of the etiquette of the links, dashed forward. Two feet to the cup, two feet for a six, and the last four holes in par! Fifty-one for the last nine—his record! Mr. Mott, gasping, clutched the putter, and struck, and heard the click of the contact, and saw a cylindrical abyss, lined with zinc, open wide to receive the Silver King. He stood up, choked with emotion.

"The—last four holes in—in *par!*" he faltered.

"Hold the flag, boy!" said Chapman.

Mr. Mott watched, fascinated. Inwardly he knew, before Chapman putted, that the stroke was too light; and as the lanky stranger strolled up for further trial, Mr. Mott, in his terrific success, blurted out his final charge.

"If you don't mind my telling you," he said, "rest your right hand on your knee, and—"

The ball rattled into the cup. From a camp-chair under the awning, a member of the Board of Governors rose and sauntered toward them.

"Mr. Chapman!" said Mr. Mott. He offered his hand across the hole.

"Thank you, Mr. Mott." Chapman's clasp was convincing.

"I was par for the last four holes! If I'd only got back on my game sooner! Listen! If you didn't hook so much—"

"Yes?" The voice of the stranger was dull with weariness.

"Well, you saw what *I* did! I came back in fifty-one, and the last four in par! Why, if you can play an even game with me *now*—"

"Hello, Chap," said the Governor at his elbow. "How are you going?"

"Fine!" said Mr. Mott, answering for him. "If he only didn't hook so much! How *did* we come out? I was a hundred and fourteen, and you—"

"Eighty-one," said Chapman. "Not bad for a starter." His tone was utterly serious; he wasn't jesting.

Mr. Mott's eyes widened. His mouth sagged. A spot of color appeared above his cheek-bones.

"Why, that's impossible. That's—"

"Forty-one for first nine, and forty for the last." Mr. Mott shook as though with palsy, and the putter fell from his hands. He had ignored Chapman's medal score, but now he was recalling incident after incident which seemed to suggest that Chapman had made recoveries, and got distance, and dropped occasional putts. . . .

"Why . . . why . . . I thought we were going about even!"

"Count 'em up," said Chapman, soberly. "6, 5, 4, 5, 5, 3, 4, 4, 5; isn't that forty-one? 5, 4, 4, 2, 6, 5, 4, 5, 5; isn't that forty? "

"You—you didn't get—a two on the thirteenth!"

"Certainly I did. I holed out while you were in the pit."

Mr. Mott now that he flogged his memory for the facts, seemed dimly to recognize that even those swerving shots of Chapman's had gone off smoothly, and that Chapman had approached sweetly, and putted with distinction. But an eighty-one! And he had volunteered to coach this man; he had showed him in detail how various shots should be made; he had claimed the privilege of instructing a stranger who had hit hardly a straight ball, and still scored close to eighty.

"Wh—what's your handicap?" he stammered. "You—you aren't *that* Chapman—are you?"

The Governor put his arm over the shoulders of the lanky stranger.

"He had three in New England," he said, "but in the Met. I suppose they'll give him four. How were *you* going, Mr. Mott?"

"Oh, pretty fair—for me," said Mr. Mott, feebly.

But when, bathed and ennobled by fresh linen, he left the club-house his heart was once more proud and high. Now and then, to be sure, he experienced a spasm of mortification at the ridiculous figure he had cut before Chapman; nevertheless he was sustained and soothed by the remembrance of the last nine holes in fifty-one and the last four in par. He felt a sturdy manhood, confident and unafraid. Today he had scored a hundred and fourteen; tomorrow it might be that he, too, should play the full round as he had played the last four holes today; upon such dreams is founded the wealth of the club-makers and the athletic outfitters. Timidity in the presence of hazards had gone from him, he believed, forever. Timidity on the greens was a thing of the past. If he could lower his average to a hundred and five by the end of the season,—and with four holes in par today he could conceivably do five in par next Saturday, or perhaps as many as six or seven,—he might get down to, say, ninety by next year. If a slim built Bostonian with no style to speak of could approximate eighty, why not Mr. Mott? If a man with a chronic hook could merit a four handicap, why not Mr. Mott? He saw roseate visions of himself at scratch; Walter Travis was already middle-aged before *he* took up the game.

"The last four in par!" whispered Mr. Mott as he went up the steps of his house.

"Well" said Mrs. Mott, pathetically, as she came to greet him, "was it worth a thousand dollars to you, Val, to stay away *all* this lovely afternoon?"

"Every cent of it!" cried Mr. Mott, hilariously. "Say, let's motor up the road somewhere; want to? Let's have dinner out! Here, I know! We'll run up to Tumble Inn. Get the Smithsons, and we'll have a party."

"I thought you said you couldn't go out to-night!" She was frankly suspicious.

"Rot! I never said that, did I? Must have been a slip of the tongue. Call the Smithsons, will you?"

"It *must* have been worth while, your staying," said Mrs. Mott, brightening.

"Well, it was," said Mr. Mott. "And I got the last four holes in par! Hurry up and telephone!"

And as he waited for her report, the man who had played a hundred and fourteen stood before the long mirror in the hallway, and gripped an imaginary club, and swung it, and finished gloriously, with the body well twisted and the hands close to the neck, and grinned happily at the reflection of another champion in the making. For this is at once the faith and the hope, the Credo and the Te Deum of the golfer of all time and of whatever ability,—Thank God for tomorrow!

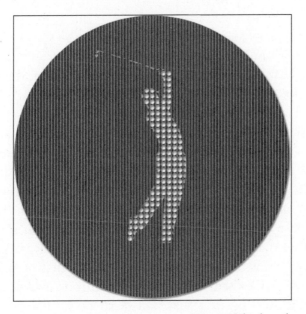

THE STORY OF THE HONG-KONG MEDAL

W. G. VAN T. SUTPHEN

At the age of thirty-five but one illusion remained to Henry Alderson, rich, single, and a member in good and regular standing of the Marion County Golf Club. It is hardly necessary to add that it was only in his capacity as a golfer that he lived again in the rose-colored atmosphere of youth, for after the third decade there is no other possible form of self-deception.

And it is equally superfluous to remark that he was a very poor golfer, for it is only the duffers at the royal and ancient game who have any leisure for the exercise of the imagination; the medal-winners are obliged to confine their attention to hitting the ball clean and to keeping their eye in for short putts. It was for Henry Alderson and his kind to keep trade brisk for the ball and club makers, and to win phenomenal matches against the redoubt-able *Col. Bogey*—a game which may be magnificent, but which is certainly not golf. Still, the diversion was unquestionably a harmless one, and served to keep him in the open air and from an overclose application to business. Moreover, it was absolutely certain that the secret of success lay well within his grasp. A few more days of practice, the final acquisition of that peculiar turn of the wrist, and then!—Henry Alderson took a fresh grip on the familiar lofting-iron that had deceived him so often, and topped another ball along the turf. Of course the delusion was a hopeless one, but he was happy in its possession; and if we who look on have become wiser in our day and generation—why, so much the worse for us.

It was a bright autumn morning, and Henry Alderson stood at the tee looking at the little red flag that marked the location of the tenth hole, two hundred and thirty yards away. He had done fairly well on the outgoing course, but this hole had always been a stumbling-block to him, and that dreadful double hazard, a scant hundred yards down the course, looked particularly savage on this particular morning. On the left lurked an enormous sand-pit, which was popularly known as the "Devil"; and the "Deep Sea," in the shape of an ice pond, was only a few yards to the right. Straight between them lay the path to glory, but for a "slice" or a "foozle" there remained only destruction and double figures.

Henry Alderson shuddered as he looked, and incontinently forgot all about "slow back." Crack! and the "gutty" had disap-peared beneath the treacherous waters of the "Deep Sea." With painful deliberation he teed another ball and mentally added two to his score. The club-head swung back, and for one fatal instant his eye wandered from the ball. Bang! and it had gone to the "Devil." Without a word Mr. Alderson took his expensive collection of seventeen clubs from the hands of his caddie and descended into the bunker to meet the Evil One.

It was just fifteen minutes after eleven when Henry Alderson entered upon his ghostly conflict with all the Powers of Darkness. At twenty minutes of twelve the caddie, tired of inaction, crept cautiously to the edge of the bunker and looked in. His master held in his hand a costly patented "driver" that was alleged to be unbreakable. Placing one foot upon the head of the club, he kicked judiciously but with determination at the precise place where the "scare" is whipped to the shaft, and then carefully added the fragments to the heap of broken putters, cleeks, and brasseys that lay before him. The boy, who was wise in his generation, waited for no more, but fled to the club-house.

Henry Alderson came up out of the bunker, took half a dozen new balls from the pocket of his red coat, and deliberately flung them into the "Deep Sea." He then tore his score-card into bits, divested himself of cap and shoes, laid his watch and purse where they would be readily observed, and walked with a firm step to the border of the pond.

Suddenly a quickly moving shadow projected itself over his shoulder, and a cheerful, albeit an unfamiliar, voice hailed him. He turned and saw a stranger standing close beside him. The newcomer was an odd-looking personage, dressed in a semiclerical suit of rusty black, and carrying an old cotton umbrella and a well-stuffed carpet-bag. He had a keen-looking, smooth-shaven face, with piercing black eyes and an aggressive nose. His complexion was of a curious pallor, as though untouched by wind or sun, but there was nothing in his appearance to indicate either ill-health or decrepitude.

"Possibly a colporteur," thought Henry Alderson. "At any rate, he's no golfer."

"How are you making out?" inquired the stranger, in a tone of polite interest.

It was on the tip of Henry Alderson's tongue to answer, "Fifty-five for nine holes" (his actual score being sixty-three), but at this awful moment, when all the solid realities of life were crumbling away beneath his feet, the lie seemed so small, so pitiful, so mean, and he replied, "Came out in forty-two, but then I lost a shot through having my ball lifted by a dog."

The stranger did not seem to be visibly impressed. "Pooh!" he said, airily; "I should hardly call that golf."

"Perhaps you play yourself," returned Alderson, with what he considered to be a sarcastic inflection.

"Not as a general thing, though I do a round or so occasionally," said the dark gentleman, placidly. Then opening his carpet-bag and taking out a golf- ball, "It's a very pretty drive from where we stand. If you will allow me."

He teed the ball, and, with what seemed to be an almost contemptuous disregard of all rules for correct driving, swung against it the crook handle of his old cotton umbrella. Crack! and it went away like a rifle-bullet, close to the ground for one hundred and twenty yards, and then, towering upward in the manner of a rocketing pigeon, caught the full strength of the breeze for a hundred yards of further carry, and dropped dead on the putting-green. Henry Alderson gasped.

"Shall we walk on?" said the stranger. It was a long putt on the green, but the umbrella was again equal to the occasion. Henry Alderson's eyes sparkled. This was an umbrella worth having.

"It makes no difference what kind of a club you use," said the gentleman in black, apparently reading his thoughts. "But with this particular make of ball you can accomplish any shot at will, no matter how difficult."

"I'd like to try that kind of ball," said Alderson, eagerly. "Can you give me the maker's address?"

"If you will accept this one, it is entirely at your service."

Henry Alderson stretched out his hand, and then as quickly withdrew it. He remembered now that when the obliging stranger had opened his bag it had appeared to be filled with what looked like legal papers—contracts perhaps—and there was a dreadful significance in the fact that all the signatures were in red. Of course it might have been carmine ink, and probably was, but it looked suspicious.

"If it's a question of signing my name to anything," he faltered, "I don't think that I can accept. I've made it a rule—er—never to go upon anybody's paper. It's—er—business, you know."

The stranger smiled indulgently. "You are quite right. Nevertheless, you need have no scruples about accepting my gift, for there is no obligation of any kind involved in the transaction."

Henry Alderson trembled, and looked furtively at the dark gentleman's feet, which, as he now observed, were encased in a pair of arctic galoshes some four sizes too large. Clearly there was no definite information to be gained in that quarter; and as the field that they were in was used as a pasture for cattle, the presence of hoof-marks could mean nothing either way. There was nothing to do but to chance it, and he was not long in making up his mind. He took the ball and stowed it away in his pocket.

The stranger nodded approvingly. "I think that I may congratulate you in advance upon your success in winning the club handicap this afternoon."

"But suppose that I lose the ball?" said Alderson, with a sudden accession of doubtfulness.

"Impossible. If your caddie has been negligent, you have only to whistle, and the ball will keep on answering ' Here ' until you come up with it. And, moreover, it is indestructible."

"It makes no difference what club I use?"

"None whatever. If you care to, you can drive that ball two hundred yards with a feather bolster."

"I shall endeavor to do so," laughed Alderson. "You won't—er—come and have a bite of luncheon with me?"

"Not today," said the stranger, politely. "But we shall probably meet again. Good luck to you, and may your success end only with the winning of the Hong-Kong Medal."

The two men bowed, and the dark gentleman walked off. He went to the edge of the "Devil" sand-bunker, marched straight into it, and disappeared. Moved by a sudden impulse, Henry Alderson followed and looked in. There was nothing to be seen, but he thought that he could detect a slight trace of sulphur in the air. However, one may be easily deceived in such matters.

As Henry Alderson trudged back to the club-house it seemed as though the events of the last half-hour had been nothing more than the disordered fancies of a noon-day nightmare. But there was the ball in his hand, the tangible evidence of what had happened. And, after all, the bargain had been entirely in his favor. Whoever the dark gentleman may have been, and Henry Alderson shuddered as he reflected upon one unholy possibility, he was certainly no business man. The wonderful ball was in his, Henry Alderson's, possession, and his chances of eternal salvation were as good as ever.

"Somebody has been stupid," chuckled Mr. Alderson to himself as he entered the grill-room of the club and took up the luncheon card.

The handicap match had been put down for three o'clock. It was a monthly affair, and the winner had the proud distinction of wearing a silver cross for the following period of thirty days. It was a coveted honor, but of course not to be compared with the Hong-Kong Medal, which was always played for at the end of the golfing year. No one knew why it was called the Hong-Kong Medal, and it was certain that its donor had never in his life been out of the Middle States. But the appellation seemed to chime in with the somewhat fanciful phraseology that prevails in all things pertaining to golf, and it possessed a sonorous clang tint that was suggestive of tomtoms and barbaric victories.

It is needless to say that Henry Alderson invariably entered all the club competitions, and as invariably came out at the bottom of the list. And yet no one had worked harder to insure success. He was absolutely saturated with the theory and literature of golf, and could rattle off the roster of open and amateur champions with the fluency of a prize Sunday-school scholar reciting the names of the kings of Judah and Israel. He neglected nothing in the way of precept or practice, and when the club champion got married he had even thought of following his example for its possible effect upon his game. But when he ventured to propose the expedient to Miss Kitty Crake he met with a decided rebuff.

"I shall never," said Miss Crake, "marry a man who is not on the scratch list. When you have won the Hong-Kong Medal, why then we shall see."

Of course, such an answer could be nothing less than the most absolute of refusals. Even in his wildest dreams he had never hoped to come in better than fourth in the monthly handicaps, and that too with an allowance of thirty-six strokes. It is true that there were other young ladies who might have accepted a less heroic standard of excellence than the winning of the Hong-Kong, but Henry Alderson felt that the matrimonial experiment was not worth trying unless Kitty Crake could be induced to take part in it. And so there the matter rested.

When Mr. Alderson stepped to the teeing-ground that afternoon for his first drive he felt unaccountably cool and collected, in spite of the fact that Miss Crake stood in the very forefront of the "gallery." It was one hundred and seventy-seven yards to the first hole, and he usually "hooked" his ball into the "Punch-bowl" hollow at the left, or else feebly topped it along the ground in the one consuming desire to get away from the spectators. But today there should be another tale to tell. For an instant he thought of directing the magic ball to land upon the putting-green dead at the hole, but he reflected that such a phemonenal stroke would undoubtedly be put down as a fluke. It was the part of wisdom to go quietly, and so he picked out a spot some twenty yards short of the green, but in good line, and affording a generous "lie."

As he lifted his club and swung through he was uncomfortably conscious of having transgressed at least eighteen out of the twenty-three cardinal precepts for correct driving, but already the ball was on its way, and, amidst a hearty burst of applause, led, as he could see, by Kitty Crake, it fell precisely as he had determined. A skilful approach laid him dead, and the hole was his in three. A subdued buzz ran around the circle of the "gallery," and everybody bent forward to watch his second drive across the "Punch-bowl." Straight over the yawning hollow flew the ball, and the crowd clapped again; but the play was now too far away to watch, and there were others ready to drive off. Henry Alderson disappeared in the direction of the "meadow" hole, and Miss Crake went to the club-house piazza to make tea. "Poor fellow," she thought, "his foozling will be all the worse when it does come."

It was a very successful tournament, and Henry Alderson won it by the credible score of eighty net. He blushed as the President handed him the silver cross, but the spectators clapped vigorously; for he had always been a good fellow, albeit a bad golfer, and his victory was a popular one.

"Splendid!" said Miss Kitty Crake, and Henry Alderson ascended forthwith into the seventh heaven.

During the month that followed there were some tremendous surprises in store for the record-holders. Three days after the handicap Alderson did the course in eighty-two, thereby breaking the amateur record, and that same afternoon he tied the best professional score. The Green Committee promptly reduced him to the scratch list, and there was some informal talk of sending him to represent the club at the National Amateur meeting. Montague, the holder of the Hong-Kong Medal for two years running, was visibly uneasy. He began to spend more time on the links, and held surreptitious conversations with Alderson's favorite caddie.

But there was a friend as well as an enemy to keep close watch upon Henry Alderson. There was a change in him that only Kitty Crake noticed at first—a change that both annoyed and alarmed her. The becoming modesty with which he had achieved his first successes had entirely disappeared. Almost imperceptibly he had grown self-sufficient and opinionated, and his attitude towards his fellow-players was at times little short of offensive. He seemed to take an insolent delight in openly flouting the hoary traditions of the game, and in giving the lie direct to each and every venerable truism incrusted in golfing lore. He invariably used a wrong grip; he played with a full swing for all distances, including the shortest of putts, and he never under any circumstances condescended to keep his eye upon the ball. It was maddening to his fellow-golfers, but his scores were a sufficient answer to all remonstrances. Indeed, it may be said that his steadily decreasing averages were beginning to cause the Green Committee considerable uneasiness. For a player to return cards of sixty-four and then fifty-six and then forty-nine seemed to argue unfavorably for the sporting character of the links. Such kind of play was plainly injuring the reputation of the club, and at least the Honorary Secretary was emboldened to hint as much. The very next day Henry Alderson returned a total of eighteen for the full round of holes, and handed it with a mocking smile to the Honorary Secretary himself. This was too much, and Henry Alderson was promptly summoned to appear before the outraged majesty of the Green Committee. But it all ended in smoke. No one could deny that extraordinary scores of a hole in one stroke had been made on several occasions, and in this case it was simply an established phenomenon multiplied by itself eighteen times. "And, gentlemen," concluded Henry Alderson. "I did it all with a wooden putter."

The Green Committee had nothing more to say, but they were plainly dissatisfied, and at once set about putting in some new hazards.

And yet—will it be believed?—'Henry Alderson was not a happy man. Egotistical and arrogant as he had become, he yet could not fail to perceive that he had lost immensely in the esteem of his clubmates. Nobody cared to play a match with him; and although at first he had put it down to jealousy, he was gradually forced to admit to himself that the reason lay deeper. Worst of all, Kitty Crake was decidedly cool in her manner towards him. He could not understand it, for his golf was certainly above reproach, and he knew that nothing now could prevent him from winning the Hong-Kong Medal. Once it was pinned upon his breast he would be in a position to demand an explanation and the fulfilment of her promise. But there was still another reason for his wishing that the match was over. Strange as it may appear, the very name of golf had become an abhorrence to him. And yet it was not so strange, after all, when one stops to consider. There is nothing so tiresome as perfection, and this especially applies to golf, as possessing an essentially feminine nature. It is the capriciousness, the inconstancy, of golf that makes it a folly so adorable, and Henry Alderson's game had arrived at a pitch of intolerable perfection. He had long ago discovered that the ball would not be a party to a poor shot. Goaded into fury by the monotonous consistency of his play, he had tried the experiment of ordering the ball into a bunker, or at least a bad lie. But the soulless piece of gutta-percha would have none of his foozling. It simply would not be denied, and after a few trials Henry Alderson resigned himself to his fate, comforting himself with the reflection that, having won the medal (and Kitty Crake), he would give up golf forever.

The day of the contest for the Hong-Kong Medal had come at last, and all golfdom had assembled to see the battle. A round-robin protesting against the admission of Henry Alderson as a competitor had been presented to the Green Committee, but that autocratic body had decided to ignore the protest. "It will be better," said a wise man, "to let him win rather than to give him a handle for a grievance. Let him take the medal, and then we can settle upon some pretext to expel him from the club. Montague has had detectives on the case, and thinks he can prove that Alderson has been playing tennis within the last two months. That will be sufficient in the eyes of all true golfers."

As it happened, Alderson and Montague were paired for the great event, and, of course, they had the gallery with them. Just before they started Alderson mustered up his courage and walked over to where Kitty Crake was standing. She did not raise her eyes as he approached, and he was obliged to speak twice before he could gain her attention.

"I trust that I am to have the benefit of your good wishes," he said, meaningly.

She looked at him in frosty surprise.

"I don't think that they will help you much." And then, with cutting deliberation, "I devoutly wish that the Hong-Kong Medal had never existed."

"Mr. Montague and Mr. Alderson," called out the referee. The two contestants came forward, and Kitty Crake ostentatiously turned her back as the play began.

In all the annals of the Marion County Golf Club a closer and more exciting match had never been played. Montague was certainly putting up the game of his life; and Alderson, while not showing any phenomenal work, was nevertheless returning a faultless score. Not a mistake had been made on either side, and at the end of the seventeenth hole honors were exactly even. But Montague was visibly breaking under the strain.

When Montague stepped forward to drive for the home hole it was plain that he was very nervous. Twice he tried to tee his ball, but his trembling fingers refused their office, and he was obliged to call upon a caddie for assistance. As he came up for the "address" he was deathly pale, and little beads of sweat were standing upon his forehead. The club swung back, and then descended upon the ball, but with a feeble, crooked blow that "sliced" it hopelessly into the bushes. A groan went up. Montague had "cracked," and the match was lost.

Up to this point Henry Alderson had played as though in a dream. At last he understood—those cold, stinging words of Kitty Crake could have but one meaning. *She did not wish him to win!* It was only too plain that she had never loved him, and that she regretted her idle words about the winning of the medal and the promise that they implied. What was he to do?

One thing was certain: he had no chance, in any event, with Kitty Crake. Of course he might go on and win the medal, and then humiliate her by contemptuously refusing to press his claim; but the revenge was an unmanly one, and he could not bring himself to adopt it. Again, he might withdraw, and so give the prize to Montague. He knew that the latter was desperately anxious to retain possession of the trophy. It was the pride, the joy, the treasure, of his otherwise empty life. The Montague infants had all cut their teeth upon the medal's firm and glittering edge. It was the family fetich; the one thing that distinguished them from the common herd of their neighbors, who lived in precisely the same pattern of suburban villa, but whose interest in life never rose above the discussion of village improvements or the election of a vestryman. Henry Alderson hesitated; his heart grew soft within him. And yet to give it up after it had cost him so much!

"Oh yes, a fair enough player, but a trifle short in his driving."

It was Montague who spoke, and Henry Alderson felt instinctively that the remark referred to him. His cheeks burned as he heard the half-veiled insult that only a golfer can understand in its full significance, and he incontinently forgot all about his generous resolution to withdraw. He stepped up to the tee.

"I dare say I can reach the green in two," he said, carelessly.

The hole was some four hundred yards away, and Montague smiled sarcastically. His enemy was about to be delivered into his hands.

"I've done two hundred and forty yards of straight carry," continued Alderson.

"Hym!" coughed Montague.

"And I'd back myself to make it three hundred."

"Why not four?" said Montague.

"Six hundred, if you say so," returned Alderson, hotly.

"Or perhaps out of sight," sneered Montague.

"Off the earth," retorted Alderson.

Montague made no reply, but turned away to hide his satisfaction. Alderson was deliberately going to "press," and every student of the art of golf knows what that implies. But there is nothing more uncertain than a certainty—in golf.

Henry Alderson swung down upon the ball. Shades of St. Rule! but was there ever such a mighty drive? Three hundred yards away, and it was still rising into the blue ether. Another instant and it had passed entirely out of sight, lost in infinite space. The spectators gasped, and Montague turned livid. But stop a bit. Where *was* the ball? The referee looked puzzled, and the caddies stared open-mouthed into the sky. And then in a flash it dawned upon Henry Alderson that his boast had been literally made good. *He had driven his ball off the earth.*

For a moment his heart stood still. With the ball was gone his golfing reputation, and gone forever. Was there anything else for him in life? The answer came in another flash of inspiration. Yes; he was a free man; now he could play golf again—his *own* game. Forgotten was the Hong-Kong Medal; forgotten for the nonce was Kitty Crake herself. The fit was upon him—the berserker rage of the true duffer. He turned to the referee.

"I acknowledge," he said, "the penalty for lost ball, and play a new one."

He teed a ball, an ordinary gutta-percha, and, swinging down upon it, made the most bungling of "tops." A roar of laughter went up, and Henry Alderson joined in it, the heartiest of all. He caught Kitty Crake's eye, and she was smiling too. Taking a brassey, he advanced for his second shot, and "missed the globe" twice running. But what a delightful sensation it was!—this was something like golf.

Finally, he succeeded in playing inside of Montague, who followed with a splendidly played iron shot out of the bushes. Alderson drove into a bunker, and noted, with an exquisite thrill of pleasure, that his ball had buried itself completely in the sand. It took him three to get out, and the crowd applauded. He "foozled" a shot into a clump of evergreens, and Kitty Crake clapped her hands. Montague made a phenomenal approach, and landed his ball dead at the hole. Alderson "hooked" one ball, "sliced" another, and banged a third into the flag, securing a lucky "rub." He missed two short putts, and then managed to hit Montague's ball, holing it, and leaving his own outside. The laughter of the "gallery" gods cleft the skies, and the referee stepped forward.

"Mr. Montague eighty strokes, Mr. Alderson ninety-six. Mr. Montague wins the tournament, and retains possession of the Hong-Kong Medal."

Curiously enough, it seemed as though the applause that followed the announcement was intended for Alderson rather than for the victor. Men with whom he had not been on speaking terms for months crowded around him to shake his hand. From being the most unpopular man in the club he had suddenly become a hero. It was incomprehensible. Last of all came up Kitty Crake. The crowd had drifted away, and they were alone. Her eyes were wet and shining, and she held out her hand. He took it, trembling inwardly.

"Well," said she at length, "the match is over: have you nothing to say to me!"

"But—but I lost it," faltered Henry Alderson.

"Exactly; and in so doing you just managed to save yourself. You have evidently no idea how simply intolerable a champion at golf may be."

"Oh, Kitty—"he began; but they were already at the club-house.

After they were married he told her the whole story.

"But there is one thing I never understood," he concluded, thoughtfully. "If it really were the enemy of mankind, he certainly acted very stupidly in not getting my signature in the good old orthodox way. What had he to show for his side of the bargain?"

"Oh, that is plain enough," answered Mrs. Alderson. "So long as pride continues to be one of the seven deadly sins—"

"Well?"

"Why, the devil is quite justified feeling cocksure of a medal-winner golf. Poor Mr. Montague!"

Comstock/Thinkstock

THE STORY OF ONE GOLF CHAMPION'S PREDICTIONS FOR THE FUTURE OF THE GAME

BY JOHN G. ANDERSON

Clairvoyancy departed in volume with the faded red coats of Musselburgh golfers. To prophesy what seemed possible in golf, even if not at all probable, a score of years ago seemed a foolish undertaking, indeed. Why mock at truth? Why say that 700,000 Americans would supplant the 50,000 of 1900? Why risk a statement that the money invested in this outdoor sport would quadruple any other three games which please the rank and file?

But may not a dreamer dream dreams? We had these men 20 years ago, men with a vision who builded better than they knew. Golf of today is greater than their dreams or apparently their wildest utterings.

So, too, then, can we dream of golf in 1950. But it is more difficult now to guarantee fulfillment. Years ago the progress which the game made in Scotland and England, the varying fortunes and evolutions through which it passed, seemed to have a ready counterpart in this country. First the apeing of dress, then of clubs, then of club customs and rules, and what not. Then style of play, imitative attempts to reproduce a champion's efforts, of the pitch-and-run, the style of course architecture—everything, in fact, which for a couple of centuries had been developed through the pitfalls of experience.

Then, lo and behold, America and Americans caught up! Not only in links portrayal and refined architecture, in dress and stylistic methods, but in the calibre of golf, so that for the first time in the world's history there was played for on American soil the supremacy title of the world in 1921, by the holder of the British honors opposed to the American champion, both long residents of the United States. What wonderful achievements! And in a score of years. Must we not preforce dream and try to catch a vision when we foolhardily speak of golf in future years.

By 1950 golf will be a self-defense sport, not taught after the fashion dictated by Marquis of Queensberry rules but a more or less luxurious necessity. A man will have to take up golf in self-defense if he wishes to keep the fellowship of his boyhood and business companions. Already it takes little vision to see the trend of things towards that end.

In 1950 golf will have become a game where tourneys will be fashioned by age limits. Each state will have its seniors' championship with 50 or 55 years as the scratch of a handicap basis. The champions of the many states will gather together for the seniors' championship title of the land. Even at the present time it takes four days to run off a championship event for the Seniors' Association with all of 350 entries. In the combined entry lists of two-score states, what with the intense interest of the players of the present day who will be eligible, if living, for such events, we may expect thousands upon thousands who will look forward to this annual event with the keenest sort of pleasure and joyful anticipation.

National championships will be restricted to those golfers who will be invited by the governing bodies to attend and the numbers will be limited to 128 at the most. We believe that there will be sent in by the secretaries of the various states a small list of golfers' names, those who are entitled to a handicap of not over two, and that the participants will be made up from this number. State championships throughout the land will act as the qualifying basis for these bigger tourneys and the play will be all the keener for the new methods.

Open championship events will not differ so much from today, since the test at 72 holes provides the finest average. But here again we feel that assistants, caddie-masters and happy-go-lucky mortals will not be permitted to send in their entries. Moreover, amateurs will not be permitted to enter unless they have shown open championship capabilities. In other words, by 1950 professional golf will be on a strictly business basis with abundant spoils to the winners.

The best golfers of all countries in the professional ranks will not be engaged by golf clubs. They will spend their whole time giving exhibitions, and, we fancy, talks on how to improve one's game. Every season will see an international contest between the grand prize winners of the medal and match play champions of the various nations. The money for these trips for highest titles will come from sums set aside after exhibition contests preceding the grand finale.

The teaching processes will have undergone a great change or we sadly miss our guess. We expect mechanical contrivances which will aid the teaching professional. Even today there are on the market mechanical conveniences which purpose to lend a guiding hand in the making of a putt or a short mashie approach. They are of very little assistance because of their heaviness and rigidity. But someone will have invented by that time an arc arrangement calculated to aid the speed of learning. It will be the professional's duty to arrange the arcs so that they correspond to the physical swing fitness of the beginner or learner.

Driving nets will be scattered all over the land, far and near from golf links. For the youth man and the young miss there will be set aside at clubs driving apparatus and putting-greens where they may play to their heart's content, always looking yearningly towards the real golf links to which they will graduate when over 16 or 17 years old; that is, of course, if they have spent sufficient time on the practice, driving, putting, and mashie-shot links provided for that very purpose.

Golf should be less expensive in 1950. Long before then golf holes will be standardized so that future changes will not be contemplated except in the unusual instance. When, therefore, all that needs to be cared for is a settled series of fairways and putting-greens, attention can be centered all the time upon the scientific analysis pertaining to the continued growth of good grass. When this has become a settled fact fewer men will be needed. Here, too, the mechanical contrivances to save man labor has shown wonderful progress but greater are in store. At a minimum of expense golf courses will be veritable runways of green, with grooming a delight to the eye.

There will be less freedom in the choice of clubs if improvement develops in play in the same ratio as over the past five years. In this respect we believe there will be less change, fortunately so, than in any other section of the game except, perhaps, in the rules where public opinion leading towards one set for nil will ultimately prevail.

There will be a doubling of the golfing population of the United States and Canada, perhaps a tripling in Canada. To permit this to be brought about, the small towns, as George Ade pointed out, will have to be the standard-bearers. There has been a spurt in this direction lately, and there will be a steady increase in the number of courses spread all over the country, mounting in number probably to another 2,000 at least when a half of this century shall have been reached.

In short, while we might expatiate upon a hundred other features showing expansion, particularly in the literary field covered by the golfing magazine, the whole can be summed up in the statement that by 1950 the game of golf will have become a dominating influence in the life of the nation, health-giving, health-bringing, and the accepted national sport.

SOURCES

Anderson, John G. "Gabbling About Golf." *Golfer's Magazine*, Volume 38. 1921.

Bangs, John Kendrick. *The Idiot at Home*. New York and London: Harper & Brothers, 1902.

Bantock, Miles. *On Many Greens: A Book of Golf and Golfers*. New York: Grosset & Dunlap, 1901.

Barbour, Ralph Henry. *The Half-Back: A Story of School, Football, and Golf*. New York: D. Appleton and Company, 1907.

Barrett, David. *Miracle at Merion: The Inspiring Story of Ben Hogan's Amazing Comeback and Victory at the 1950 U.S. Open*. New York: Skyhorse, 2012.

Barrett, David. *Making the Masters: Bobby Jones and the Birth of America's Greatest Golf Tournament*. New York: Skyhorse, 2012.

Bowden, Tripp. *Freddie & Me: Life Lessons from Freddie Bennett, Augusta National's Legendary Caddy Master*. New York: Skyhorse, 2009.

Braid, James. *Advanced Golf: Or, Hints and Instruction for Progressive Players, Second Edition*. London: Methuen & Co., 1908.

Chapin, Anna Alice. "*Straight Golf.*" The Century Illustrated Monthly Magazine. New York: The Century Co., 1911-1912.

Darwin, Bernard. *Tee Shots and Others*. Toronto: The Musson Book Company, 1911.

Duncan, George, and Bernard Darwin. *Present-Day Golf*. New York: George H. Doran Company, 1921.

Edgar, J. Douglas. *The Gate to Golf*. St. Albans: Edgar & Co., 1920.

Evans Jr., Charles. *Chick Evans' Golf Book: The Story of the Sporting Battles of the Greatest of all Amateur Golfers.* Chicago: Thos. E. Wilson & Co., 1921.

Gunderson, Sarah. "How the Quakers Became Reconciled to the Golfers," in *Golf,* edited by United States Golf Association, 24-25. 1898.

Hall, Holworthy. *Dormie One: And Other Golf Stories.* New York: The Century Co., 1917.

Harman, H. E. *"An Intimate Story of Miss Alexa Stiling's Golf Victories."* Golfer's Magazine, Volume 38. 1921.

Hezlet, May. *Ladies' Golf.* London: Hutchinson and Co., 1907.

Hilton, Harold H. *Modern Golf.* New York: Outing Publishing Company, 1913.

Hilton, Harold H. "Physique in Golf." *The Outing Magazine, Volume LXII.* New York: Outing Publishing Company, 1913.

Hunter, David Smith. *Golf Simplified: Cause and Effect.* Garden City: Doubleday, Page & Company, 1922.

Jerome, Jerome Klapka. *Idle Ideas in 1905.* London: Hurst and Blackett, Limited, 1906.

Leach, Henry. *The Happy Golfer: Being Some Experiences, Reflections, And A Few Deductions of a Wandering Player.* London: Macmillan and Co., 1914.

Leitch, Cecil. *Golf.* Philadelphia: J. B. Lippincott Company, 1922.

Macdonald, Charles B. "Golf: The Ethical and Physical Aspects of the Game." *Golf, Volume 2.* United States Golf Association. J. Newman, 1898.

Marshall, Robert. *The Enchanted Golf Clubs.* Gundy: Toronto, 1900. [Editor's note: this book was originally published as *The Haunted Major.*]

McPherson, J. Gordon. *Golf and Golfers: Past and Present.* Edinburgh and London: William Blackwood and Sons, 1891.

McSpadden, Joseph Walker, ed. *How to Play Golf: Compiled from the Best English and American Authorities.* New York: Thomas Y. Crowell & Co., 1907.

Miller, Jeff. *Crown at Glen Garden: Ben Hogan, Byron Nelson, and the Little Texas Golf Course that Propelled them to Stardom.* New York: Skyhorse, 2012.

Milne, A. A. *The Holiday Round.* London: Methuen & Company, 1912.

Milne, A. A. *Not That it Matters.* New York: E.P. Dutton & Company, 1920.

Ouimet, Francis. *Golf Facts for Young People.* New York: The Century Co., 1921.

Player, Gary. *Don't Choke: A Champion's Guide to Winning Under Pressure.* New York: Skyhorse, 2010.

Proudfoot, W. *"Beginning Golf."* Golf, Volume 2. United States Golf Association. J. Newman, 1898.

Silverman, Matthew. *Golf Miscellany: Everything You Always Wanted to Know About Golf.* New York: Skyhorse, 2012.

Smith, Garden Grant. *The World of Golf.* London: A.D. Innes & Company, 1898.

Steele, Chester K. *The Golf Course Mystery.* Cleveland: George Scully and Company, 1919.

Sutphen, W. G. Van T. *The Golficide and other Tales of the Fair Green.* New York: Harper & Brothers, 1898.

Taylor, John Henry. *Taylor on Golf: Impressions, Comments, and Hints.* London: Hutchinson & Co., 1905.

Travers, Jerome Dunstan. *Travers' Golf Book.* New York: The Macmillan Company, 1913.

Van Loan, Charles E. *Fore! Golf Stories* New York: George H. Doran Company, 1918.

Vardon, Harry. *The Complete Golfer.* New York: McClure, Phillips & Co., 1905.

Wethered, Roger Henry, and Joyce Wethered. *Golf from Two Sides.* London: Longmans, Green, and Co., 1922.

Wodehouse, P. G. *The Man Upstairs and Other Stories.* Penguin, 1914.